I0015755

Building Interactive Dashboards in Microsoft 365 Excel

Harness the new features and formulae in M365 Excel
to create dynamic, automated dashboards

Michael Olafusi

Building Interactive Dashboards in Microsoft 365 Excel

Copyright © 2024 Packt Publishing

All rights reserved. No part of this book may be reproduced, stored in a retrieval system, or transmitted in any form or by any means, without the prior written permission of the publisher, except in the case of brief quotations embedded in critical articles or reviews.

Every effort has been made in the preparation of this book to ensure the accuracy of the information presented. However, the information contained in this book is sold without warranty, either express or implied. Neither the author, nor Packt Publishing or its dealers and distributors, will be held liable for any damages caused or alleged to have been caused directly or indirectly by this book.

Packt Publishing has endeavored to provide trademark information about all of the companies and products mentioned in this book by the appropriate use of capitals. However, Packt Publishing cannot guarantee the accuracy of this information.

Group Product Manager: Kaustubh Manglurkar
Publishing Product Manager: Apeksha Shetty
Book Project Manager: Aparna Nair
Senior Editor: Rohit Singh
Technical Editor: Rahul Limbachiya
Copy Editor: Safis Editing
Proofreader: Safis Editing
Indexer: Hemangini Bari
Production Designer: Aparna Bhagat
DevRel Marketing Coordinator: Nivedita Singh

First published: February 2024

Production reference: 1080224

Published by Packt Publishing Ltd.
Grosvenor House
11 St Paul's Square
Birmingham
B3 1RB, UK.

ISBN 978-1-80323-729-9

www.packtpub.com

To my wife, Hannah Olafusi, for the support throughout the two years of writing this book. And to my daughter, Sophia Olafusi, for adding to the fun with unplanned battles for the keyboard and mouse.

– Michael Olafusi

Foreword

Data is the new oil, and I live in an oil continent where nobody is drilling. This quote summarizes my early passion for data analysis. Data-driven decision-making has become indispensable in the modern business world – to drill data, organizations need robust systems and processes to collect, organize, analyze, and visualize data in order to derive actionable insights. This book, *Building Interactive Dashboards in Microsoft 365 Excel*, by Michael Olafusi is a timely knowledge box for every data professional as it empowers you with the knowledge and skills required to meet business needs via dashboards in Excel.

Excel has emerged as one of the most popular tools for building dashboards, owing to its ubiquity, ease of use, and powerful data visualization capabilities. However, not all Excel versions are created equal when it comes to dashboarding. That's where **Microsoft 365 (M365)** Excel comes in. The latest iterations of Excel pack some amazing new features that can help users build dynamic, automated, and visually appealing dashboards much more efficiently.

In this practical guide, Michael leverages his over 15 years of experience in business intelligence, financial analysis, and Excel training to unlock the dashboarding superpowers in M365 Excel. Right from the outset, he demystifies dashboards and how they differ from regular reports. He then outlines the definitive characteristics that set truly intuitive and actionable dashboards apart.

Before diving into dashboard creation techniques, Michael rightly stresses the paramount importance of connecting to primary data sources rather than using static Excel sheet exports or copies. This approach allows dashboards to always reflect the latest data with a simple refresh. Here, he introduces one of my personal favorite Excel tools – Power Query.

Excel Power Query has completely transformed how analysts can ingest, transform, and consolidate data from disparate sources. Michael aptly calls it the "ultimate data transformation tool." He walks you through all the key steps from establishing live connections to different data sources to shaping, cleaning, merging, and mashing up datasets with ease. The skills you will gain in this section will prove invaluable even outside of pure dashboarding needs.

With the data pipeline set up, he moves on to analytics and visualization techniques – including using Excel's time-tested PivotTables and the newer Power Pivot tools. You will learn how to crunch large datasets while still keeping dashboards dynamic and allowing end users to slice and dice data on the fly. Of course, he also covers the latest game-changing features exclusive to M365 Excel – such as dynamic arrays and lambda functions.

While most Excel books tend to focus largely on number-crunching, Michael rightly gives visualization its due importance in the context of dashboards. You will gain mastery over Excel's 19 chart types and also learn creative ways of building visually engaging dashboards using conditional formatting, custom number formatting, shapes, and form controls, among other techniques.

The icing on the cake is the hands-on dashboard creation project using a sample company's data. This end-to-end implementation allows you to apply all the concepts covered earlier. You'll gain priceless real-world experience in Excel-based dashboarding.

Michael's conversational style, ample illustrations, and simple explanations make this guide accessible yet comprehensive at the same time. While M365 Excel contains features galore, he focuses sharply on the tools and techniques needed specifically in the context of building automated, interactive dashboards. I love his systematic approach and the logical flow of topics.

By the end of this book, you will no longer dread dashboard-building activities. Instead, you'll have fun turning static datasets into visual stories and uncover actionable insights faster than ever before! I highly recommend this book whether you're just getting started with Excel analytics or looking to take your skills up a notch using M365's latest and greatest features.

Olanrewaju Oyinbooke

Ex-senior cloud advocate at Microsoft

Contributors

About the author

Michael Olafusi is a 9x Microsoft **Most Valuable Professional** (**MVP**) and a business intelligence consultant. He is the lead consultant and founder of MHS Analytics Inc. in Canada and UrBizEdge Limited.

He has been consulting for clients across North America, Europe, and Africa on data analysis, business intelligence, and financial modeling for the past 10 years. Outside of his consulting business, he is a member of Rotary and the **Southern Cruisers Riding Club** (**SCRC**) Chapter 373. He is a proud member of the Canadian Red Cross friendly calls volunteer team. He is also a faculty member at WorldQuant University, USA.

I would like to thank the amazing team of editors and experts at Packt who made the completion of this book possible. You all rock!

About the reviewer

Brandon Tarr has a diverse background, with expertise in IT infrastructure, software support and dev, cloud, and multi-SaaS product solutions. In his latest role, Brandon is deeply immersed in architecting collab and SaaS solutions such as M365, Atlassian, and Miro, with a heavy focus on Slack Enterprise Grid. Brandon excels in use case discovery, definition, develop, and delivery, contributing to workplace transformation, business solutions development, and digital workplace strategy and roadmap management.

I'd like to thank my wife, best friend, and love of my life, Samantha. Also, my twin girls, who mean the world to me. Lastly, all the people who have given me a chance and opportunity to work for them. It's always an honor.

Table of Contents

Preface   xv

Part 1 – Dashboards and Reports in Modern Excel

1

Dashboards, Reports, and M365 Excel   3

Introducing dashboards and reports	4	Excel 2021	12
Meeting modern business needs	6	Older versions of Excel	19
The characteristics of a dashboard	7	Summary	22
The different versions of Microsoft Excel	7	Further reading	22
Excel 365	10		

2

Common Dashboards in Large Companies   23

Major types of dashboards	24	Understanding the supply chain and logistics dashboard	35
Understanding the sales dashboard	26		
Understanding the financial analysis dashboard	31	Understanding the marketing dashboard	38
Understanding the HR dashboard	33	Summary	43

Part 2 – Keeping Your Eyes on Automation

3

The Importance of Connecting Directly to the Primary Data Sources   47

The different ways to bring data into Excel	47	Connecting directly to the primary data source	65
Copying and pasting data into Excel	53	Common issues and how to overcome them	68
Importing data from flat files	54	Summary	70
Importing data from databases	59		
Importing data from cloud platforms	60		

4

Power Query: the Ultimate Data Transformation Tool   71

Introduction to Power Query	72	Keep Rows and Remove Rows	99
Connecting to over 100 different data sources	81	Unpivot Columns and Pivot Columns	101
		Group By	104
Transforming data in Power Query	84	Fill Series and Remove Empty	105
Appending data from multiple sources in one data table	85	Replace Values	113
Merging data from two tables into one table	91	Important tips	114
		Understanding Close & Load To	119
Common data transformations	98	Demystifying the underlying M code	121
Choose Columns	98	Summary	124

5

PivotTable and Power Pivot   125

Mastering Pivot Tables	125	Power Pivot and Data Models	167
The role of Slicers	145	DAX	182
Dynamic reports with PivotTables	151	Summary	184

6

Must-Know Legacy Excel Functions   185

Math and statistical functions	**186**	TEXT	202
SUM	186	LEN	203
SUMIFS	187	**Date manipulation functions**	**204**
COUNT	188	TODAY	204
COUNTIFS	188	DATE	205
MIN	189	YEAR	205
MAX	190	MONTH	206
AVERAGE	191	DAY	207
Logical functions	**192**	EDATE	207
IF	193	EOMONTH	208
IFS	194	WEEKNUM	209
IFERROR	194	**Lookup and reference functions**	**210**
SWITCH	195	VLOOKUP	211
OR	197	HLOOKUP	212
AND	197	INDEX	212
Text manipulation functions	**198**	MATCH	213
LEFT	199	OFFSET	214
MID	199	INDIRECT	215
RIGHT	200	CHOOSE	215
SEARCH	200	**Summary**	**216**
SUBSTITUTE	201		

7

Dynamic Array Functions and Lambda Functions   217

Dynamic array functions	**218**	BYCOL	238
UNIQUE	218	BYROW	239
FILTER	221	MAKEARRAY	239
SEQUENCE	225	MAP	241
SORT	229	REDUCE	242
SORTBY	233	SCAN	243
Lambda functions	**235**	**Summary**	**244**
LAMBDA	235		

Part 3 – Getting the Visualization Right

8

Getting Comfortable with the 19 Excel Charts   247

Column chart	248	Radar chart	273
Bar chart	255	Treemap chart	275
Line chart	260	Sunburst chart	276
Area chart	262	Histogram chart	277
Pie chart	263	Box and whisker chart	278
Doughnut chart	265	Waterfall chart	279
XY (scatter) chart	267	Funnel chart	281
Bubble chart	270	Filled map chart	282
Stock chart	271	Combo chart	283
Surface chart	272	Summary	284

9

Non-Chart Visuals   285

Conditional formatting	286	Shapes	306
Highlight Cells Rules	291	SmartArt	309
Top/Bottom Rules	293	Sparkline	311
Data bars	295	Images	312
Color scales	297	Symbols	313
Icon sets	299	Summary	317
Custom formula conditional formatting	302		

10

Setting Up the Dashboard's Data Model   319

Adventure Works Cycle Limited	319	Purchasing schema	322
HR schema	321	Production schema	323
Sales schema	321	Person schema	324

Building business-relevant
dashboards   325

Data transformation in Power Query 326
Summary   352

11

Perfecting the Dashboard   353

Building the HR manpower
dashboard   353
Inserting PivotTables   355
Inserting PivotCharts   358
Inserting picture, shapes, and icons 360

Building the sales performance
dashboard   362
Creating measures   363

Inserting slicers and timelines   365
Inserting a PivotTable and a PivotChart 367
Inserting shapes and a picture   369
Connecting slicers to the PivotTables and
PivotCharts   370

Building the supply chain inventory
dashboard   371
Summary   376

12

Best Practices for Real-World Dashboard Building   377

Gathering the dashboard
requirements   377
Existing established analysis dashboards 378
Newly established analysis dashboards   380
Ad hoc analysis dashboards   380

An overview of different
data professionals   381
Data analyst   381

Business intelligence analyst   382
Data engineer   382
Data scientist   383
Database administrator   383

Advantages and limitations
of Excel dashboards   384
Summary   385

Index   387

Other Books You May Enjoy   396

Preface

Microsoft 365 Excel is a modern version of Excel that is constantly updated with features that make creating and automating analyses, reports, and dashboards very easy compared to older Excel versions. This book focuses on creating dashboards using this modern version of Excel. Some of the modern Excel features covered are Power Query and Power Pivot. With a hands-on approach, this book will help you create at least three dashboards from scratch. You will also learn the best practices for building robust data models and designing dashboards.

Who this book is for

This book is for all Microsoft Excel users, especially those who work in a business environment and need to create dynamic reports and dashboards that reflect new data and help support decision-makers with actionable insights that are visually engaging. Other users who will greatly benefit from this book are financial analysts, MIS analysts, sales analysts, marketing executives, supply chain analysts, business analysts, BI professionals, customer experience executives, management consultants, operations analysts, and investment bankers.

The book assumes that you are familiar with the Microsoft Excel interface and have it installed on your computer. You are expected to practice the concepts and skills taught in this book in order to master them and get the most value from this book.

What this book covers

Chapter 1, Dashboards, Reports, and M365 Excel, explains the difference between dashboards and reports and what is special about Microsoft 365 Excel. It is often common to see people use the words *dashboards* and *reports* interchangeably, but they are different. Also, Microsoft Excel has changed a lot in the last four years, in terms of both its capabilities and product versions. This chapter will help you understand the difference between dashboards and reports, and also the concept of modern Excel.

Chapter 2, Common Dashboards in Large Companies, covers the five major types of dashboards the companies require: sales dashboard, financial analysis dashboard, human resources dashboard, supply chain dashboard, and marketing dashboard. You will become aware of the types of needs dashboards address and why businesses require dashboards.

Chapter 3, The Importance of Connecting Directly to the Primary Data Sources, presents different ways of bringing data into Excel, the importance of always connecting to the primary source, and how to overcome common data source challenges. The concepts covered in this chapter can be the difference between a dashboard that is built once and used for years without any reworking and a dashboard that keeps breaking down.

Chapter 4, Power Query: the Ultimate Data Transformation Tool, gives an overview of the amazing data transformation features of Power Query and some demonstrations of its use. Power Query is the most commonly known tool for modern Excel users and is vital for creating repeatable data transformations.

Chapter 5, PivotTable and Power Pivot, presents a clear explanation of how to use pivot tables to achieve interactive analysis and the use of Power Pivot to build robust data models. The chapter covers a deep dive into Pivot Tables and the use of slicers and **Data Analytics Expressions (DAX)**.

Chapter 6, Must-Know Legacy Excel Functions, includes coverage of key math functions, logical functions, text manipulation functions, date manipulation functions, and lookup functions. These form the bedrock of most Excel sheet-based data transformation and aggregation.

Chapter 7, Dynamic Array Functions and Lambda Functions, helps you understand what dynamic array functions are and their special use, with a special focus on Lambda functions. The chapter also walks you through the key dynamic array functions to master and some interesting uses of Lambda functions.

Chapter 8, Getting Comfortable with the 19 Excel Charts, gives a demonstration of each of the 19 chart types in Excel. The chapter explains what each chart is best used for and gives a practical illustration per chart.

Chapter 9, Non-Chart Visuals, shows the use of conditional formatting, shapes, smart art, sparklines, images, and symbols to visually communicate insights. These, when properly used, can greatly enhance the readability, ease of use, and visual appeal of a dashboard.

Chapter 10, Setting Up the Dashboard's Data Model, presents a hands-on demonstration of how to set up the foundation of a proper dashboard. The chapter takes you through the typical reporting needs in a company and transforming data in Power Query.

Chapter 11, Perfecting the Dashboard, gives a practical walk-through of building a human resources dashboard, a sales performance dashboard, and a supply chain dashboard.

Chapter 12, Best Practices for Real-World Dashboard Building, lists the important guidelines for gathering dashboard requirements and deciding on what dashboards are worth building in Excel.

To get the most out of this book

This book does not assume you have prior knowledge of any tool or any technical experience to follow the given instructions.

Software/hardware covered in the book	Operating system requirements
Microsoft Excel	Windows

If you are using the digital version of this book, we advise you to type the code yourself or access the code from the book's GitHub repository (a link is available in the next section). Doing so will help you avoid any potential errors related to the copying and pasting of code.

Download the example code files

You can download the example code files for this book from GitHub at `https://github.com/PacktPublishing/Building-Interactive-Dashboards-in-Microsoft-365-Excel`. If there's an update to the code, it will be updated in the GitHub repository. For large-sized images used in the book, you can also refer to them in the `Large images` folder in this GitHub repository.

We also have other code bundles from our rich catalog of books and videos available at `https://github.com/PacktPublishing/`. Check them out!

Conventions used

There are a number of text conventions used throughout this book.

`Code in text`: Indicates code words in text, database table names, folder names, filenames, file extensions, pathnames, dummy URLs, user input, and Twitter handles. Here is an example: "Save this Excel file as `Sales Dashboard.xlsx`."

A block of code is set as follows:

```
=IFS(B28="A","Excellent",B28="B","Very Good",B28="C ", "Good",B28="D",
"Poor",B28="E","Very Poor",B28="F","Fail")
```

When we wish to draw your attention to a particular part of a code block, the relevant lines or items are set in bold:

```
Table.Group(#"Changed Type1", {"SalesOrderID"}, {{"SalesReasonIDs",
each Text.Combine([SalesReasonID],","), type nullable text}})
```

Bold: Indicates a new term, an important word, or words that you see onscreen. For instance, words in menus or dialog boxes appear in **bold**. Here is an example: "To know what version of Excel you are using, go to **File | Account**, and in the upper-right section, you will see your Excel version."

> **Tips or important notes**
> Appear like this.

Get in touch

Feedback from our readers is always welcome.

General feedback: If you have questions about any aspect of this book, email us at `customercare@packtpub.com` and mention the book title in the subject of your message.

Errata: Although we have taken every care to ensure the accuracy of our content, mistakes do happen. If you have found a mistake in this book, we would be grateful if you would report this to us. Please visit `www.packtpub.com/support/errata` and fill in the form.

Piracy: If you come across any illegal copies of our works in any form on the internet, we would be grateful if you would provide us with the location address or website name. Please contact us at `copyright@packt.com` with a link to the material.

If you are interested in becoming an author: If there is a topic that you have expertise in and you are interested in either writing or contributing to a book, please visit `authors.packtpub.com`.

Share Your Thoughts

Once you've read *Building Interactive Dashboards in Microsoft 365 Excel*, we'd love to hear your thoughts! Scan the QR code below to go straight to the Amazon review page for this book and share your feedback.

`https://packt.link/r/1-803-23729-5`

Your review is important to us and the tech community and will help us make sure we're delivering excellent quality content.

Download a free PDF copy of this book

Thanks for purchasing this book!

Do you like to read on the go but are unable to carry your print books everywhere?

Is your eBook purchase not compatible with the device of your choice?

Don't worry, now with every Packt book you get a DRM-free PDF version of that book at no cost.

Read anywhere, any place, on any device. Search, copy, and paste code from your favorite technical books directly into your application.

The perks don't stop there, you can get exclusive access to discounts, newsletters, and great free content in your inbox daily

Follow these simple steps to get the benefits:

1. Scan the QR code or visit the link below

https://packt.link/free-ebook/9781803237299

2. Submit your proof of purchase
3. That's it! We'll send your free PDF and other benefits to your email directly

Part 1 –
Dashboards and Reports
in Modern Excel

This part provides an introduction to dashboards, reports, and M365 capabilities. By the end of this section, you will have a clear understanding of what dashboards are meant to achieve and how you can leverage the new capabilities in M365 Excel to build very effective and dynamic dashboards.

This part has the following chapters:

- *Chapter 1, Dashboards, Reports, and M365 Excel*
- *Chapter 2, Common Dashboards in Large Companies*

1

Dashboards, Reports, and M365 Excel

Many Excel users use the words dashboard and report interchangeably and are not able to clearly delineate them. This is often because most people learn to use Excel on the job and not before they are mandated by superiors to churn out reports and dashboards for them. It is not uncommon to have a manager who calls everything with a beautiful chart in it a dashboard and another who believes only specialist software (other than Excel) can create dashboards. Sadly, no analyst who is bounced endlessly between these two types of managers will understand the real difference between a dashboard and a report.

Microsoft sadly adds to the woes analysts face at work by creating different versions of Microsoft Excel. Almost every week, I come across an analyst spending hours and using complex formulas they copied from an online forum without understanding how the 100-plus-characters cocktail of functions works to achieve what is now an easy single function in the recent versions of Excel. My first recommendation to everyone learning how to build dashboards in Excel is to get Microsoft 365 Excel or Excel 2021. The difference between using those versions and using an older version can be likened to the difference between a horse-drawn carriage and a modern car.

This chapter will cover what dashboards are and what they are used for. Then, we will go on to explain what reports are and how they are different from dashboards. Some people may argue that all analyses from a dataset are reports and that a dashboard is a report. That is a valid argument; however, when working as a data analyst or any role that requires carrying out data analysis within a company, it is important to think of them separately. You would not want to give your CEO a report if what they are expecting is a dashboard. And if you are in a decision-making position, you will want to be clear with your team regarding what you want. After the clarification on dashboards and reports, the chapter will explain the different Excel versions and which versions you should use if you want to create dashboards easily.

By the end of this chapter, you will understand in a clear and practical way the difference between dashboards and reports, the importance of dashboards in modern companies, and why Microsoft 365 Excel or Excel 2021 should be your chosen version of Excel for building dashboards.

In this chapter, we will cover the following topics:

- Introducing dashboards and reports
- Meeting modern business needs
- The characteristics of a dashboard
- The different versions of Microsoft Excel

Introducing dashboards and reports

Dashboards are visual representations of key metrics and actionable insights to be primarily consumed by decision makers. Many self-acclaimed dashboard experts say it should always be set to fit within a screen view, and the reason for this is a very valid one. Imagine needing to scroll down to see the fuel gauge on your car's dashboard; seeing everything in one ever-present view is a much better user experience than having to scroll. The trouble, however, lies with *whose screen*. Screen resolution, monitor size, and Excel zoom settings are never the same for all parties concerned – the dashboard builder and the dashboard users. So it can be a very tricky clause to include in the dashboard definition, but knowing this, it is always good to aim to avoid the need for your dashboard users to scroll right or down when viewing your dashboard.

Reports are well-formatted presentations of data and are often the outcome of all data analysis processes. The very interesting thing to note is that all dashboards are reports, but not all reports are dashboards. A table of all employees showing their biodata, professional qualifications, and payroll information, one row per employee, is a report.

The following screenshot shows what such a table might look like:

Department							
Document Control	Engineering	Executive	Facilities and Maintena...	Finance	Human Resources	Information Services	Marketing
Production	Production Control	Purchasing	Quality Assurance	Research and Develop...	Sales	Shipping and Receiving	Tool Design

Name	BirthDate	Gender	MaritalStatus	JobTitle	Department	Rate	VacationHours	HireDate	StartDate	EndDate
A. Scott Wright	9/17/1968	M	S	Master Scheduler	Production Control	$23.56	44	12/12/2008	12/12/2008	(blank)
Alan J Brewer	3/29/1984	M	M	Scheduling Assistant	Production Control	$16.00	47	2/13/2009	2/13/2009	(blank)
Alejandro E McGuel	12/5/1988	M	S	Production Technician - WC40	Production	$15.00	52	12/6/2008	12/6/2008	(blank)
Alex M Nayberg	4/13/1990	M	M	Production Technician - WC45	Production	$10.00	77	2/8/2009	2/8/2009	(blank)
Alice O Ciccu	1/26/1979	F	M	Production Technician - WC50	Production	$11.00	95	12/7/2008	12/7/2008	(blank)
Amy E Alberts	9/20/1957	F	M	European Sales Manager	Sales	$48.10	21	4/16/2012	4/16/2012	(blank)
Andreas T Berglund	3/28/1989	M	M	Quality Assurance Technician	Quality Assurance	$10.58	84	2/2/2009	2/2/2009	(blank)
Andrew M Cencini	9/24/1988	M	S	Production Technician - WC45	Production	$10.00	73	3/6/2009	3/6/2009	(blank)
Andrew R Hill	9/6/1988	M	S	Production Supervisor - WC10	Production	$25.00	65	2/22/2009	2/22/2009	(blank)
Andy M Ruth	10/20/1983	M	M	Production Technician - WC30	Production	$9.50	39	1/31/2009	1/31/2009	(blank)
Angela W Barbariol	5/31/1991	F	S	Production Technician - WC50	Production	$11.00	92	1/20/2009	1/20/2009	(blank)
Anibal T Sousa	9/5/1974	F	S	Production Technician - WC20	Production	$14.00	8	2/23/2009	2/23/2009	(blank)
Annette L Hill	1/29/1978	F	M	Purchasing Assistant	Purchasing	$12.75	50	12/6/2010	12/6/2010	(blank)
Annik O Stahl	12/26/1976	M	M	Production Technician - WC60	Production	$12.45	17	12/17/2008	12/17/2008	(blank)
Arvind B Rao	8/21/1974	M	M	Buyer	Purchasing	$18.27	60	2/28/2009	2/28/2009	(blank)
Ashvini R Sharma	3/27/1977	M	S	Network Administrator	Information Services	$32.45	70	12/4/2008	12/4/2008	(blank)
Barbara C Moreland	1/4/1976	F	M	Accountant	Finance	$26.44	58	2/18/2009	2/18/2009	(blank)
Barbara S Decker	7/2/1979	F	M	Production Technician - WC20	Production	$14.00	17	1/22/2009	1/22/2009	(blank)
Baris F Cetinok	10/7/1990	M	S	Production Technician - WC40	Production	$15.00	72	2/15/2009	2/15/2009	(blank)
Barry K Johnson	3/26/1956	M	S	Production Technician - WC10	Production	$13.45	88	1/7/2008	1/7/2008	(blank)
Belinda M Newman	9/17/1969	F	S	Production Technician - WC45	Production	$10.00	83	2/20/2009	2/20/2009	(blank)
Ben T Miller	6/3/1973	M	M	Buyer	Purchasing	$18.27	55	3/9/2010	3/9/2010	(blank)
Benjamin R Martin	1/5/1986	M	S	Production Technician - WC30	Production	$6.75	28	1/27/2009	1/27/2009	(blank)
Benjamin R Martin	1/5/1986	M	S	Production Technician - WC30	Production	$7.25	28	1/27/2009	1/27/2009	(blank)
Benjamin R Martin	1/5/1986	M	S	Production Technician - WC30	Production	$9.50	28	1/27/2009	1/27/2009	(blank)
Betsy A Stadick	12/17/1966	F	S	Production Technician - WC10	Production	$13.45	99	12/18/2009	12/18/2009	(blank)
Bjorn M Rettig	11/6/1989	M	S	Production Technician - WC30	Production	$9.50	43	1/7/2009	1/7/2009	(blank)
Bob N Hohman	8/16/1979	M	S	Production Technician - WC50	Production	$11.00	12	12/24/2008	12/24/2008	(blank)
Bonnie N Kearney	9/10/1996	F	M	Production Technician - WC10	Production	$13.45	89	1/1/2010	1/1/2010	(blank)
Brandon G Heidepriem	1/10/1977	M	M	Production Technician - WC60	Production	$12.45	22	2/8/2009	2/8/2009	(blank)
Brenda M Diaz	2/28/1983	F	M	Production Supervisor - WC40	Production	$25.00	71	3/5/2009	3/5/2009	(blank)
Brian P LaMee	8/11/1984	M	M	Scheduling Assistant	Production Control	$16.00	48	3/3/2009	3/3/2009	(blank)
Brian Richard Goldstein	12/23/1970	M	S	Production Technician - WC40	Production	$15.00	63	12/11/2009	12/11/2009	(blank)
Brian S Welcker	6/6/1977	M	S	Vice President of Sales	Sales	$72.12	10	2/15/2011	2/15/2011	(blank)
Brian T Lloyd	2/10/1977	M	S	Production Technician - WC40	Production	$15.00	55	1/29/2009	1/29/2009	(blank)
Britta L Simon	9/28/1989	F	M	Production Technician - WC60	Production	$12.45	14	1/29/2009	1/29/2009	(blank)
Bryan Baker	8/27/1973	M	S	Production Technician - WC60	Production	$12.45	35	1/21/2009	1/21/2009	(blank)
Bryan A Walton	9/20/1984	M	S	Accounts Receivable Specialist	Finance	$19.00	62	1/24/2009	1/24/2009	(blank)
Candy L Spoon	2/23/1976	F	S	Accounts Receivable Specialist	Finance	$19.00	61	1/6/2009	1/6/2009	(blank)
Carol M Philips	10/17/1988	F	M	Production Technician - WC30	Production	$9.50	45	2/12/2009	2/12/2009	(blank)

‹ › ... HumanResources EmployeePayHisto   HumanResources EmployeeDepartme   **Report Demo**   HumanResources Employee   HumanResources Department   +

Figure 1.1 – An overview of table of employee biodata and payroll data

And as simple as it sounds, it might involve a **Human Resources** (**HR**) officer working for hours to put together that report. It could be that the biodata is in PDF files of one page per employee, the payroll data is in a **Comma-Separated Values** (**CSV**) file export from the payroll software, and the updated qualifications are acquired via a survey form to all employees. However, that table is not a dashboard.

To create a dashboard from the same dataset, the HR officer will need to identify what key HR metrics the decision makers who will use his dashboard are interested in and what type of decisions they would need the dashboard to enlighten them on. It is not uncommon for the head of HR and the management team to want to track the productivity level of the staff measured in average revenue per total staff, average revenue per sales staff, and average revenue per operations staff, and then be shown this information (metrics) in a way that helps them see the trend over the years and compare it with the industry average. Another common actionable insight decision makers look for in an HR dashboard is to understand the effectiveness of their hiring and staffing process, often captured by metrics such as time to hire, employee turnover, and average tenure by job role and department, and again they are used to compare with the industry benchmarks. So, when creating a dashboard, the HR officer looks beyond the data to what the users use their dashboard for and the best ways to provide those insights in a visually engaging way, which prompts taking the right actions or business decisions.

The following screenshot shows an example of what the final HR dashboard looks like:

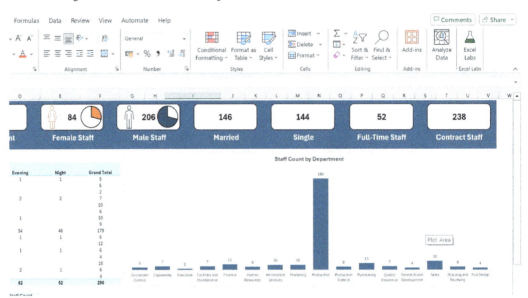

Figure 1.2 – An overview of dashboard from the same employee dataset

In the next section, we will learn why dashboards are an important need of all modern businesses.

Meeting modern business needs

Modern businesses are drowning in data as technology has made it both easy and cheap to gather data around every aspect of business operations. Even a company's website can generate thousands of data points monthly, and this is data the business often does not do much to set up the collection of. Now imagine how much more data is being collected from the more intentionally set up accounting tool, customer relationship management tool, distribution management tool, sales management tool, vendor management, procurement tool, and HR management tool.

Increasingly, business managers are getting frustrated with fragmented reports that show activities but have no meaningful or actionable insights. What is now on every modern business manager's lips to their subordinates is *give me dashboards*. It is no longer acceptable to just create hundreds of reports covering every single aspect of business operations. An analyst is now expected to build a dashboard that ties together in one visually engaging layout all the important metrics and actionable insights, just like the car's dashboard shows in one view all the driver needs to be abreast of as they drive the car. Similarly, business managers who are the drivers of the company to the desired destination also want a dashboard they can take a look at every day and see how well or poorly they are doing. And just like an abnormally high-temperature signal on the car's dashboard will make you pop open the bonnet to start digging around for the cause, a poor performance metric will necessitate the business manager to request the hitherto mundane reports to fish out the probable cause and remedy for the poor performance.

Without exaggeration, dashboards are a vital need for all modern business managers.

In the next section, we will take a look at the main characteristics of all dashboards.

The characteristics of a dashboard

Search for the word *dashboard* online, and you will be presented with a list of articles about dashboards that seem to have little in common. The reason is that most online articles that are at the top of search results are by professional content writers and not data analysts, and many were hired to promote a specific tool. For data analysts, a dashboard has some clear characteristics that set it apart from other types of reports.

A dashboard has the following definitive characteristics:

- It is designed to be very visually engaging
- It must be easy to read and understand
- It must present actionable insights, using the key business metrics decision makers need to be on top of
- It must be interactive, allowing users to dynamically view dimensions or aspects of the analysis (this is often achieved with slicers and filters in Excel)
- It must be in its own dedicated sheet and occupy as close to a one-screen view as possible
- It must be automated to reflect new insights as the source data grows or is updated

In the next section, we will examine the different versions of Microsoft Excel in use today and discuss which versions you should use in order to have a more enjoyable experience in building dashboards.

The different versions of Microsoft Excel

Since the first Excel, Excel 1.0 for Apple Macintosh, in 1985, there have been over 25 versions of Excel by Microsoft, but 99% of Excel users today are spread across the following versions:

- Excel 365, which is a subscription-based version with constantly updated features and can be referred to as the most recent version.
- Excel 2021, which came out in October 2021, is the most recent non-subscription-based version of Excel. Unlike the subscription-based Excel 365, it only gets security updates after its initial release, while Excel 365 gets additional monthly features.
- Excel 2019, which came out in October 2019.

- Excel 2016, which was released in September 2015.

- Excel 2010, which was released in June 2010.

- Excel 2007, which was released in November 2006.

To know what version of Excel you are on, go to **File**, **Account**, and in the upper right section, you will see your Excel version. See *Figure 1.3* to *Figure 1.5* for a helpful illustration of the steps to identify your Excel version. If you do not have **File** but have Excel sheets with 1,048,576 rows, then you are on Excel 2007. If your Excel sheets have less than 1 million rows, you are on a version earlier than Excel 2007 and should not continue reading this book until you have upgraded your version of Excel.

The following screenshot shows you how to get to **File**:

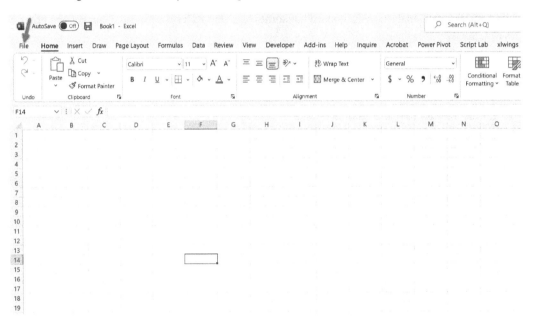

Figure 1.3 – Navigating to File within Excel

The following screenshot shows you how to locate **Account**:

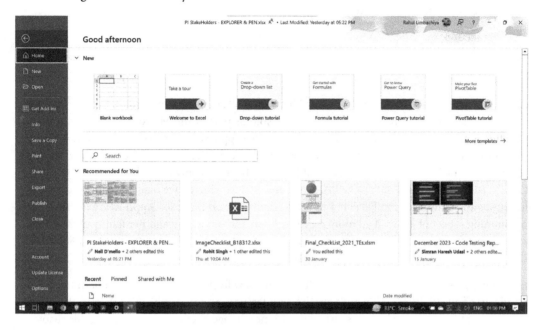

Figure 1.4 – An overview of navigating to Account

The following screenshot shows you where to look to see the Microsoft Excel version:

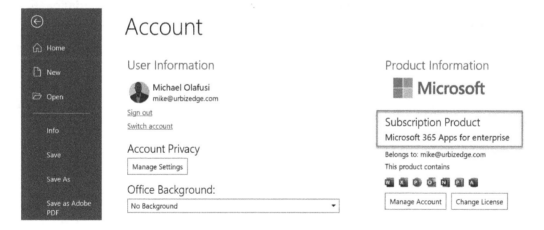

Figure 1.5 – Identifying the Excel version

In interpreting the version, you can swap out **Microsoft** with **Excel**, so my version shown in the preceding figures then reads as **Excel 365**.

In the next section, we will take a look at what is special about the Excel 365 version.

Excel 365

Excel 365 is the subscription-based version of Microsoft Excel that constantly pushes feature updates and is the most feature-rich version of Excel. It is sold as part of the Microsoft 365 productivity suite, often giving the buyer access to all Microsoft Office applications and some other productivity applications, such as OneDrive and Teams. For dashboard creation, it is the most recommended version to use as it has all the time-saving features. It has new dynamic array formulas, such as UNIQUE, FILTER, SEQUENCE, SORTBY, RANDARRAY, and SORT, which have made possible the type of calculations and automation in Excel that used to require **Visual Basic for Applications** (**VBA**), the programming aspect of Excel. And more recently, Microsoft has added another family of functions that further stretch the automation capabilities of Excel: LET, LAMBDA, BYROW, BYCOLUMN, MAP, REDUCE, SCAN, MAKEARRAY, and ISOMITTED.

The advantages of Excel 365 are not just limited to the new formulas it has that are not in the other versions. In addition, its charting and visualization features are more advanced than in the other versions, except Excel 2021, which was just released 3 months ago as of the time of writing this chapter.

> **Important note**
> You can always keep track of the updates for Excel 365 at https://docs.microsoft.com/en-us/officeupdates/update-history-microsoft365-apps-by-date.

The following screenshot shows the version history as detailed in the preceding link:

Version History

Year	Release date	Current Channel	Monthly Enterprise Channel	Semi-Annual Enterprise Channel (Preview)	Semi-Annual Enterprise Channel
2022	January 12	Version 2112 (Build 14729.20260)			Version 2008 (Build 13127.21856)
2022	January 11	Version 2112 (Build 14729.20248)	Version 2111 (Build 14701.20290) Version 2110 (Build 14527.20364)	Version 2108 (Build 14326.20738)	Version 2108 (Build 14326.20738) Version 2102 (Build 13801.21106)
2022	January 04	Version 2112 (Build 14729.20194)			
2021	December 17		Version 2110 (Build 14527.20344) Version 2109 (Build 14430.20386)		
2021	December 16	Version 2111 (Build 14701.20262)		Version 2108 (Build 14326.20702)	Version 2102 (Build 13801.21092) Version 2008 (Build 13127.21846)
2021	December 14	Version 2111 (Build 14701.20248)	Version 2110 (Build 14527.20340) Version 2109 (Build 14430.20380)	Version 2108 (Build 14326.20692)	Version 2102 (Build 13801.21086) Version 2008 (Build 13127.21842)
2021	December 03	Version 2111 (Build 14701.20226)			
2021	December 01	Version 2110 (Build 14527.20312)			
2021	November 09	Version 2110 (Build 14527.20276)	Version 2109 (Build 14430.20342) Version 2108 (Build 14326.20600)	Version 2108 (Build 14326.20600)	Version 2102 (Build 13801.21050) Version 2008 (Build 13127.21820)

Figure 1.6 – Microsoft 365 updates history

The best Excel 365 channel to be on is the **current channel** because it gets new features more quickly than the **monthly enterprise channel** and the **semi-annual enterprise channel**. Do note that if your license was assigned to you by a company IT admin, the admin invariably controls what channel you will be on. In the next section, we will discuss Excel 2021 version.

Excel 2021

Excel 2021 is the most recent perpetual license version of Excel. It has all the feature updates of Excel up to October 2021, spanning new formulas to new data transformation tools.

> **Important note**
> You can read Microsoft's official listing of the new features above Excel 2019 that Excel 2021 has at `https://support.microsoft.com/en-us/office/what-s-new-in-excel-2021-for-windows-f953fe71-8f85-4423-bef9-8a195c7a1100`.

Now let us understand the features in depth:

Coauthoring: Coauthoring is collaborative working on the same Excel file by two or more people. This method is recommended over the **Share Workbook** feature under the **Review** tab in the older versions of Excel.

The following screenshot shows us what the coauthoring experience is like:

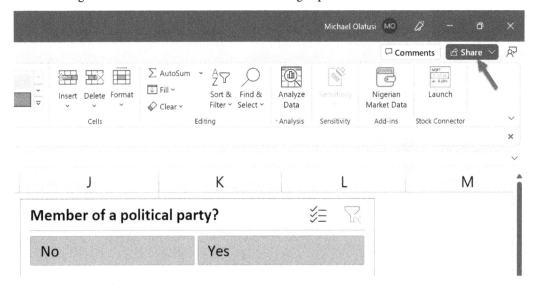

Figure 1.7 – Coauthoring

Let us look at this feature in more detail in the following screenshot:

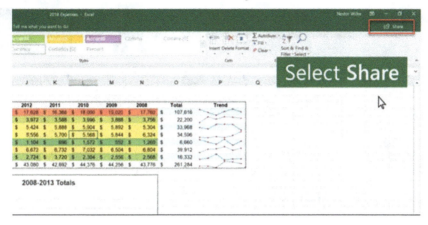

Figure 1.8 – An overview of coauthoring

Modern comments: This is a threaded comment experience with the ability to mention/tag a colleague. The following screenshot shows what modern comments look like:

Figure 1.9 – An overview of modern comments

Know who's in your workbook: This works hand in hand with coauthoring. You now can now see the names of people co-working with you on a shared Excel file.

The following screenshot illustrates the feature:

Figure 1.10 – Know who's in your workbook

Visual refresh: This is more of a UI design change that aims at making the menu tabs cleaner and more action aligned.

The following screenshot illustrates the feature:

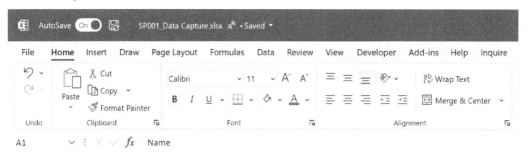

Figure 1.11 – Visual refresh

The XLOOKUP function: This is a replacement for VLOOKUP and HLOOKUP. It allows you to search across rows or columns and pick values to the left or right, or above or below your found lookup value. It also contains error handling.

The following screenshot illustrates the feature:

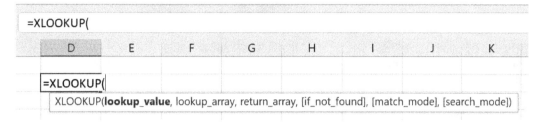

Figure 1.12 – The XLOOKUP function

The LET function: LET is a function that allows you to create the equivalent of reusable variables within a formula.

The following screenshot shows an example of using LET to assign a value to a variable called *radius* and using it for calculation:

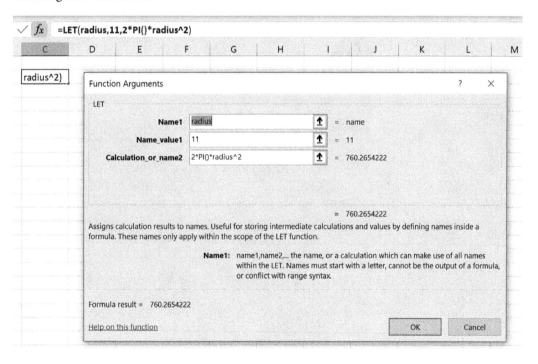

Figure 1.13 – The LET function

Dynamic arrays: Dynamic arrays are the biggest update in Excel 2022. It is what makes it a great version for dashboard creation. We have a separate section on dynamic arrays in *Chapter 4, Power Query: the Ultimate Data Transformation Tool*.

Dynamic arrays allow calculations that spill into multiple cells and also automatically shrink or expand. Before dynamic arrays, people tried to achieve this by using array formulas, but they don't shrink and can be very difficult to work with.

In the following screenshot is the use of UNIQUE, a dynamic array function, to get the unique entries from a range:

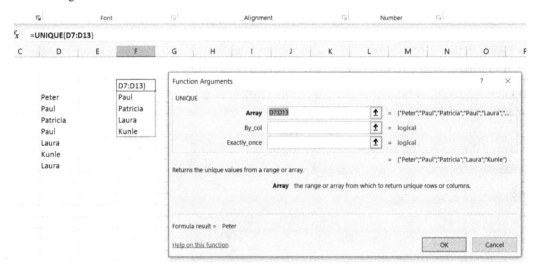

Figure 1.14 – Dynamic arrays

The XMATCH function: Like XLOOKUP, this is a replacement for the MATCH function.

The following screenshot illustrates the feature:

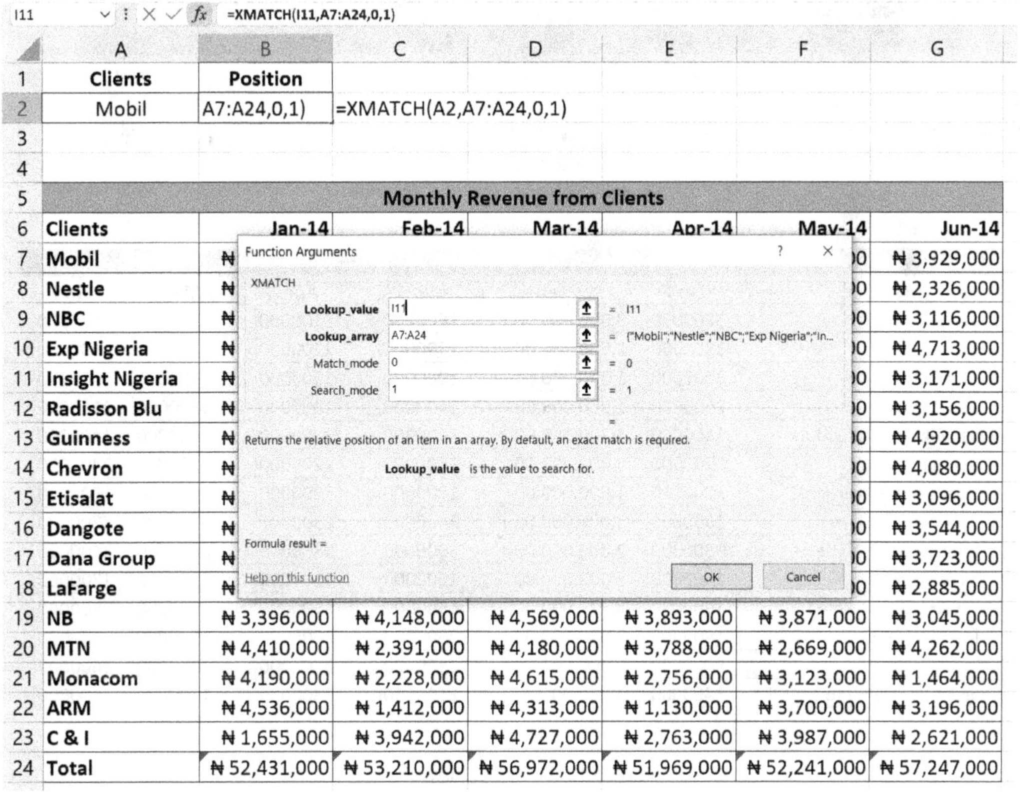

Figure 1.15 – The XMATCH function

Sheet views: This feature allows you to create many saved, customized, filtered, and/or sorted views of a table. It is a huge convenience when working on a shared file so that each person's view is retained.

The following screenshot illustrates the feature:

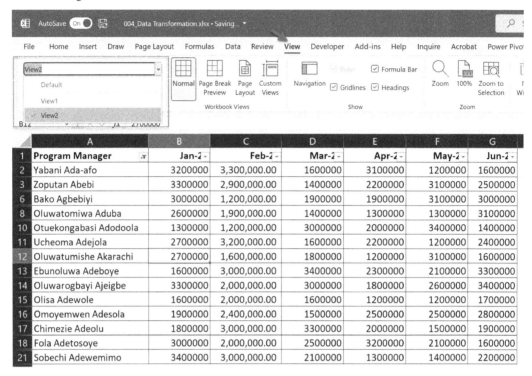

	A	B	C	D	E	F	G
1	Program Manager	Jan-2	Feb-2	Mar-2	Apr-2	May-2	Jun-2
2	Yabani Ada-afo	3200000	3,300,000.00	1600000	3100000	1200000	1600000
3	Zoputan Abebi	3300000	2,900,000.00	1400000	2200000	3100000	2500000
6	Bako Agbebiyi	3000000	1,200,000.00	1900000	1900000	3100000	3000000
8	Oluwatomiwa Aduba	2600000	1,900,000.00	1400000	1300000	1300000	3100000
10	Otuekongabasi Adodoola	1300000	1,200,000.00	3000000	2000000	3400000	1400000
11	Ucheoma Adejola	2700000	3,200,000.00	1600000	2200000	1200000	2400000
12	Oluwatumishe Akarachi	2700000	1,600,000.00	1800000	1200000	3100000	1600000
13	Ebunoluwa Adeboye	1600000	3,000,000.00	3400000	2300000	2100000	3300000
14	Oluwarogbayi Ajeigbe	3300000	2,000,000.00	3000000	1800000	2600000	3400000
15	Olisa Adewole	1600000	2,000,000.00	1600000	1200000	1200000	1700000
16	Omoyemwen Adesola	1900000	2,400,000.00	1500000	2500000	2500000	2800000
17	Chimezie Adeolu	1800000	3,000,000.00	3300000	2000000	1500000	1900000
18	Fola Adetosoye	3000000	2,000,000.00	2500000	3200000	2100000	1600000
21	Sobechi Adewemimo	3400000	3,000,000.00	2100000	1300000	1400000	2200000

Figure 1.16 – Sheet views

Performance improvements: Many formulas have been optimized to compute faster, and to improve the overall stability of Excel. This is a big plus when working with large datasets, as is commonly the case with dashboards.

Unhide many sheets at once: This is a feature for people who work with many sheets and often need to hide/unhide sheets live.

The following screenshot illustrates the feature:

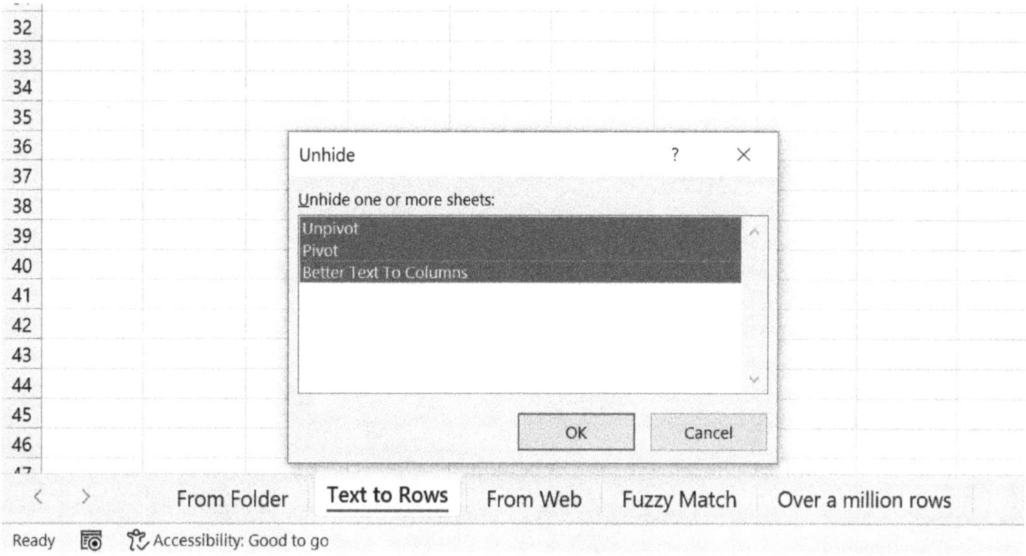

Figure 1.17 – Unhide many sheets at once

Altogether, these features make Excel 2021 a great tool to use for modern business reporting and dashboard building.

In the next section, we will discuss the other Excel versions.

Older versions of Excel

Excel 2019 and earlier are the older versions that I am referring to. Excel 2019 was released barely 3 years ago, and many people are still trying to catch up with the added features in Excel 2016 (especially the additional charts and forecast tool). So some people may find it shocking to classify Excel 2019 as an outdated version. However, when it comes to creating modern dashboards, you will do yourself good by accepting that all versions earlier than Excel 2021 are outdated.

One great thing about Excel is that the features are incremental, so the newer versions have the features of the older versions retained. To give you a good idea of the other features in Excel 365 and Excel 2021 we will be focusing on as we build dashboards, I have created a listing of all the notable features that come with each version of Excel, dating back to Excel 2007, in the following subsections.

Excel 2019

Excel 2019 was released in September 2018 and came preloaded with the following functions that were not in the earlier version:

- New functions, such as `CONCAT`, `IFS`, `MAXIFS`, `MINIFS`, `SWITCH`, and `TEXTJOIN`
- Map charts and funnel charts
- Insert vector graphics and 3D models
- New themes (especially the famous black theme)
- Customizable default PivotTable layout
- PivotTable automatic date and time grouping
- PivotChart drill-down buttons
- Automatic relationship detection in the data model
- Search in the PivotTable field list
- Power Query improvements

Excel 2016

Excel 2016 was released in September 2015 and created a big buzz in the user community due to its very popular new charts. Before it, Excel had not delivered any major chart updates for over a decade. The following is a listing of the new features it introduced:

- New chart types: treemap, sunburst, histogram, box and whisker, waterfall, and Pareto
- Power Query (known in this version as Get and Transform Data)
- 3D maps

Excel 2013

Excel 2013 was released in January 2013 and came with a major UI upgrade. The following is a full listing of the new features it delivered:

- Flash Fill
- Chart recommendations
- Filter tables with slicers
- One workbook, one window (this fixed a big issue of needing to work with two different Excel files opened and displayed at the same time on one or two monitors)
- Power Query (a huge time-saving and data transformation tool)

- Drill down, drill up, and cross drill in Pivot Table
- Standalone PivotChart
- 51 new functions

Excel 2010

Excel 2010 was released in June 2010 and was another delight to the user communities because of its sparkline feature. Excel fans around the world were churning out interesting use cases for sparklines, and it was positioned as a great-to-have visual in a dashboard. The following is a listing of its new features:

- Sparklines
- Slicers
- Improved tables and filters
- Paste previews
- More conditional formatting options
- Improved PivotTable calculation options

Excel 2007

Excel 2007 was released in January 2007 and caused an uproar in the user community as people expressed their displeasure with the new ribbon style of the menu. Today, it is, however, considered one of the most important versions ever released, as it was the first to have 1,048,576 rows and 16,384 columns. The following list shows the new features in the version:

- The now well-loved ribbon system
- Increased number of cells per sheet
- Themes and styles
- Sort by color, add levels in filters, and many additions to sort and filter functionality
- New functions, including `IFERROR`, `AVERAGEIFS`, `SUMIFS`, `COUNTIFS`, and `Cube` formulas
- Improved charts
- Improved PivotTable

We are now at the end of the chapter; it has been a very enlightening one on dashboards, reports, and Microsoft Excel versions. In the next section, we will do a quick summary of the entire chapter.

Summary

In this chapter, we have covered the key foundational things to know as we progress into building modern dashboards. Just to reiterate, the major learning highlights from this chapter are as follows: we started with the difference between dashboards and reports. We then learned about why dashboards are important for modern businesses. We then learned about the definitive characteristics of dashboards. Next, we went through the different Excel versions and why Excel 365 and Excel 2021 are the recommended versions for building dashboards.

And that's it for this chapter; in the next chapter, we will dive into the common dashboards required by most modern companies.

Further reading

You can read more on the Excel features mentioned in this chapter at this official Microsoft documentation pages:

- *What's new in Excel 2021 for Windows*: https://support.microsoft.com/en-us/office/what-s-new-in-excel-2021-for-windows-f953fe71-8f85-4423-bef9-8a195c7a1100

- *What's new in Office 2021*: https://support.microsoft.com/en-us/office/what-s-new-in-office-2021-43848c29-665d-4b1b-bc12-acd2bfb3910a

- *What's the difference between Microsoft 365 and Office 2021?*: https://support.microsoft.com/en-us/office/what-s-the-difference-between-microsoft-365-and-office-2021-ed447ebf-6060-46f9-9e90-a239bd27eb96

2
Common Dashboards in Large Companies

Congratulations on the progress you are making. Now you are no longer unclear about the differences between dashboards and reports. In this chapter, we will take it a few steps further. Building on what we learned in *Chapter 1, Dashboards, Reports, and M365 Excel*, in this chapter, we will be exploring the common categories of dashboards used in the business world. Businesses – especially large companies where analytics and report automation are a must-have – have teams creating these categories of dashboards.

By the end of this chapter, you will have a good understanding of the major dashboard types and the insights they are meant to reflect. You will be exposed to common insights, also known as **Key Performance Indicators (KPIs)**, that decision-makers want to see captured. Together, we will examine, from a business manager's point of view, how dashboards must be set up to enable KPIs to be seen and acted on. At the same time, we will get a good grasp of the necessary datasets you will require to build dashboards.

In this chapter, we will cover the following topics:

- Major types of dashboards
- Understanding the sales dashboard
- Understanding the financial analysis dashboard
- Understanding the **Human Resources (HR)** dashboard
- Understanding the supply chain and logistics dashboard
- Understanding the marketing dashboard

Major types of dashboards

There are at least five major categories of dashboards that all large companies require. They are listed as follows:

- The **Sales dashboard** tracks the sales amount, sales quantity, average sales invoice amount, average quantity per invoice, sales calls, active customers, and sales discounts often dimensioned by region, product categories, date, sales officers, and customer type, and compared with already set targets. It is one of the most important dashboards in a company and is of particular interest to the company's managing director, head of sales, and head of finance.

- The **Financial analysis dashboard** tracks a company's financial transactions and financial position. A major aspect of the dashboard is tracking financial expenses by cost categories, cost centers, and date. Usually, these are departments and functional units within the company that have their own budget allocation, and then do a comparison of the actual expenditure versus the budget. Many companies also analyze the revenue generated by product lines against the associated costs and analysis of employee productivity as a ratio of revenue against the employee headcount. The analysis of revenue against the employee headcount is often done for the overall company employee headcount and a separate one is done for the sales employee headcount. Another important aspect of this dashboard is visually displaying the company's financial performance ratios: the gross profit margin, operating profit margin, net profit margin, operating expenses efficiency, asset management ratio, liquidity ratio, leverage ratio, and balance sheet ratio.

- The **HR dashboard** displays the metrics about the people in a company, the resources allocated for their use, and all activities under the HR department. A typical HR dashboard will track headcounts by branch and department, personnel expenses, learning and development activities, leaves and vacations, employee performance evaluations, and staffing activities.

- The **Supply chain and logistics dashboard** tracks everything that relates to a company's procurement activities, distribution activities, production activities, inventory management, and vendors. Usually, the focus is on reporting efficiency, in terms of time and the costs of operations for the supply chain department. The dashboard is of particular importance to the managing director, head of operations, and head of finance because a huge chunk of the company's expenses is tied to the activities monitored by the dashboard.

- The **Marketing dashboard** tracks all of a company's marketing activities across traditional media and digital media, as dimensioned by partners, periods, regions, and products. It is often built to integrate data from third-party vendors who carry out marketing and advertising activities for the company. The vendors can range from digital agencies that manage the company's Facebook ads, Google ads, and Twitter ads, to traditional media agencies doing on-the-street and in-person product activations. It aims to measure the company's return on marketing activities and uncover the most effective marketing channel combination to generate the most sales for the same expenditure.

Throughout this chapter and the entire book, we will use a 25,000-employee company that has the following functional organogram as an easy example of how to build dashboards for it. The reason for this approach is twofold:

- This will help those of you who are completely new to how a typical large company is structured functionally. You will not confuse the aberrations you see in poorly structured sole entrepreneurship businesses and young start-ups with the proper structure that a large company typically has.

- Some of you will be from a **Software-as-a-Service (SaaS)** business space, and others will be from a more conventional business space. As much as people like to talk up the differences between a SaaS company and a non-SaaS company, they are more alike than not. The organogram we are using aligns with them and makes it easy for you to apply the learning from this book to your SaaS and non-SaaS companies. Only the supply chain dashboard will be very different for SaaS and non-SaaS companies.

The following diagram is a functional organogram for a large company:

Figure 2.1 – The functional organogram of a large company

This structure applies to most large organizations, whether they are SaaS companies, financial institutions, manufacturing companies, retail companies, telecoms companies, publishing houses, professional services companies, hospitality companies, or airlines. A SaaS company's operations team might be mostly software engineers. An accounting services company's operations team will be its army of certified accountants. Essentially, the specific roles and titles in the functional breakdowns listed in

Figure 2.1 will change from company to company, but the analytics needs will still be very much alike. All companies with the preceding structure will need a sales dashboard, a financial analysis dashboard, an HR dashboard, an operations/logistics dashboard, and a marketing dashboard.

Understanding the sales dashboard

Every company's primary activity is sales. Businesses exist to generate sales. Even non-profit organizations and public service organizations that do not charge for their services are primarily driven to grow the usage of their services. Sales is simply the acquisition of your products or services. It does not matter whether the acquirer does not pay you. You could even run an organization that is funded by the government to provide free Covid-19 vaccinations to rural community dwellers. Though you are not charging the end users for the vaccine, your organization's existence is to ensure the number of people using your services is growing. You would definitely be worried if people stopped using your services or if the numbers did not meet the goals you agreed on with your funding partner.

Sales dashboards are used to track all that is strategically important to the company about the acquisition of its products and services. To make it less clumsy to explain the sales dashboard, I will be focusing on a for-profit business scenario. Additionally, I will use the term *products* to represent both products and services.

Sales managers either love or hate dashboards. The ones who love it always have new ideas on what more to add to the dashboard and can easily overload it with too many details so that it becomes only useable for them, while everyone else finds it overwhelming or confusing. For people like that, I suggest that you start with a wireframe or sketch of the dashboard. Ask them to manage their expectations and requests before you start doing the actual modeling and design in Excel. If you take a laxer approach with them, every review meeting will include the addition of new metrics and design changes.

Often, the sales managers who loathe dashboards were once field sales officers who were victims of analytics that had no sensible relation to what was happening on the field. For them, they see the dashboard as a fancy tool that the company management wants, and there's nothing wrong with that. Do understand that when you are dealing with them, much more than the insights to run their sales team better, you are first of all freeing them from a boring management request. So, you want to start by understanding what they need to show management before trying to win them over on how you can help them with insights that will take their sales team from good to great.

A typical for-profit company will want to track some or all of the following KPIs:

- **Sales growth**: A report might stop at showing just the sales figures, but a dashboard goes further to help managers see the sales trend. Sales growth can be presented as a percentage figure or on a trend-showing chart. Often, it will be dimensioned by products, sales channels, regions, and the time period. In simpler terms, the user might want to see sales growth by product lines, sales channels, regions, and other meaningful categories. And while using those, you might want to see a year-to-year comparison, a quarter-to-quarter comparison, and a month-to-month comparison. When there is an already set sales growth target, you will need to show the actual sales growth against the sales growth target. Often, people assume sales must be shown in a currency value, but that's not always the case. Some companies' internal setup of budgeting and forecasts are tied to sales volume, and for them, the sales volume is more important than the sales value. You will want to check with the company's head of sales to understand the strategic insights they want. From my personal experience, most sales dashboards will have a mix of sales value and sales volume insights.

- **Sales channels performance**: Companies sell their products through different sales channels and all sales are not equal. Some channels are more costly and problematic for a company than other channels. A retail company might value sales from its online store more sales via its distributor's store. The company might be getting a higher sales margin for the online store as it might just be the payment processor it's paying a small percentage of the sales' full value. In contrast, with the distributor channel, it is giving a significant percentage of its recommended retail value (the full sales value) to the distributor. So, companies are usually looking for ways to achieve a higher ratio of their sales being made via the more favorable sales channels. Have you ever wondered why your bank wants you to do everything via their phone app? Usually, this KPI is expressed as a percentage value of total sales. It shows the percentage value of the selected sales channel as a ratio of total sales. Again, the sales can be a currency value or sales volume.

- **Average sales per customer**: For SaaS companies where revenue is more important than sales volume in their forecast and demand planning, this is referred to as **Average Revenue Per User** (**ARPU**). The KPI's name says it all. Its power is in showing the company how much, on average, they make from each customer. This is then compared with the industry average to understand whether the company is doing poorly in generating sales compared to its competitors. Also, some companies set a goal for this. This metric enables them to see whether they are achieving the goal. In one of my data analytics roles for a telecoms company, which involved creating a sales dashboard for their Africa operations, this KPI was even more important than the total sales value. A lot of the company's plans and budget around marketing expenditure and sales bonuses revolved around it. The usual formula for this KPI is total sales divided by the total number of customers sold to.

- **Average order value**: This measures the average amount of spending per order placed with the company. Do not confuse it with the average sales per customer because the formula for this is the total sales divided by the total orders placed. Not all companies will include this in their top 10 sales KPIs, but for some B2B companies, it can be a big insight. It can show whether clients are ignoring them in favor of their competition for high-value orders. Ever heard of the quote, *no one ever gets fired for buying IBM*? Well, in the corporate procurement space, decision-makers feel more at ease buying from big names even if they could have gotten a better deal from a different supplier. It is a worrisome thing to experience, and companies at a disadvantage due to that perception in their industry typically track this to see whether their strategies to break into the big order value space yield any fruit.

- **Active customers versus total customers**: I can hear someone asking whether there can be a customer who's not active. The interesting thing in the business world is how hard we try to let go of a customer. A customer is someone who has bought your product. Unfortunately, even if that was 10 years ago, technically, they are still your customer. Aside from some local laws prohibiting you from keeping their records, you can still always reach out to them unlike someone else who has never had a business transaction with you and is non-existent in your records. Common sense tells us that a customer who just purchased from you yesterday should not be classified in the same way as a customer who last bought from you 10 years ago. The application of that common sense is the reason for the different classifications of customers in the business space. A broad classification is active customers, inactive customers, and churned customers. Active customers are those who bought from you recently. For companies in sectors where customers use the products weekly or monthly, active customers can be set as customers who purchased your product in the last 30 days. Still, for the same type of companies, inactive customers can be set as customers who last purchased your product 31 to 90 days ago, and churned customers can be set as customers who last purchased over 90 days ago. This KPI is often expressed as active customers divided by the sum of active and inactive customers. Naturally, the higher the ratio, the fewer customers who end up in the churn category.

- **Market share**: This is one of the few KPIs that requires an external data source. Market share is a measure of the dominance of your products in the addressable market space. Usually, it is presented at a per-product-line level, and it requires buying market research data from third-party providers. Often, it is shown as a pie chart or 100% stacked-column chart showing your company's sales compared to the sales of your major competitors' sales in the market. It's more insightful when shown over the last couple of time spans – especially years. It provides a balance to the sales growth KPI, allowing sales managers to know whether they are losing or gaining market share regardless of their sales growth.

- **Sales per headcount**: This is a measure of the productivity of the company's staff. The primary view is the sales-per-sales-staff headcount, which is then checked against the industry average to understand whether the sales team is doing better than the competitors' sales teams. A secondary view can be the sales-per-staff headcount, which is sales divided by the total company staff count. The main reason some companies do this is to check whether they are more people-efficient than their competition. It can be a terrible thing to have twice the employee size of your competitors for the same amount of yearly revenue. Many CEOs use this as a compelling basis to transition to a more technology-dependent operations model if they find that they need more employees per sales amount than their competition.

- **Productive calls ratio**: Not every sales call by a sales officer leads to sales; however, in reality, a company's resources are used up for these sales calls, and the sales officers are paid to bring in sales. Hence, it's natural for the management to want to see how well their sales generation process is working. Is the lead generation process lousy and sending unqualified leads to the sales team? Or is it the sales team that is not doing a good job of converting qualified leads into sales? For a sales manager, a very insightful chart is one that shows the average productive calls ratio of their sales team and the quartiles. A box plot does this perfectly but might require some initial work to teach the sales manager how to interpret it. With this visual depiction of the KPI, the sales manager will know whether all their team members are struggling to make productive calls or it's just a segment of the sales officers who are not doing well.

- **Net Promoter Score (NPS)**: NPS is a customer satisfaction metric that enables a company to know the ratio of highly satisfied clients (promoters) to very unhappy clients (detractors). It uses a very simple but powerful customer survey question: *On a scale of 0 to 10, how likely are you to recommend our product to a friend or colleague?* Submissions that are of the range 0 to 6 are marked as detractors, 7 to 8 are marked as passives, and 9 to 10 are marked as promoters. The NPS value is the percentage of promoters minus the percentage of detractors. The NPS value can itself range from -100 to 100. -100 is when all your customers submit a rating of 6 and below. 100 is when all your customers submit a rating of 9 or 10. This KPI is very instructional for management to determine the success rate of customer loyalty and satisfaction strategies. And for companies looking to ride on a positive network effect (that is, seeing their products go viral), getting a high NPS is necessary.

- **Sales conversion rate**: Often, sales people work leads passed to them by marketing as potential customers (qualified leads) into becoming active customers. The process can be long and multi-stage. Sales managers want to see the leads count, the deals count, and the deals value for each stage in the sales conversion process. It is very well known that a company should not expect to generate a sales revenue that exceeds the total deals value it has in its sales pipeline. So, managers, over time, along with the help of sale conversion ratios, can reliably estimate how much deals value to have at each stage of the sales conversion process in order to meet a sales target.

- **Sales cycle length**: This KPI tracks the average number of days it takes the sales team to close a deal. For management, the sales conversion rate and sales cycle length are two sides of the same coin. While sales conversion rates show how well the sales team is converting sales opportunities into actual sales, the sales cycle length shows the time it takes them to make the sale. The target for sales managers is to have high sales conversion rates and low sales cycle lengths. Often, this KPI is dimensioned by the sales cycle stage, deal size, region, customer class, and new/existing customers.

The preceding list is not exhaustive, but depending on the company, there can be other metrics that are important to show on the sales dashboard. The rule to observe is don't mix a report and a dashboard, but I see it happen too frequently. Let reports be separate from dashboards. If you find yourself creating a dashboard that will cater to what the CEO, global sales head, regional sales head, branch sales head, channel sales manager, and field sales officers want to see, then you are on the wrong track. You will eventually do a report with some dashboard concepts – I have been in that situation before. You might need to show them this book and this paragraph so that they understand why it is not the right thing. Usually, dashboards are for decision-makers. A field sales officer should probably be looking at a sales report and not a sales dashboard. And the further apart the concerns of the decision-makers, the more likely it is that you should have separate dashboards for them. Having a management-level sales dashboard separate from a regional sales dashboard can be a more reasonable choice than giving the CEO and regional sales managers the same dashboard.

The usual datasets you will need to build the sales dashboard are the **Customer Relationship Management (CRM)** application data, the **Enterprise Resource Planning (ERP)** application data, the Salesforce management platform data, the employee headcount data, which is regularly updated, the customer survey responses for NPS calculations, the market research data on the market share and industry averages, and data from any other sales support tool the company uses.

For companies that use Microsoft Dynamics 365 or Salesforce, you can easily pull in the data in real time into Excel. See the following screenshot of the connector to Dynamics and Salesforce:

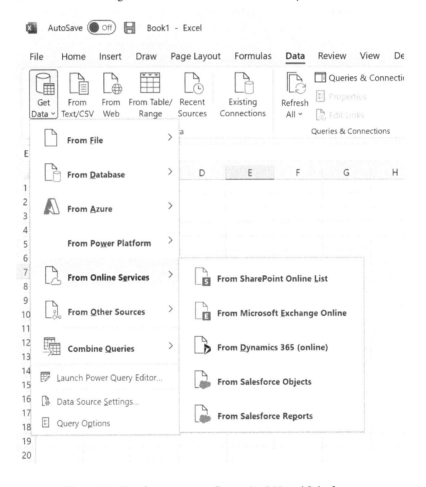

Figure 2.2 – Excel connector to Dynamics 365 and Salesforce

To help you see what a sales dashboard with all the KPIs mentioned can look like, see the following screenshot:

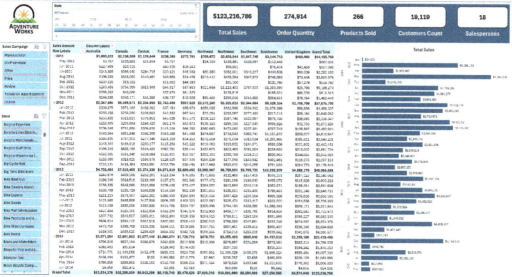

Figure 2.3 – An overview of a typical sales dashboard

Next, we will move on to examine the financial analysis dashboard.

Understanding the financial analysis dashboard

The lifeblood of every organization is its finances. Financial analysis dashboards are very important and should show the company's financial state. Unsurprisingly, the first dashboards that companies set up are around their financial activities. The finance department already creates many financial analysis reports both for internal use and external (such as tax, bank, investors, and more) use. And the finance managers are usually the first set of people, alongside the operations managers, to ask for dashboards.

The typical KPIs in a financial analysis dashboard are listed as follows:

- **Sales trend**: Just as the sales team like to keep tabs on sales, the finance team is also always monitoring sales. They are often displayed in comparison with last year's date and target.

- **Gross profit margin**: This is calculated as the gross profit divided by sales revenue. It measures the percentage left after deducting the cost of sales. The cost of sales (which is often labeled as the cost of goods sold for physical goods companies and the cost of revenue for service-only companies) are the direct costs incurred to produce the goods sold or service rendered. Care must be taken not to read too much meaning into the standalone value of this KPI. Different industries have different cost structures and having a high or low gross profit margin means nothing in itself except that you have a negative gross profit margin and should close the business. This KPI is more meaningful when it is shown as a trend over the years. Also, it can be compared to the industry average, thereby allowing management to know whether they are an efficient or inefficient producer. If a company's gross profit margin is less than the industry average, that means they are incurring production costs that are higher than their competition's.

- **Operating profit margin**: This is calculated as the operating profit divided by sales revenue. It reflects the percentage left after the production costs and business operations costs are deducted. For most companies without loans and interest-earning investments, this is the same as their profit before tax. So, it is a very important identifier of the actual profitability of a company. In every sector, the best-run companies are the ones that have very well-tuned operations that allow them to spend less of their sales revenue on operations compared to their competitors. Company executives are always looking for ways to be cost-effective and retain more of their sales revenue as profit. And as mentioned, for the gross profit margin, showing this as a trend and/or in comparison with the industry average is a more meaningful way to present this KPI rather than showing its one-time value.

- **Net profit margin**: This is calculated as the profit after tax divided by the sales revenue. It measures what the percentage left for the owners of the business after all business expenses have been covered. Investment returns and some valuation methods are dependent on this KPI. Company executives try to raise this as high as possible. It is not uncommon for them to look for ways to reduce taxes and put excess cash to income-earning use so as to boost the net profit margin. A more meaningful use of this KPI is to show the trend over the years and/or compare it with the industry average.

- **Account receivables aging**: Account receivables are sales made, but the associated money has not been collected from the customers. Every company's head of finance wants to see how much of the company's sales are still uncollected and in age brackets. For a company whose sales policy is Net-5 (meaning they are expecting payment in no more than 5 days after sales), the finance managers might want to see receivables in age brackets of 0 to 5 days old, 6 to 15 days old, 16 to 30 days old, 31 to 90 days old, and more than 90 days old. Often, this is visualized as a conditionally formatted table, bar chart, or column chart.

- **OpEx by cost center**: Every finance expense report shows a very lengthy breakdown of expenses by expense category or general ledger accounts and cost centers. You will want to avoid replicating that large endless scrolling table on your finance dashboard. So, a good compromise that still shows the major insights the decision-makers want to see is a table of expenses by cost center response sliced into the major cost categories they might want to drill down into.

- **Assets trend**: Assets are what drive a company's revenue generation process, and in the book world, we should be filling our dashboard with asset management ratios such as total asset turnover, fixed assets turnover, and inventory turnover. In practice, I have found that most finance managers don't think in those terms and are rather looking for clear trends in their asset positions and asset mix. They prefer a trend line that shows a sudden rise or dip in their assets and a general direction of the asset level. Often, that is enough for them. The key takeaway is not to hit an imaginary assets turnover value, but to see any trend they cannot explain as expected or desirable. Be sure to check with the dashboard users the particular assets they want to see on the dashboard, and remind them that they should use a fixed assets report for all deep probing needs.

- **Working capital lines**: This is one of the few KPIs where the trend is not as important as the current state. Working capital is a mix of current assets and current liabilities. It shows the ability of the company to meet its immediate financial obligations. Finance managers often want to see the company's current cash at hand, total account receivables, total account payables, inventories, bank overdraft drawn, other current assets, and other current liabilities.

- **Debt service**: Outstanding debts, the accrued debt service value, the next debt service payment date and amount, and the current value of any term sheet guard ratio (such as the debt service coverage ratio, interest coverage ratio, and debt service reserve account value) are important values to show regarding the company's debt financing. For the dashboard, the current values are of more importance than showing the trend or forecast.

- **Capital structure**: Company executives will appreciate seeing their companies current capital structure at a quick glance. Visually show the total equity, total debt, debt-to-equity ratio, return on equity, and if you can, the company's **Weighted Average Cost of Capital** (**WACC**).

- **Cash flow trend**: A trend of the cash flow from operating activities, cash flow from investing activities, and cash flow from financing activities is another very helpful insight for company executives. It shows, in a very clear and unmistakable way, the cash profile of a company. It helps them understand whether the cash is coming from unsustainable activities such as asset disposal and capital raises or from actual business operations.

The typical users of a high-level financial dashboard are the managing director, the finance director, senior finance managers, and some members of the board of directors. You want to be careful not to replicate the financial statements report in the financial dashboard or fill it with long tables of financial transactions. You can have the reports on separate Excel sheets but have just high-level insights on the dashboard.

Usually, the data for the financial dashboard will come from the company's ERP, any dedicated accounting application used, and market research data on industry averages.

The next category of the dashboard we will be examining is the HR dashboard.

Understanding the HR dashboard

The HR department is no longer what it used to be 20 years ago. Now they do more proactive planning than they used to do and are increasingly relying on analytics to ensure that their company is energized with the right people, who are treated correctly and are provided with the right resources.

The list of KPIs that will fill the HR dashboard of one company will usually be very different for another company, as the world of work has changed drastically in the last decade and companies are moving away from the traditional way of managing their staff. And with every new people management strategy comes a bucket list of KPIs to track. Luckily, there are some universally relevant KPIs.

The following is a list of these must-know KPIs by segment:

- **Headcount spread**: Company executives want to know the total staff and their spread by regions, departments, and for diversity goals, by race/gender. Showing this as a column or bar chart that can be stacked or clustered is a very common way to visualize this. Additionally, companies that have manpower plans per department might want to show the current headcount side by side with the target headcount. If you can show how the company headcount compares to competing companies with similar annual revenue, that is also a good insight for the company management team. Also, you can show a card of the ratio of HR staff to other staff in the company.

- **Employee attrition**: Employees leave companies for various reasons, and companies also let go of employees. What management is often interested in is seeing are the attrition rates over the years, seeing the most recent year's value by department, and other important categories. In addition, some HR managers want to see the attrition by the tenure of the employees: 0 to 1 year, 2 to 5 years, 5 to 10 years, and above 10 years. This can help them understand whether they are losing a lot of their recent hires or whether the old staff members are suddenly leaving. A combo chart (that is, a line chart and column chart combination) can help show both the attrition count and the attrition rate.

- **Personnel costs**: HR managers are expected to know the overall personnel costs of the company, so giving them this metric is a good thing. You will want to show a card of the most recent year's value with a growth indicator alongside it. Then, a clustered column chart or clustered bar chart showing the last 2 years' value by department is equally valuable. Have another card showing the average personnel cost and a growth indicator and a third card showing revenue per employee. Lastly, have a chart that breaks down the personnel costs by payroll cost, incentives, retirement benefits, and stock options.

- **Training**: A major aspect of an HR manager's planning involves employee learning and development. Each year, they work with all departments in the company to come up with training plans and budgets. They definitely want to track that expenditure and those activities on a dashboard. Valuable metrics to show are the total training spend, total training hours, training expenditure by department, training expenditure by region, training expenditure versus the budget, training hours by type of training, and the average rating of training relevance. Many companies have compliance, **Health**, **Safety, and Environment** (**HSE**), company policies, company culture, and regulatory required training that all or some staff must go through yearly. Having a bullet chart that tracks the achievement of this is a great add-on for this section of the HR dashboard.

- **Leave**: Companies have paid and unpaid leave broken down into categories such as earned leave, sick leave, casual leave, maternity leave, paternity leave, marriage leave, bereavement leave, sabbatical leave, and compensatory off leave. Not all companies have these many leave types, as some find it more convenient to bundle some leave types. However, showing the total leave days taken as a card and having a stacked clustered column or bar chart showing paid and unpaid leave across the different leave categories is often enough to capture the quick insights HR managers want to see.

- **Recruitment**: Often, HR teams are stressed by the never-ending cycle of hiring and ensuring no team lacks the manpower they need. Having a section of the dashboard reflect how they are performing and where they can do better in the hiring process is always a good thing. Have visuals showing the average time to fill open roles, interview-to-offer ratio, offer acceptance rate, and cost per hire.

- **Retention and productivity**: Have a small section of the dashboard to show the absenteeism rate, the employee satisfaction rating, the average performance rating, the dismissal rate, and the average employee tenure.

Usually, HR managers are more willing to let you have more control over the design and layout of their dashboard as long as you are giving them the insights they find valuable, and they do not need to do much to update the dashboard. What can be very problematic is that in many companies, the HR systems are not as digitalized and centralized as the sales and finance systems. You might need to help the HR managers restructure their data gathering process in such a way that their fragmented data sources are linkable. Explain to them that there must be a unique identifier in their recruitment data tables to eventually link with the staff database rather than expecting to use names to trace an employee's journey from recruitment to exit.

We will now examine the supply chain and logistics dashboard category.

Understanding the supply chain and logistics dashboard

The supply chain and logistics dashboards are particularly important for physical goods companies. The supply chain management unit of a company is a critical part of the company's operations. They are in charge of ensuring the timely procurement of raw materials, the effective coordination of the production and product distribution process, demand planning, and information systems integration with external parties to ensure a seamless logistics workflow.

Excel directly connects to some of the popularly used supply chain and resource planning platforms such as SAP and Microsoft Dynamics. For ones without a direct way to connect to Excel, a common alternative is to connect to the database the platforms are sitting on.

The following screenshot shows the SAP connector in Microsoft Excel:

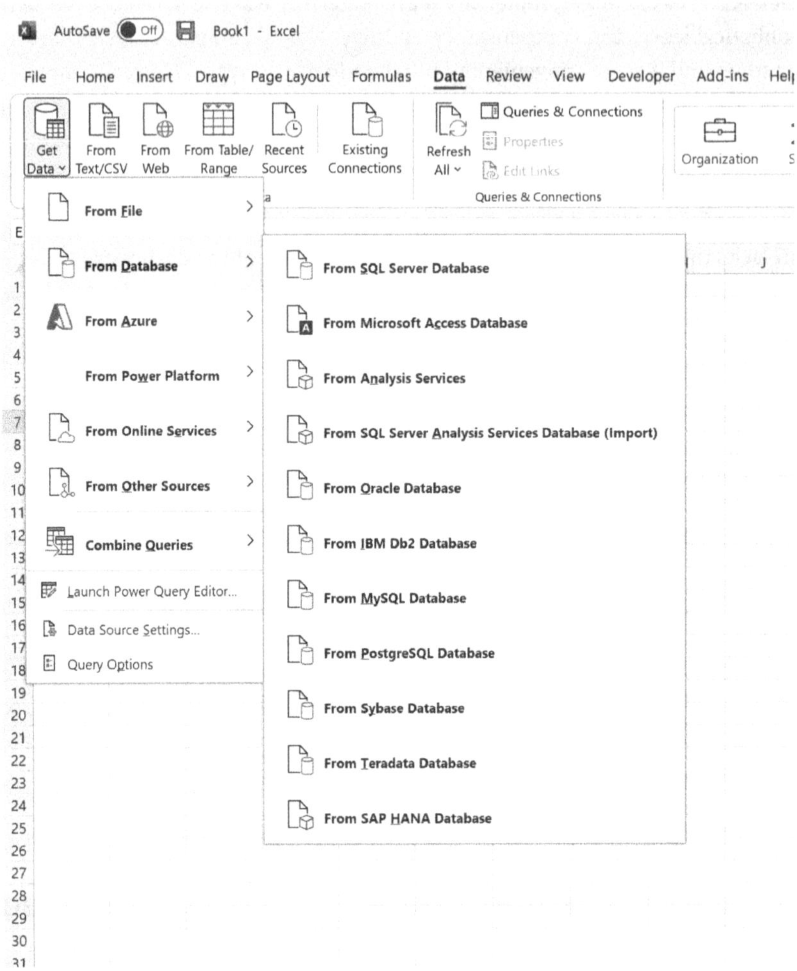

Figure 2.4 – Connectors to SAP and common databases

The head of operations, logistics managers, and other supply chain managers will benefit from a dashboard that helps them keep track of the following KPIs:

- **Capacity utilization**: Companies spend a lot to set up production factories, raw materials warehouses, finished goods warehouses, and distribution vehicles. Company executives want to see how well those assets are put to use. Is the factory operating close to its installed capacity? Are the warehouses less than half-filled and need to be scaled down? Are the trucks spending more time parked than on the road? You should provide the answers to these important questions in your supply chain dashboard. A pie chart or 100% stacked-column chart can be used to show these capacity utilization metrics.

- **Throughput**: Optimization of the distribution network for the time to deliver to the customer, the best fill rate, and the transportation cost is a major concern of the supply chain team. Have a section of your dashboard that shows a visual of the distribution network on a map and the sales throughput from the major distribution nodes. This will help supply chain managers see bottlenecks in their distribution networks and identify where to create new distribution nodes.

- **Order cycle time**: This is a measure of the time it takes for a confirmed order from a customer to be delivered to the customer. If you have ordered merchandise online, you will be familiar with the stages that your order goes through: order created, order accepted/confirmed, order shipped, and order delivered. This metric shows the average time it takes to go from order accepted/confirmed to order delivered. Most companies have a service-level commitment to deliver to customers within a set timeline, and this is only realizable if the supply chain team proactively works to meet the timeline. Having a way for them to see this easily and as close to real time as possible in your dashboard is a big aid to the supply chain managers.

- **Vendor performance**: Companies often rely on third-party entities (vendors) to carry out many of the activities necessary to ensure smooth operations. The procurement team of the operations and supply chain unit are responsible for sourcing the right vendors and setting the service agreements to ensure an acceptable quality of service is provided by the vendors. A robust supply chain dashboard will show the performance of the vendors in living up to the set service quality levels. And to help prevent over-dependence on a vendor, a visual analysis of actively used vendors is important. For companies with large numbers of vendors, doing a vendor concentration-clustered column chart might be better. You can show the major operations activities contracted out, along with how many vendors were used in the reporting period.

- **Days inventory outstanding**: This is a measure of the number of days for which inventory is stored before being used up. For companies using inventory management methods such as just-in-time, which aim to minimize the cost of holding inventory, the aim would be to keep the number of days as minimal as possible. For some other companies where there are cyclical price and availability issues with the supplies they need, inventory planning is usually more complex and can reflect a seasonality that the days inventory outstanding metric can reflect.

- **Distribution cost per sales**: Company executives want to see the costs incurred to get the manufactured goods to the paid customer. Usually, you provide more actionable insights by showing this as a ratio of the sales revenue. Seeing that the company spends $2 on warehousing and $20 on shipping goods to a customer is more instructive that showing an absolute amount of $20,000,000 as the distribution cost.

- **Perfect order rate**: This is a measure of order delivery accuracy. It tracks the ratio of orders delivered without incidents (for example, damages, inaccurate orders, or late deliveries). The higher the rate, the better. This can be shown as a gauge visual.

Typically, companies spend a lot to set up the most expensive and robust supply chain management platform they can afford, yet the complexity of supply chain management means it is never perfect. It is not uncommon for some business logic to be unclear or not reflected in the system's data, often causing you to work with incomplete data in your dashboard-building process. You want to work closely with a high-ranking supply chain staff member in the company to guide you through the labyrinth that most supply chain setups in companies usually are.

The following screenshot is an example of a supply chain and logistics dashboard:

Figure 2.5 – An overview of a supply chain dashboard example

Finally, we will examine the marketing dashboard category.

Understanding the marketing dashboard

The marketing department of a company is responsible for product design, unlocking sales channels, and boosting demand for the company's products, while at the same time, positioning the company as a strong and reputable brand. Marketing dashboards are meant to reflect the effectiveness of all the company's marketing activities in creating product acceptance, generating demand, and increasing the company's brand value.

A large part of marketing activities is strategy-based and that often creates the problem of tracking and reporting their effectiveness. It is not unusual that you will have to help the marketing team create numeric ways of tracking the effectiveness of some of their activities. For example, how do you track and report the effectiveness of the marketing department's social media activities? How do you assign a meaningful number to the thousands of tweets, Facebook posts, Instagram posts, TikTok posts, and LinkedIn posts they put out monthly? One way is to carry out sentiment scoring on the conversations and engagements. And in Excel, it is easy once you add the **Azure Machine Learning** add-in from the Office app store. You can see the add-in in the following screenshot:

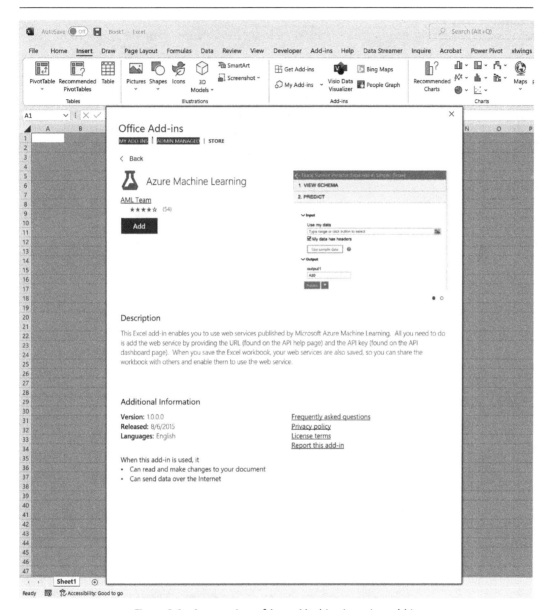

Figure 2.6 – An overview of Azure Machine Learning add-in

The other issue is how to get the data from social media platforms. There's usually the option to download or export data, which is thanks to the **General Data Protection Regulation (GDPR)** rules that mandate social media platforms to allow users to download their data. But that could be very impractical to do daily, and you might be limited to an account's posts without the other users' engagements. A more common approach is to connect via an **Application Programming Interface**

(**API**) – either the platform's or a third-party API – to the live data feed from the platforms for use within Excel.

Another challenge that is often faced in marketing dashboard creation is the over-reliance on contracted agents or media platforms analytics. It is not uncommon to see companies use Google Analytics to track user activities on their websites and mobile apps. Google Analytics automatically generates hundreds of analytics, which they present to all companies and individuals that use their platform.

The following is a screenshot of the Google Analytics dashboard:

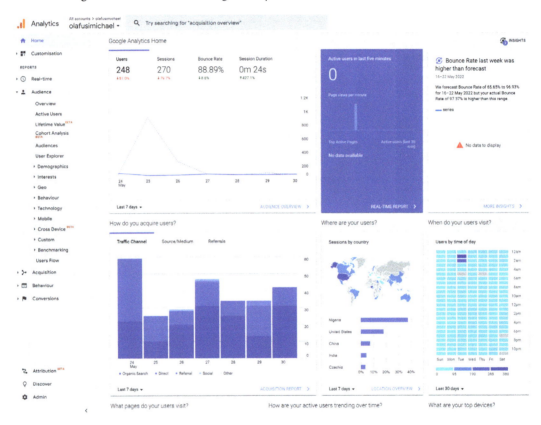

Figure 2.7 – An overview of the Google Analytics auto-created dashboard

And as you can imagine, there is no consideration for your unique needs or strategic goals. You will want to pull out the data you need from Google Analytics and other platforms the company uses for marketing activities, and then create the actionable insights the marketing team actually needs. You will also find yourself relating the data across the different sources to actual sales and customer activities recorded on the company's internal data.

The following is a list of common marketing KPIs you will typically be tracking on the marketing dashboard:

- **Customer acquisition cost**: This is one of the most important marketing KPIs to track. How much does the company spend, on average, to gain a new customer? The answer is the basis for most marketing plans and budgets. This is usually calculated as the total marketing expenditure divided by the number of new customers acquired. It is more insightful to show this as a trend and in comparison to the industry average (if the data exists).

- **Customer lifetime value**: This is another important marketing KPI, as it gives an estimate of what each customer is worth to the company. It is an average value but still the best figure to work with when spending to get new customers. For companies that have customer segmentation where each segment demonstrates very different purchasing power, having this metric computed by the different customer segments might be more meaningful. The usual calculation for customer lifetime value is to multiply the average amount spent by the customer by the average number of times a customer buys from the company throughout the time the customer engages with the company. Let's say the average order customers place is $50 and they buy on average once a month for a 2-year period before suddenly no longer purchasing from the company. The customer lifetime value will be $50 x 24 lifetime purchases = $1,200. Many companies peg marketing expenditure to a fraction of this. A company with a strategy of not spending more than 10% of the customer lifetime value on customer acquisition will typically set a budget that reflects how many customers they aim to acquire multiplied by 10% of the customer lifetime value.

- **Cost per lead**: Advertising campaigns, promotional campaigns, and online campaigns are usually used to capture potential leads who are then further engaged and filtered down to qualified leads for the sales team to work into making a purchase. The right way to track the success of marketing campaigns is to figure out how many qualified leads they generate. And usually, companies want to spend the least amount to get a qualified lead. This KPI shows how much marketing expenditure is incurred per qualified lead. Usually, you want to show the total and the breakdown by the marketing campaign.

- **Customer retention**: This is a measure of how frequently your customers make new purchases. A quick and easy computation is to divide your active customer base by your total (not churned) customer base. Present this as a ratio on a card and indicate its growth over the previous year. You will likely want to also have a separate report on the **Recency, Frequency, and Monetary (RFM)** value score across the company's non-churned customers. Then, show the average RFM score on the dashboard in a card that also indicates the growth over the previous year.

- **Customer engagement**: The response time to customer inquiries on the different web platforms the company interfaces with the public is a critical metric to track. Additionally, the quality of those engagements is usually measured by the average feedback rating users and customers leave at the end of the engagements. These two KPIs are useful to marketing managers in assessing the quality of work their team do and protecting the integrity and brand of the company. These two can be shown as cards and made responsive to filters by using an engagement platform.

- **Website and app usage**: Metrics such as users, site visits, click-through rates, bounce rates, sessions, app downloads, user registrations, and other important digital platform usage metrics should be shown as cards with growth indicators.

- **Audience reach**: Social media reach and traditional media reach should be tracked on the dashboard. If the media platforms are not too many, you can show each separately as a card: Facebook reach, Twitter reach, LinkedIn reach, Google ads reach, radio ads reach, newspaper ads reach, and TV ads reach. The trouble might be getting this data for all of the platforms. Some social media platforms readily make the daily, weekly, and monthly audience reach available. A weekly or monthly reach can be a more manageable periodicity than a daily reach. The following screenshot shows how to access audience reach data on LinkedIn. Notice the **Export** button on the right-hand side:

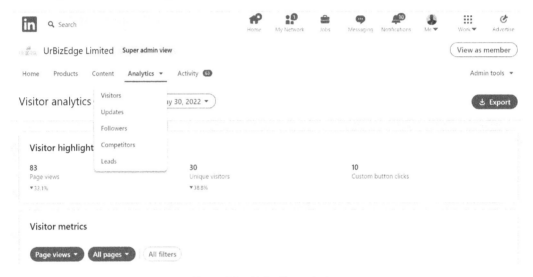

Figure 2.8 – LinkedIn analytics

There are many other marketing KPIs that can be tracked, but you want to be careful not to fill your dashboard with vanity metrics. Vanity metrics are metrics that have no impact on sales conversion or meaningful use for the marketing team.

We have come to the end of this chapter, and in the next section, we will run through what we have learned.

Summary

In this chapter, we covered the major types of business dashboards and what KPIs each type is expected to track for company executives. You should no longer be unclear as to what a sales dashboard is meant to track and what datasets you need to use to build it. The same goes for the financial dashboard, HR dashboard, supply chain dashboard, and marketing dashboard. Visual examples of each dashboard type were provided to help you have a clear idea of what your final dashboard may look like.

That sums up this chapter. In the next chapter, we will go through how to properly connect to the needed datasets in an easy-to-refresh way and do some data preparation at the data ingestion stage.

Part 2 –
Keeping Your Eyes
on Automation

This part gives you the skills to properly bring in your datasets, transform the data, link different data together, analyze the data, extract the business-relevant metrics, and set up the reporting framework the dashboard will sit on.

This part has the following chapters:

- *Chapter 3, The Importance of Connecting Directly to the Primary Data Sources*
- *Chapter 4, Power Query: the Ultimate Data Transformation Tool*
- *Chapter 5, PivotTable and Power Pivot*
- *Chapter 6, Must-Know Legacy Excel Functions*
- *Chapter 7, Dynamic Array Functions and Lambda Functions*

3

The Importance of Connecting Directly to the Primary Data Sources

The most important part of dashboard-building is accessing the relevant data sources. Without data, you can't have any dashboard. Data is to a dashboard what flour is to cake, and there are many ways to get the needed data into Excel for dashboard creation. A very common way is to paste a copy of the data into an Excel sheet. People log in to their social media platforms, accounting software, resource-planning applications, sales applications, and HR software to grab an export of the data they need for their dashboard-building. For them, the convenient way to get data into Excel is to export data from the source and paste it into Excel.

There are many ways to get data into Excel other than by exporting it from the source and copy-pasting it into Excel. In this chapter, we will examine all the different ways to get data into Excel and what the peculiarities of each way are. For dashboard-building, you should connect to the primary data source. A primary data source is the original source of the data, the first place the data is recorded.

In this chapter, we will cover the following topics:

- The different ways to bring data into Excel
- Connecting directly to the primary data source
- Common issues and how to overcome them

The different ways to bring data into Excel

Excel is the world's most used data analysis tool and that's in part due to how easily it allows you to bring in data from all types of sources. You can go online and copy a web page and paste it into Excel, and it won't complain nor give an error. You can even paste an image into Excel; in fact, it is difficult to find what you can't copy and paste into Excel. The built-in flexibility of Excel makes it a very beginner-friendly tool.

The following screenshot shows an example of copying a table of populations by country from `https://en.wikipedia.org/wiki/List_of_countries_by_population_(United_Nations)` and pasting it into Excel:

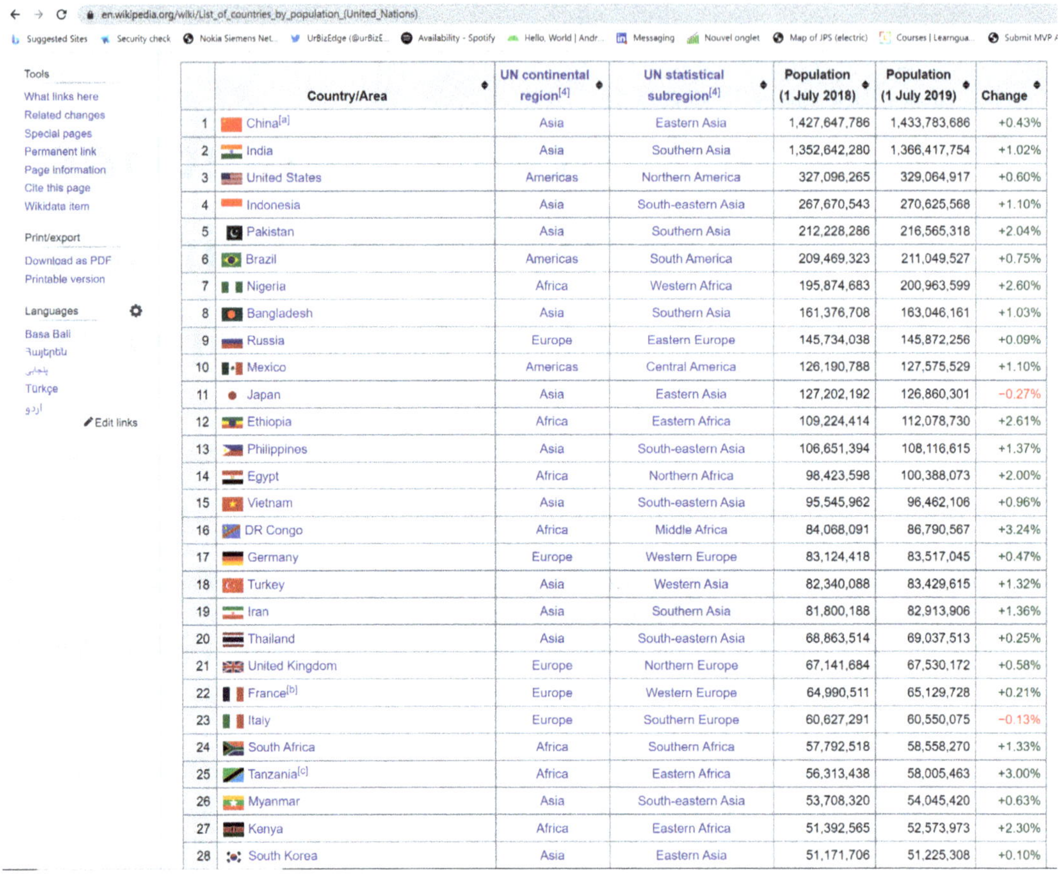

#	Country/Area	UN continental region[4]	UN statistical subregion[4]	Population (1 July 2018)	Population (1 July 2019)	Change
1	China[a]	Asia	Eastern Asia	1,427,647,786	1,433,783,686	+0.43%
2	India	Asia	Southern Asia	1,352,642,280	1,366,417,754	+1.02%
3	United States	Americas	Northern America	327,096,265	329,064,917	+0.60%
4	Indonesia	Asia	South-eastern Asia	267,670,543	270,625,568	+1.10%
5	Pakistan	Asia	Southern Asia	212,228,286	216,565,318	+2.04%
6	Brazil	Americas	South America	209,469,323	211,049,527	+0.75%
7	Nigeria	Africa	Western Africa	195,874,683	200,963,599	+2.60%
8	Bangladesh	Asia	Southern Asia	161,376,708	163,046,161	+1.03%
9	Russia	Europe	Eastern Europe	145,734,038	145,872,256	+0.09%
10	Mexico	Americas	Central America	126,190,788	127,575,529	+1.10%
11	Japan	Asia	Eastern Asia	127,202,192	126,860,301	−0.27%
12	Ethiopia	Africa	Eastern Africa	109,224,414	112,078,730	+2.61%
13	Philippines	Asia	South-eastern Asia	106,651,394	108,116,615	+1.37%
14	Egypt	Africa	Northern Africa	98,423,598	100,388,073	+2.00%
15	Vietnam	Asia	South-eastern Asia	95,545,962	96,462,106	+0.96%
16	DR Congo	Africa	Middle Africa	84,068,091	86,790,567	+3.24%
17	Germany	Europe	Western Europe	83,124,418	83,517,045	+0.47%
18	Turkey	Asia	Western Asia	82,340,088	83,429,615	+1.32%
19	Iran	Asia	Southern Asia	81,800,188	82,913,906	+1.36%
20	Thailand	Asia	South-eastern Asia	68,863,514	69,037,513	+0.25%
21	United Kingdom	Europe	Northern Europe	67,141,684	67,530,172	+0.58%
22	France[b]	Europe	Western Europe	64,990,511	65,129,728	+0.21%
23	Italy	Europe	Southern Europe	60,627,291	60,550,075	−0.13%
24	South Africa	Africa	Southern Africa	57,792,518	58,558,270	+1.33%
25	Tanzania[c]	Africa	Eastern Africa	56,313,438	58,005,463	+3.00%
26	Myanmar	Asia	South-eastern Asia	53,708,320	54,045,420	+0.63%
27	Kenya	Africa	Eastern Africa	51,392,565	52,573,973	+2.30%
28	South Korea	Asia	Eastern Asia	51,171,706	51,225,308	+0.10%

Figure 3.1 – Web page of countries and their populations

And yes, the desired goal of having a copy of the data in Excel seems to have been achieved here:

Figure 3.2 – The web page pasted into Excel

What many people do not know is that Excel offers other ways to bring data into it besides pasting the copied data. We could have connected Excel directly to the web page by using the **From Web** tool in Excel.

To grab data directly from a web page, you go to the **Data** menu, then **Get Data**, and then **From Other Sources**, as shown in the following screenshot:

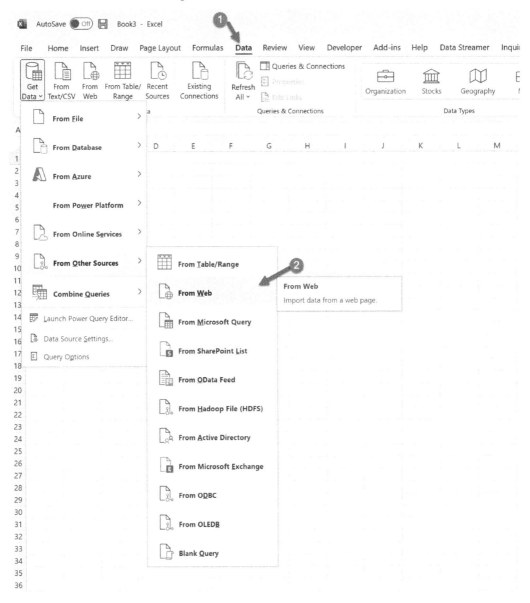

Figure 3.3 – Getting data from the web in Excel

You simply put in the web page URL and click on **OK**, as shown in the following screenshot:

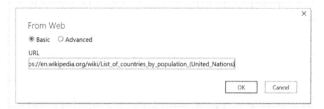

Figure 3.4 – Indicating the web page address to pull data from

A navigator window comes up with a preview of the website data, as seen in the following screenshot:

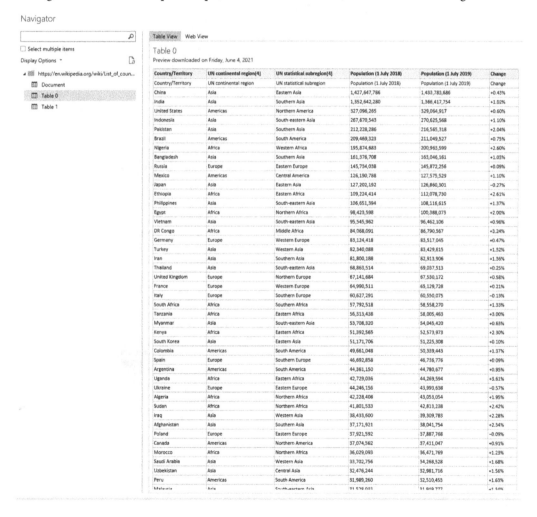

Figure 3.5 – Window with a preview of the web page data

This approach comes with the benefit of getting updates easily when you need to grab updated data from the web page. As opposed to having to do the entire copy-paste process each time, you just need to update the data in Excel. With this **From Web** approach, a simple refresh is all that is required. The following screenshot shows how to carry out the refresh:

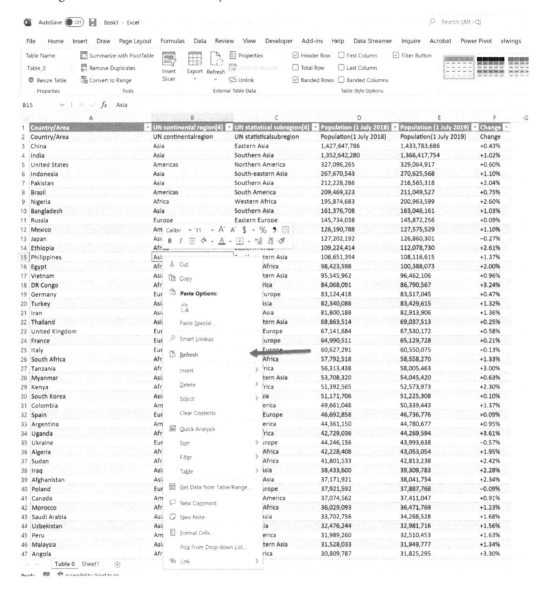

Figure 3.6 – Refreshing the data in Excel

There are five different ways to bring data into Excel and some of these ways are tied to the nature of the data source. The five ways are as follows:

- Copying and pasting data into Excel
- Importing data from flat files
- Importing data from databases
- Importing data from cloud platforms
- Importing data through custom connectors

We will dive deeper into these five methods and how they differ from one another in the following sub-sections.

Copying and pasting data into Excel

Copy and pasting data into Excel can be an error-free way to get data into Excel but it comes with the downside of no option to live-refresh to pull in updates from a data source. For one-time reports and analysis, this limitation is not an issue, but for dashboards that must be easy to update, it is a major concern. Hence, you'll want to avoid using copy and paste to bring in data for your dashboard-building.

In the following screenshot, I emphasize that the **Paste** tool in Excel is forbidden for bringing data into Excel for dashboard-building:

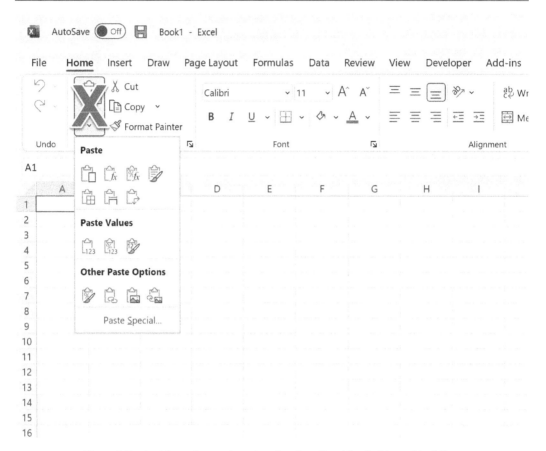

Figure 3.7 – Avoid copying and pasting data into Excel for dashboard-building

Next, we will examine importing data from flat files.

Importing data from flat files

Flat files are standalone data files such as **Comma-Separated Values (CSV)** files, text files, **JavaScript Object Notation (JSON)** files, **Extensible Markup Language** (**XML**) files, Parquet files, **Portable Document Format** (**PDF**) files, **XML Paper Specification** (**XPS**) files, **OpenDocument Spreadsheet** (**ODS**) files, and Excel files. Yes, you can import an Excel file into another Excel file. This is generally better than copying and pasting for repeatedly used reports and dashboards. Excel also allows you to import multiple flat files in one go if you put them all in one folder.

You can access these import tools by going to the **Data** menu, **Get Data**, and then **From File**, as shown in the following screenshot:

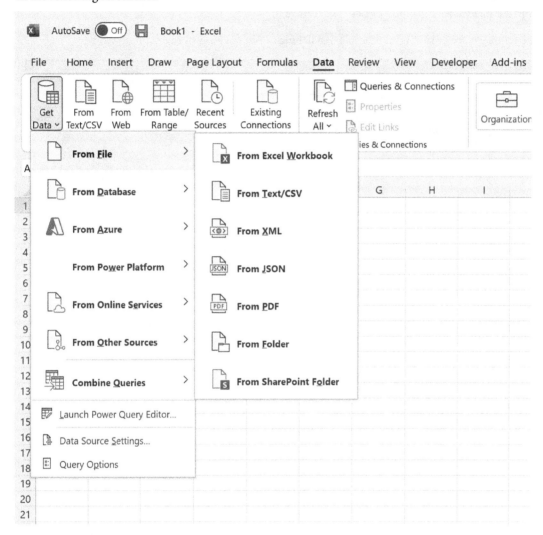

Figure 3.8 – Getting data from a file in Excel

How is this better than copying the data from the flat file and pasting it into Excel? When you import data from a flat file, Excel maintains the connection to that file and allows you to refresh it when you need to pull updated data from the file. This is the big advantage of importing data from a flat file rather than copy-pasting it.

It is understandable to think that only data from files on your PC can be imported via this method, but that's not the case. Once you combine this with an import from the web, you can import data from flat files that are in cloud or network storage.

The following screenshot is an example of a flat file in Azure cloud storage:

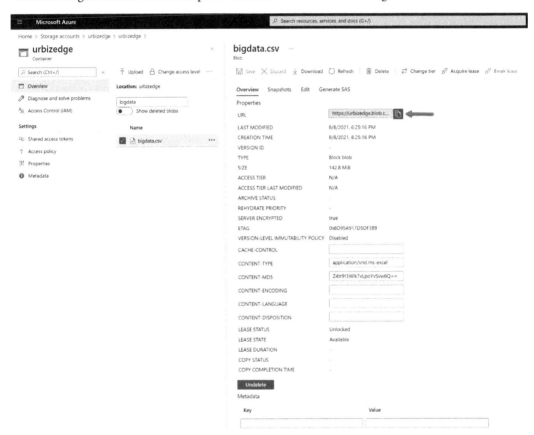

Figure 3.9 – A flat file in cloud storage

To connect to this cloud-hosted file, I grab its public URL; then, I go through **Get Data** and **From Web** in Excel, as shown in the following screenshot:

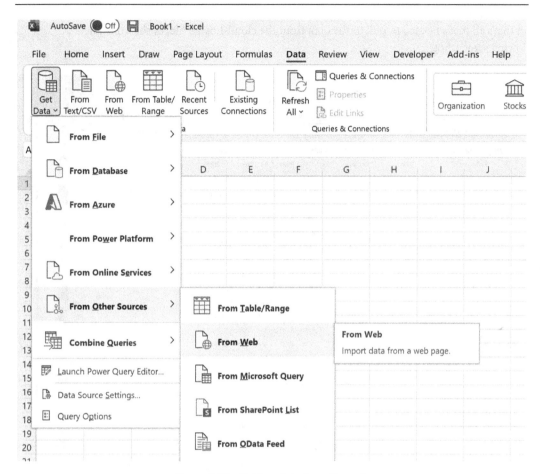

Figure 3.10 – Getting data from the web

I put in the file's URL, as shown in the following screenshot:

Figure 3.11 – Putting in the file's URL

And that's all that's needed to pull in the data from the cloud-hosted file, as shown in the following screenshot:

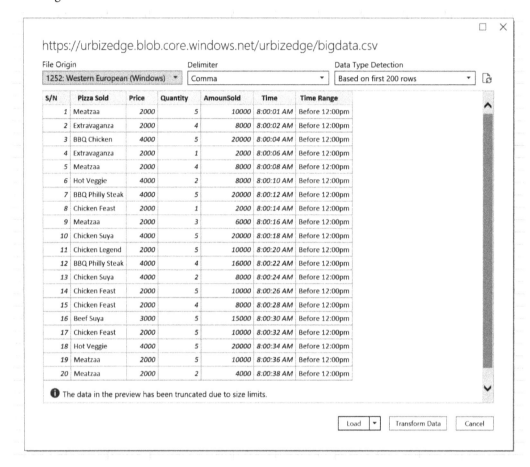

Figure 3.12 – Preview of the cloud-hosted file's data

There's an advantage to being able to connect to flat files via the web – it makes it easy to turn manually updated flat files into a pseudo-cloud database. There are many instances in which certain data can only be provided as flat files, which are manually updated. For one company, I built dashboards for currency translation exchange rates, which were sourced from the central bank's website every month and input manually into an Excel file. Putting this Excel file on OneDrive instantly made it a lot easier to dashboard-build and pull in the monthly opening, average, and closing exchange rates.

Importing data from databases

Databases are the best data sources to work with because they have validation and consistency logic already built into them. No one enjoys seeing their dashboards break because a column that is meant to hold numbers suddenly has text input. With databases, especially relational databases, reliable validation or data ingestion logic prevents inconsistent value types from being input into a field. Also, most enterprise applications that power the different aspects of a company's operations – from sales to staff clock-in – store their data in a database. Hence, connecting to the underlying database for those enterprise applications is an important step toward achieving data integrity.

Excel makes it possible to connect directly to many of the popular databases – a Microsoft SQL Server database, Oracle database, IBM Db2 database, MySQL database, PostgreSQL database, Sybase database, or SAP HANA database. The following screenshot shows the list of direct connectors Excel has to common databases:

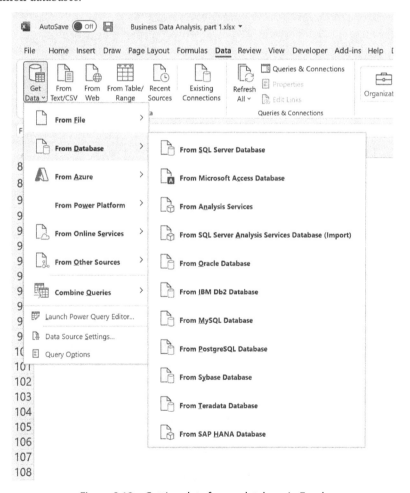

Figure 3.13 – Getting data from a database in Excel

When opting to either export data from an enterprise application or connect to the database underneath the enterprise application, always go with connecting to the database.

Importing data from cloud platforms

Cloud platforms are web-powered applications and are typically accessed over the internet. Excel allows direct connection to some of these commonly used cloud platforms and direct connection to a large number of Azure cloud applications.

The following screenshot highlights the Azure cloud applications that you can connect to directly in Excel:

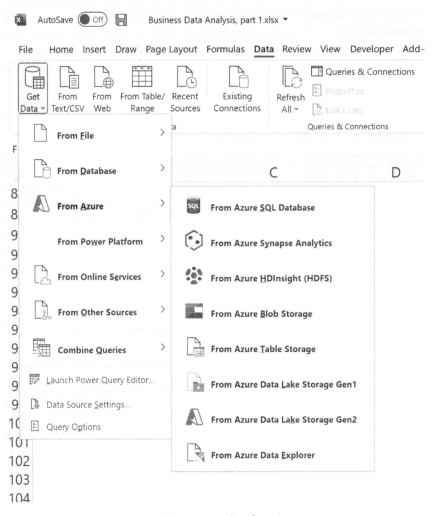

Figure 3.14 – Getting data from Azure

Also, for companies that use the Microsoft Power Platform suite of applications, there are native connectors to Power BI datasets and Dataverse, as shown in the following screenshot:

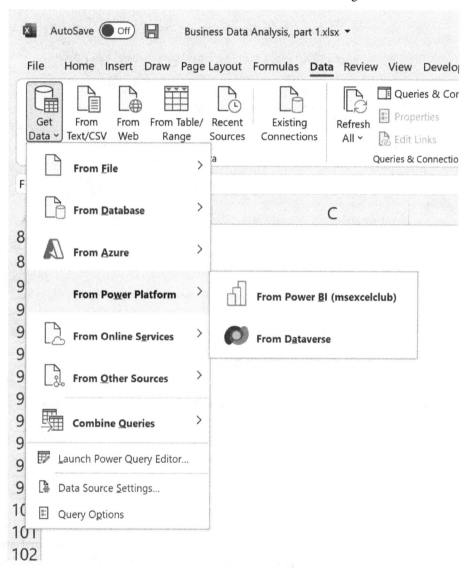

Figure 3.15 – Getting data from Power Platform

Connectors to online applications such as Salesforce, SharePoint, Dynamics, and Microsoft Exchange can be found under the **From Online Services** section, as shown in the following screenshot:

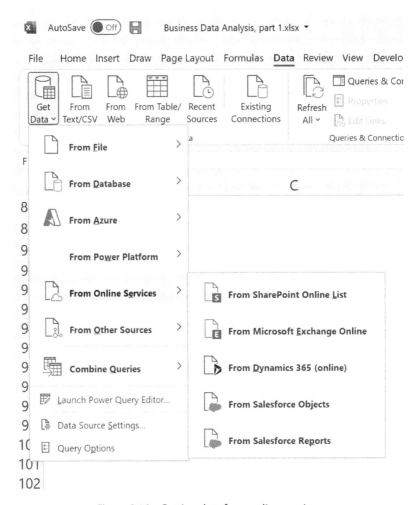

Figure 3.16 – Getting data from online services

SharePoint is widely used in organizations and is fast becoming a source of data for analysts as companies adopt cloud-based file storage and document-sharing systems. When you select **From SharePoint Online List** in the options under **From Online Services**, you will get a dialog prompt to key in the SharePoint **Site URL** info. This is the root URL, which should not include subfolders and other strings. It will usually be in the following format – `https://msexcelclub.sharepoint.com/sites/msexcelclub/` – meaning you'll have to delete all the ending strings when you copy the SharePoint URL from your web browser or Teams. See the following screenshot for an example of providing the site URL:

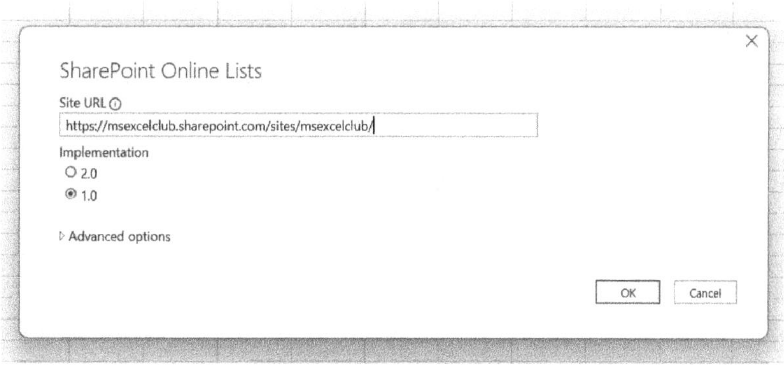

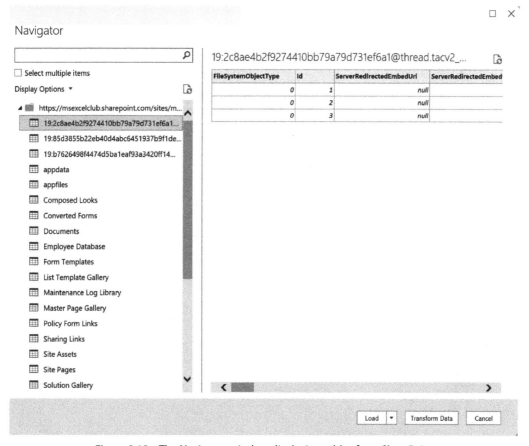

Figure 3.17 – Connecting to SharePoint Lists

And upon successful connection, you'll be presented with the familiar **Navigator** window, as shown in the following screenshot:

Figure 3.18 – The Navigator window displaying tables from SharePoint

Moving on from the options under **From Online Services**, we will explore **From Other Sources**.

In the **From Other Sources** section, you will find some other online cloud application connectors, as shown in the following screenshot:

Figure 3.19 – Getting data from other sources

Presented with the choice between exporting data from a cloud platform and connecting directly via the native connectors shown in the preceding screenshot, you should always go for connecting via the built-in connectors.

Next, we will examine the importance of connecting directly to the primary data source when building a dashboard.

Connecting directly to the primary data source

A major requirement for all dashboards is to be able to easily update them as new activities occur in the business processes the dashboards track, meaning you should set up your dashboard to easily pull in new data and reflect updated metrics and analysis on a daily, weekly, or monthly basis. Achieving this requires connecting directly to the primary data source.

Primary data sources are the original and first source of the data used for analysis and reporting. If a company uses an accounting application for its financial transactions and record-keeping and has staff who post transactions on the application daily, that application is the primary data source for a financial analysis dashboard. As a consultant or internal data analyst for the company, creating organization-wide dashboards, you might be given Excel or CSV exports of data from the accounting application to use in building the financial analysis dashboards.

> **Note**
> With this knowledge of the need to connect directly to the primary data source, it's your duty to ask where the exported data came from and figure out a way to directly connect to the original source of the data. You don't want to build dashboards that are connected to exported data or data sources that are many levels away from the original source.

The dangers that come with connecting to exported data or non-primary data sources are as follows:

- **Loss of data integrity**: The further you move away from the original data source, the higher the likelihood that the data has been altered and that analysis done with the data will generate incorrect insights.

- **Update delays**: It's not unusual for non-primary data sources to not update according to or sync with the primary data in real time. Exported data, unless there's an automated process that periodically fetches newly updated data exports, doesn't capture new updates at all.

Due to these two drawbacks, it is always preferable to connect directly to primary data sources. You also have to be aware that some companies keep multiple instances of their business data. Some have backup databases that are updated only once a day. Although their dashboards may not need to capture hourly updates, you will want to ask for a connection to a more frequently updated data source. Due to performance concerns, companies try to limit the amount of reporting queries sent to their production database. This is a valid concern, but rather than making you connect to a database for a logistics dashboard that is meant to reflect hourly production and freight metrics but is synced daily, you will want to connect to one that is synced hourly.

In *Chapter 13, Hands-on – Building Company-Wide Dashboards for AdventureWorks LLC*, we will connect to a company's **enterprise resource planning** (**ERP**) database to create dashboards. The database is the primary data source for the company's operations activity management.

The following screenshot is an illustration of how we can connect to the SQL Server database that houses AdventureWorks LLC's business data. First, you pick **From SQL Server Database** under **From Database** in the **Get Data** option under the **Data** menu:

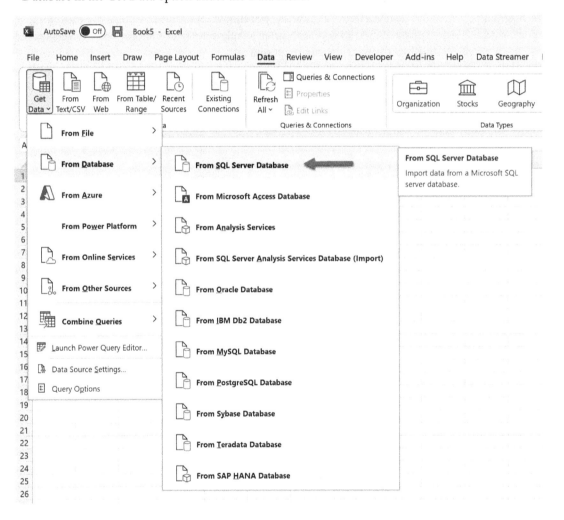

Figure 3.20 – Getting data from an SQL Server database

A small, detached pane will appear asking for the SQL Server database address and connection credentials. On providing them correctly, a **Navigator** window will come up like the one shown in the following screenshot, and in it, you see all the tables in the database:

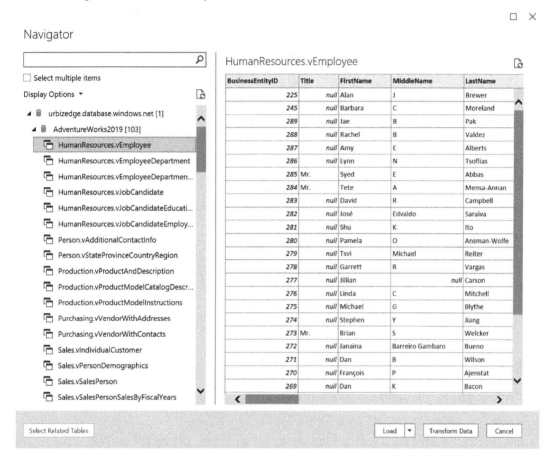

Figure 3.21 – Preview of the SQL database tables

In reality, however, it is not always as simple as just demanding to connect to the primary data source. There will be times when Excel has no connector for the primary data source. Other times, you just won't be allowed to connect to the primary data source.

In the next section, we will explore these common issues and practical ways to overcome them.

Common issues and how to overcome them

There are some common issues you are bound to face in the quest to connect directly to the primary data source. We will examine these issues and explore practical ways to overcome them.

- **No connector in Excel**: You have identified the primary data source and you don't have any objections from the organization regarding connecting directly to the data source. The issue is you can't find any connector for the data source within Excel. How do you proceed then? Fortunately, there are many custom connectors. The most common one is the **Open Database Connectivity (ODBC)** connector. You can always try to get the organization's technical team to set up an ODBC connector for you. The following screenshot shows what the ODBC setup window looks like:

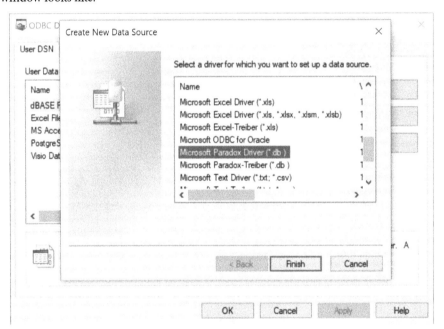

Figure 3.22 – The ODBC connector setup window

In situations where no one is able to set up an ODBC connector for you, you can buy ODBC drivers with setup instructions online. Popular providers of ODBC drivers are CData, Devart, and Progress.

- **No permission to connect to the primary data source**: Due to performance and security concerns, organizations may not allow you to connect directly to the primary data source. I have encountered situations where connecting to the primary data source meant the company had to open up a port, which is very susceptible to external hacking attacks, so they decided against allowing me to connect directly to the primary data source. I have also had situations where concerns around performance and operations disruptions were the reason the company wouldn't let me connect to the production database. In all these instances, I took the pragmatic approach of discussing the need to connect as closely as possible to the primary data source for my dashboards to work as intended. In all these cases, a workaround that was better than a manual export of data was implemented for me. This ranged from having me connect to a replica database, which synced with the production database as frequently as my dashboards needed to be updated, to finding a more secure way of letting me connect to the primary data source. An example was a company that wouldn't allow me to connect directly to their Dynamics NAV database via the usual SQL path. but upon my insistence on the need to connect to the live data for my dashboards to work as expected, they eventually allowed me to connect via **Open Data Protocol (OData)** to the database. There is usually more than one way to connect to all data sources. If the concern is security, you just have to find a way that overcomes the security concerns in question.

- **The primary data source is a flat file**: There are situations where the primary data does not exist in any enterprise application or database but in an Excel or text file. This is common for small companies where there are not enough resources – in terms of both budget and staff – to move all business operation activities to enterprise applications. You often find aspects of the business activities still primarily recorded on flat files such as Excel sheets, Google Sheets, and other spreadsheets. A quick low-resistance way to get your dashboards set up is to find a way to get those flat files onto a cloud storage solution such as OneDrive, SharePoint, Azure Storage, and so on. That way, you can connect to them right within Excel to build dashboards that are shared with users without any worries about losing the connection to the source data. However, I have had real-world cases where it was more appropriate to get the company to move away from using flat files and toward using a proper application designed for the activities they managed on a spreadsheet. A common example is accounting and finance activities. Every company should use a proper accounting tool for their business accounting and bookkeeping. The risks, failure points, and scalability issues that come with using a spreadsheet for all their business accounting are not worth the cost savings. Also, due to the huge market size for accounting software and the stiff competition among thousands of software providers, there is good accounting software that costs the same as Excel (Microsoft Office Suite). Even if the company tries to make a case for using Excel for their accounting, sales management, HR management, supply chain management, and marketing management, the company will spend more on fixing the errors and issues that will eventually crop up due to using spreadsheets to handle all its business activities. In dealing with situations where the primary data source is a flat file, you want to think long-term. You should examine the reasons why the company is not using the proper software and be certain that the reasons are valid, with no costly risks attached.

We are now at the end of this chapter. Although it was a short chapter, the message contained in it must be taken very seriously. The foundation of a dashboard is the data powering it, and properly getting the data into Excel is even more important than what you do with the data within Excel.

Summary

In this chapter, we examined the different ways Excel allows you to bring data into it. We saw the disadvantages of copying and pasting data into Excel for dashboard-building, even though it can seem very convenient. We went through the peculiarities of working with flat files. We established that connecting to the primary data source is the best path to follow, and it's usually a database or an enterprise application. Lastly, we went through the different issues that can come up and how to overcome them while still connecting as closely as possible to the primary data source.

In the next chapter, we will take our learning to the next natural stage: working with the data in Excel. We will do a deep-dive into Power Query, which is the recommended data transformation engine for all dashboard-creators.

4

Power Query: the Ultimate Data Transformation Tool

The most important update to Excel in the last 12 years has been Power Query. Power Query is a powerful data connectivity and data transformation tool. Its purpose is to enable report and dashboard builders that connect directly to the data they need, wherever it is stored, transform the data as desired, and have a repeatable process of generating updated reports and dashboards as the underlying data changes.

Much of what Power Query makes possible out of the box for the modern Excel user is transformations that used to be only possible via **Visual Basic for Applications (VBA)** code in Excel. There are daily, weekly, and monthly reports that were not possible to fully automate in earlier versions of Excel without using VBA but are now possible by using Power Query. Power Query makes it possible to build fully automated dashboards in Excel without writing VBA code or complex formulas.

In this chapter, we will get you well acquainted with Power Query by covering the following topics:

- Introduction to Power Query
- Connecting to over 100 different data sources
- Transforming data in Power Query
- Appending data from multiple sources into one data table
- Merging data from multiple sources into one data table
- Common data transformations
- Important tips
- Understanding Close & Load To
- Demystifying the underlying M code

Introduction to Power Query

Power Query was officially released by Microsoft in 2013 as an add-in that was installable in Excel 2010 and Excel 2013. It was originally designed to help Excel users connect to data directly, especially data not housed in an Excel file. Examples of such data are relational database tables, SharePoint lists, text files, and cloud data sources. It creates a pathway to connect to these types of data, transform the data, and then load the data into Excel sheets, tables, or PivotTables. In essence, Power Query is an **Extract, Transform, and Load** (**ETL**) tool.

Power Query has changed a lot since the first version. In Excel 2010 and Excel 2013, it had a dedicated menu and was a **Component Object Model** (**COM**) add-in that could be enabled or disabled after installing the Power Query add-in. The following screenshot shows what it was like in the early versions in Excel 2010 and Excel 2013:

Figure 4.1 – Power Query in Excel 2013

The following screenshot shows how to disable or enable Power Query as a COM add-in after installing the Power Query for Excel 2010/2013 add-in:

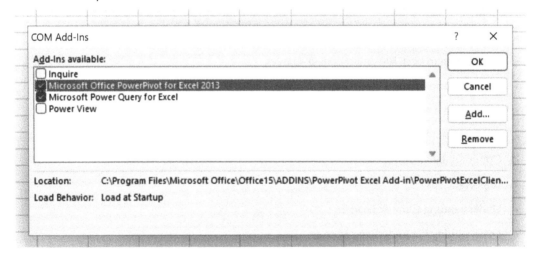

Figure 4.2 – Power Query was an optional COM add-in

Microsoft made Power Query an integrated feature of Excel in Excel 2016; it is no longer an add-in that must be installed and enabled. In Excel 2016 and above, you automatically have Power Query and access it from the **Data** menu. The following screenshot shows Power Query in Excel 2016, where it was referred to as **Get & Transform**:

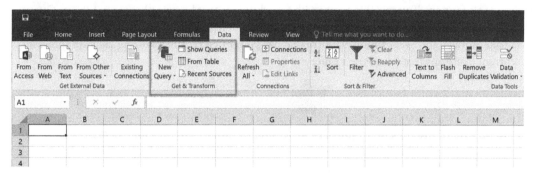

Figure 4.3 – Power Query as Get & Transform in Excel 2016

The following screenshot shows the current (July 2023) generally available version in Excel 365:

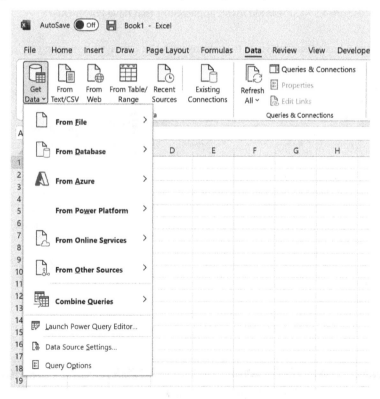

Figure 4.4 – Power Query in Excel 365

Power Query originally started as a tool in Microsoft Excel, but over the years, Microsoft has made it available in other Microsoft applications. Currently, Power Query is available in Microsoft Excel, Power BI, Microsoft Dataverse, and Microsoft Azure Data Lake Storage. The goal of Microsoft is to make Power Query the primary data extraction, transformation, and loading engine in all its data analysis tools for non-IT users. This comes with the advantage that knowing how to use Power Query in Excel means you will be automatically proficient at using it in Power BI, Microsoft Dataverse, Azure Data Lake Storage, and every future platform that has Power Query. The following diagram shows all the current platforms that have Power Query:

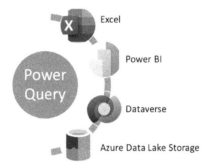

Figure 4.5 – Current Microsoft applications that have Power Query

Power Query in Excel has a user interface that aligns with the Office ribbon menu style, as shown in the following screenshot:

Figure 4.6 – Power Query in Microsoft Excel

Similarly, Power Query in Power BI maintains a ribbon menu user interface style, as shown in the following screenshot:

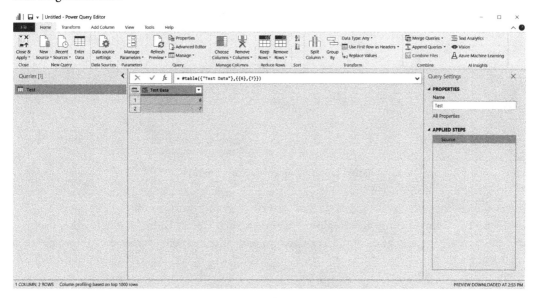

Figure 4.7 – An overview of Power Query in Power BI

In Dataverse and Azure Data Lake Storage, Power Query is an online in-browser tool with a subset of the functionality available in the Power BI desktop application. The following screenshot shows Power Query online:

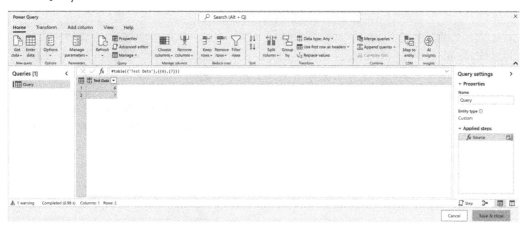

Figure 4.8 – An overview of Power Query online

The Power Query menu is a functionally laid out one with four primary sections – the **Home**, **Transform**, **Add column**, and **View** menus.

The **Home** menu houses commonly used commands such as **New Source** to connect to a new data source, **Merge Queries**, **Append Queries**, **Use First Row as Headers**, **Manage Parameters**, and **Advanced Editor**. The following screenshot shows what the **Home** menu houses:

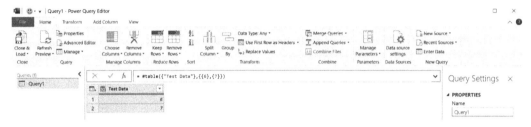

Figure 4.9 – Power Query Home menu

The **Transform** menu houses commands that are primarily for transforming data in place. You'll find **Group By**, **Unpivot Columns**, **Replace Values**, **Extract**, **Detect Data Type**, and other useful data transformation commands in the **Transform** menu. The following screenshot shows us the **Transform** menu:

Figure 4.10 – Power Query Transform menu

The **Add Column** menu houses commands that create new columns. Most prominent is the **Custom Column** command, used to create formula-based columns. There are some commands such as **Extract** that also exist in the **Transform** menu, but they are not the same. For example, while **Extract** in the **Transform** menu will replace the original column with the extracted data, **Extract** in **Add Column** will extract the data into a new column, leaving the original column intact. The following screenshot shows the commands under the **Add Column** menu:

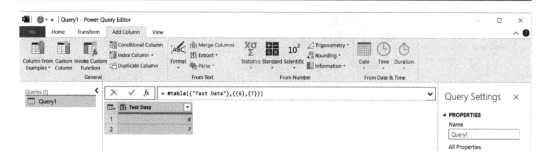

Figure 4.11 – Power Query Add Column menu

The **View** menu houses the commands that control what is displayed within the Power Query window. You can hide or make the **Query Settings** pane visible, hide or display **Formula Bar**, and show **Advanced Editor**. The following screenshot shows the commands under the **View** menu:

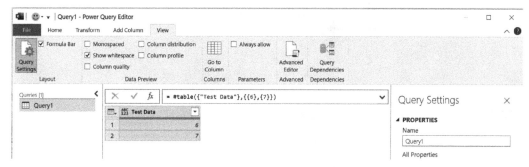

Figure 4.12 – Power Query View menu

In addition to these four standard menus, you get dynamic menus that come up only when you are performing some special operations. One such operation is when working on a *list* in Power Query, a new **Transform** menu shows up and has a set of different commands than the ones under the **Transform** menu mentioned earlier. See the following screenshot and notice the purple header indicating **List Tools**:

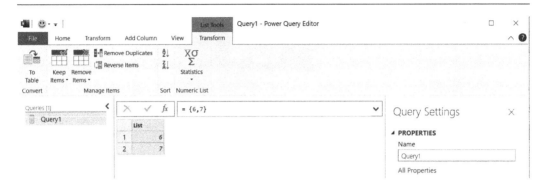

Figure 4.13 – List Tools for working with lists in Power Query

When dealing with *records* in Power Query, another menu, called **Convert**, shows up. See the following screenshot and notice the blue header indicating **Record Tools**:

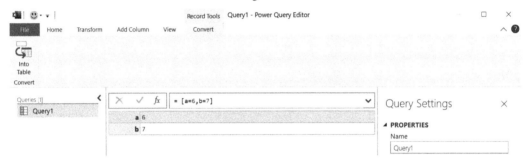

Figure 4.14 – Record Tools for working with records in Power Query

Power Query allows working with data in four output structures: single-entry values, tables, lists, and records. A **single-entry value** is a single literal value such as **123**, **Michael**, or false. The following is a screenshot of a single-entry value:

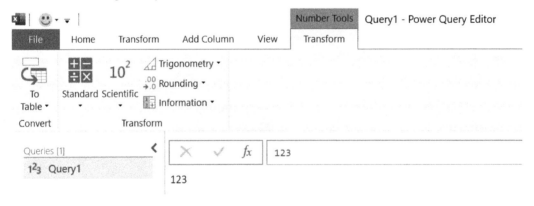

Figure 4.15 – Single-entry value in Power Query

A **table** is a collection of rows and columns of data. It is the most common structure of data we will encounter in Power Query as most data sources automatically reflect their data in a table structure within Power Query. The following screenshot shows a table showing the syntax for creating a table from literal values:

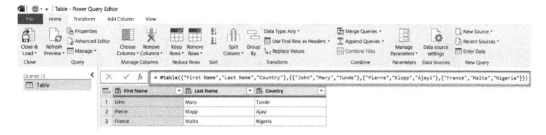

Figure 4.16 – A Power Query table

A **list** is single-dimension array of values. Think of a list of names, a list of numbers, a list of places, and a list of emails. These are typically what will be a column's values in a table. To create a list, you type in the entries in a comma-separated way within a pair of curly brackets. You can see an example of a list in the following screenshot:

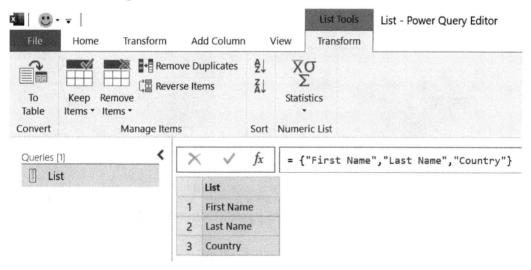

Figure 4.17 – A Power Query list

A **record** is a named collection of *key-value pairs*. The format makes it look like a transposed table with columns that hold just one value. You can create a record by typing key-value pair entries within a square bracket. See the following screenshot to see what a record looks like:

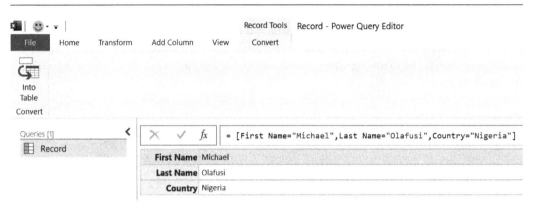

Figure 4.18 – A Power Query record

You can rightly say a table is a *record of lists*. A table's column is a list and a table's row is a *record*. And that's exactly how Power Query handles tables. When you grab a table's row, you get a *record*. The following is a screenshot of grabbing the second row in the table shown earlier. Notice that the rows are zero-indexed, hence the need to put in 1 instead of 2 when specifying the row number at the end of the table expression:

Figure 4.19 – Grabbing a row from a table

And when you grab a table's column, you get a *list*; see the example in the following screenshot. Notice that you need only to provide the column name in square brackets at the end:

Figure 4.20 – Grabbing a column from a table

The main purpose of Power Query in dashboard building is to bring in your business data in a way that allows auto-refresh, does the necessary data transformations, combines fragmented data, and loads it into Excel.

In the next section, we will go through how to connect to your business data using Power Query.

Connecting to over 100 different data sources

Power Query has connectors for over 100 different data sources. This means you can connect directly to most data sources without the need to first export the data and re-import the static export into Excel. This direct, live connection to data sources is one of the major advantages of using Power Query for report building.

However, there's a catch with the current connector setups – their availability can be limited by the host application. This means some connectors are available for Power Query in Power BI and not available for Power Query in Excel. You can access the list of Power Query connectors on the Microsoft official page for Power Query, `https://powerquery.microsoft.com/en-us/connectors/`, and via this GitHub page: `https://github.com/olafusimichael/B18312`.

If there's a data source you want to directly connect to and it's in the preceding list but not available for Power Query in Excel, there's a likelihood that there's a *custom connector* for it. So, check online first for a custom connector or other ways to connect to it. For instance, the Google Sheets connector is only available for Power Query in Power BI but there's a popular way to connect to Google Sheets using the **Web** connector. It has some flaws, but my main point is that it's better to check online than to assume that Excel cannot connect directly to the data source. Lastly, Microsoft and its partners keep adding to the connectors collection and expanding the availability of existing ones. This means that by the time you are reading this book, some of the connectors shown in the preceding table as not available in Power Query for Excel may already be available.

In Excel 2016, there was no connector for the *SAP HANA* database, but it now exists in Excel 2021. See the following two screenshots:

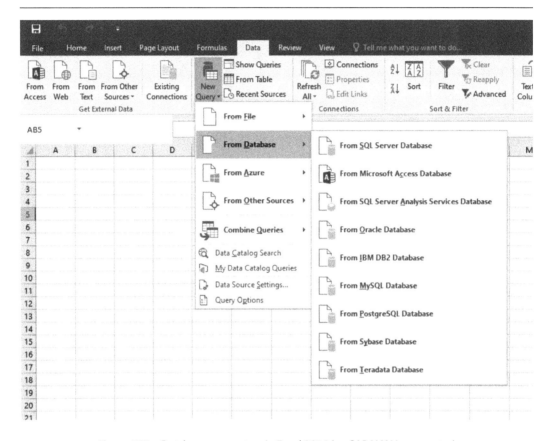

Figure 4.21 – Database connectors in Excel 2016 (no SAP HANA connector)

The following screenshot shows the database connectors in Excel 365 and you'll notice that it has the *SAP HANA* connector at the bottom of the list:

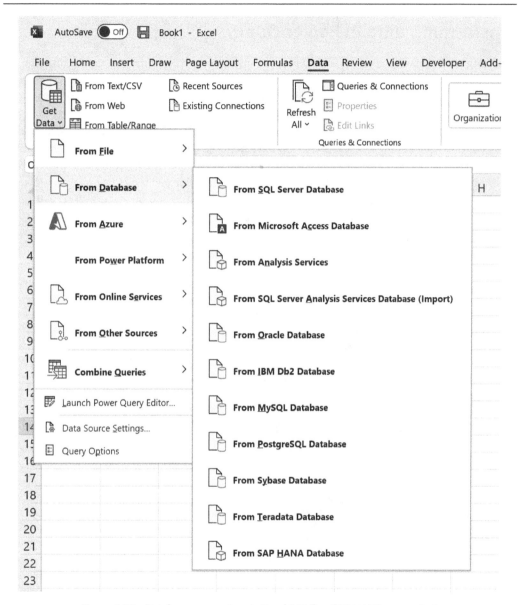

Figure 4.22 – Database connectors in Excel 365 (has SAP HANA connector)

A major requirement in all dashboards is to be easily updated as new activities occur in the business processes that the dashboards track. This means you should set up your dashboards to easily pull in new data and reflect updated metrics and analysis on a daily, weekly, or monthly basis. Achieving this requires connecting directly to the primary data source. We have gone through the different data sources you can connect to directly in Power Query. In the next section, we will go through how to transform your data in Power Query.

Transforming data in Power Query

Connecting to the data you need is a critical part of your dashboard building, and equally important is cleaning and shaping the data correctly. Power Query is Excel's most powerful tool for data cleaning and transformation. You can easily combine data from multiple sources in Power Query using **Merge Queries** or **Append Queries**. You can remove duplicate entries, split a column into multiple columns, fill values down an empty range, fill values up an empty range, extract values from a column, unpivot a table (which might be new to Excel users who have not used Power Query before), and do many other data transformations necessary to get your data ready for analysis. Most of these transform tools can be found in the **Transform** menu, the **Add Column** menu, and the **Home** menu of Power Query. For convenience, if you right-click on a column name in Power Query, you will see a list of the commonly used transform tools, as shown in the following screenshot:

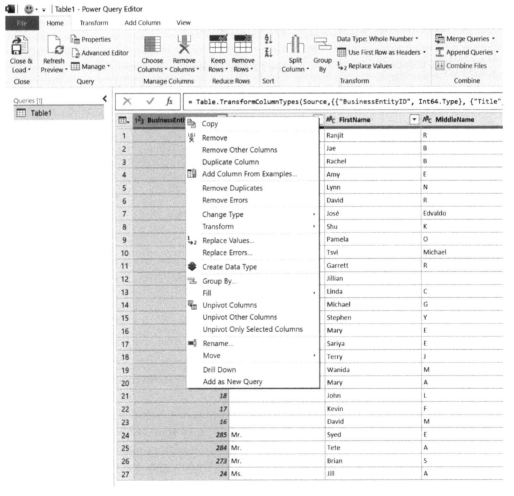

Figure 4.23 – Accessing common transform tools by right-clicking on a column name

Next, we will go through some practical demonstrations of some important transformations you must be proficient at carrying out in Power Query.

Appending data from multiple sources in one data table

A common issue you will face as you work with data from multiple sources is the need to consolidate data that is best used as a single table. An example that we will walk through is the consolidation of departmental tables that will best serve our analytical purpose if modeled into just one table. You can access the practice file in the companion folder for this book. The filename is `AdventureWorks - Employees by Dept.xlsx`, and it is a collection of employees by department in a fictitious company, AdventureWorks Limited.

The following screenshot shows the data in the practice file:

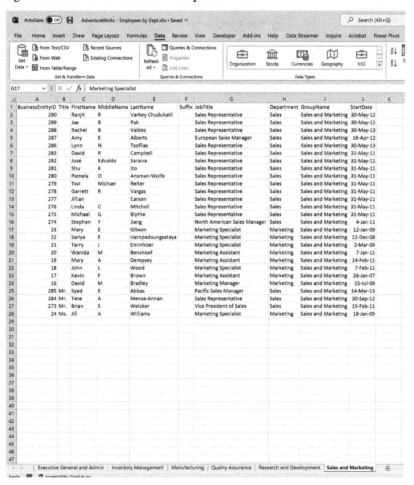

Figure 4.24 – An overview of table of employees by department

How do we go from these multiple tables of employees to one consolidated table of all employees? With Power Query, this is easily achieved by using **Append Queries**.

You start by pulling in all the tables in the Excel file into Power Query. In this demonstration, you will open a blank Excel file, go to the **Data** menu, click on **Get Data**, click on **From File**, and select **From Excel Workbook**. See the following screenshot:

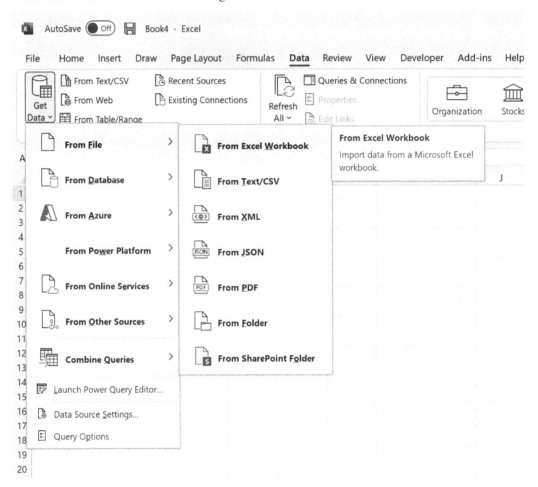

Figure 4.25 – Importing data from an Excel file

Browse to the Excel file and select it in the window that pops up. A navigator window will come up, showing you all the sheets and tables within the Excel file. Enable **Select Multiple Items** and check all the department sheets in the file. Then, click on **Transform Data**. See the following screenshot:

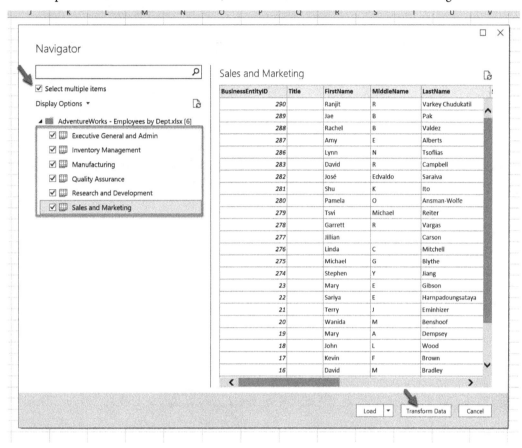

Figure 4.26 – Power Query Navigator window

This will launch the Power Query window where we will carry out the actual consolidation process. On the **Home** menu, select **Append Queries as New**. This will allow us to create the consolidated table as a standalone table with the departmental tables left intact. See this step in the following screenshot:

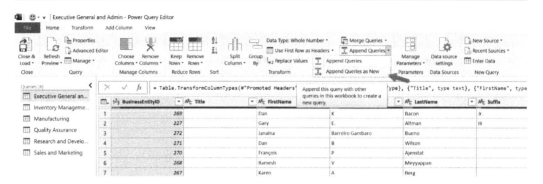

Figure 4.27 – Append queries as a new table in Power Query

An **Append** window will come up. Make sure to select all the tables and ensure no table is selected more than once. Click on **OK**. The following screenshot shows the selection pane:

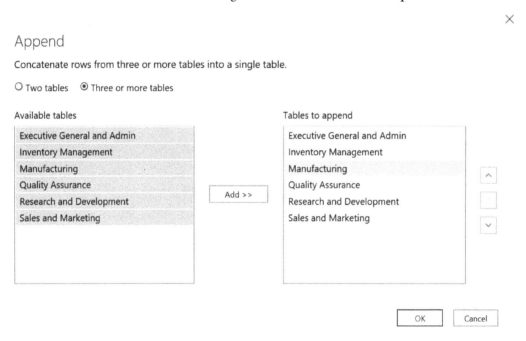

Figure 4.28 – Append queries setup window

A new table will be created. Rename the table from the default `Append1` name and remove nulls from the ID column. It is not uncommon for empty rows to be pulled into Power Query when you import data from an Excel sheet. The following screenshot shows the expected actions:

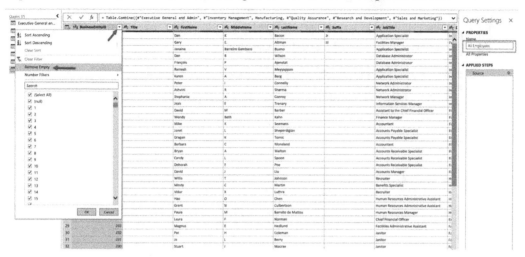

Figure 4.29 – An overview of renaming the table and removing nulls from the ID column

As a hint, if the data is already formatted as a table in Excel, it will also show during the import stage. You will see the sheet and the formatted table separately during the import stage shown in *Figure 4.26*. Selecting the formatted table rather than the sheet can be a way to prevent Excel from importing empty rows that are not part of the table.

And that is how you consolidate data across different tables into one table. It is a very common task you will need to do as you work with business data more and, especially, data captured in flat files. It is very common to encounter a collection of flat files capturing data by day, month, year, location, brand, department, sales channel, or some other dimension. Now, you know how to append those data tables as one consolidated table.

If your data tables are in different flat files, you may achieve consolidation faster by putting all the files in one dedicated folder and importing the folder into Power Query. Select **Get Data**, **From File**, and **From Folder** to access this functionality. See the following screenshot for a visual illustration of the steps:

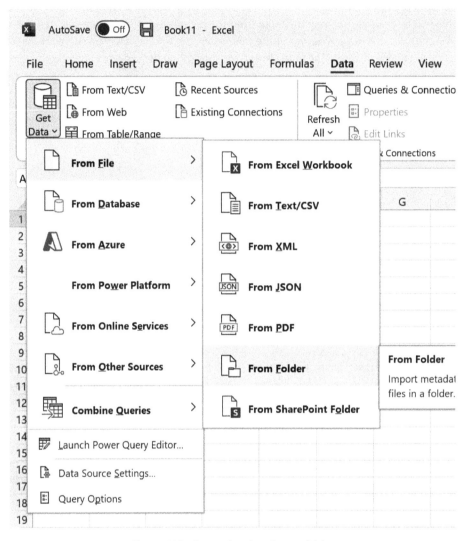

Figure 4.30 – Importing data from a folder

See the following screenshot, which reflects the window that shows after selecting the desired folder. Notice that there is a **Combine** button in the navigator window, which will do the auto append if selected:

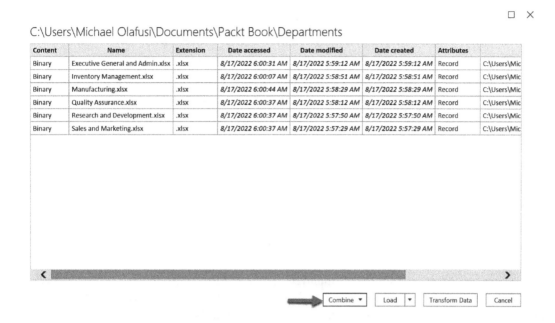

C:\Users\Michael Olafusi\Documents\Packt Book\Departments

Content	Name	Extension	Date accessed	Date modified	Date created	Attributes	
Binary	Executive General and Admin.xlsx	.xlsx	8/17/2022 6:00:31 AM	8/17/2022 5:59:12 AM	8/17/2022 5:59:12 AM	Record	C:\Users\Mic
Binary	Inventory Management.xlsx	.xlsx	8/17/2022 6:00:07 AM	8/17/2022 5:58:51 AM	8/17/2022 5:58:51 AM	Record	C:\Users\Mic
Binary	Manufacturing.xlsx	.xlsx	8/17/2022 6:00:44 AM	8/17/2022 5:58:29 AM	8/17/2022 5:58:29 AM	Record	C:\Users\Mic
Binary	Quality Assurance.xlsx	.xlsx	8/17/2022 6:00:37 AM	8/17/2022 5:58:12 AM	8/17/2022 5:58:12 AM	Record	C:\Users\Mic
Binary	Research and Development.xlsx	.xlsx	8/17/2022 6:00:37 AM	8/17/2022 5:57:50 AM	8/17/2022 5:57:50 AM	Record	C:\Users\Mic
Binary	Sales and Marketing.xlsx	.xlsx	8/17/2022 6:00:37 AM	8/17/2022 5:57:29 AM	8/17/2022 5:57:29 AM	Record	C:\Users\Mic

Combine ▼   Load ▼   Transform Data   Cancel

Figure 4.31 – Letting Power Query automatically combine the files in the folder

Next, we will explore another very common task you must be comfortable carrying out in Power Query: merging data across two tables.

Merging data from two tables into one table

There will be instances where you have data split across two tables but need them just in one table. For people with SQL knowledge, this is often achieved with an SQL JOIN clause. There are different types of joins: inner join, left outer join, right outer join, self join, cross join, and so on. In Power Query, **Merge Query** achieves many of these joins in a very easy-to-understand way.

As an example, we will merge data in the employees table we just worked on and a payroll table. You can access the practice files in the companion folder. The filename is Merge Data.xlsx.

Load the data from the two sheets in the file into Power Query. Go to the **Home** menu and click on **Merge Queries as New**. See the following screenshot:

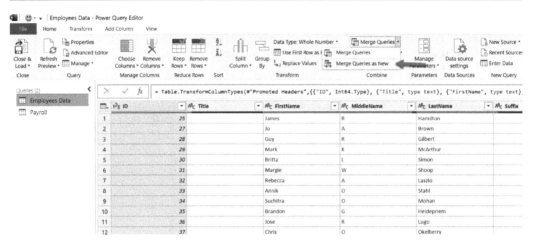

Figure 4.32 – Merge Queries as New table in Power Query

In the **Merge** pane that comes up, select **Employees Data** as the first table and **Payroll** as the second table. The order is actually important. Click on the **ID** column of both tables to let **Merge** know that it is the unique identifier column common to both tables. See the following screenshot. Notice that there are six options to select from for the join type:

Figure 4.33 – Merge queries settings

A clear explanation of the different types of join is given here:

- **Left outer join** means all records in the first (top) table will be matched to records in the second (bottom) table. The merged table will have the same rows and number of records as the first table, and for records it could not match, it will show null for the second-table columns.

- **Right outer join** means all records from the second table will be retained in the merged table and matching records from the first table will be included. Where there are no matching records in the first table, the merged table will show null for the columns from the first table.

- **Full outer join** shows all records from both tables, putting null in columns of each table where it could not find a match for the record in the other table.

- **Inner join** shows only records present in the two tables. It omits records that are present in just one table.

- **Left anti join** shows records that are only present in the first table. It omits all records that can be found in the second table.

- **Right anti join** shows records that are only present in the second table. It omits all records that can be found in the first table.

For our demonstration, we need all the records in the **Employees Data** table and would like to see them alongside the matching **Payroll** data. If no **Payroll** data was found for a record, it should show null for the **Payroll** column. And since we have specified that the **ID** column is the column to be used for the matching, a matched record means the same ID value was found in both tables. In essence, we are carrying out a left outer join. The merged table will look like the following screenshot:

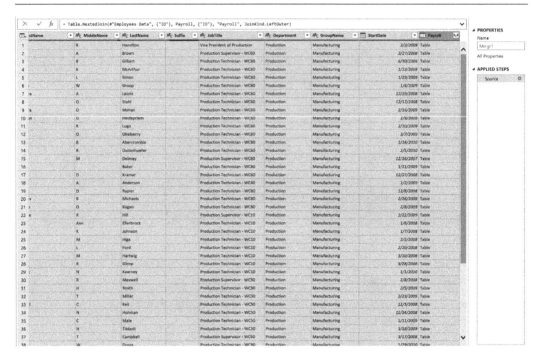

Figure 4.34 – An overview of merging the Employees Data table with the Payroll table

Clicking on the dropdown beside the **Payroll** column allows us to select the columns from the **Payroll** table that should be extracted into the merged table. For our demonstration, we will select all the columns but deselect **Use original column name as prefix**. See the following screenshot for the exact step:

Figure 4.35 – Expanding the Payroll table to display the selected columns

The merged table now shows the columns from the **Payroll** table. See the following screenshot:

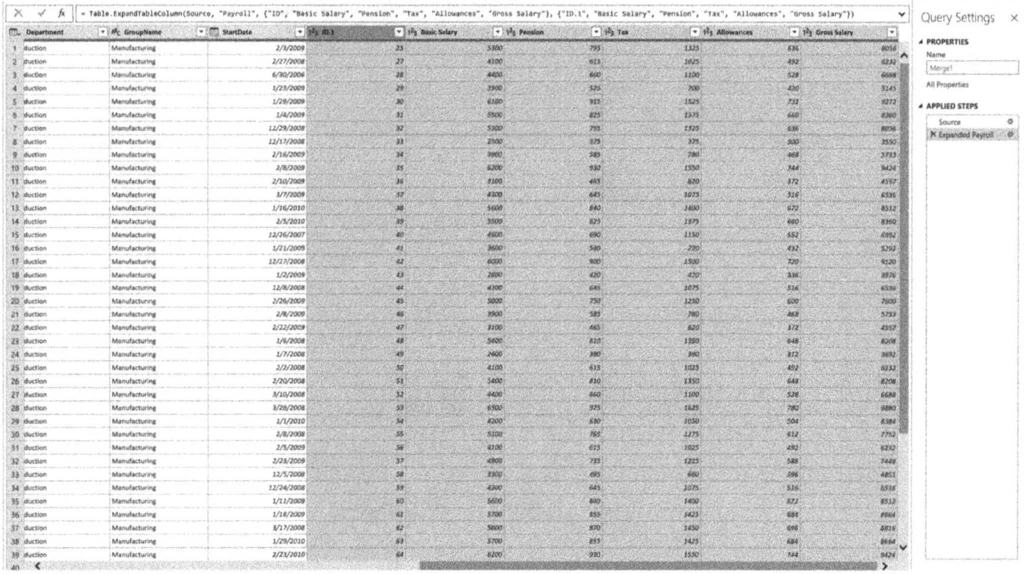

Figure 4.36 – An overview of the merged Employees Data and Payroll tables

Merging tables can be a very convenient way to get related data from two tables into one table, but you have to avoid merging tables unless it is absolutely necessary. When you merge tables, you eventually duplicate data and add to the time-consuming processes happening underneath your reports. You could argue away the performance slowdown is negligible for small tables, but there is a bigger reason not to merge tables that is at the core of proper data modeling. A proper data model involves relying more on proper relationships between tables rather than merging tables into one. As you build professional reports and dashboards, you must let go of the temptation to use Merge Query, VLOOKUP, and other lookup functions to duplicate data across related tables. Rely more on creating relationships between related tables. We will cover how to do this in *Chapter 5, PivotTable and Power Pivot*, in the *Power Pivot and Data Model* section.

There is one very special use of Merge Query in Power Query. It has the ability to match text with slight spelling differences. This is a very powerful use of Merge Query. We will explore how it does this by carrying out a merge on two tables from a sample file named Fuzzy Match.xlsx, which can be accessed from the companion folder.

The first table is a listing of expat staff for a company who get paid on a weekly basis at a set hourly rate:

Expat Staff	Hourly Rate
Adetosoye Chuku	$74
Uwailomwan Akintunde	$86
Efe Zoputa	$110
Afiba Adeolu	$90
Aduba Adesehinwa	$89
Ibironke Abolanle	$108
Toben Ekong	$98
Chinwe Chimezie	$72
Uloaku Omolola	$109
Adedeji Daraja	$90

Table 4.1 – Expat staff and their hourly rate

The second table is a listing of how many hours they have worked in four weeks:

Staff	Week 1	Week 2	Week 3	Week 4
Adedeji M. Daraja	14	24	21	21
Adetosoye Chuku	12	21	16	14
Aduba O. Adesehinwa	22	15	14	13
Afiba Adeolu	11	14	21	22
Chinwe Chimezie	20	19	18	16
Efe Ken Zoputa	17	14	15	18
Ibironke Bolanle	16	14	14	25
Toben Ekong	11	12	16	17
Uloaku Yves Omolola	14	10	19	17
Uwailomwan Akintunde	11	20	25	22

Table 4.2 – Weekly logged time worked by staff

Notice that the names do not match exactly. In the first table, only first names and last names are recorded, while in the second table, some have a middle name or middle initial. With a regular merge, those staff whose names are not written the same way in the two tables will not be matched correctly. However, we can achieve correct matching by enabling fuzzy matching options in **Merge Query** and you can indicate the level of strictness in similarity consideration. Exact spelling is the same as a 100% (written as 1) similarity threshold. If left blank, the default value of a 0.80 (80%) similarity threshold is applied. For this demonstration, I have set it to a 0.70 (70%) similarity threshold. See the settings in the following screenshot:

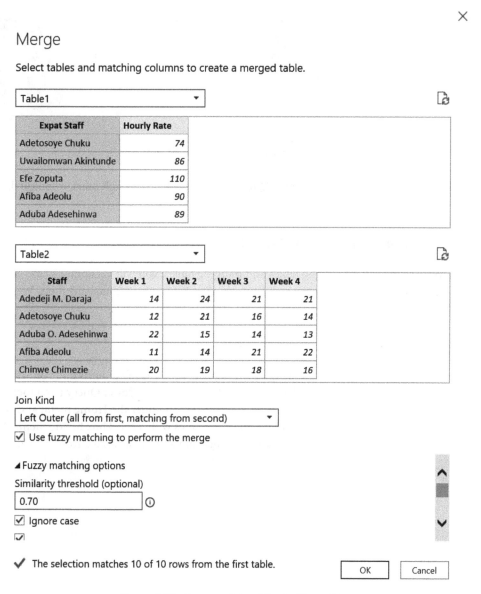

Figure 4.37 – Fuzzy match setting in Merge Query

On clicking **OK**, you'll be presented with similar output as in the following screenshot:

	Aᴮᴄ Expat Staff	1²₃ Hourly Rate	1²₃ Week 1	1²₃ Week 2	1²₃ Week 3	1²₃ Week 4
1	Adetosoye Chuku	74	12	21	16	14
2	Uwailomwan Akintunde	86	11	20	25	22
3	Efe Zoputa	110	17	14	15	18
4	Afiba Adeolu	90	11	14	21	22
5	Aduba Adesehinwa	89	22	15	14	13
6	Ibironke Abolanle	108	16	14	14	25
7	Toben Ekong	98	11	12	16	17
8	Chinwe Chimezie	72	20	19	18	16
9	Uloaku Omolola	109	14	10	19	17
10	Adedeji Daraja	90	14	24	21	21

Figure 4.38 – Outcome of the fuzzy matching

Now you know how to merge tables in Power Query. Next, we will go through other common data transformations you should be proficient at.

Common data transformations

In addition to being great at appending tables and merging tables, you will encounter many other data transformation needs that will necessitate using some of Power Query's amazing tools. We will cover the common ones in this section.

Choose Columns

It might sound simplistic, but if you are working with tables with lots of columns and you want a quick way to select the columns you need, then you will appreciate that Power Query has a tool for just that. All you need to do is click the **Choose Columns** button under the **Home** menu and you will be presented with a window showing all the column names with a checkbox beside them. For ease of spotting the required columns, you can set the column names to be sorted from A to Z. See the following screenshot:

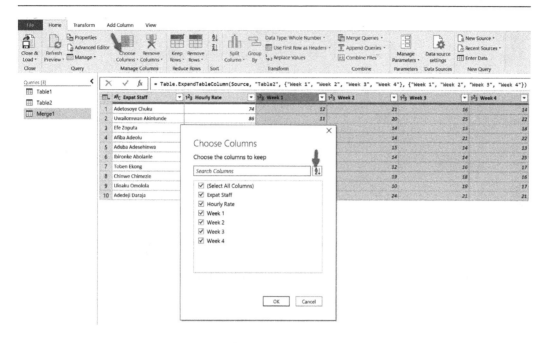

Figure 4.39 – Choose Columns in Power Query

Choose Columns is a fast and convenient way to select the columns needed in a table that has lots of columns.

Keep Rows and Remove Rows

There will be times you need to remove unwanted rows from a table – these could be rows where one or more of the columns have errors, rows that are completely blank, or duplicate rows in the table. It's also possible, but not as common as the need to remove rows, to indicate which rows you want to keep. The following are screenshots of the **Keep Rows** options and **Remove Rows** options:

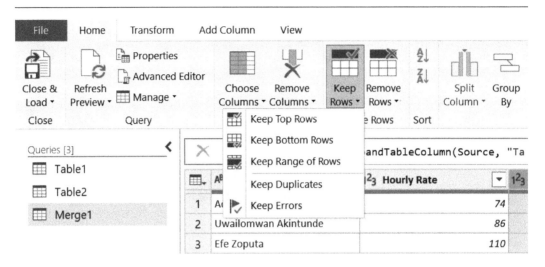

Figure 4.40 – Keep Rows in Power Query

The next screenshot shows the options under **Remove Rows**:

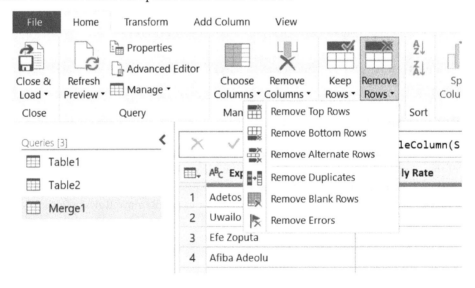

Figure 4.41 – Remove Rows in Power Query

With that, we are done with exploring how to keep or remove rows from a table in Power Query. We will now go on to another import tool within Power Query.

Unpivot Columns and Pivot Columns

You can wrangle more insights from a table if it is structured to have few columns and lots of rows rather than the same table being structured to have more columns with fewer rows. For instance, the merged table of expat staff pay rates and weekly logged hours would be better structured to have all the weeks in a column rather than each week being its own column. To achieve this restructuring, **Unpivot Columns** is the go-to tool. It is easily found under the **Transform** menu; just ensure you have the columns you want to collapse before clicking on **Unpivot Columns**.

The following screenshot shows a table with weeks set as columns and we would like to collapse those columns into one column of weeks and another column of values:

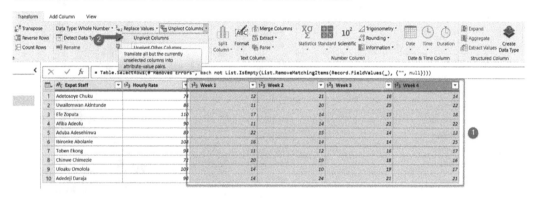

Figure 4.42 – Unpivot Columns in Power Query

The following screenshot is the outcome after renaming the default column names of **Attribute**, **Value to Week**, and **Hours Logged**, respectively:

| ✕ | ✓ | fx | = Table.RenameColumns(#"Unpivoted Columns",{{"Attribute", "Week"}, {"Value", "Hours Lo |

▦▾	AᴮC Expat Staff	▾	1²₃ Hourly Rate	▾	AᴮC Week	▾	1²₃ Hours Logged	▾
1	Adetosoye Chuku		74		Week 1		12	
2	Adetosoye Chuku		74		Week 2		21	
3	Adetosoye Chuku		74		Week 3		16	
4	Adetosoye Chuku		74		Week 4		14	
5	Uwailomwan Akintunde		86		Week 1		11	
6	Uwailomwan Akintunde		86		Week 2		20	
7	Uwailomwan Akintunde		86		Week 3		25	
8	Uwailomwan Akintunde		86		Week 4		22	
9	Efe Zoputa		110		Week 1		17	
10	Efe Zoputa		110		Week 2		14	
11	Efe Zoputa		110		Week 3		15	
12	Efe Zoputa		110		Week 4		18	
13	Afiba Adeolu		90		Week 1		11	
14	Afiba Adeolu		90		Week 2		14	
15	Afiba Adeolu		90		Week 3		21	
16	Afiba Adeolu		90		Week 4		22	
17	Aduba Adesehinwa		89		Week 1		22	
18	Aduba Adesehinwa		89		Week 2		15	
19	Aduba Adesehinwa		89		Week 3		14	
20	Aduba Adesehinwa		89		Week 4		13	
21	Ibironke Abolanle		108		Week 1		16	
22	Ibironke Abolanle		108		Week 2		14	
23	Ibironke Abolanle		108		Week 3		14	
24	Ibironke Abolanle		108		Week 4		25	
25	Toben Ekong		98		Week 1		11	
26	Toben Ekong		98		Week 2		12	
27	Toben Ekong		98		Week 3		16	
28	Toben Ekong		98		Week 4		17	
29	Chinwe Chimezie		72		Week 1		20	
30	Chinwe Chimezie		72		Week 2		19	
31	Chinwe Chimezie		72		Week 3		18	
32	Chinwe Chimezie		72		Week 4		16	
33	Uloaku Omolola		109		Week 1		14	
34	Uloaku Omolola		109		Week 2		10	
35	Uloaku Omolola		109		Week 3		19	
36	Uloaku Omolola		109		Week 4		17	
37	Adedeji Daraja		90		Week 1		14	
38	Adedeji Daraja		90		Week 2		24	
39	Adedeji Daraja		90		Week 3		21	
40	Adedeji Daraja		90		Week 4		21	

Figure 4.43 – Outcome of the unpivot

And if you want to do the reverse, there's **Pivot Columns**. It is right before the **Unpivot Columns** button under the **Transform** menu. See the following screenshot:

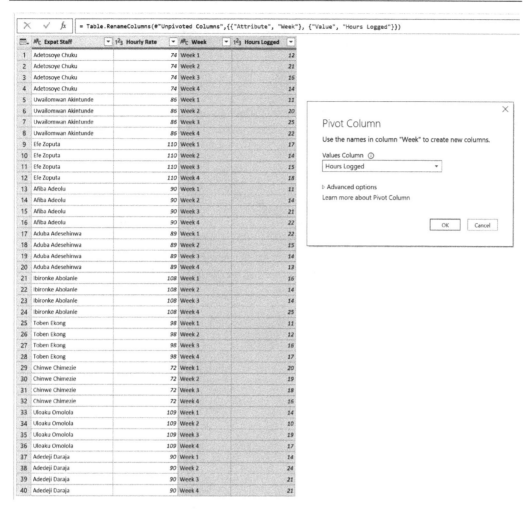

Figure 4.44 – Pivot Columns in Power Query

Notice that the result is exactly the table we had before the unpivoting. See the following screenshot:

	Expat Staff	Hourly Rate	Week 1	Week 2	Week 3	Week 4
1	Adedeji Daraja	90	14	24	21	21
2	Adetosoye Chuku	74	12	21	16	14
3	Aduba Adesehinwa	89	22	15	14	13
4	Afiba Adeolu	90	11	14	21	22
5	Chinwe Chimezie	72	20	19	18	16
6	Efe Zoputa	110	17	14	15	18
7	Ibironke Abolanle	108	16	14	14	25
8	Toben Ekong	98	11	12	16	17
9	Uloaku Omolola	109	14	10	19	17
10	Uwailomwan Akintunde	86	11	20	25	22

Figure 4.45 – Outcome of the pivot

That wraps up **Unpivot Columns** and **Pivot Columns**. We will examine **Group By**, which is another important transformation, in the next section.

Group By

If we want to summarize a table, **Group By** is the very tool for that. Going on with our example table, imagine we want to summarize the table by weeks and show the total hours logged. **Group By**, found under the **Home** menu, achieves that easily for us. See the following screenshot:

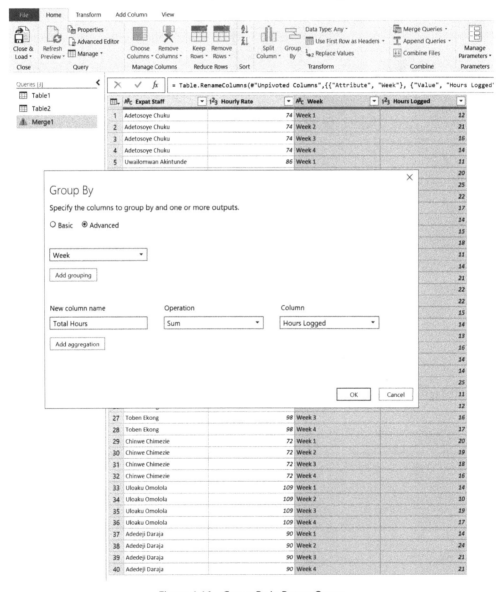

Figure 4.46 – Group By in Power Query

The resulting table is shown in the following screenshot:

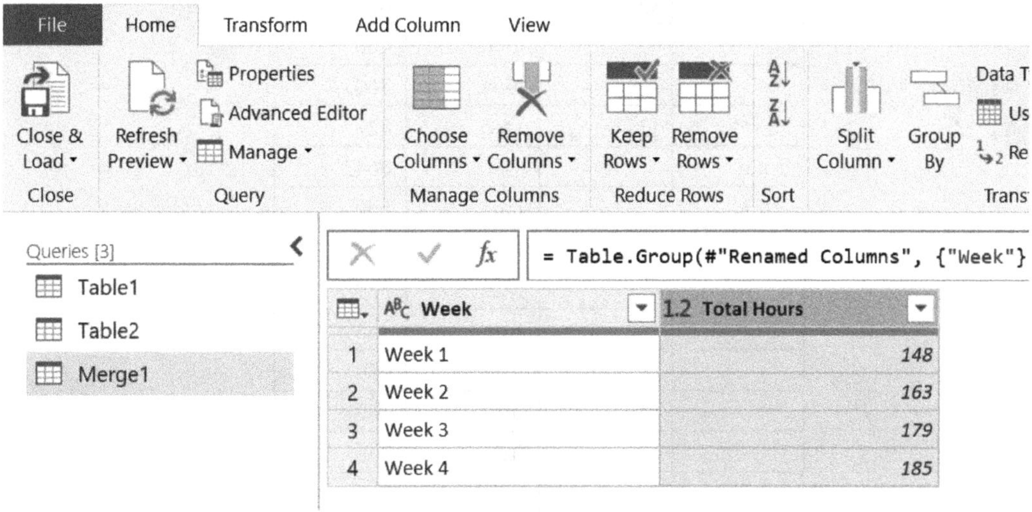

Figure 4.47 – Outcome of the table group by week

In the next section, we will cover how to handle missing values within your data.

Fill Series and Remove Empty

Another very common transformation you will find yourself doing when you deal with tables with some columns that are not fully populated is the need to replace the null values with valid entries. There are usually two ways to handle missing values: you fill in data from other rows or you remove the entire row.

As an example, we will consider the following table of date periods and values but with some missing values. You can find the practice data in the file named Fill Down and Fill Up.xlsx in this book's companion folder:

Year	Quarter	Month	Value
2021		Jan	514
		Feb	630
	Q1	Mar	496
		Apr	831
		May	697
	Q2	Jun	439
		Jul	404
		Aug	358

Year	Quarter	Month	Value
	Q3	Sep	627
		Oct	460
		Nov	360
	Q4	Dec	827
Total			6643
2022		Jan	650
		Feb	777
	Q1	Mar	329
		Apr	453
		May	659
	Q2	Jun	389
		Jul	248
		Aug	546
	Q3	Sep	272
		Oct	841
		Nov	388
	Q4	Dec	892
Total			6444

Table 4.3 – Practice data for Fill Series and Remove Empty transformations

Notice that the year is partially filled. We will fix this by using the fill series fill down option to populate the blank rows with the appropriate year. Fill Series is under the **Transform** menu. For the **Year** column, we will do a fill down to fix the missing values. Select the **Year** column, go to the **Transform** menu, click **Fill**, and select **Down**. The following screenshot shows setting fill down on the **Year** column:

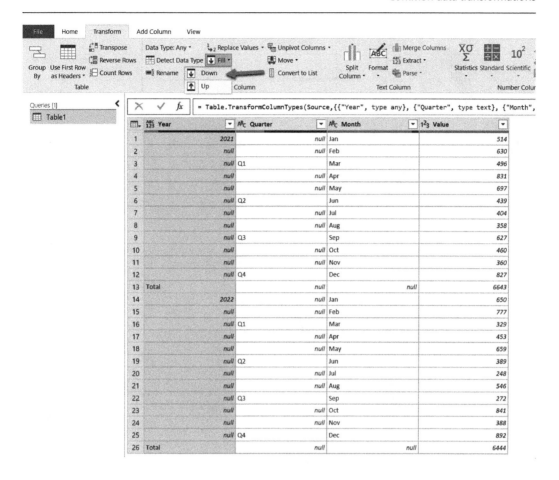

Figure 4.48 – Fill Down in Power Query

In the following screenshot of the outcome, notice how the **Year** value is filled down to replace the null values.

```
= Table.FillDown(#"Changed Type",{"Year"})
```

	Year	Quarter	Month	Value
1	2021	null	Jan	514
2	2021	null	Feb	630
3	2021	Q1	Mar	496
4	2021	null	Apr	831
5	2021	null	May	697
6	2021	Q2	Jun	439
7	2021	null	Jul	404
8	2021	null	Aug	358
9	2021	Q3	Sep	627
10	2021	null	Oct	460
11	2021	null	Nov	360
12	2021	Q4	Dec	827
13	Total	null	null	6643
14	2022	null	Jan	650
15	2022	null	Feb	777
16	2022	Q1	Mar	329
17	2022	null	Apr	453
18	2022	null	May	659
19	2022	Q2	Jun	389
20	2022	null	Jul	248
21	2022	null	Aug	546
22	2022	Q3	Sep	272
23	2022	null	Oct	841
24	2022	null	Nov	388
25	2022	Q4	Dec	892
26	Total	null	null	6444

Figure 4.49 – Outcome of the fill down transformation

Also notice that for the **Quarter** column, only the last month of the quarter is populated. To fix this, we will use the fill up option. Select the **Quarter** column, go to the **Transform** menu, click **Fill**, and select **Up**. The following screenshot is an example of using **Fill Up** to populate the **Quarter** column, which only has the last month of the quarter populated.

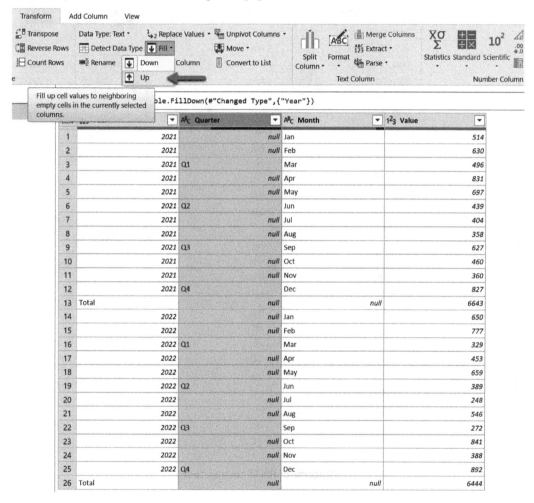

Figure 4.50 – Fill Up in Power Query

Notice in the following screenshot how the quarters are now filled upward to ensure there are no null records in the **Quarter** column:

	Year	Quarter	Month	Value
		`= Table.FillUp(#"Filled Down",{"Quarter"})`		
1	2021	Q1	Jan	514
2	2021	Q1	Feb	630
3	2021	Q1	Mar	496
4	2021	Q2	Apr	831
5	2021	Q2	May	697
6	2021	Q2	Jun	439
7	2021	Q3	Jul	404
8	2021	Q3	Aug	358
9	2021	Q3	Sep	627
10	2021	Q4	Oct	460
11	2021	Q4	Nov	360
12	2021	Q4	Dec	827
13	Total	Q1	null	6643
14	2022	Q1	Jan	650
15	2022	Q1	Feb	777
16	2022	Q1	Mar	329
17	2022	Q2	Apr	453
18	2022	Q2	May	659
19	2022	Q2	Jun	389
20	2022	Q3	Jul	248
21	2022	Q3	Aug	546
22	2022	Q3	Sep	272
23	2022	Q4	Oct	841
24	2022	Q4	Nov	388
25	2022	Q4	Dec	892
26	Total	null	null	6444

Figure 4.51 – Outcome of the fill up transformation

Lastly, we need to remove the rows where **Month** is blank. Those rows are where the total for each year is recorded under the **Value** column. They will cause problems with double counting in the **Value** column, causing inaccuracy in our analysis by quarter, as **Q1** is shown for the 2021 **Total** row, and they will make the year column difficult to use as it is now a mix of numbers and text. Because of these reasons, we will use **Remove Empty** to delete the rows where the **Month** column entry is blank. To achieve this, click on the drop-down icon beside the **Month** column name, and select **Remove Empty**. See the following screenshot of where to access the **Remove Empty** feature:

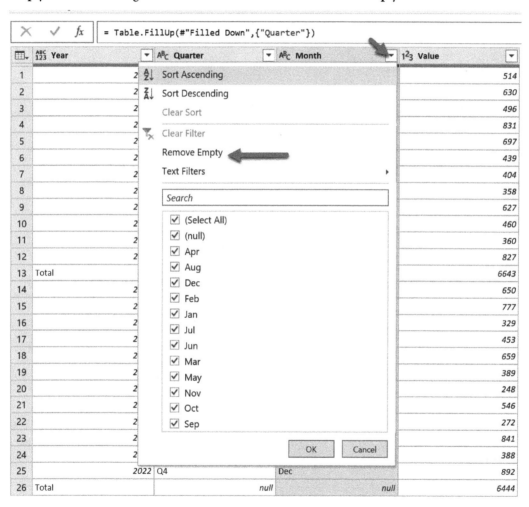

Figure 4.52 – Remove Empty in Power Query

The outcome will be the removal of rows that have empty or null values in the selected column, as shown in the following screenshot:

ABC 123 Year	ABC Quarter	ABC Month	123 Value
1	2021 Q1	Jan	514
2	2021 Q1	Feb	630
3	2021 Q1	Mar	496
4	2021 Q2	Apr	831
5	2021 Q2	May	697
6	2021 Q2	Jun	439
7	2021 Q3	Jul	404
8	2021 Q3	Aug	358
9	2021 Q3	Sep	627
10	2021 Q4	Oct	460
11	2021 Q4	Nov	360
12	2021 Q4	Dec	827
13	2022 Q1	Jan	650
14	2022 Q1	Feb	777
15	2022 Q1	Mar	329
16	2022 Q2	Apr	453
17	2022 Q2	May	659
18	2022 Q2	Jun	389
19	2022 Q3	Jul	248
20	2022 Q3	Aug	546
21	2022 Q3	Sep	272
22	2022 Q4	Oct	841
23	2022 Q4	Nov	388
24	2022 Q4	Dec	892

The formula bar reads: `= Table.SelectRows(#"Filled Up", each [Month] <> null and [Month] <> "")`

Figure 4.53 – Outcome of the Remove Empty transformation

There will be times when you will want to do a find and replace, and that's what we will cover in the next section.

Replace Values

Just like in Excel's find and replace feature, Power Query allows you to find and replace by using **Replace Values** under the **Transform** menu. As a convenient illustration, we will replace the **Q** in the **Quarter** column with Qtr. To achieve this, select the **Quarter** column and click on **Replace Values** under the **Transform** menu. See the following screenshot on the use of **Replace Values** to replace **Q** in the **Quarter** column with Qtr.

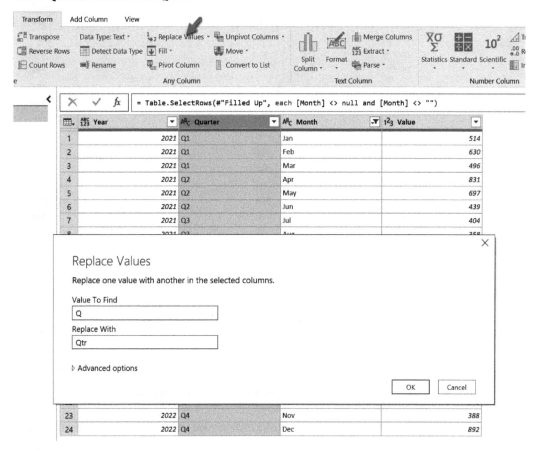

Figure 4.54 – Replace Values in Power Query

The outcome is a **Quarter** column that displays **Qtr 1**, **Qtr 2**, **Qtr 3**, and **Qtr 4**, as shown in the following screenshot:

	X ✓ fx	= Table.ReplaceValue(#"Filtered Rows","Q","Qtr ",Replacer.ReplaceText,{"Quarter"})		
	ABC 123 Year	ABC Quarter	ABC Month	123 Value
1	2021	Qtr 1	Jan	514
2	2021	Qtr 1	Feb	630
3	2021	Qtr 1	Mar	496
4	2021	Qtr 2	Apr	831
5	2021	Qtr 2	May	697
6	2021	Qtr 2	Jun	439
7	2021	Qtr 3	Jul	404
8	2021	Qtr 3	Aug	358
9	2021	Qtr 3	Sep	627
10	2021	Qtr 4	Oct	460
11	2021	Qtr 4	Nov	360
12	2021	Qtr 4	Dec	827
13	2022	Qtr 1	Jan	650
14	2022	Qtr 1	Feb	777
15	2022	Qtr 1	Mar	329
16	2022	Qtr 2	Apr	453
17	2022	Qtr 2	May	659
18	2022	Qtr 2	Jun	389
19	2022	Qtr 3	Jul	248
20	2022	Qtr 3	Aug	546
21	2022	Qtr 3	Sep	272
22	2022	Qtr 4	Oct	841
23	2022	Qtr 4	Nov	388
24	2022	Qtr 4	Dec	892

Figure 4.55 – Outcome of the Replace Values transformation

Now that we have covered some of the common transformations you will need to do as you manipulate data in Power Query, we will move on to important tips you should be aware of.

Important tips

At the first launch of Power Query in Excel, you may notice that the formula bar is not visible. You can easily enable it by going to the **View** menu and checking the checkbox beside **Formula Bar**. See the following screenshot:

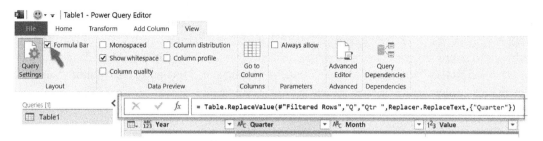

Figure 4.56 – Enabling the formula bar in Power Query

Most of the commonly used transformations can be easily accessed upon right-clicking on the column name. See the following screenshot:

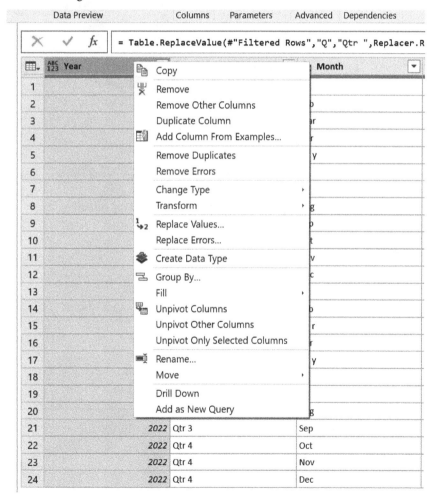

Figure 4.57 – Right-clicking on a column to reveal common transformations

Always set the column data type. It might not cause you much trouble in Excel, but as you begin to apply your Power Query knowledge in Power BI and other platforms, you will face issues that are linked to improperly set column data types. A quick way to set the data types for all columns at once is to use **Detect Data Type** under the **Transform** menu after selecting all the columns. See the following screenshot:

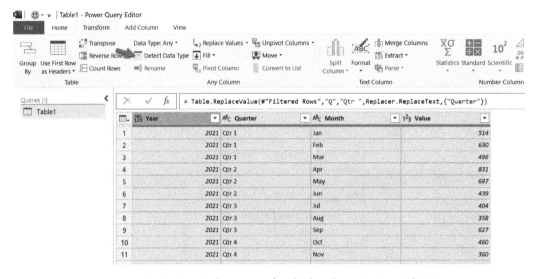

Figure 4.58 – Detecting data types of multiple columns in Power Query

You can set it for a column at a time by clicking on the data type icon beside the column name. See the following screenshot:

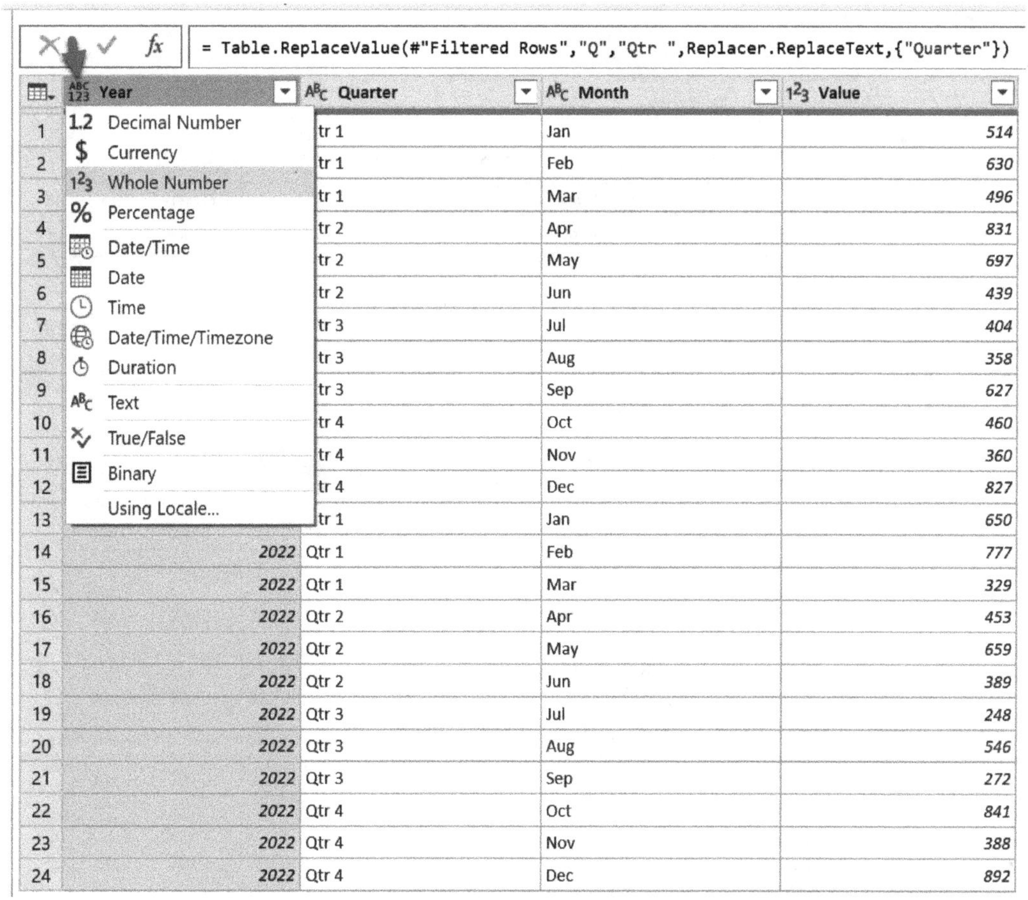

Figure 4.59 – Setting the data type of a single column in Power Query

You can get a visual summary of the column's valid entries, errors, and missing entries by enabling **Column quality** under the **View** menu. See the following screenshot:

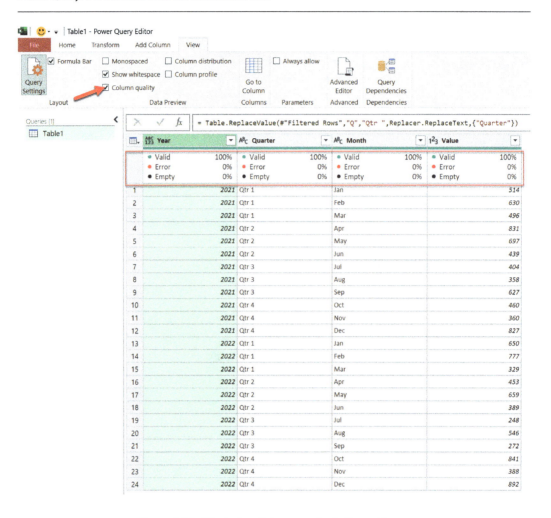

Figure 4.60 – Displaying Column quality in Power Query

Lastly, you can access the M code behind all your applied steps (transformations) by clicking on **Advanced Editor** under the **Home** menu. This can help you become more familiar with the M code and also makes for a nifty way to copy transformations from one file to another. See the following screenshot:

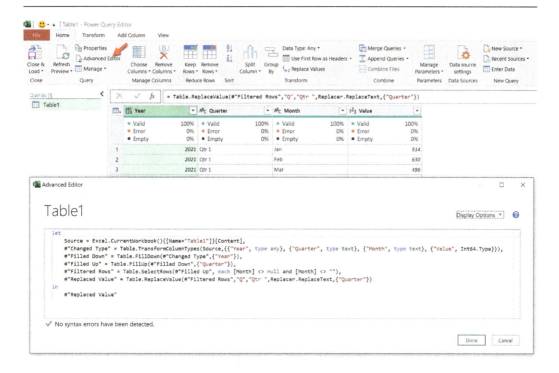

Figure 4.61 – Displaying Advanced Editor in Power Query

There are many more other tips that will speed up your work within Power Query but the preceding ones are the only ones we can cover without making the chapter unnecessarily long. I picked them because I strongly believe they are the undisputable high-value tips everyone should know. We will now move on to another important aspect of your work within Power Query. We will deal with how to load your transformed data back into Excel.

Understanding Close & Load To

When you are done with your Power Query data ingestion and transformation, you will have to load the transformed data for access within Excel's main application area. You can access the load feature under the **Home** menu. You will be presented with **Close & Load** and **Close & Load To....** See the following screenshot of the **Close & Load** options:

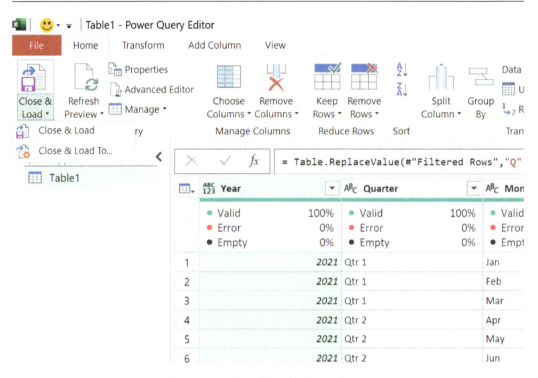

Figure 4.62 – Close & Load in Power Query

You might wonder what the difference is between **Close & Load**, and **Close & Load To**.

Close & Load loads the transformed data using your default settings. If you have not altered the default settings since Excel's installation, it will load each table into a separate Excel sheet and also into the data model. The data model is essentially *Power Pivot*, which we will discuss in *Chapter 5, PivotTable and Power Pivot*.

Close & Load To presents you with all the options for where you can load the Power Query tables. See the following screenshot:

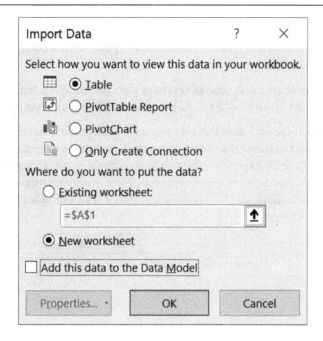

Figure 4.63 – Close & Load To in Power Query

The options allow you to load the data into Excel tables, directly into a PivotTable or PivotChart, or to have it just as a data connection. Also, you can indicate whether to add the data to Excel's *Data Model* or not. If you would like to have a copy of the table displayed in an Excel sheet, you can select the **Table** option. If you would rather go straight to creating a PivotTable report from the data you are loading, then it's best to select **PivotTable Report**. And if you want a PivotChart straightaway, then select **PivotChart**. **Only Create Connection** is an interesting option. It allows you to make the data available in Excel without creating a table or PivotTable. It is usually used if you just want to load the data into a data model and do some additional work on it in Power Pivot before bringing it in for report or dashboard creation in regular Excel sheets.

The next section is about the different value types in Power Query, which are at the core of all M code.

Demystifying the underlying M code

The language in which the formulas and transformations you do in Power Query are written is called M. To master Power Query, you have to be familiar with the general syntax of the M language. At the core of all things done in Power Query, there are five value types:

- **Primitive values**: These are single entries such as numbers, text, logic, and `null`. Examples are `2012`, `"Michael Olafusi"`, `false`, and `null`.

- **List values**: We touched on these briefly in the introduction. They are an ordered collection of entries or values within curly brackets. An example is `{23, 45, 78, 95}`, which is a list of primitive values. However, a list can be a collection of a list, a record, a primitive value, or a combination of different types of values. Hence, {34, "Olafusi", {23, null, 10}, 25} is a valid list.

- **Record values**: These are a collection of key-value pairs within square brackets. An example is [John = 18, Michael = 24, Mary = 29]. The key is never put in quotes.

- **Function values**: These are values that take arguments and output a different value type. They have a special syntax of listing the function's parameters within a parenthesis on the left, then typing => and putting the expression that manipulates those parameters at the right of =>. An example is (a,b) => a + b, which is the equivalent of a summation of any two numbers when the function is invoked. The following screenshot is an example of the function being invoked in Power Query:

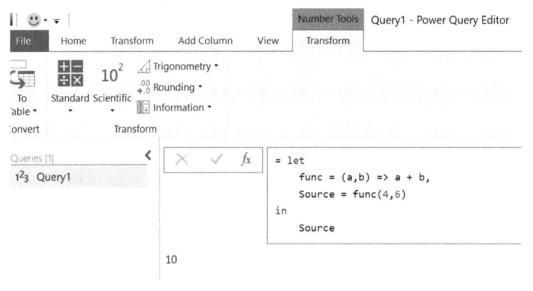

Figure 4.64 – Function value in Power Query

- **Table values**: These are the most used value type in Power Query as most data imported into Power Query is auto-transformed into a table. There are many ways to create a table, but if you want to create a literal table, it can be easily achieved by using the #table keyword. An example is #table({"Name", "Age"}, { {"John", 22}, {"Jane", 24} }). See the following screenshot of the created table:

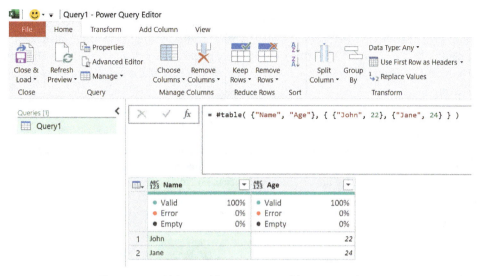

Figure 4.65 – Using #table to create a table in Power Query

Every transformation you do in Power Query creates M code. You can see all the code your transformations have automatically created by going to **Advanced Editor** under the **Home** menu. You can also examine the M code for the currently selected transformation or query in the formula bar. The following is a screenshot of the M code showing in **Advanced Editor** for the fill series and **Remove Empty** transformations we carried out earlier:

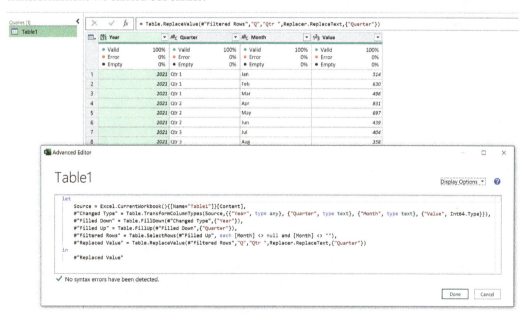

Figure 4.66 – Advanced Editor in Power Query

Notice that the code started with the `let` keyword and had the `in` keyword toward the end. The different transformations are written line by line, with each line ending with a comma except the last line before the `in` keyword. Each line has a variable name and then an = sign before the actual transformation expression. The expression that should be returned is the one whose variable name is put after the `in` keyword.

> **Important note**
>
> You don't actually need to use the `let` ... `in` syntax. The code block or query will always run if it returns a value. This means you can type in just a value and see the result returned to you. Remember that a value can be any of the five values we have discussed.

The following screenshot is an example of typing in just a primitive value:

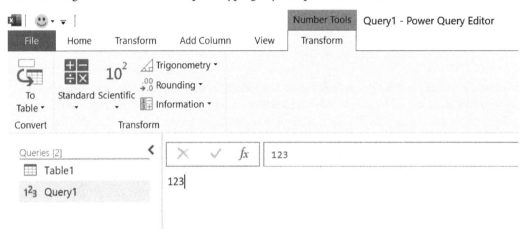

Figure 4.67 – Typing in a value in Power Query

And that brings us to the end of this chapter on Power Query.

Summary

This has been a very long chapter as we went through special uses of Power Query – how it allows you to connect directly to over 100 data sources and carry out data transformations. We went through some common transformations such as appending data, merging data, unpivoting columns, filling series, and replacing values. I also shared with you some important tips to keep in mind as you work toward boosting your competence in the use of Power Query. Lastly, we examined how to load your transformed data and get a hang of the M code that powers everything in Power Query.

In the next chapter, we will explore the use of PivotTables and Power Pivot to create the analysis and dashboards you desire after using Power Query to pull in the clean data required.

5
PivotTable and Power Pivot

Pivot Tables have been at the core of dynamic reports in Excel for over 25 years, since their introduction in Excel 5 in 1994. They're often the quickest route to creating high-level or summary reports from large record sets. In the business world, most datasets are a growing set of daily transactions and business activities, which can be overwhelming for decision makers. The decision makers are often interested in summarized reports at a monthly or weekly level, grouped by a business relevant dimension (product, region, cost center, department, and so on). And for those responsible for creating these types of reports, a Pivot Table is a very convenient way to build them and capture new data in them automatically. The extremely important role a Pivot Table plays in the work life of a data analyst moved Microsoft to create Power Pivot as a more advanced version of a Pivot Table.

Pivot Tables and Power Pivot are indispensable tools for the modern data analyst who intends to build automated dashboards in Excel. Once you've gone through the rigmarole of connecting to datasets and doing the transformations that must happen at the Power Query stage, you want a way to create the analysis and desired dashboards with an automatic refresh. Pivot Tables and Power Pivot make that happen.

In this chapter, we will make you proficient in the use of Pivot Tables and Power Pivot as we cover the following topics:

- Mastering Pivot Tables
- The role of slicers
- Dynamic reports with Pivot Table slicers s
- Power Pivot and Data Models
- DAX

Mastering Pivot Tables

A Pivot Table is what I call Excel's special tool for analyzing large datasets. It allows you to create meaningful summary reports from large tables. Imagine you have a table of records that spans thousands of rows, and you need to create an insightful report from this table. Usually, a meaningful report will be one that won't have the same thousands of rows. Rather, it will be a report that is a summary of that large table. Also, it is impossible to fit a chart on a thousand-row table. However, the summary table created via a Pivot Table can be plotted on a chart. Thus, the two major components of a dashboard, aggregated values and charts, are easily created with a Pivot Table.

We will attempt to use a Pivot Table to create a sales report from a sales orders table. You can access the practice file, `AdventureWorks -Sales SalesOrderHeader.xlsx`, in the `companion` folder. It holds over 30,000 records of sales spanning four years for Adventure Works LLC. You can see in *Figure 5.1* the structure of the sales order table:

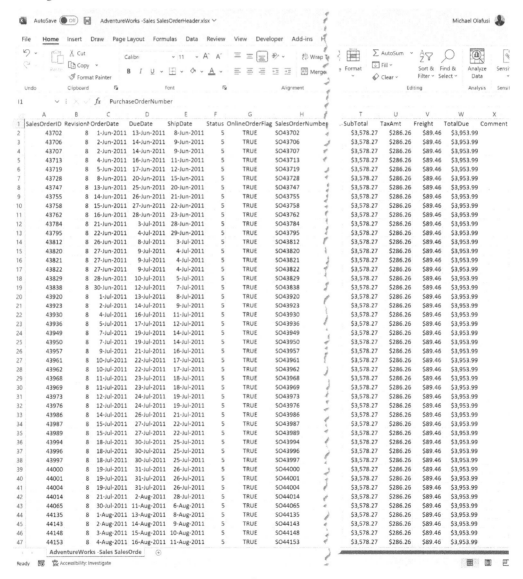

Figure 5.1 – An overview of AdventureWorks sales orders

How can we create a dynamic report of sales by period across the sales territories using a Pivot Table, a report that will look like the one shown in *Figure 5.2*?

	A	B	C	D	E	F	G	H	I	J	K	L
1	OnlineOrderFlag (All)											
2												
3	Sales Amount	Territories										
4	Period	Australia	Canada	Central	France	Germany	Northeast	Northwest	Southeast	Southwest	United Kingdom	Grand Total
5	⊞2011	1693032.742	2106905.873	1126645.7	236268.627	272780.9066	705672.2	2620943.826	1847744.58	3144713.099	400991.929	14155699.53
6	⊟2012	2347885.461	6599971.022	3334868	1743487.654	607828.1753	3272239.8	5325813.056	3344683.61	9329154.343	1769769.215	37675700.31
7	⊟Qtr1	699057.2978	1675437.009	956756.7	125024.5666	179789.406	489448.83	1683300.691	1239410.57	2264399.12	131112.6328	9443736.816
8	Jan	209974.675	871163.4814	469301.67	37454.1576	56676.2204	258034.65	882585.5744	539891.587	1076397.706	56857.7258	4458337.444
9	Feb	233156.22	292250.1394	108503.33	42531.5294	67541.0576	72290.753	202967.399	277432.231	317214.9712	35164.2718	1649051.9
10	Mar	255926.4028	512023.3877	378951.7	45038.8796	55572.128	159123.43	597747.7171	422086.75	870786.4432	39090.6352	3336347.472
11	⊞Qtr2	595597.2137	1850590.56	861354.27	549951.9247	161640.0973	973552.32	1458175.958	705765.027	2358439.026	420428.7769	9935495.173
12	⊞Qtr3	502526.5164	1776428.588	826944.73	609309.3153	111889.1	1024627	1202129.176	759198.587	2700939.273	650414.5341	10164406.83
13	⊞Qtr4	550704.4332	1297514.866	689812.28	459201.8472	154509.572	784611.65	982207.232	640309.427	2005376.924	567813.2711	8132061.495
14	⊞2013	4702404.05	7010449.699	3374336.3	4271019.266	2869491.971	2965567	6759500.671	2705730.97	10239209.34	4068178.667	48965887.96
15	⊞2014	3071053.842	2681602.594	1077449.2	1868973.799	1729718.522	876730.61	3355402.818	985940.211	4437517.808	2335108.897	22419498.32
16	Grand Total	11814376.1	18398929.19	8913299.2	8119749.346	5479819.576	7820209.6	18061660.37	8884099.37	27150594.59	8574048.708	123216786.1
17												

Figure 5.2 – The sales amount by period and territories

A Pivot Table is easy to use. With just a couple of mouse clicks, you are done creating most reports. The usual first step is to select the table of data from which you want to create a summary. In our case, we will select the table in the AdventureWorks -Sales SalesOrder sheet. Then, head over to the **Insert** menu and click on **PivotTable** – it is the first from the left under the **Insert** menu. A dialog box will pop up; confirm that the table range is correct, then leave the destination on the default **New Worksheet** option, and click on **OK** (see *Figure 5.3*):

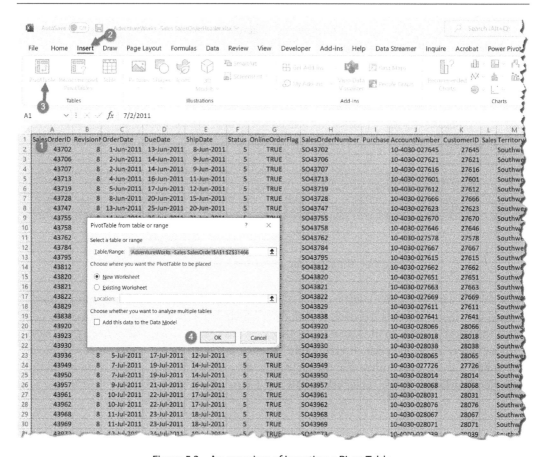

Figure 5.3 – An overview of inserting a Pivot Table

A new sheet will appear and have an interface like the one shown in *Figure 5.4*:

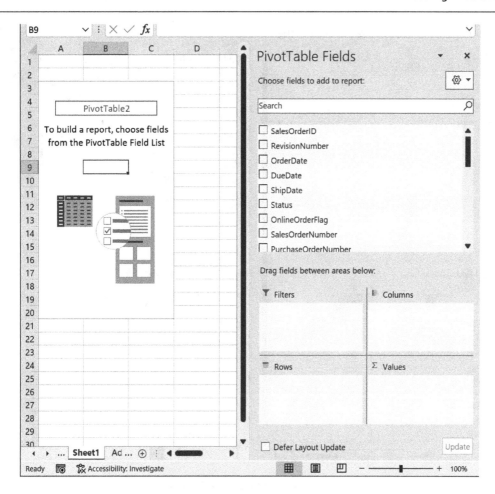

Figure 5.4 – A Pivot Table

On the left is a display placeholder that changes to the report as you place fields from the upper left into the quadrants on the lower left. The fields you see on the upper left are exactly the same as the columns in your originally selected table.

The quadrants on the lower left are very important in achieving the report structure you want. The **Filters** quadrant is where you drag fields that will act as a filter, allowing you to create reports only on the subset of data that aligns with selected filter values. For our use case, we will put **OnlineOrderFlag** in the **Filters** quadrant. This will allow us to indicate whether we want the final report to show for all orders, just online orders, or just in-store orders (see *Figure 5.5*):

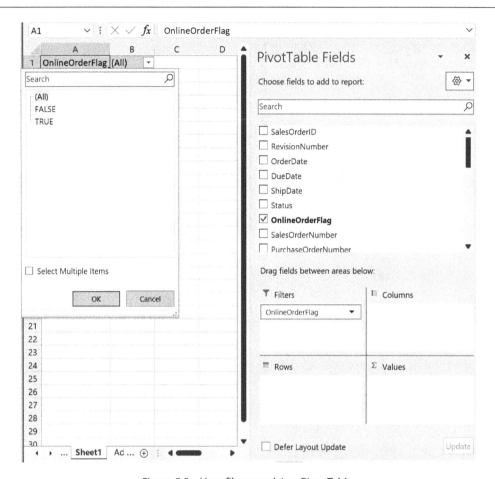

Figure 5.5 – How filters work in a Pivot Table

Next, we will examine the **Columns** quadrant. The **Columns** quadrant is where you drag fields that will become categories in your report. If you want a report that is grouped by product, then you drag the product field into **Columns**. If you want a report that is grouped by regions, then you drag regions into **Columns**. For our report, we want to see sales performance across the sales territories, so we will drag **Territory** into **Columns** (see the outcome in *Figure 5.6*):

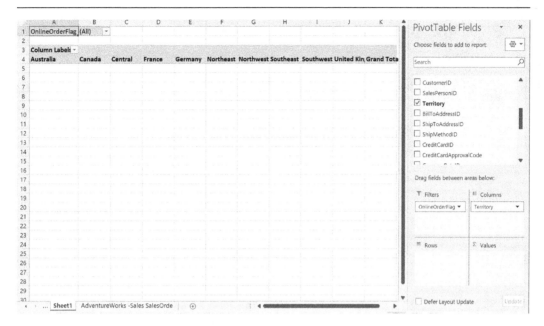

Figure 5.6 – How columns work in a Pivot Table

The **Values** quadrant is where all fields that must be aggregated are dragged to. If you need to sum up a sales amount, drag the sales amount field to **Values**. If you need to find the average sales discount, drag the sales discount to **Values**. If you need to find the percentage contribution to the total quantity, drag the quantity to **Values**. Any field that needs to have an aggregation calculation made on it goes straight to **Values**. For our use case, we want to show the total sales amount across the different territories. So, we will drag the **TotalDue** field to **Values** (see *Figure 5.7* for the outcome):

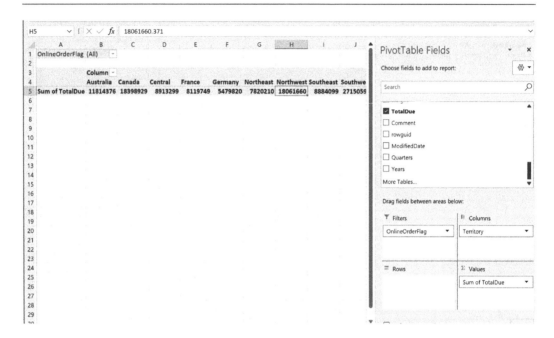

Figure 5.7 – The Values quadrant in a Pivot Table

You will see that it made a sum of **TotalDue**. To access all the possible aggregations and specify the desired formatting, click on the field in the **Values** quadrant and select **Values Field Settings…** (see *Figure 5.8*):

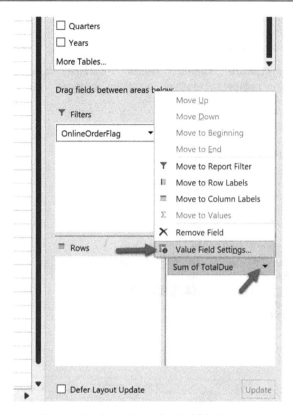

Figure 5.8 – Accessing Value Field Settings…

In the **Value Field Settings** pane that comes up, you can specify the type of aggregation you want and the number format for the values (see *Figure 5.9*):

	Australia	Canada	Central	France	Germany	Northeast	Northwes
TotalDue	11814376	18398929	8913299	8119749	5479820	7820210	18061660

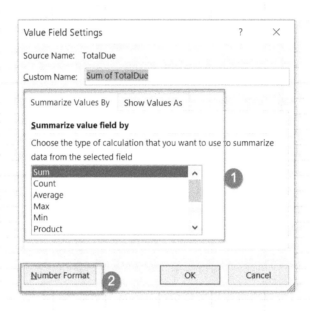

Figure 5.9 – The settings options in Value Field Settings

Now, we will explore the last quadrant – **Rows**. This has the same function as **Columns,** except that it arranges the categories row-wise and not column-wise, as is the case with **Columns**. As a quick demonstration, if we drag **Territory** from **Columns** to **Rows**, note that nothing changes in the details presented, but the orientation appears different (see *Figure 5.10*):

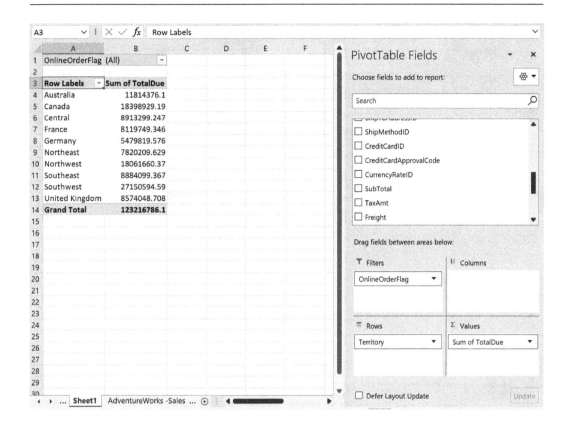

Figure 5.10 – Moving Territory from Columns to Rows

This looks easier to read than the previous orientation. Do we then leave nothing in **Columns**? Not necessarily. For our example, we could decide to want to see a categorization by date; dragging **OrderDate** into **Columns** nicely achieves this for us (see *Figure 5.11*):

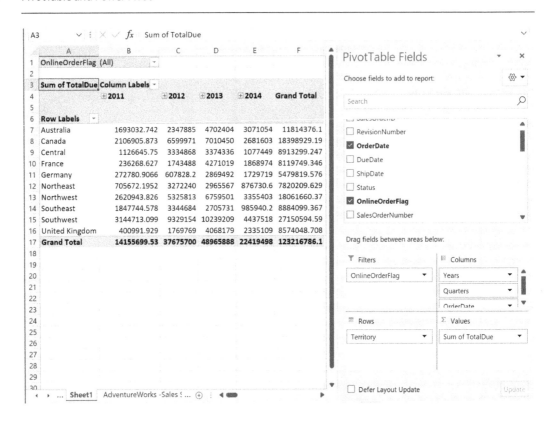

Figure 5.11 – Date in Columns and Territory in Rows

Now is a good time to revisit **Filters** and see its effect on the report. Go ahead and set the **OnlineOrderFlag** filter to **TRUE** (see *Figure 5.12*):

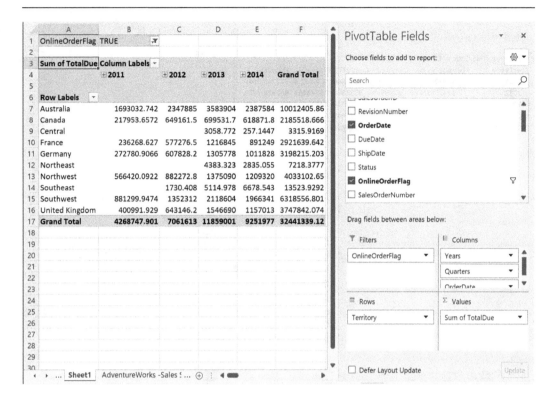

Figure 5.12 – A sample sales report

Do you remember the initial report in *Figure 5.2* that I mentioned we would be creating? Note that it is different from what we have in *Figure 5.12*. How can we achieve the report in *Figure 5.2*? It's amazingly easy! We simply swap the fields in **Rows** and **Columns**. Place **OrderDate** in **Rows** and **Territory** in **Rows**, as shown in *Figure 5.13*. Don't forget to reset **OnlineOrderFlag** to **ALL**:

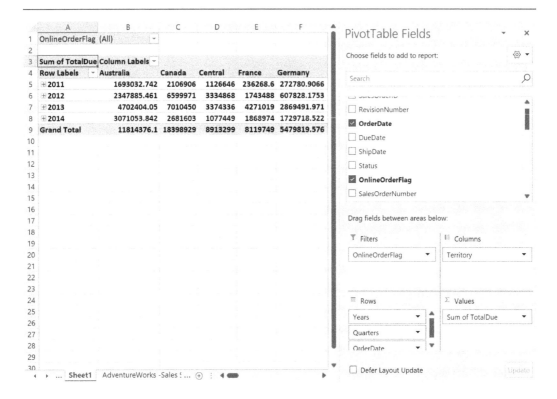

Figure 5.13 – A different orientation of the sales report

The **Values** quadrant is the one with the most features, and these features can be easily accessed in **Field Value Settings**. This allows you to specify the type of calculation you want on the field dragged to **Values**. Under **Summarize Values By**, you can set the calculation to any of the following – sum, count, average, max, min, product, count numbers, standard deviation, and variance. And under **Show Values As**, you can select percentage of total, percentage of a specific category's value, difference from a specific category's value, percentage difference from a specific category's value, running total, percentage running total, numeric rank, and index.

Each of the four quadrants allows you to drag more than one field into it. This means that you can decide to have two or more fields in **Filters**, **Columns**, **Values** and **Rows**.

When you drag dates or numeric fields into **Columns** or **Rows**, Pivot Table gives you the ability to group the categories. Did you notice how it automatically grouped the **OrderDate** field into **Years**, **Quarters**, and **OrderDate** (date)? You can create or remove grouping by right-clicking on the displayed categories and accessing the **Group...** and **Ungroup...** options (see *Figure 5.14*):

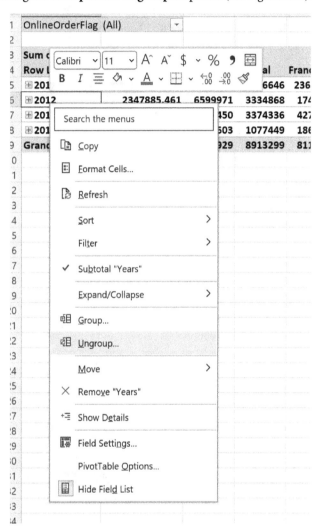

Figure 5.14 – The Group... and Ungroup... options

Whenever you are working with Pivot Table, two additional ribbon menus show up. They are the **PivotTable Analyze** menu and the **Design** menu. If you click on any cell on the Excel sheet that is not part of the Pivot Table report area, **PivotTable Fields** on the right side will disappear. It will reappear once you click within the Pivot Table report area on the upper left of the Excel window. However, if you close it using the close icon, as shown in *Figure 5.15*, it won't reappear by clicking within the Pivot Table report area. You will have to enable **Show Field Lists** in the right-click options of the report area or under the **PivotTable Analyze** menu to make it display again:

Figure 5.15 – The PivotTable Fields list close icon

The **PivotTable Analyze** menu allows you to access and edit the name of the Pivot Table. You can also generate sheets of the same Pivot Table but with each sheet set to show one of the filter values. By doing this on the Pivot Table, we have created leads to two new sheets with the same Pivot Table, but with one set to **FALSE** and the other set to **TRUE** in the **OnlineOrderFlag** filter. The setting can be accessed under **Options** on the far left of the **PivotTable Analyze** menu, as shown in *Figure 5.16*:

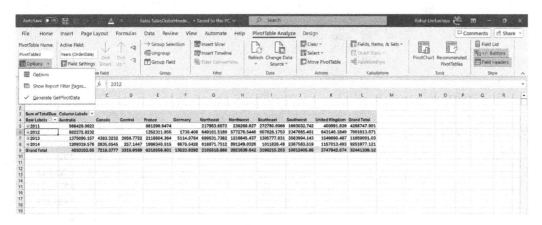

Figure 5.16 – An overview of generating sheets corresponding to the filter values

There's also a **Field Settings** feature from where you can customize the settings of any field you dragged into the quadrants. For the fields in the **Values** quadrant, you will be presented with the **Value Field Settings** window. For the fields in **Rows** and **Columns**, you will be shown a **Field Settings** window that looks different and allows you to customize the default subtotal applied, the filter behavior, the display layout, and the print layout (see *Figure 5.17* on how to access **Field Settings**):

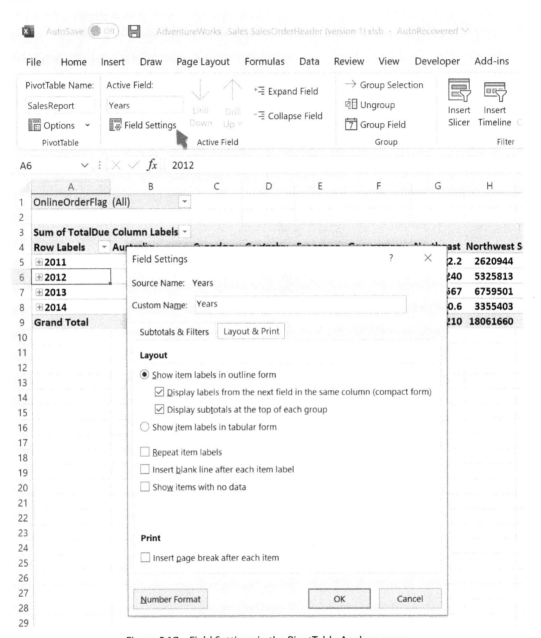

Figure 5.17 – Field Settings in the PivotTable Analyze menu

You can via the **PivotTable Analyze** menu insert a slicer and a timeline, which we will cover in detail in the next section. You can force a refresh of the Pivot Table especially if the underlying table has been updated. You can use **Change Data Source** to resize the underlying table, which is very useful when you have new fields you want to capture in the Pivot Table. With **Move PivotTable**, you can move the Pivot Table to a new sheet or to a different place in the current sheet.

There will be times you need to quickly create new calculated fields from the existing fields. With **Calculated Field** accessible under **Fields, Items & Sets**, you can create new fields easily, as shown in *Figure 5.18*:

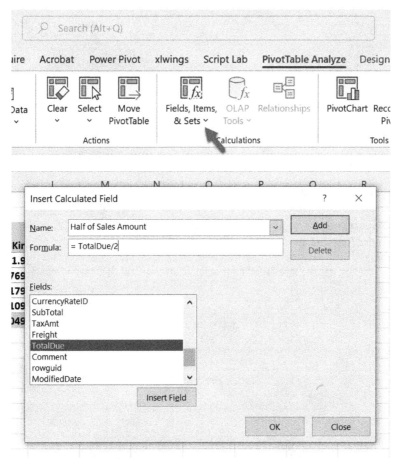

Figure 5.18 – A calculated field in a Pivot Table

On the far right under the **PivotTable Analyze** menu, also shown in *Figure 5.19*, are the buttons to turn on or off **Field List**. These are the expand/collapse buttons and the field headers:

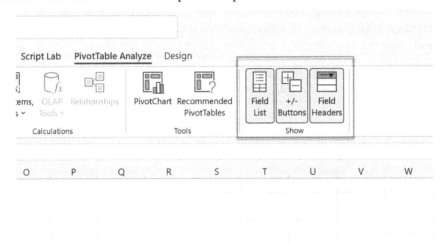

Figure 5.19 – Showing or hiding Field List, +/- Buttons, and Field Headers

The **Design** menu houses settings to enable or disable subtotals and grand totals. With **Report Layout**, you can set the display form of the report and set category labels to repeat or not. You should try **Show in Tabular Form** for reports where you have two or more fields in **Rows** (see *Figure 5.20* for the full lists of options under **Report Layout**):

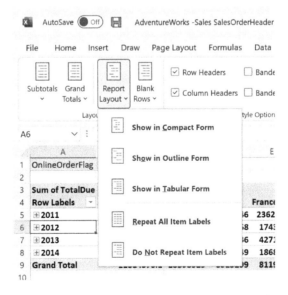

Figure 5.20 – The Report Layout setting in a Pivot Table

Still within the **Design** menu, you can set the visual display of the rows, columns, and the entire Pivot Table.

A Pivot Table can seem simple and, thus, be easily underestimated, but in the hands of a proficient user, it can replicate what only complex formulas and macros can create. The real mastery lies in being able to creatively combine all the features and use it alongside other tools, such as slicers and charts. In the next section, we will do a deep dive into **Slicers**.

The role of Slicers

Slicers are the modern version of filters in Excel. You can include a slicer in any Pivot Table report and any Excel range formatted as a table. You will always find **Slicer** under the **Insert** menu, and for a Pivot Table, you can also find it under the **PivotTable Analyze** menu. For a good illustration, we will put the **OnlineOrderFlag** field in a Slicer (see *Figure 5.21*):

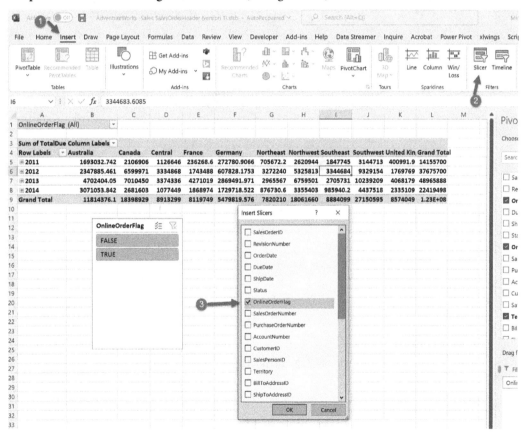

Figure 5.21 – An overview of inserting a slicer in Excel

It works exactly like a filter but comes with the added advantage of more visual customizations. To fully explore these customizations, we will take out the **OnlineOrderFlag** slicer and use a field with more distinct values so that we get a richer experience with the customizations. To remove a slicer, you can click on it and hit the *Delete* key on your keyboard. Alternatively, you can right-click on the slicer and click on **Remove OnlineOrderFlag**, as shown in the following screenshot:

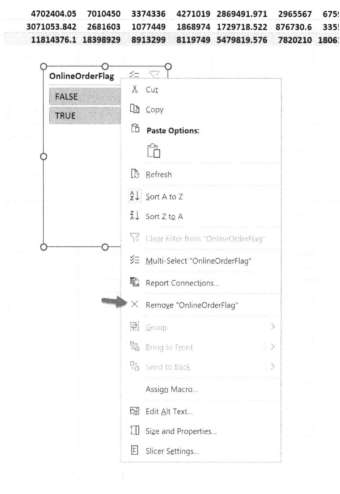

Figure 5.22 – Removing a slicer

In the place of **OnlineOrderFlag**, we will add the **Territory** field as a slicer, as shown in *Figure 2.23*:

(All)   ▼

Column Labels ▼										
Australia	Canada	Central	France	Germany	Northeast	Northwest	Southeast	Southwest	United Kin	Grand Total
1693032.742	2106906	1126646	236268.6	272780.9066	705672.2	2620944	1847745	3144713	400991.9	14155700
2347885.461	6599971	3334868	1743488	607828.1753	3272240	5325813	3344684	9329154	1769769	37675700
4702404.05	7010450	3374336	4271019	2869491.971	2965567	6759501	2705731	10239209	4068179	48965888
3071053.842	2681603	1077449	1868974	1729718.522	876730.6	3355403	985940.2	4437518	2335109	22419498
11814376.1	18398929	8913299	8119749	5479819.576	7820210	18061660	8884099	27150595	8574049	1.23E+08

Territory

- Australia
- Canada
- Central
- France
- Germany
- Northeast
- Northwest
- Southeast
- Southwest
- United Kingdom

Insert Slicers   ?   ×

- [ ] PurchaseOrderNumber
- [ ] AccountNumber
- [ ] CustomerID
- [ ] SalesPersonID
- [x] Territory
- [ ] BillToAddressID
- [ ] ShipToAddressID
- [ ] ShipMethodID
- [ ] CreditCardID
- [ ] CreditCardApprovalCode
- [ ] CurrencyRateID
- [ ] SubTotal
- [ ] TaxAmt
- [ ] Freight
- [ ] TotalDue
- [ ] Comment

OK   Cancel

Figure 5.23 – Adding the Territory field as a slicer

Slicers have a dedicated menu, **Slicer**. The menu has a collection of customizations that often make the slicer a preferred choice over the filter for dashboards and visually appealing reports (see the menu in *Figure 5.24*):

Figure 5.24 – The Slicer customization menu

You can set the slicer color, which can be very useful to ensure that the color matches your report theme. For pixel perfect positioning relative to other illustrations (pictures, shapes, icons, and smart arts) in your report, you can use the customizations grouped as **Arrange**. This has the **Bring Forward**, **Send Backward**, **Selection Pane**, **Align**, **Group**, and **Rotate** options. Perhaps the most interesting customization is the number of columns in the slicer. Dashboard builders have used it to create better blending slicers that greatly enhance the overall look of the dashboard. For illustration, see *Figure 5.25* for how it can turn the previously bland report into a better-looking one:

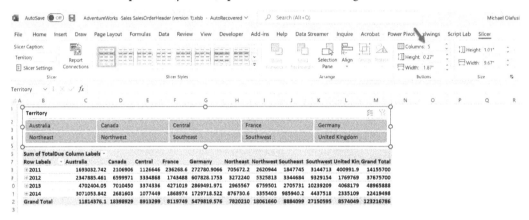

Figure 5.25 – Slicer set to numerous columns and put at top of report

Right-clicking on a slicer uncovers additional settings that can be set to achieve a more fitting slicer in your report (see *Figure 5.26* for the settings that are accessible via a right-click; of notable mention are the **Multi-Select** and **Report Connections** options to specify the Pivot Tables that the slicer can filter, and **Slicer Settings…**):

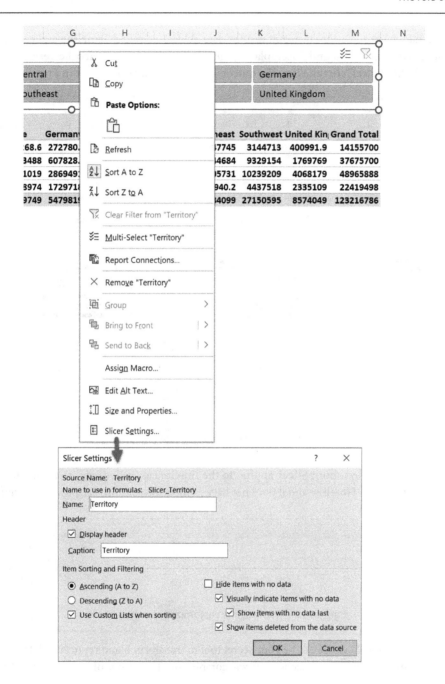

Figure 5.26 – Additional slicer settings

There's a special type of slicer that is meant just for date fields. It is called **Timeline** and can also be accessed in the same menu you find **Slicer**, placed right beside it. You can replace the **Territory** slicer we created with the **OrderDate** timeline. The outcome will look similar to what's in *Figure 5.27*:

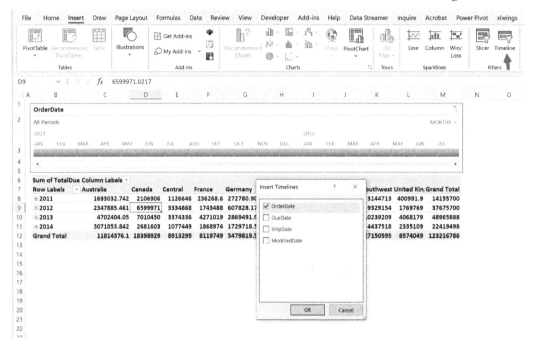

Figure 5.27 – Adding an OrderDate field timeline

All what we have discussed about **Slicer** applies to the timeline as well, except that the timeline's dedicated menu is named **Timeline** and it does not have number-of-columns settings (see *Figure 5.28* for the **Timeline** menu):

Figure 5.28 – The Timeline customization menu

And that wraps it up for slicers. It can be your secret tool to transform bland reports and dashboards into better-looking ones. In the next section, we will combine our knowledge of PivotTables and slicers to achieve more dynamic reports.

Dynamic reports with PivotTables

PivotTables make it easy to create dynamic and visually engaging reports without writing a single formula. We will demonstrate this by creating a report like the one in *Figure 5.29*, using just a Pivot Table, slicers, and a PivotChart. A Pivot Chart is essentially a chart built on the outcome of a Pivot Table:

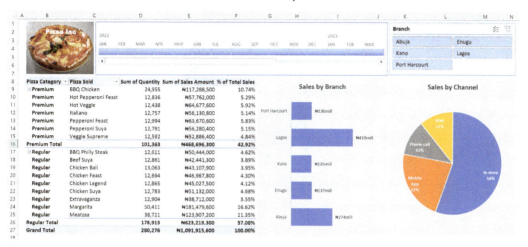

Figure 5.29 – A dynamic report created by using a Pivot Table

The practice file is `Dynamic Reports.xlsx` and can be accessed in the `companion` folder. The practice data is in the **Sales Data** sheet, as shown in *Figure 5.30*:

	A	B	C	D	E	F	G	H	I	J
1	S/N	Date	Branch	Pizza Sold	Unit Price	Quantity	Sales Amount	Sales Channel	Payment Type	Pizza Category
2	1	6/1/2022	Abuja	Chicken Bali	₦ 3,300.00	4	₦13,200.00	In store	Upfront Payment	Regular
3	2	6/1/2022	Port Harcourt	Margarita	₦ 3,600.00	1	₦3,600.00	Mobile App	Payment on Delivery	Regular
4	3	6/1/2022	Abuja	Margarita	₦ 3,600.00	5	₦18,000.00	In store	Upfront Payment	Regular
5	4	6/1/2022	Port Harcourt	Chicken Suya	₦ 4,000.00	2	₦8,000.00	In store	Upfront Payment	Regular
6	5	6/1/2022	Lagos	Margarita	₦ 3,600.00	1	₦3,600.00	In store	Upfront Payment	Regular
7	6	6/1/2022	Abuja	Meatzaa	₦ 3,200.00	4	₦12,800.00	Mobile App	Payment on Delivery	Regular
8	7	6/1/2022	Lagos	Margarita	₦ 3,600.00	1	₦3,600.00	In store	Upfront Payment	Regular
9	8	6/1/2022	Lagos	Meatzaa	₦ 3,200.00	2	₦6,400.00	In store	Upfront Payment	Regular
10	9	6/1/2022	Kano	Margarita	₦ 3,600.00	2	₦7,200.00	In store	Upfront Payment	Regular
11	10	6/1/2022	Lagos	Margarita	₦ 3,600.00	1	₦3,600.00	In store	Upfront Payment	Regular
12	11	6/1/2022	Port Harcourt	Margarita	₦ 3,600.00	1	₦3,600.00	In store	Upfront Payment	Regular
13	12	6/1/2022	Lagos	Hot Pepperoni Feast	₦ 4,500.00	3	₦13,500.00	In store	Upfront Payment	Premium
14	13	6/1/2022	Lagos	Pepperoni Suya	₦ 4,400.00	4	₦17,600.00	Web	Upfront Payment	Premium
15	14	6/1/2022	Abuja	Pepperoni Feast	₦ 4,900.00	1	₦4,900.00	Web	Payment on Delivery	Premium
16	15	6/1/2022	Abuja	Pepperoni Feast	₦ 4,900.00	6	₦29,400.00	In store	Upfront Payment	Premium
17	16	6/1/2022	Lagos	Hot Veggie	₦ 5,200.00	1	₦5,200.00	In store	Upfront Payment	Premium
18	17	6/1/2022	Abuja	Margarita	₦ 3,600.00	5	₦18,000.00	Mobile App	Payment on Delivery	Regular
19	18	6/1/2022	Lagos	Margarita	₦ 3,600.00	1	₦3,600.00	Phone call	Upfront Payment	Regular
20	19	6/1/2022	Abuja	Pepperoni Feast	₦ 4,900.00	2	₦9,800.00	Mobile App	Payment on Delivery	Premium
21	20	6/1/2022	Lagos	Beef Suya	₦ 3,300.00	1	₦3,300.00	Mobile App	Upfront Payment	Regular
22	21	6/1/2022	Port Harcourt	Beef Suya	₦ 3,300.00	1	₦3,300.00	In store	Upfront Payment	Regular
23	22	6/1/2022	Lagos	Margarita	₦ 3,600.00	2	₦7,200.00	Mobile App	Upfront Payment	Regular
24	23	6/1/2022	Port Harcourt	Margarita	₦ 3,600.00	1	₦3,600.00	In store	Upfront Payment	Regular
25	24	6/1/2022	Abuja	Meatzaa	₦ 3,200.00	1	₦3,200.00	In store	Upfront Payment	Regular
26	25	6/1/2022	Enugu	Meatzaa	₦ 3,200.00	3	₦9,600.00	Mobile App	Payment on Delivery	Regular
27	26	6/1/2022	Port Harcourt	Margarita	₦ 3,600.00	4	₦14,400.00	In store	Upfront Payment	Regular
28	27	6/1/2022	Lagos	Meatzaa	₦ 3,200.00	5	₦16,000.00	Mobile App	Payment on Delivery	Regular
29	28	6/1/2022	Lagos	Margarita	₦ 3,600.00	4	₦14,400.00	In store	Upfront Payment	Regular
30	29	6/1/2022	Lagos	Hot Veggie	₦ 5,200.00	2	₦10,400.00	In store	Upfront Payment	Premium
31	30	6/1/2022	Lagos	Chicken Legend	₦ 3,500.00	1	₦3,500.00	In store	Upfront Payment	Regular
32	31	6/1/2022	Enugu	BBQ Philly Steak	₦ 4,000.00	1	₦4,000.00	In store	Upfront Payment	Regular
33	32	6/1/2022	Enugu	Beef Suya	₦ 3,300.00	2	₦6,600.00	In store	Upfront Payment	Regular
34	33	6/1/2022	Lagos	BBQ Chicken	₦ 4,700.00	2	₦9,400.00	In store	Upfront Payment	Premium
35	34	6/1/2022	Abuja	Meatzaa	₦ 3,200.00	3	₦9,600.00	In store	Upfront Payment	Regular
36	35	6/1/2022	Enugu	Meatzaa	₦ 3,200.00	1	₦3,200.00	Phone call	Payment on Delivery	Regular
37	36	6/1/2022	Lagos	Margarita	₦ 3,600.00	2	₦7,200.00	In store	Upfront Payment	Regular
38	37	6/1/2022	Port Harcourt	Meatzaa	₦ 3,200.00	5	₦16,000.00	In store	Upfront Payment	Regular
39	38	6/1/2022	Lagos	Chicken Bali	₦ 3,300.00	2	₦6,600.00	Phone call	Upfront Payment	Regular
40	39	6/1/2022	Lagos	Hot Pepperoni Feast	₦ 4,500.00	1	₦4,500.00	Mobile App	Upfront Payment	Premium
41	40	6/1/2022	Enugu	Hot Veggie	₦ 5,200.00	1	₦5,200.00	In store	Upfront Payment	Premium
42	41	6/1/2022	Abuja	Chicken Feast	₦ 3,700.00	2	₦7,400.00	Phone call	Upfront Payment	Regular
43	42	6/1/2022	Port Harcourt	Extravaganza	₦ 3,000.00	2	₦6,000.00	In store	Upfront Payment	Regular
44	43	6/1/2022	Lagos	Chicken Suya	₦ 4,000.00	4	₦16,000.00	Web	Upfront Payment	Regular
45	44	6/1/2022	Kano	Chicken Suya	₦ 4,000.00	2	₦8,000.00	Web	Upfront Payment	Regular
46	45	6/1/2022	Lagos	BBQ Philly Steak	₦ 4,000.00	1	₦4,000.00	Web	Upfront Payment	Regular
47	46	6/1/2022	Enugu	Extravaganza	₦ 3,000.00	3	₦9,000.00	Web	Payment on Delivery	Regular

Dynamic Report · **Sales Data** · (+)

Figure 5.30 – The Pizza Inc sales data

The sales data, shown in *Figure 5.30*, is for a fictitious company called Pizza Inc that has five branches across Nigeria. They sell 16 different pizza types grouped into two categories. Pizzas priced at 4,000 naira and less are classed as regular, while pizzas selling at prices greater than 4,000 naira are classed as premium. Customers place orders over the phone, on the company's mobile app, on the company's web store, and in physical stores. For the online and phone orders, customers can choose between payment on delivery and upfront payment. The extracted data is from June 2022 to May 2023, as the company's financial year is a June-to-May cycle.

Our dynamic report will be on a dedicated Excel sheet, so we will start by inserting a Pivot Table on a selection of the sales data, as shown in the following screenshot:

S/N	Date	Branch	Pizza Sold	Unit Price	Quantity	Sales Amount	Sales Channel	Payment Type	Pizza Category
1	6/1/2022	Abuja	Chicken Bali	₦ 3,300.00	4	₦13,200.00	In store	Upfront Payment	Regular
2	6/1/2022	Port Harcourt	Margarita	₦ 3,600.00	1	₦3,600.00	Mobile App	Payment on Delivery	Regular
3	6/1/2022	Abuja	Margarita	₦ 3,600.00	5	₦18,000.00	In store	Upfront Payment	Regular
4	6/1/2022	Port Harcourt	Chicken Suya	₦ 4,000.00	2	₦8,000.00	In store	Upfront Payment	Regular
5	6/1/2022	Lagos	Margarita	₦ 3,600.00	1	₦3,600.00	In store	Upfront Payment	Regular
6	6/1/2022	Abuja	Meatzaa	₦ 3,200.00	4	₦12,800.00	Mobile App	Payment on Delivery	Regular
7	6/1/2022	Lagos	Margarita	₦ 3,600.00	1	₦3,600.00	In store	Upfront Payment	Regular
8	6/1/2022	Lagos	Meatzaa	₦ 3,200.00	2	₦6,400.00	In store	Upfront Payment	Regular
9	6/1/2022	Kano	Margarita	₦ 3,600.00	2	₦7,200.00	In store	Upfront Payment	Regular
10	6/1/2022	Lagos	Margarita	₦ 3,600.00	1	₦3,600.00	In store	Upfront Payment	Regular
11	6/1/2022	Port Harcourt	Margarita	₦ 3,600.00	1	₦3,600.00	In store	Upfront Payment	Regular
12	6/1/2022						In store	Upfront Payment	Premium

Figure 5.31 – Inserting a Pivot Table on the sales data

Drag **Pizza Category** and **Pizza Sold** into the **Rows** quadrant. Then, drag **Quantity**, **Sales Amount** and, for a second time, **Sales Amount** into the **Values** quadrant. Note that the default aggregation on the fields in the **Values** quadrant is **Sum**. Excel does sum aggregation on numeric fields and counts on non-numeric fields. We can, however, specify our desired aggregation by using **Value Field Settings**. And that's what we will do for the second **Sales Amount** field; we will set it to **% of Grand Total**. The labels on the report table are auto-generated – **Row Labels** for **Pizza Category** and **Pizza Sold**, and

Values for **Sum of Quantity**, **Sum of Sales Amount**, and **Sum of Sales Amount2**. Change **Sum of Sales Amount2** to **% of Total Sales** (see *Figure 5.32* for what the result should look like):

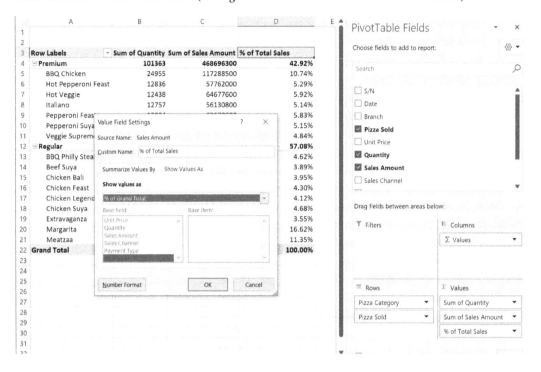

Figure 5.32 – Setting up the sales report Pivot Table

It would be good to have the quantities show in a thousand-separated format and for the sales amount to carry the reporting currency (Nigerian naira). We can achieve this by using the **Number Format** button on the **Value Field Settings** pane (see *Figure 5.33*):

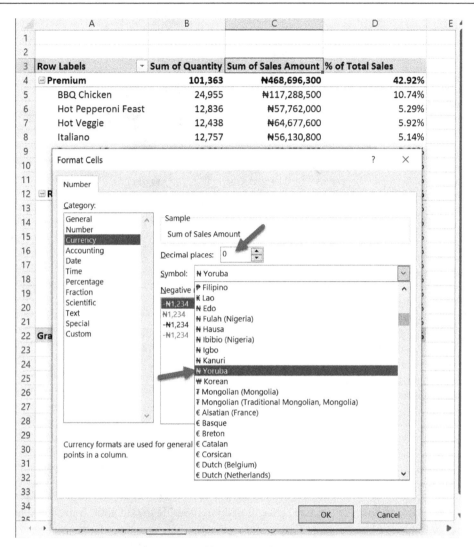

Figure 5.33 – The Number format setting

Usually, report users like being able to specify the date period for which they wish to view a report. **Timeline** is a perfect way to give them this dynamic effect. Insert a timeline and put the **Date** field in it. Also, add a Slicer with the **Branch** field in it. The outcome will look like *Figure 5.34*:

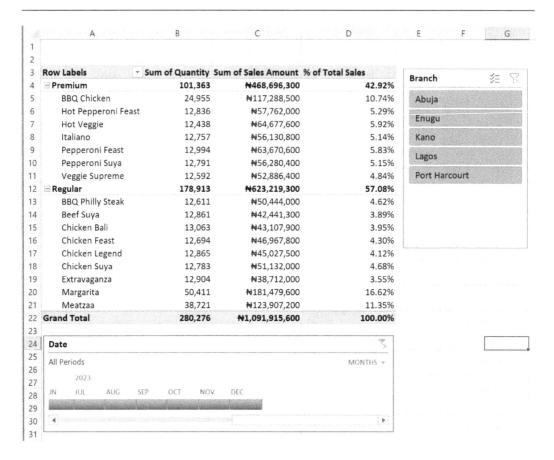

Row Labels	Sum of Quantity	Sum of Sales Amount	% of Total Sales
⊟ Premium	101,363	₦468,696,300	42.92%
BBQ Chicken	24,955	₦117,288,500	10.74%
Hot Pepperoni Feast	12,836	₦57,762,000	5.29%
Hot Veggie	12,438	₦64,677,600	5.92%
Italiano	12,757	₦56,130,800	5.14%
Pepperoni Feast	12,994	₦63,670,600	5.83%
Pepperoni Suya	12,791	₦56,280,400	5.15%
Veggie Supreme	12,592	₦52,886,400	4.84%
⊟ Regular	178,913	₦623,219,300	57.08%
BBQ Philly Steak	12,611	₦50,444,000	4.62%
Beef Suya	12,861	₦42,441,300	3.89%
Chicken Bali	13,063	₦43,107,900	3.95%
Chicken Feast	12,694	₦46,967,800	4.30%
Chicken Legend	12,865	₦45,027,500	4.12%
Chicken Suya	12,783	₦51,132,000	4.68%
Extravaganza	12,904	₦38,712,000	3.55%
Margarita	50,411	₦181,479,600	16.62%
Meatzaa	38,721	₦123,907,200	11.35%
Grand Total	280,276	₦1,091,915,600	100.00%

Branch

Abuja

Enugu

Kano

Lagos

Port Harcourt

Date

All Periods   MONTHS ▾

2023

JN   JUL   AUG   SEP   OCT   NOV   DEC

Figure 5.34 – The Date timeline and branch slicer

The positioning, however, can be better. Insert a couple of rows above the Pivot Table and put the timeline there. Also, set the Slicer to two columns and put it beside the timeline. You should have a report that looks like the one in *Figure 5.35*:

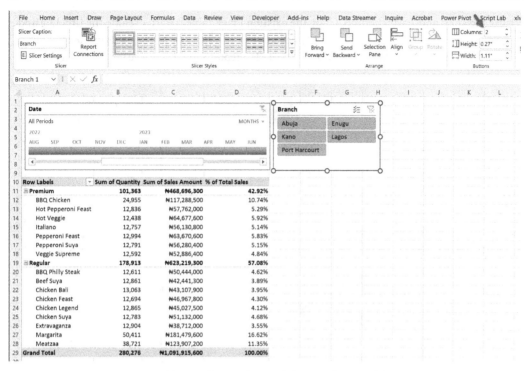

Figure 5.35 – Moving the timeline and slicer to the top of the report

Now is a great opportunity to get familiar with a must-have component in dashboards – charts. We will add two charts, a bar chart of sales by branch and a pie chart of sales by channel. To achieve this, we need to add them as Pivot Charts. This means we will add two new Pivot Tables right on the same sheet where we have the current Pivot Table. You can add the Pivot Tables from scratch using the sales data table, or you can copy and paste the one we have already created in an unused sheet area.

Let's use the copy-and-paste method. Copy the existing Pivot Table report, exclude the timeline and slicer, and then paste the report into an empty cell on the right. Remove all the fields in the quadrants, and put **Branch** in **Rows** and **Sales Amount** in **Values**. The report should look like the one in *Figure 5.36*:

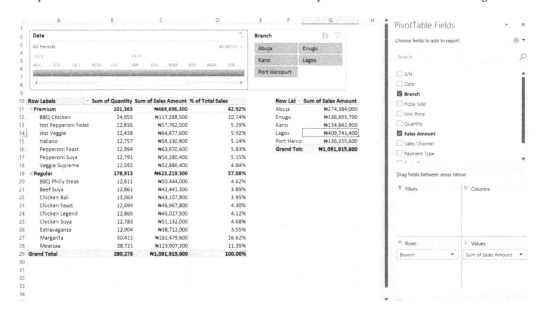

Figure 5.36 – An overview of inserting a new Pivot Table by copying and pasting an existing one

We will then insert a Pivot Chart, which can be found under the **PivotTable Analyze** menu, and then select the **Bar** chart (see *Figure 5.37*):

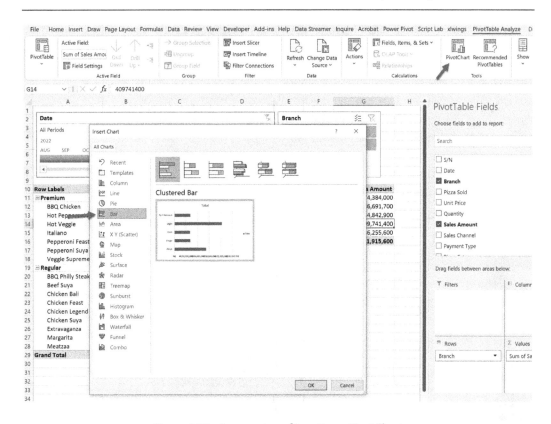

Figure 5.37 – An overview of inserting a Pivot Chart

Place the chart on top of the Pivot Table so that it covers it entirely. Set the chart title to **Sales by Branch**, and turn off **Field Buttons** under the **PivotTable Analyze** menu (see *Figure 5.38* for the step of turning off **Field Buttons**):

Figure 5.38 – Turning off Field Buttons for a Pivot Chart

We then make the chart look much better by turning off the gridlines, removing the legend, and removing the horizontal axis showing the sales figures. The outcome should look like the one in *Figure 5.39*:

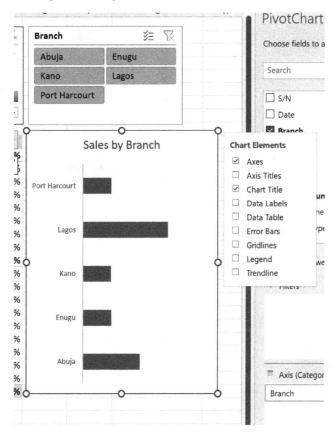

Figure 5.39 – The chart improvement formats

Set the chart fill to a light gray color, set the outline to no outline, and set the bar's series gap width to **50%**, as shown in *Figure 5.40*:

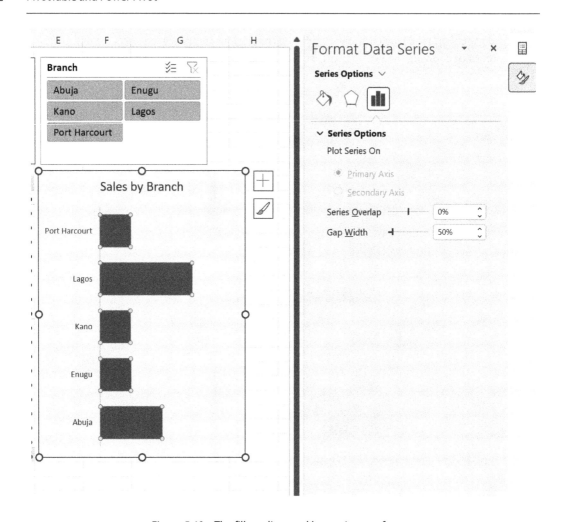

Figure 5.40 – The fill, outline, and bar series gap format

One more nice customization for the bar chart is to add a data label and set the custom format to millions. Use the custom format code [$₦-yo-NG]#,##0,,"mill" to achieve the following result:

Figure 5.41 – Setting the custom format on the added data label

Create another Pivot Table that has **Sales Channel** in **Rows** and **Sales Amount** in **Values**. Create a pie chart from it, and place it on the Pivot Table. Format the chart to have a gray fill, no outline, and no legend, and set the data label to display the category name, percentage, and leader lines. Rename the chart `Sales by Channel`. The outcome should look like *Figure 5.42*:

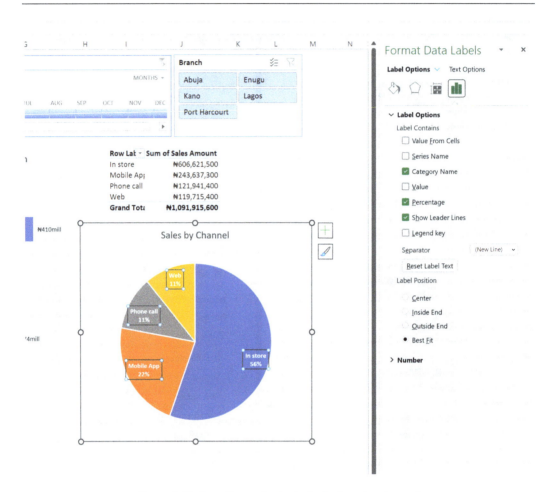

Figure 5.42 – Inserting a pie chart of sales by sales channel

Arrange the entire report to look like the following one, placing the company logo (`pizza Inc logo.jpg` in the `companion` folder) on the upper left. Click on an empty cell, go to the **View** menu, and turn off **Gridlines** (see *Figure 5.43*):

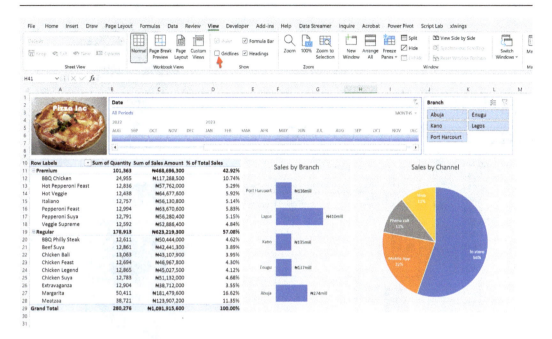

Figure 5.43 – An overview of the well-arranged report

We are almost done. Unfortunately, the charts and table do not respond correctly to the slicer and timeline. We need to set the slicer and timeline to interact with all the report components. This is easily achieved by right-clicking on the timeline and slicer and then selecting **Report Connections**, followed by selecting all the components listed in the box for the report sheet so that they will be connected to the slicer/timeline (see *Figure 5.44*):

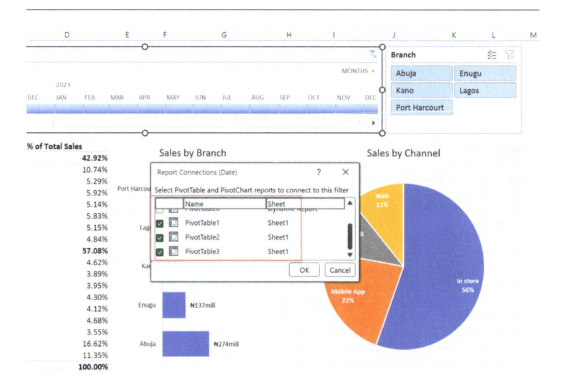

Figure 5.44 – Setting the connections within the report components

At this stage, you will want to replace the default labels in the table on the left with more meaningful names. Also, you might like a different report layout. To change the report layout, go to the **Design** menu, then **Report Layout**, and select **Show in Tabular Form** and **Repeat All Item Labels**. The results should look like *Figure 5.45*:

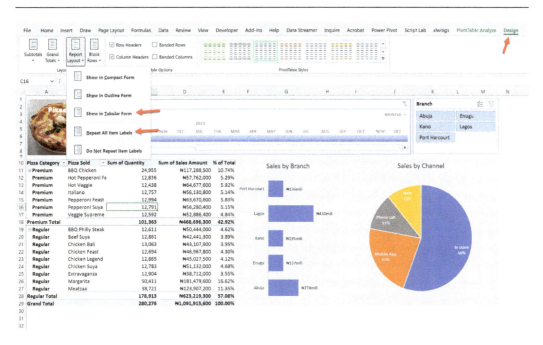

Figure 5.45 – An overview of a tabular report layout

And that's the typical way to create a dynamic report with a Pivot Table. Note that we did not type in any formulas and did nothing special to achieve this beautiful interactive report. Every time you pick an item in the slicer or timeline, the table and charts adjust accordingly. In the next section, we will examine Power Pivot and the Data Model in Excel.

Power Pivot and Data Models

Power Pivot is an advancement on the Pivot Table. It is available for Excel 2010 version and above, although for Excel 2010, you will need to install it as an external add-in, downloadable at https://www.microsoft.com/en-US/download/details.aspx?id=43348&_ga=2.91119071.49961281.1663320266-850568410.1663320266.

To get started with Power Pivot, you will often need to do one-time enabling to have it show up in the Excel ribbon. Go to **File** | **Options** | **Add-ins**, click on **COM Add-ins** on the **Manage** dropdown, and enable **Microsoft Power Pivot for Excel** (see *Figure 5.46*):

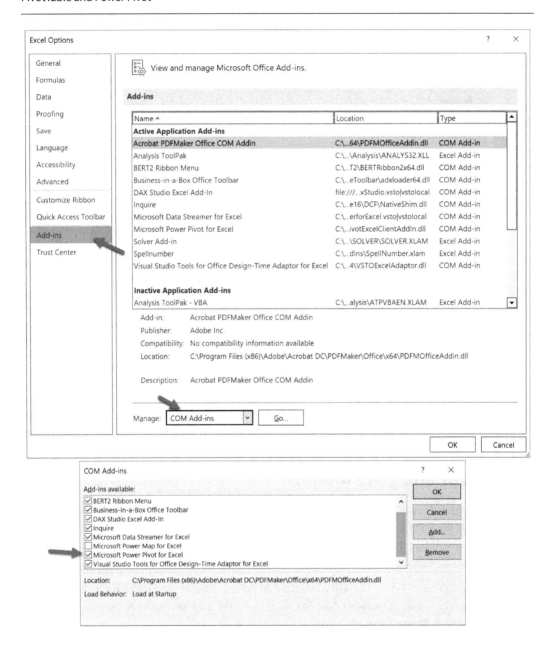

Figure 5.46 – Enabling Power Pivot in Excel

What are the additional features that Power Pivot gives a dashboard builder beyond what is possible with PivotTables? In no specific order of importance, the following is a list of the common reasons to use Power Pivot over a regular Pivot Table:

- Power Pivot allows you to analyze data with over 1,048,576 rows, while PivotTables are restricted by a hard limit on Excel rows.

- Power Pivot works well for data spread across multiple tables and sources, while a Pivot Table entails one table with all the necessary fields. Essentially, Power Pivot eliminates the need to do lookups and data duplication, as is often necessary when using PivotTables to create a table with all the necessary fields across all the data tables.

- Power Pivot allows the use of the very powerful **Data Analysis Expressions (DAX)** library to create more sophisticated reports than is possible in a Pivot Table.

- Power Pivot uses a new data compression and analysis engine that makes it much faster and more reliable for large data analysis than a Pivot Table.

- Power Pivot has KPIs to easily report values that have benchmarks or targets, while a Pivot Table does not.

- Power Pivot has additional interesting features, such as the ability to sort a column using values in a different column, and allows you to do a distinct count in **Value Field Settings**.

For a clear demonstration of the major advantages of Power Pivot and its huge importance to dashboard builders, we will use it to create a dashboard from three related tables. The practice data is in the Power Pivot Practice Data.xlsx file in the companion folder. It has three tables – Sales Data, Product Category, and Branch Data.

We will create a dashboard similar to the one shown in *Figure 5.47*:

Month_Year	Branch	Branch Manager	Sales	Sales Target	Profit	Sales Status
Jun 2022	Abuja	Uwailomwan Akintunde	21,646,200	22,865,340	4,356,734	◐
	Enugu	Efe Zoputa	10,808,600	11,390,980	2,110,540	◐
	Kano	Aduba Adesehinwa	10,455,600	11,236,910	2,105,828	◐
	Lagos	Adetosoye Chuku	34,484,800	34,145,120	6,826,628	●
	Port Harcourt	Afiba Adeolu	11,142,300	11,354,640	2,190,950	◐
Jul 2022	Abuja	Uwailomwan Akintunde	23,594,000	22,865,340	4,691,462	●
	Enugu	Efe Zoputa	12,060,700	11,390,980	2,385,840	●
	Kano	Aduba Adesehinwa	11,311,400	11,236,910	2,253,339	●
	Lagos	Adetosoye Chuku	35,702,200	34,145,120	7,094,812	●
	Port Harcourt	Afiba Adeolu	10,742,900	11,354,640	2,137,642	◐
Aug 2022	Abuja	Uwailomwan Akintunde	22,846,500	22,865,340	4,549,876	◐
	Enugu	Efe Zoputa	11,825,800	11,390,980	2,338,221	●
	Kano	Aduba Adesehinwa	11,714,800	11,236,910	2,321,956	●
	Lagos	Adetosoye Chuku	34,429,100	34,145,120	6,843,673	●
	Port Harcourt	Afiba Adeolu	11,608,300	11,354,640	2,321,447	●
Sep 2022	Abuja	Uwailomwan Akintunde	23,091,200	22,865,340	4,617,098	●
	Enugu	Efe Zoputa	10,998,300	11,390,980	2,182,645	◐
	Kano	Aduba Adesehinwa	11,300,000	11,236,910	2,255,968	●
	Lagos	Adetosoye Chuku	33,883,400	34,145,120	6,748,195	◐
	Port Harcourt	Afiba Adeolu	11,481,600	11,354,640	2,296,808	●
Oct 2022	Abuja	Uwailomwan Akintunde	23,856,600	22,865,340	4,756,856	●
	Enugu	Efe Zoputa	11,836,400	11,390,980	2,332,481	●
	Kano	Aduba Adesehinwa	11,520,600	11,236,910	2,296,418	●
	Lagos	Adetosoye Chuku	35,164,700	34,145,120	7,036,921	●
	Port Harcourt	Afiba Adeolu	11,817,700	11,354,640	2,367,046	●
Nov 2022	Abuja	Uwailomwan Akintunde	22,149,500	22,865,340	4,378,115	◐

Figure 5.47 – A sample Power Pivot dashboard

The first step is to get the tables into Power Query. For the first table, **Sales Data**, click a cell within the table, go to the **Data** menu, and click on **From Table/Range**, as shown in *Figure 5.48*:

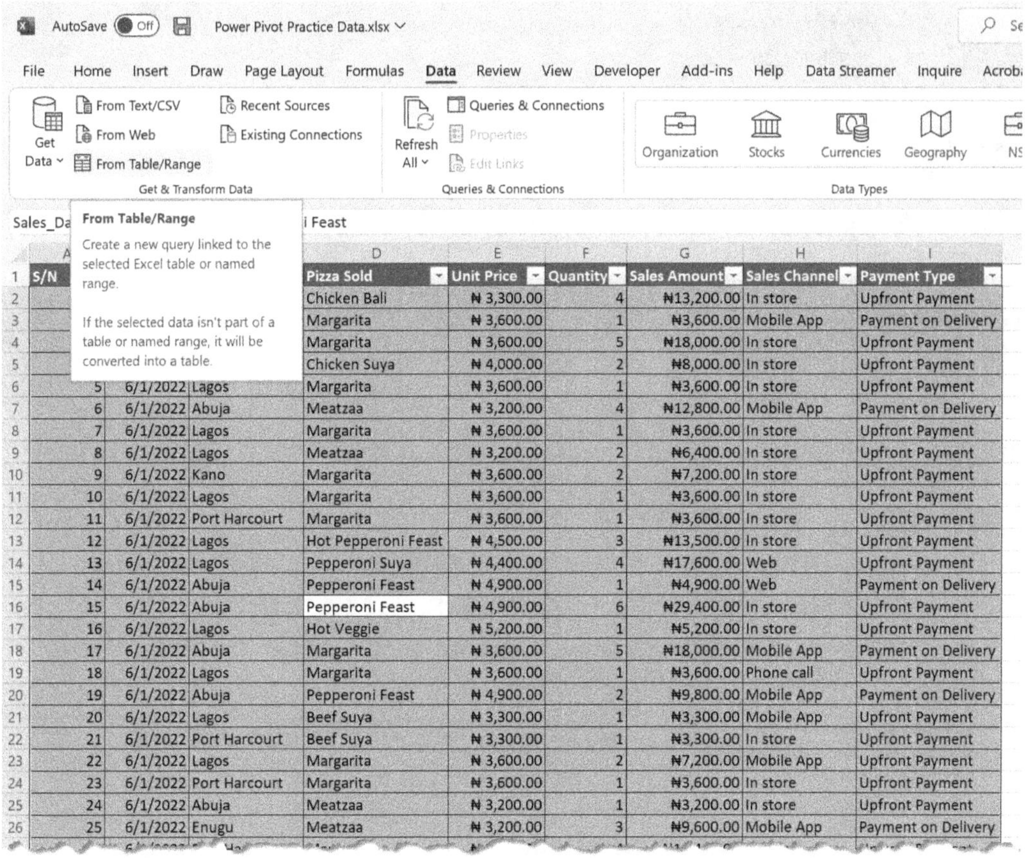

Figure 5.48 – Importing the sales data into Power Query

This will import the data into Power Query. The challenge now is how to import the other two tables, as Power Query locks the Excel sheets, preventing you from doing anything there until you close Power Query. One way is to close and load to a connection with a Data Model enabled, as shown in *Figure 5.49*. Then, repeat the process for the other two tables:

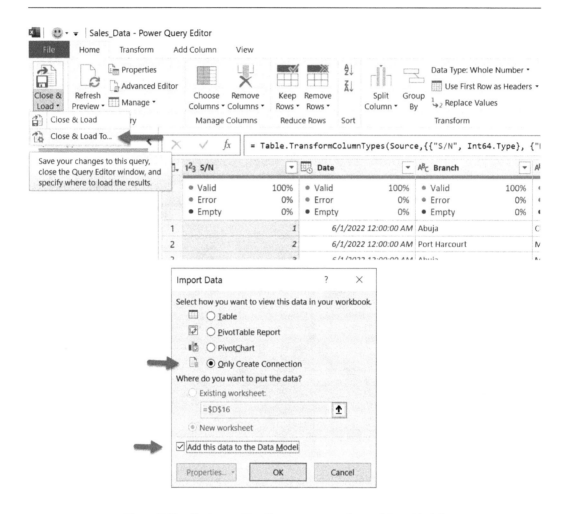

Figure 5.49 – Closing and loading to a connection and Data Model

Interestingly, you can import the same Excel file that we are working on as a new source and select the two tables (**Branch Data** and **Product Category**) in one import step (see *Figure 5.50*):

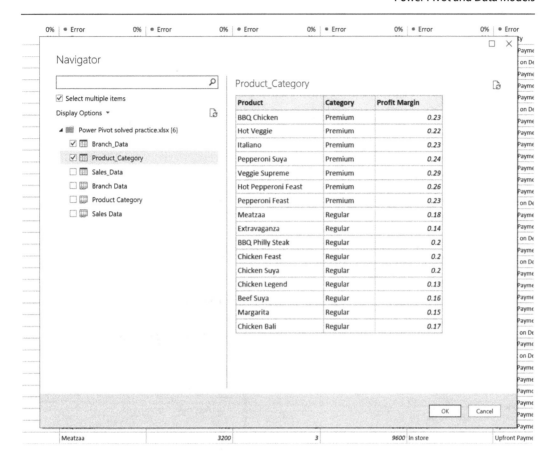

Figure 5.50 – Importing the other tables from the Excel file

With the three tables now in Power Query, you can now close and load to the Pivot Table, as shown in *Figure 5.51*. This is, however, not compulsory, as you can still access the tables in Power Pivot if you load them with any other option, as long as **Add this data to the Data Model** is ticked during loading:

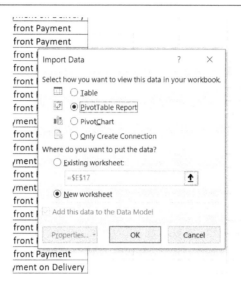

Figure 5.51 – Loading the tables into a Pivot Table

Loading to a Pivot Table will show a sheet that looks like the one shown in *Figure 5.52*:

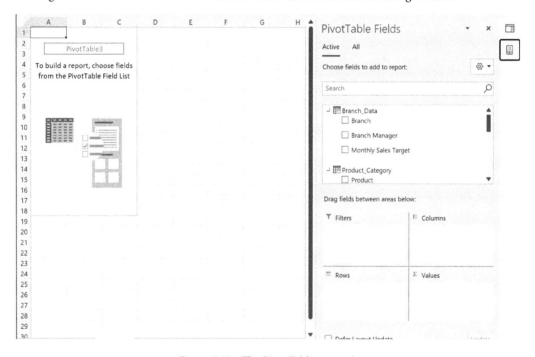

Figure 5.52 – The Pivot Table created

Note the subtle difference in the field list pane – it shows all three tables. Once you load tables into a Data Model in Excel, tools such as the Pivot Table and Power Pivot can access all the tables at once. It's just that Power Pivot gives more control and features that feed back to the Pivot Table.

We can now access the tables in Power Pivot by going to the **Power Pivot** menu and clicking on **Manage**, as shown in *Figure 5.53*:

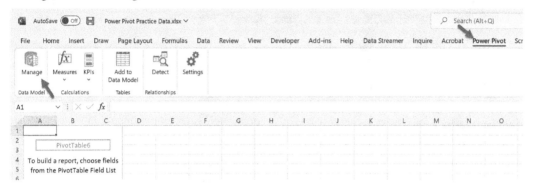

Figure 5.53 – Launching the Power Pivot window

Clicking the **Manage** button brings up a Power Pivot window with a look very distinct from a regular Excel sheet window. It has four parts:

- A menu to access its data manipulation tools
- A context-aware view of the data, which can be set to a data view or a diagram view in the menu
- A section to write DAX measures in the data view
- All the tables in the Data Model, listed in the data view

See *Figure 5.54* for the layout of these four parts:

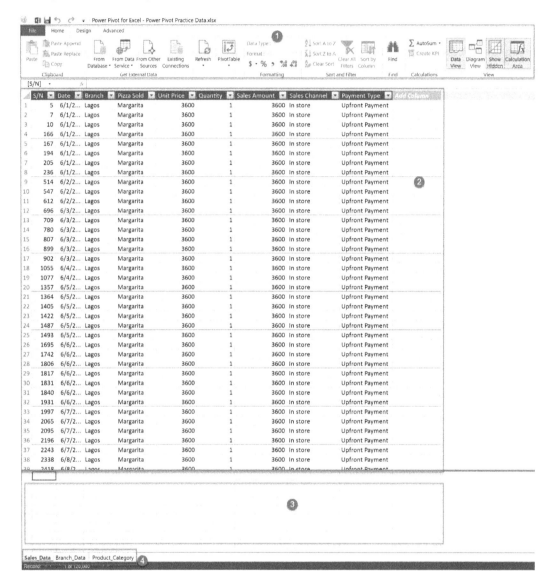

Figure 5.54 – An overview of the different parts of the Power Pivot window

We will start by switching to the diagram view and creating the relationships that must be between the tables we have. It is easy to create a relationship. All you need to do is drag the related column from one table on top of its corresponding column in a second table. The relationship line will pop up. We will do this for **Pizza Sold** in the **Sales Data** table with **Product** in the **Product Category** table, and **Branch** in the **Sales Data** table with **Branch** in the **Branch Data** table (see *Figure 5.55*):

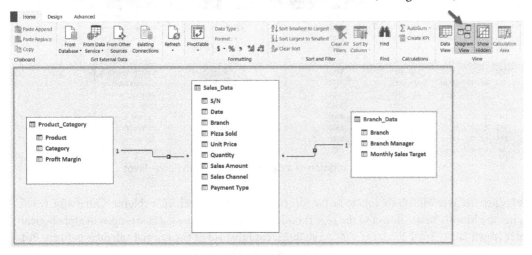

Figure 5.55 – Creating relationships in a Pivot Table

We then switch back to **Data View**. To make our dashboard richer and analysis more robust, we will create two new columns (called **calculated columns**) and three measures. Measures are usually aggregations that output one value, unlike calculated columns, which output as many values as there are rows in the table.

To create a calculated column, you select **Add Column** on the right of the last column in your table and type in the formula bar, using the following syntax – Column Name =: Formula.

Using that approach, we will create a column for the date in a month and year format using Month Year := FORMAT(Sales_Data[Date], "mmm yyyy") and another for Year Month := VALUE(FORMAT(Sales_Data[Date],"yyyymm")) (see the formula step in *Figure 5.56*):

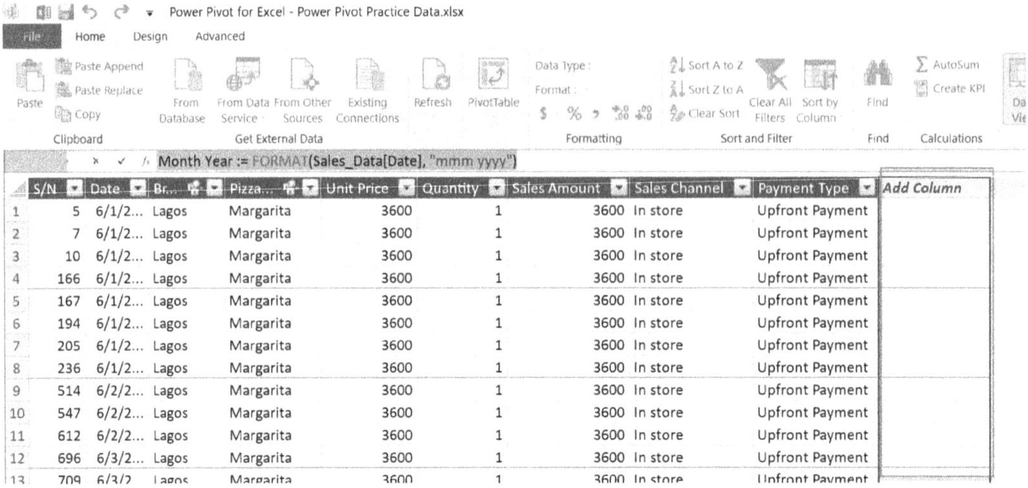

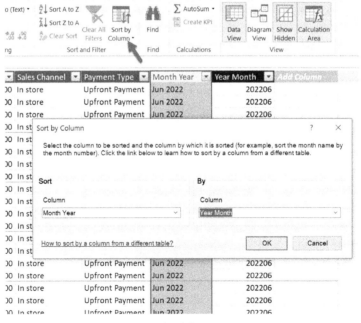

Figure 5.56 – The addition of a calculated column in Power Pivot

We created the **Year Month** column to be the sort column for the **Month Year** column. Otherwise, when we use the **Month Year** column in the report building, we will get the dates arranged in alphabetical order (April 2022, April 2022, Feb 2022, Feb 2023, etc.) instead of the normal calendar pattern. But with **Year Month**, we can force **Month Year** to sort correctly. All we need to do is to select the **Month Year** column and set **Sort By Column** in the menu to **Year Month**, as shown in *Figure 5.57*:

Figure 5.57 – Sort by Column in Power Pivot

With the columns added, we will move on to adding the measures. We will start with putting to use the relationships we have created between our tables. The product category table has the profit margin for each pizza product, and by multiplying this margin with the sales generated by the related pizza, we will get the profit. In regular Excel, you will likely the VLOOKUP on the profit margin in the sales data table and use it to create a second column that will be the profit. Thus, two new columns will be created, with values across all the 100,000 rows of data in the sales data table. This is the main reason why many Excel reports tend to bulk up and start having performance issues.

Power Pivot allows us to achieve same profit computation without creating even a single additional column. We will create a measure by putting the following formula in a measures cell within the data view – `Profit:=SUMX(Sales_Data,Sales_Data[Sales Amount]*RELATED(Product_Category[Profit Margin]))` (see the outcome in *Figure 5.58*):

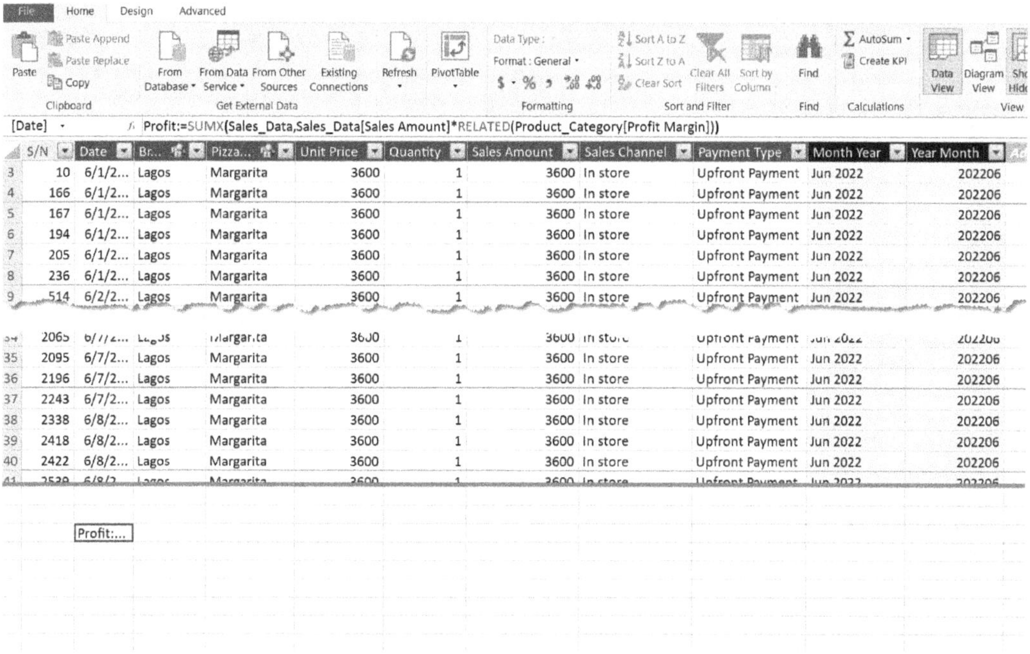

Figure 5.58 – Creating profit measure

Power Pivot has a KPI feature that we will use to achieve the conditional formatting icon that indicates sales performance against monthly targets, as seen in the previous final dashboard screenshot. However, we need a total sales measure and a sales target measure to feed into the KPI tool. Create the following measures – `Sales := SUM(Sales_Data[Sales Amount])` and `Sales Target := SUM(Branch_Data[Monthly Sales Target])`.

Select the **Sales** measure, and on the menu, click on **Create KPI**. The KPI base field is already set to the **Sales** measure; you only need to set the target value to the **Sales Target** measure. Edit the yellow area to begin at 80% and the green to begin at 100%. This ensures that only when sales equal or exceed the target will the KPI show green, while yellow will show from 80% to just below 100% achievement of the target:

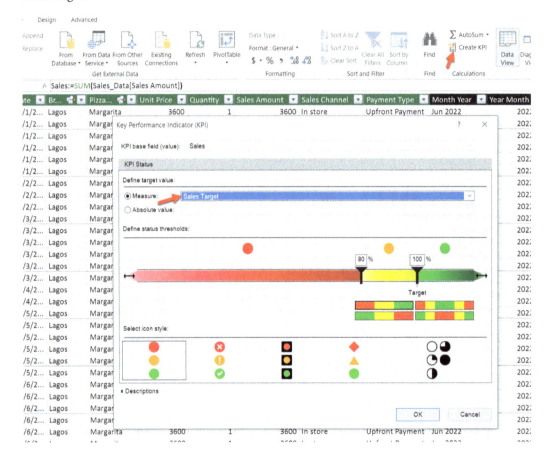

Figure 5.59 – Setting up a KPI in Power Pivot

All that we need to create our dashboard is now in place, so we can close Power Pivot and see that all that we did is now reflected in the Pivot Table created earlier in *Figure 5.52* (see *Figure 5.60*):

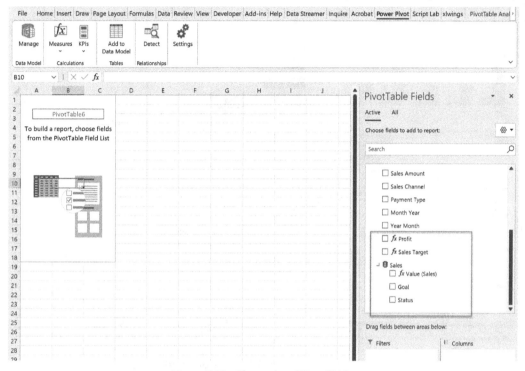

Figure 5.60 – The updated Pivot Table

Create a slicer with **Branch** from the **Branch Data** table. For the main Pivot Table, drag **Month Year**, **Branch**, and **Branch Manager** into **Rows**, in that order. Drag the **Sales** measure, the **Sales Target** measure, and **KPI Status** into **Values**.

Using the same approach of copying and pasting an existing Pivot Table and editing it, create a Clustered Column Pivot Chart of **Sales** and **Profit** against **Branch**. Create a Stacked Bar Pivot Chart of **Sales** against **Sales Channel** and **Payment Type**. Use the number formatting that we have already learned about to set the data labels in the #,##0,,"M" custom format. With the color formats and arrangement similar to what we had in the Pivot Table dynamic report in the previous section, you will achieve a dashboard similar to the one in *Figure 5.61*:

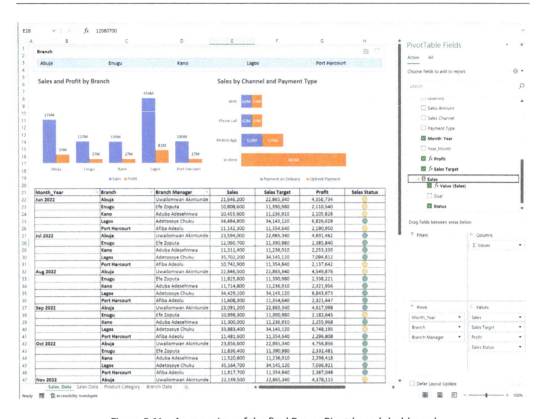

Figure 5.61 – An overview of the final Power Pivot-based dashboard

And that brings us to the end of this practical demonstration of the use of Power Pivot to create more feature-rich reports and dashboards.

In the next section, we will do a basic walk-through of the formula that powers Power Pivot.

DAX

DAX is the technical name for the formulas you type in Power Pivot. It is very much like the regular formulas we use in Excel cells but has two major differences:

- Rather than referencing cell addresses, you reference tables, columns, and other formulas (measures)

- It has functions that are not in Excel sheets while, at the same time, lacking some functions that are in Excel sheets

DAX in Excel allows you to create calculated columns and measures as we did in the last section. Calculated columns are very similar to the columns you create in a formatted table in Excel, where you reference the table name and its columns. It is not possible to enter different formulas for rows in the same column. This is the first adjustment people with only a background in Excel sheet formulas grapple with. You always have to think of one formula you'll input that will generate the results you want across all the rows in the column. If you want different calculations for different segments of your data table, you don't enter one type of formula for a group of rows and another type of formula for another group of rows, as you could in Excel sheets. You have to critically think through the logic behind the outcome you want and work out just one formula that will provide all the different outcomes at once.

Measures are another unfamiliar concept to the regular Excel sheet user. They are formulas that you type, referencing tables and columns, but the result is not static even when the values referenced did not change. Unlike regular Excel formulas, which reference a static range of cells, a measure is always affected by filters, and not just slicers or explicit filters but also what can be termed **implicit filters**. When you create a Pivot Table that has a measure in the **Values** quadrant, the measure output values are filtered or altered by the field entries in the **Rows** and **Columns** quadrants. This means that you have to consider this behavior when you write measures. If you want a measure that will always show total sales, regardless of what fields are in **Rows**, **Columns**, **Filters**, and the slicer, then you write the formula in such a way that it will not be affected by those fields. This is easily the most difficult part of creating measures; this filter effect that you should always keep in mind is technically referred to as the **filter context**.

There are over 250 DAX functions, but you will find yourself using just a couple as you build dashboards and reports using Power Pivot. There are many DAX functions that have exactly the same name as the Excel functions and the same use. Some of the popular ones are SUM, AVERAGE, DATE, EOMONTH, EDATE, PRODUCT, IF, OR, AND, LOOKUP, and SWITCH. It's never a bad idea to try out the Excel function you know, as chances are high that the same function exists in DAX. And there are a couple that are named differently in DAX – FORMAT, which does the exact thing that TEXT does in Excel. However, you can't escape needing to learn the DAX formulas that have no Excel counterparts. The need to correctly handle filter context made it mandatory for DAX to have many formulas that will be strange to regular Excel sheet users.

Some of the most notable DAX-specific formulas are CALCULATE, FILTER, SUMX, AVERAGEX, RELATED, and ALL:

- **CALCULATE** is arguably the most important DAX function, as it is the default formula to manipulate the filter context and ensure that your measures output the desired results. You will typically use it as a wrapper around another DAX function and then add a filter context-altering argument toward the end. An example is a measure to always show total sales in a sales table, regardless of what is set in other fields of the table (date, product, customer, etc.). To create such a measure, you will use Total Sales := CALCULATE(SUM(Sales_Table[Sales_Amount]),ALL(Sales_Table)).

- That brings us to what ALL is used for. **ALL** is a DAX function that removes the filter effect of the fields specified within the ALL function. It is often used within the CALCULATE function, which we discussed previously. It can accept a table, meaning all the fields within the table, and it can accept a table and specific columns within the table. If we wanted to create a measure to compute all products sales, removing the filter effect of the product field, we would use ALL as follows – `All_Product_Sales := CALCULATE(SUM(Sales_Table[Sales_Amount]),ALL(Sales_Table, Sales_Table[Product])))`.

- What does `FILTER` do? **FILTER** creates a filtered subset of a table or column. It is often used to make the CALCULATE work on the subset rather than on the entire table or column. An example is if we want a measure that will show just online sales, then we need to do a sum of sales for a subset of the data that has the sales channel column set as `Online`. The formula will look very much like `Online Sales := CALCULATE(SUM(Sales_Table[Sales_Amount]),FILTER(Sales_Table, Sales_Table[Sales_Channel]="Online")))`.

For more on DAX functions and how to use them, read the official documentation at `https://learn.microsoft.com/en-us/dax/dax-function-reference`.

We have now come to the end of this interesting chapter; we have covered a lot, and I hope you followed along using the practice data.

Summary

The Pivot Table is a very important tool in the toolbox of a modern data analyst, and Power Pivot adds more power to it. We have extensively covered the practical use of the Pivot Table and Power Pivot by creating interactive and beautiful dashboards. You have learned many useful concepts and report layout tricks. We have, thus, set you on the path to getting comfortable with DAX and its peculiarities.

In the next chapter, we will cover Excel functions and how to make your reports and dashboards fully responsive and automated by leveraging the many powerful functions of Excel.

6
Must-Know Legacy Excel Functions

Functions are a very important part of Excel and make many of the reports and analyses carried out in Excel possible. The ability to have reports that recompute the very instant the underlying data changes is what makes Excel a preferred choice by company executives and business managers who don't want complex IT-driven applications. The ease with which reports can be created, edited, and shared is why Excel is widely used by all the functional departments of most companies. Functions in Excel are the biggest enablers of that ease of report creation.

Functions are what make it possible to carry out quick computations and complex analyses in Excel with a few keystrokes. There are over 460 Excel functions and Microsoft keeps adding new ones almost yearly. From Excel 2021 and above, Excel completely changed how functions work within Excel and gave rise to the classification of prior versions of Excel as **Legacy Excel**. Thus, Excel 2021 and above are referred to as **Modern Excel**. Also, some new sets of functions were added to Modern Excel and termed **dynamic array functions**.

In this chapter, we will explore the Excel functions that have always been in Excel, before the new dynamic array functions were introduced, and focus on the must-know ones. These functions are must-know for data analysis and dashboard building. You will want to pay attention to all the functions covered in this chapter and be confident that you can use them on your own.

The following topics will be covered:

- Math and statistical functions
- Logical functions
- Text manipulation functions
- Date manipulation functions
- Lookup and reference functions

Math and statistical functions

The most used functions in Excel are math and statistical functions such as SUM, COUNT, AVERAGE, MIN, MAX, SUMIFS, COUNTIFS, AVERAGEIFS, and ABS. They allow people to grab quick insights from a range of numeric data. SUM is, perhaps, the most used Excel function as it allows people to quickly see the sum of a range of cells.

In this section, we will cover the most well-known math functions that a data analyst and dashboard creator must be well versed in. You may perceive them as very simple functions that do not require much explanation, but their importance warrants we cover them. Also, when combined with dynamic array functions, which we will learn about in *Chapter 7, Dynamic Array Functions and Lambda Functions*, they become very formidable tools.

Every data analyst using Excel should be proficient in using the following math and statistical functions:

- SUM
- SUMIFS
- COUNT
- COUNTIFS
- MIN
- MAX
- AVERAGE

We will explore these must-know functions in the next subsections.

SUM

SUM has the following syntax: SUM(range/cells). It sums up all the values in the provided range or cells. It skips non-numeric values. The following screenshot shows an example of using SUM to add up values in a range:

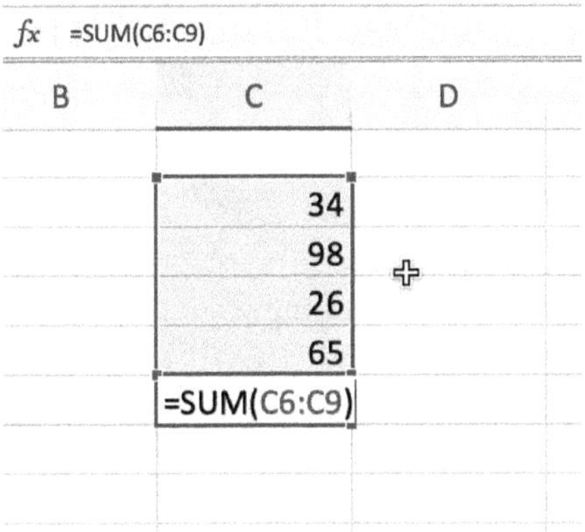

Figure 6.1 – SUM function example

`SUM` is often described as Excel's most used function. Now, let's look at the next must-know function.

SUMIFS

`SUMIFS` is an extension of the `SUM` function and allows you to specify a condition that must be met for each row of the data selection to be included in the final summation. Its syntax is `SUMIFS(sum_range,criteria_range_1,criteria_1, criteria_range_2,criteria_2,…)`. Only the first three arguments are compulsory. The following screenshot shows an example of using `SUMIFS` to sum sales for iPhones:

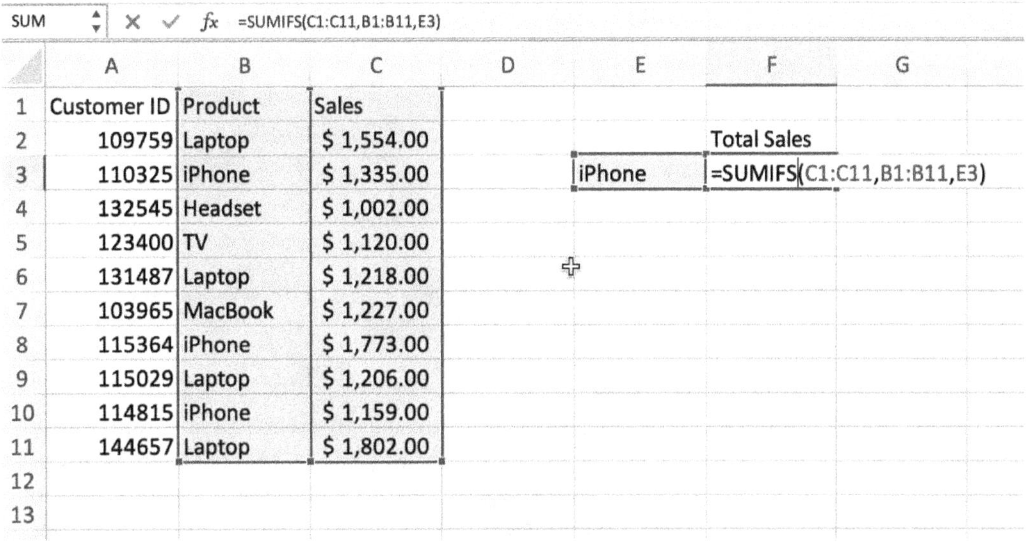

	A	B	C	D	E	F	G
1	Customer ID	Product	Sales				
2	109759	Laptop	$ 1,554.00			Total Sales	
3	110325	iPhone	$ 1,335.00		iPhone	=SUMIFS(C1:C11,B1:B11,E3)	
4	132545	Headset	$ 1,002.00				
5	123400	TV	$ 1,120.00				
6	131487	Laptop	$ 1,218.00				
7	103965	MacBook	$ 1,227.00				
8	115364	iPhone	$ 1,773.00				
9	115029	Laptop	$ 1,206.00				
10	114815	iPhone	$ 1,159.00				
11	144657	Laptop	$ 1,802.00				
12							
13							

Figure 6.2 – SUMIFS function example

SUMIFS is one of the most versatile functions in Excel and is useful for aggregating values for a summary or management report creation. Next, we will explore another important function.

COUNT

COUNT is an Excel function that gives the total occurrences of numeric value cells in a selected range. Its syntax is COUNT(range/cells). The following screenshot shows an example of using COUNT to get the total paid transactions in a sales table:

	A	B	C	D	E	F	G
1	Sales ID	Status	Sales Value	Paid Amount			
2	43659	Executed	$23,153.23	$ 23,153.23			
3	43660	Executed	$ 1,457.33	$ 1,457.33			
4	43661	Executed	$36,865.80	$ 36,865.80			
5	43662	Executed	$32,474.93	$ 32,474.93			
6	43663	Executed	$ 472.31	$ 472.31			
7	43664	Executed	$27,510.41	$ 27,510.41			
8	43665	Executed	$16,158.70	$ 16,158.70			
9	43666	None	$25,072.79				
10	43667	Executed	$ 6,876.36	$ 6,876.36		Paid Sales	
11	43668	None	$13,123.56			18	
12	43669	Executed	$ 807.26	$ 807.26		=COUNT(D2:D21)	
13	43670	Executed	$ 6,893.25	$ 6,893.25		COUNT(**value1**, [value2], …)	
14	43671	Executed	$ 9,153.61	$ 9,153.61			
15	43672	Executed	$ 6,895.41	$ 6,895.41			
16	43673	Executed	$ 4,216.03	$ 4,216.03			
17	43674	Executed	$ 2,955.05	$ 2,955.05			
18	43675	Executed	$ 6,434.08	$ 6,434.08			
19	43676	Executed	$15,992.74	$ 15,992.74			
20	43677	Executed	$ 8,773.68	$ 8,773.68			
21	43678	Executed	$11,036.40	$ 11,036.40			
22							
23							

Figure 6.3 – COUNT function example

The formula outcome of 18 represents the number of non-empty cells in the selected range.

COUNTIFS

COUNTIFS is an extension of the COUNT function in the same manner that SUMIFS is to SUM. It allows you to count only numeric value cells that meet set conditions. Its syntax is COUNTIFS(criteria_range_1,criteria_1, criteria_range_2,criteria_2,…). The following screenshot shows an example of COUNTIFS used to count the number of transactions whose status is set to **None**:

SUM		⌄ ┆ ✕ ✓	*fx*	=COUNTIFS(B2:B21,"None")				

	A	B	C	D	E	F	G
1	Sales ID	Status	Sales Value	Paid Amount			
2	43659	Executed	$23,153.23	$ 23,153.23			
3	43660	Executed	$ 1,457.33	$ 1,457.33			
4	43661	Executed	$36,865.80	$ 36,865.80			
5	43662	Executed	$32,474.93	$ 32,474.93			
6	43663	Executed	$ 472.31	$ 472.31			
7	43664	Executed	$27,510.41	$ 27,510.41		Status: None	
8	43665	Executed	$16,158.70	$ 16,158.70		2	
9	43666	None	$25,072.79			=COUNTIFS(B2:B21,"None")	
10	43667	Executed	$ 6,876.36	$ 6,876.36			
11	43668	None	$13,123.56				
12	43669	Executed	$ 807.26	$ 807.26			
13	43670	Executed	$ 6,893.25	$ 6,893.25			
14	43671	Executed	$ 9,153.61	$ 9,153.61			
15	43672	Executed	$ 6,895.41	$ 6,895.41			
16	43673	Executed	$ 4,216.03	$ 4,216.03			
17	43674	Executed	$ 2,955.05	$ 2,955.05			
18	43675	Executed	$ 6,434.08	$ 6,434.08			
19	43676	Executed	$15,992.74	$ 15,992.74			
20	43677	Executed	$ 8,773.68	$ 8,773.68			
21	43678	Executed	$11,036.40	$ 11,036.40			
22							

Figure 6.4 – COUNTIFS function example

The formula result of 2 represents the count of transactions with the status set to **None**.

MIN

MIN is an Excel function for getting the minimum value in a selected range. Its syntax is MIN (range/ cells). On the surface, it looks more relevant to an academician than to a business data analyst. I'll warn you not to be deceived – MIN provides an elegant way to cap values of computations, such as transaction fees or bonus calculations. See the following example of using MIN to implement a transaction fee of **3%** capped at **$200**:

SUM		∨ ⋮ ✕ ✓ ƒx	=MIN(3%*D5,200)	

	A	B	C	D	E
1	Sales ID	Status	Sales Value	Paid Amount	Transaction Fee (3% capped at $200)
2	43659	Executed	$23,153.23	$23,153.23	$200.00
3	43660	Executed	$1,457.33	$1,457.33	$43.72
4	43661	Executed	$36,865.80	$36,865.80	$200.00
5	43662	Executed	$32,474.93	$32,474.93	=MIN(3%*D5,200)
6	43663	Executed	$472.31	$472.31	$14.17
7	43664	Executed	$27,510.41	$27,510.41	$200.00
8	43665	Executed	$16,158.70	$16,158.70	$200.00
9	43666	None	$25,072.79		$0.00
10	43667	Executed	$6,876.36	$6,876.36	$200.00
11	43668	None	$13,123.56		$0.00
12	43669	Executed	$807.26	$807.26	$24.22
13	43670	Executed	$6,893.25	$6,893.25	$200.00
14	43671	Executed	$9,153.61	$9,153.61	$200.00
15	43672	Executed	$6,895.41	$6,895.41	$200.00
16	43673	Executed	$4,216.03	$4,216.03	$126.48
17	43674	Executed	$2,955.05	$2,955.05	$88.65
18	43675	Executed	$6,434.08	$6,434.08	$193.02
19	43676	Executed	$15,992.74	$15,992.74	$200.00
20	43677	Executed	$8,773.68	$8,773.68	$200.00
21	43678	Executed	$11,036.40	$11,036.40	$200.00
22					

Figure 6.5 – MIN function example

Using MIN, we can pick the lower (minimum) value between the $200 cap and 3% of the transaction value. This effectively caps the transaction fee at $200.

MAX

MAX is syntactically the same as MIN except that it gets the maximum value in a range. Its syntax is MAX(range/cells). And like MIN, it delivers excellent value to a business data analyst as much or even much more than it does for an academician interested in descriptive statistics. With MAX, you can set a lower limit for calculations such as fees, loan repayment installments, and more. See the following example of MAX being used to set a transaction fee as the higher value of **$200** and **3%**:

	A	B	C	D	E	F
	SUM	✓ : ✗ ✓ fx		=MAX(3%*D4,200)		
1	Sales ID	Status	Sales Value	Paid Amount	Transaction Fee (3% or $200, whichever is higer)	
2	43659	Executed	$23,153.23	$23,153.23	$694.60	
3	43660	Executed	$1,457.33	$1,457.33	$200.00	
4	43661	Executed	$36,865.80	$36,865.80	=MAX(3%*D4,200)	
5	43662	Executed	$32,474.93	$32,474.93	$974.25	
6	43663	Executed	$472.31	$472.31	$200.00	
7	43664	Executed	$27,510.41	$27,510.41	$825.31	
8	43665	Executed	$16,158.70	$16,158.70	$484.76	
9	43666	Executed	$25,072.79	$25,072.79	$752.18	
10	43667	Executed	$6,876.36	$6,876.36	$206.29	
11	43668	Executed	$13,123.56	$13,123.56	$393.71	
12	43669	Executed	$807.26	$807.26	$200.00	
13	43670	Executed	$6,893.25	$6,893.25	$206.80	
14	43671	Executed	$9,153.61	$9,153.61	$274.61	
15	43672	Executed	$6,895.41	$6,895.41	$206.86	
16	43673	Executed	$4,216.03	$4,216.03	$200.00	
17	43674	Executed	$2,955.05	$2,955.05	$200.00	
18	43675	Executed	$6,434.08	$6,434.08	$200.00	
19	43676	Executed	$15,992.74	$15,992.74	$479.78	
20	43677	Executed	$8,773.68	$8,773.68	$263.21	
21	43678	Executed	$11,036.40	$11,036.40	$331.09	
22						

Figure 6.6 – MAX function example

MAX returned the higher (maximum) value between $200 and 3% of the transaction amount. The outcome is that the transaction fee will never be less than $200.

AVERAGE

AVERAGE is an Excel function for calculating the mean or average of values in a range or group of cells. Its syntax is AVERAGE (range/cells). The following screenshot shows an example of using AVERAGE to get the average sales value for a set of sales transaction records:

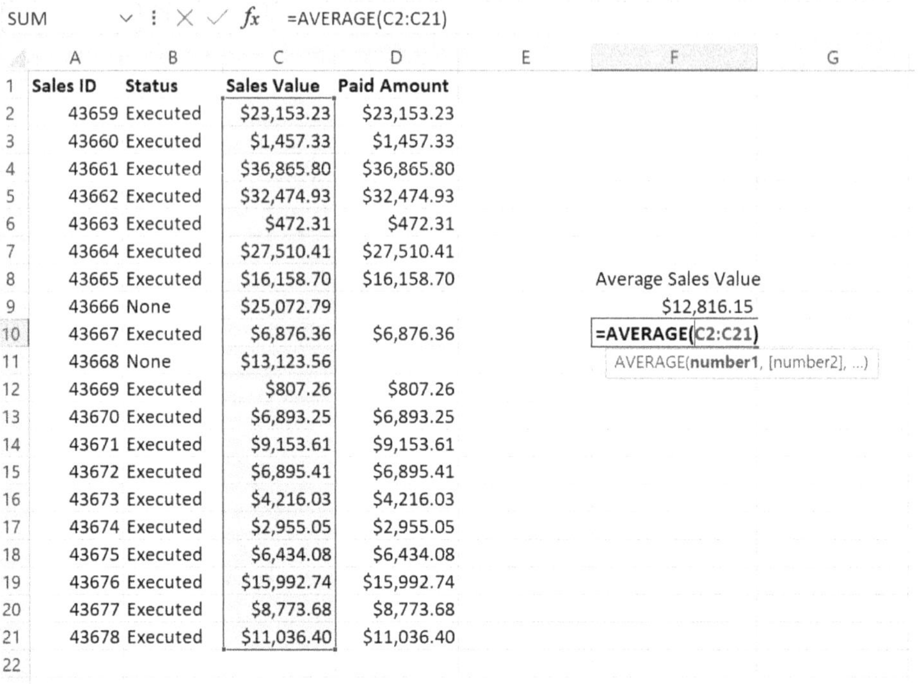

Figure 6.7 – AVERAGE function example

The result of $12,816.15 given by AVERAGE represents the mean value of all the sales transactions under consideration. It can be useful for comparing with other period sales to understand whether customers are placing large sales orders or small sales orders.

In the next section, we will cover some logical functions that you must be proficient at using.

Logical functions

In Legacy Excel, logical functions are functions that carry out logical comparisons or return a logical value (TRUE or FALSE). You can find a full list of the logical functions that are available, as well as their documentation, at https://support.microsoft.com/en-us/office/logical-functions-reference-e093c192-278b-43f6-8c3a-b6ce299931f5. They make a lot of condition-based calculations possible in Excel.

The logical functions that we will cover in this section are as follows:

- IF
- IFS
- IFERROR

- SWITCH

- OR

- AND

The first of these logical functions we will cover is IF.

IF

IF is an Excel function that carries out a specified logical check and allows us to have different outputs for when the check equals TRUE and for when the check equals FALSE. It is one of the most important functions in Excel as it allows us to wrap other functions in a condition-based implementation. Think of any computation you need to do but you must factor in a condition that must be met. A common example in the business domain is bonus computation. It is not uncommon for bonuses to be tied to a condition being met.

The syntax for the IF function is IF(logical_test,value_if_true,value_if_false). The value_if_true and value_if_false values are optional. When value_if_true is not provided, the default is TRUE, while for value_if_false, the default is FALSE. The following screenshot shows an example of using IF to compute a **10%** cash back for sales transactions that are above **$20,000**:

IF		fx	=IF(C4>20000,C4*10%,0)			
	A	B	C	D	E	F	G
1	Sales ID	Status	Sales Value	Paid Amount	Cash Back		
2	43659	Executed	$23,153.23	$23,153.23	$2,315.32		
3	43660	Executed	$1,457.33		$0.00		
4	43661	Executed	$36,865.80	$36,865.80	=IF(C4>20000,C4*10%,0)		
5	43662	Executed	$32,474.93	$32,474.93	IF(**logical_test**, [value_if_true], [value_if_false])		
6	43663	Executed	$472.31	$472.31	$0.00		
7	43664	Executed	$27,510.41	$27,510.41	$2,751.04		
8	43665	Executed	$16,158.70	$16,158.70	$0.00		
9	43666	None	$25,072.79		$2,507.28		
10	43667	Executed	$6,876.36	$6,876.36	$0.00		
11	43668	None	$13,123.56		$0.00		
12	43669	Executed	$807.26	$807.26	$0.00		
13	43670	Executed	$6,893.25	$6,893.25	$0.00		
14	43671	Executed	$9,153.61	$9,153.61	$0.00		
15	43672	Executed	$6,895.41	$6,895.41	$0.00		
16	43673	Executed	$4,216.03	$4,216.03	$0.00		
17	43674	Executed	$2,955.05	$2,955.05	$0.00		
18	43675	Executed	$6,434.08	$6,434.08	$0.00		
19	43676	Executed	$15,992.74	$15,992.74	$0.00		
20	43677	Executed	$8,773.68	$8,773.68	$0.00		
21	43678	Executed	$11,036.40	$11,036.40	$0.00		
22							

Figure 6.8 – IF function example

IF is a powerful function that makes conditional computation possible. Next, we will examine a closely related function.

IFS

IFS is an extension of the IF function. While IF is designed to handle just one logical test, IFS allows you to have as many logical tests as you need without having to nest functions within functions. IFS was added to Excel in Excel 2016, so you have to be on that version or higher to use it. The syntax for IFS is IFS(logical_test1,value_if_true1, logical_test2,value_if_true2,…). The following screenshot shows an example of using IFS to give **20%** cash back for sales transactions that are higher than **$30,000**, **15%** cash back for transactions higher than **$25,000** but not higher than **$30,000**, and **10%** for transactions higher than **$20,000** but not higher than **$25,000**:

	✓ : ✕ ✓ *fx*		=IFS(C5>30000,C5*20%,C5>25000,C5*15%,C5>20000,C5*10%,C5<=20000,0)						
	A	B	C	D	E	F	G	H	I	J

Sales ID	Status	Sales Value	Paid Amount	Cash Back			
43659	Executed	$23,153.23	$23,153.23	$2,315.32			
43660	Executed	$1,457.33		$0.00			
43661	Executed	$36,865.80	$36,865.80	$7,373.16			
43662	Executed	$32,474.93	$32,474.93	=IFS(C5>30000,C5*20%,C5>25000,C5*15%,C5>20000,C5*10%,C5<=20000,0)		
43663	Executed	$472.31	$472.31	IFS(**logical_test1**, value_if_true1, [logical_test2, value_if_true2], [logical_test3, value_if_true3]
43664	Executed	$27,510.41	$27,510.41	$4,126.56			
43665	Executed	$16,158.70	$16,158.70	$0.00			
43666	None	$25,072.79		$3,760.92			
43667	Executed	$6,876.36	$6,876.36	$0.00			
43668	None	$13,123.56		$0.00			
43669	Executed	$807.26	$807.26	$0.00			
43670	Executed	$6,893.25	$6,893.25	$0.00			
43671	Executed	$9,153.61	$9,153.61	$0.00			
43672	Executed	$6,895.41	$6,895.41	$0.00			
43673	Executed	$4,216.03	$4,216.03	$0.00			
43674	Executed	$2,955.05	$2,955.05	$0.00			
43675	Executed	$6,434.08	$6,434.08	$0.00			
43676	Executed	$15,992.74	$15,992.74	$0.00			
43677	Executed	$8,773.68	$8,773.68	$0.00			
43678	Executed	$11,036.40	$11,036.40	$0.00			

Figure 6.9 – IFS function example

The formula extract is =IFS(C5>30000,C5*20%,C5>25000,C5*15%,C5>20000,C5*1 0%,C5<=20000,0). Notice that I had to put a fourth logical test to identify sales values that are $20,000 or less and give a bonus value of 0.

IFERROR

IFERROR is a function that allows you to trap errors in your formula and output something else in place of the error. Not all errors in Excel are due to an actual data entry or formula issue. Many lookup functions in Excel will give an #N/A! error when they can't find the value to be looked up. This in no way means something is wrong, and, sometimes, showing zero or blank in place of an error is preferable.

With IFERROR, you enter the formula as you normally do, and then wrap an IFERROR function around it. The syntax is IFERROR(formula, value_if_error). In the following example, we are using if IFERROR to trap a #DIV/0 error, replacing the error with a blank entry:

IF		: X ✓ fx	=IFERROR(B13/C13,"")			
	A	B	C	D	E	F
1	**Date**	**Daily Sales (₦)**	**₦/$ Exch. Rate**	**Daily Sales ($)**		
2	1-Dec-22	₦12,410,133.37	536	$23,153.23		
3	2-Dec-22	₦798,616.18	548	$1,457.33		
4	3-Dec-22	₦20,460,519.67	555	$36,865.80		
5	4-Dec-22	₦17,698,838.16	545	$32,474.93		
6	5-Dec-22	₦252,686.28	535	$472.31		
7	6-Dec-22	₦14,855,621.89	540	$27,510.41		
8	7-Dec-22	₦8,774,171.98	543	$16,158.70		
9	8-Dec-22	₦13,890,325.66		#DIV/0!	=B9/C9	
10						
11						
12	**Date**	**Daily Sales (₦)**	**₦/$ Exch. Rate**	**Daily Sales ($)**		
13	1-Dec-22	₦12,410,133.37	=IFERROR(B13/C13,"")			
14	2-Dec-22	₦798,616.18	548	$1,457.33		
15	3-Dec-22	₦20,460,519.67	555	$36,865.80		
16	4-Dec-22	₦17,698,838.16	545	$32,474.93		
17	5-Dec-22	₦252,686.28	535	$472.31		
18	6-Dec-22	₦14,855,621.89	540	$27,510.41		
19	7-Dec-22	₦8,774,171.98	543	$16,158.70		
20	8-Dec-22	₦13,890,325.66		=IFERROR(B20/C20,"")		
21						

Figure 6.10 – IFERROR function example

The formula extract is =IFERROR(B13/C13,""). The "" value at the end indicates a blank entry. If we wanted 0, we would have written the formula as =IFERROR(B13/C13,0). The concept is to put whatever you want in place of the error in the last IFERROR last argument.

SWITCH

SWITCH is a function that acts very much like IFS but is much simpler for logical tests that involve just the equal-to operator. Its syntax is SWITCH(expression,value1,result1,value2,result2,...).

A very relatable illustration is a formula that writes a comment in front of grade letters. Let's say there are six possible grade letters – A, B, C, D, E, and F – and you have a Comment column that will be set to Excellent for A, Very Good for B, Good for C, Poor for D, Very Poor for E, and Fail for F. With IFS, the formula will look very much like this:

```
=IFS(B28="A","Excellent",B28="B","Very
Good",B28="C","Good",B28="D","Poor",B28="E","Very
Poor",B28="F","Fail")
```

See the following screenshot for the IFS function's implementation in this case:

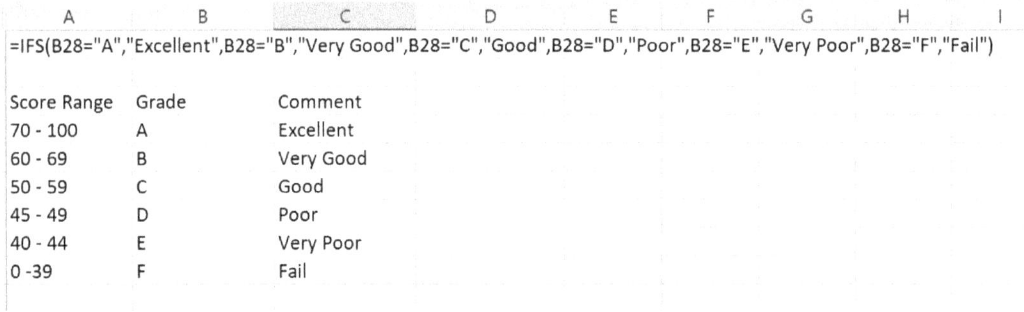

A	B	C	D	E	F	G	H	I
=IFS(B28="A","Excellent",B28="B","Very Good",B28="C","Good",B28="D","Poor",B28="E","Very Poor",B28="F","Fail")								
Score Range	Grade		Comment					
70 - 100	A		Excellent					
60 - 69	B		Very Good					
50 - 59	C		Good					
45 - 49	D		Poor					
40 - 44	E		Very Poor					
0 -39	F		Fail					

Figure 6.11 – Grade to Comment using the IFS function

With SWITCH, the same outcome can be achieved with =SWITCH(B28,"A","Excellent","B","Very Good","C","Good","D","Poor","E","Very Poor","F","Fail"), which is much easier to read, as well as being shorter. See the following screenshot for the SWITCH function's implementation:

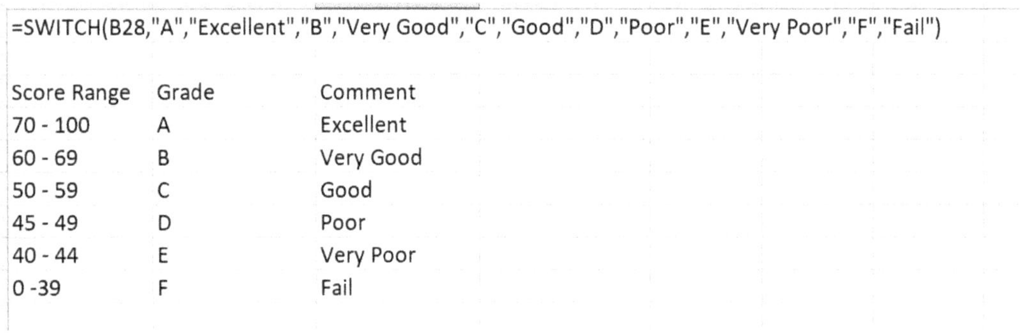

=SWITCH(B28,"A","Excellent","B","Very Good","C","Good","D","Poor","E","Very Poor","F","Fail")			
Score Range	Grade		Comment
70 - 100	A		Excellent
60 - 69	B		Very Good
50 - 59	C		Good
45 - 49	D		Poor
40 - 44	E		Very Poor
0 -39	F		Fail

Figure 6.12 – Grade to Comment using the SWITCH function

And with that, we have come to the end of looking at SWITCH. Now, let's look at another logical function.

OR

OR is an Excel function that accepts one or more logical tests and returns TRUE if at least one of the tests evaluates to TRUE. It is usually used in conjunction with IF to allow multiple logical tests within an IF function. Its syntax is OR (logical_test1, logical_test2, …). The following screenshot shows an example of using **OR** within the **IF** function to give a store bonus of **5%** for sales greater than **$20,000** for all sales made on weekends:

IF	⌄ ⦂ ✕ ✓ *fx*	=IF(OR(C4>20000,B4="Sat",B4="Sun"),C4*5%,0)		
	A	B	C	D	E
1	**Date**	**Day**	**Daily Sales ($)**	**Store Bonus**	
2	1-Dec-22	Thu	$23,153.23	$1,157.66	
3	2-Dec-22	Fri	$1,457.33	$0.00	
4	3-Dec-22	Sat	=IF(OR(C4>20000,B4="Sat",B4="Sun"),C4*5%,0)		
5	4-Dec-22	Sun	OR(logical1, **[logical2]**, [logical3], [logical4], …)		
6	5-Dec-22	Mon	$472.31	$0.00	
7	6-Dec-22	Tue	$27,510.41	$1,375.52	
8	7-Dec-22	Wed	$16,158.70	$0.00	
9	8-Dec-22	Thu	$14,881.23	$0.00	
10	9-Dec-22	Fri	$4,275.75	$0.00	
11	10-Dec-22	Sat	$25,476.14	$1,273.81	
12	11-Dec-22	Sun	$26,268.28	$1,313.41	
13	12-Dec-22	Mon	$40,567.40	$2,028.37	
14	13-Dec-22	Tue	$31,353.09	$1,567.65	
15	14-Dec-22	Wed	$36,224.94	$1,811.25	
16	15-Dec-22	Thu	$25,709.15	$1,285.46	
17					

Figure 6.13 – Using OR to capture multiple conditions

The formula extract is =IF (OR (C4>20000, B4="Sat", B4="Sun"), C4*5%, 0).

The OR part, OR (C4>20000, B4="Sat", B4="Sun"), will output TRUE so long as one of the three conditions is met.

AND

AND acts similarly to OR in that it accepts one or more logical tests, but it only returns TRUE if all the logical tests return TRUE. It is also used mostly in conjunction with IF to capture multiple conditions that must be satisfied. Its syntax is AND (logical_test1, logical_test2, …). The following screenshot shows an example of using AND within IF to give out a store bonus of **5%** for sales that happen on Sundays that are above **$20,000**:

IF	∨ ⋮ ✕ ✓	*fx*	=IF(AND(C6>20000,B6="Sun"),C6*5%,0)		

⧸	A	B	C	D	E
1	**Date**	**Day**	**Daily Sales ($)**	**Store Bonus**	
2	1-Dec-22	Thu	$23,153.23	$0.00	
3	2-Dec-22	Fri	$1,457.33	$0.00	
4	3-Dec-22	Sat	$36,865.80	$0.00	
5	4-Dec-22	Sun	$32,474.93	$1,623.75	
6	5-Dec-22	Mon	=IF(AND(C6>20000,B6="Sun"),C6*5%,0)		
7	6-Dec-22	Tue	$ AND(logical1, **[logical2]**, [logical3], …)		
8	7-Dec-22	Wed	$16,158.70	$0.00	
9	8-Dec-22	Thu	$14,881.23	$0.00	
10	9-Dec-22	Fri	$4,275.75	$0.00	
11	10-Dec-22	Sat	$25,476.14	$0.00	
12	11-Dec-22	Sun	$26,268.28	$1,313.41	
13	12-Dec-22	Mon	$40,567.40	$0.00	
14	13-Dec-22	Tue	$31,353.09	$0.00	
15	14-Dec-22	Wed	$36,224.94	$0.00	
16	15-Dec-22	Thu	$25,709.15	$0.00	

Figure 6.14 – AND function example

The formula extract is =IF(AND(C6>20000,B6="Sun"),C6*5%,0). The AND part is AND(C6>20000,B6="Sun"), which will return TRUE if both conditions are met.

That's it for the must-know logical functions. In the next section, we will cover text manipulation functions.

Text manipulation functions

Most datasets are a mix of text fields and numeric fields. A good data analyst should be adept at manipulating text fields. In this section, we will cover the major text manipulation functions you should be proficient at using:

- LEFT
- MID
- RIGHT
- SEARCH
- SUBSTITUTE
- TEXT
- LEN

The first of these text manipulation functions that we will cover is LEFT.

LEFT

LEFT is an Excel function that extracts the first set of characters in a provided value. Its syntax is `LEFT(text,number_of_characters)`. It is often useful for extracting a categorizing substring from a text field. The following screenshot shows an example involving extracting a country code from an asset tag:

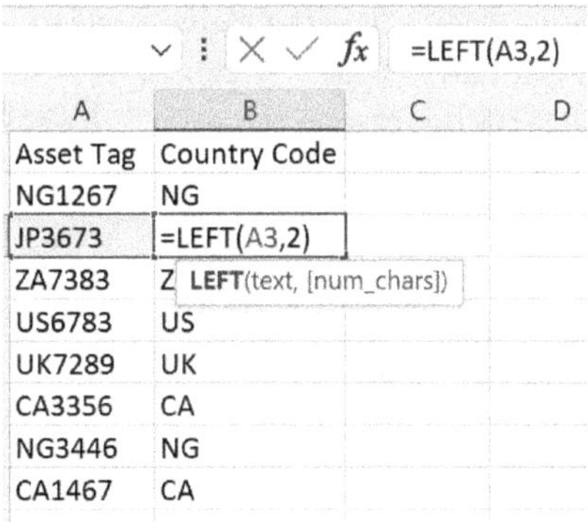

			fx	=LEFT(A3,2)	
	A	B	C	D	
	Asset Tag	Country Code			
	NG1267	NG			
	JP3673	=LEFT(A3,2)			
	ZA7383	Z LEFT(text, [num_chars])			
	US6783	US			
	UK7289	UK			
	CA3356	CA			
	NG3446	NG			
	CA1467	CA			

Figure 6.15 – LEFT function example

The formula extract is `=LEFT(A3,2)`. It extracts the first two characters from the selected cell.

MID

MID is an Excel formula for extracting characters from a provided value starting from a desired position. Its syntax is `MID(text,start_position,number_of_characters)`. The following screenshot shows an example of using MID to extract item size from item codes for a company that combines the item name, item size, and item color when creating their finished goods item code:

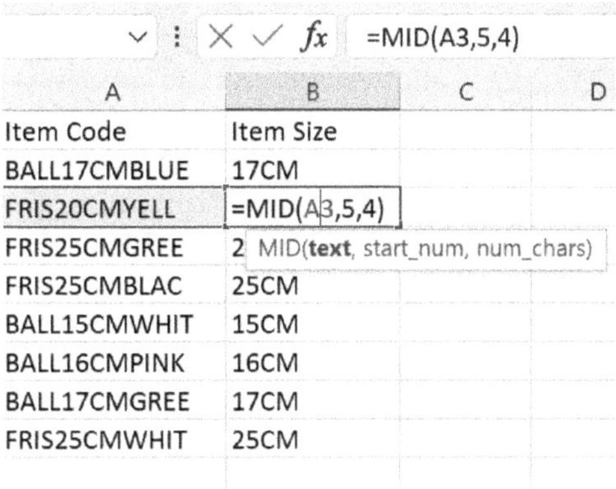

			fx	=MID(A3,5,4)	
	A	B	C	D	
	Item Code	Item Size			
	BALL17CMBLUE	17CM			
	FRIS20CMYELL	=MID(A3,5,4)			
	FRIS25CMGREE	2 MID(text, start_num, num_chars)			
	FRIS25CMBLAC	25CM			
	BALL15CMWHIT	15CM			
	BALL16CMPINK	16CM			
	BALL17CMGREE	17CM			
	FRIS25CMWHIT	25CM			

Figure 6.16 – MID function example

The formula extract is =MID(A3,5,4) and it extracts four characters starting from the fifth character of the item code.

RIGHT

RIGHT is an Excel formula for extracting a specified number of characters at the end of a provided value. It's almost like the opposite of LEFT as it extracts the specified number of characters starting with the last character. Its syntax is RIGHT(text,number_of_characters). For the same data we used MID on, with RIGHT, we can extract the color code as it's the last four characters of the item code:

	⌄ : ✕ ✓ *fx* =RIGHT(A3,4)			
A	B	C	D	E
Item Code	Item Size	Color Code		
BALL17CMBLUE	17CM	BLUE		
FRIS20CMYELL	20CM	=RIGHT(A3,4)		
FRIS25CMGREE	25CM	G RIGHT(text, [num_chars])		
FRIS25CMBLAC	25CM	BLAC		
BALL15CMWHIT	15CM	WHIT		
BALL16CMPINK	16CM	PINK		
BALL17CMGREE	17CM	GREE		
FRIS25CMWHIT	25CM	WHIT		

Figure 6.17 – RIGHT function example

The formula extract is =RIGHT(A3,4). It extracts the last four characters of the selected cell.

SEARCH

SEARCH is an Excel function that searches for a provided piece of text in a selected cell and returns the starting character position if the text is found. If the search text is not found, it returns a #VALUE! error. The function syntax is SEARCH(find_text,within_text,start_num), with start_num being optional. The following screenshot shows an example of using SEARCH to search for **25CM** within the item codes. It returns the character position of the searched text for instances it's found within the item code:

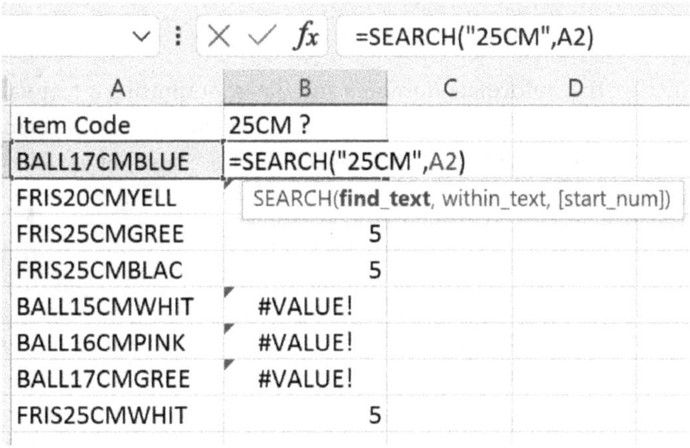

Text manipulation functions   201

Figure 6.18 – SEARCH function example

The formula extract is =SEARCH("25CM",A2), which translates to searching for 25CM in cell A2 and returning the position if found.

SUBSTITUTE

SUBSTITUTE is an Excel function that finds and replaces text within a selected cell. Its syntax is SUBSTITUTE(text,old_text_to_replace,new_text,instance_num), with instance_num being optional. The following screenshot shows how to use SUBSTITUTE to replace **25CM** with **26CM** in the item codes:

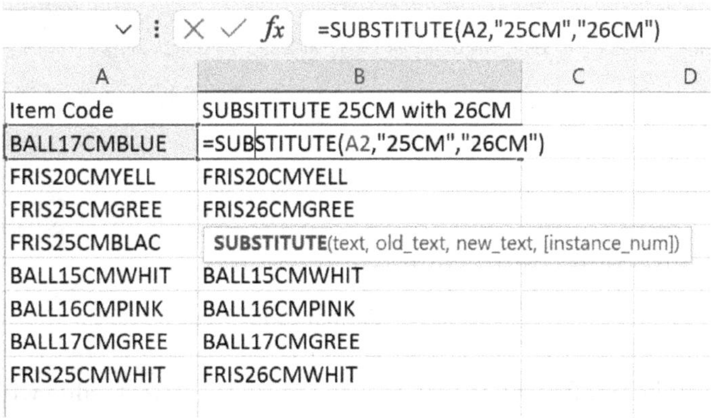

Figure 6.19 – SUBSTITUTE function example

The formula extract is =SUBSTITUTE(A2,"25CM","26CM"). It replaces 25CM with 26CM in the selected cell.

TEXT

TEXT is an Excel function that reformats numbers and dates, outputting a text value. Its syntax is TEXT(value_to_be_formatted, format_code_to_apply). The format codes are the same format codes that you can find in Excel's **Format Cells** tool, as shown in the following screenshot:

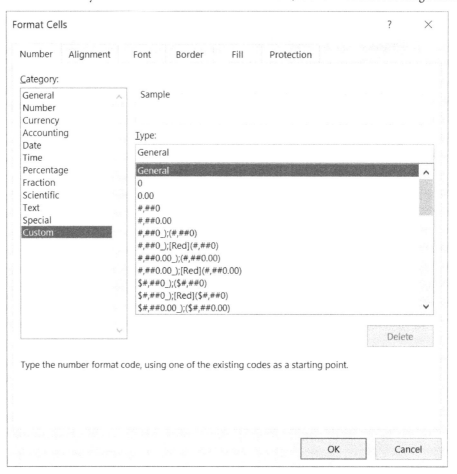

Figure 6.20 – Format codes

A TEXT-based formula that formats a date as a day of the week text value will be printed as =TEXT(A2, "dddd"). This makes TEXT a very useful function for extracting date components from dates or reformatting dates into a persistent text value. The following screenshot shows how to extract the day from date values:

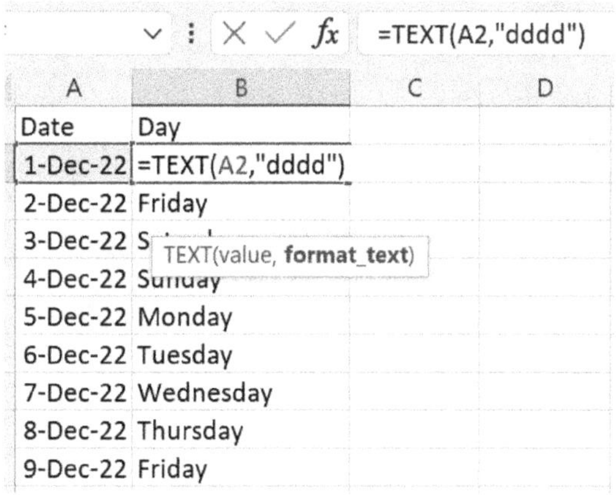

| | | fx | =TEXT(A2,"dddd") |

	A	B	C	D
	Date	Day		
	1-Dec-22	=TEXT(A2,"dddd")		
	2-Dec-22	Friday		
	3-Dec-22	S TEXT(value, **format_text**)		
	4-Dec-22	Sunday		
	5-Dec-22	Monday		
	6-Dec-22	Tuesday		
	7-Dec-22	Wednesday		
	8-Dec-22	Thursday		
	9-Dec-22	Friday		

Figure 6.21 – TEXT function example

TEXT comes in handy when you need to generate dynamic texts from numeric or data values that must be formatted in a specific way. Next, we will explore the LEN function.

LEN

LEN is an Excel function that extracts the number of characters in a selected value. Its syntax is LEN (value). It's mostly used for text values but also works for numeric values. The following screenshot shows an example of using LEN to extract the total character count of the item codes:

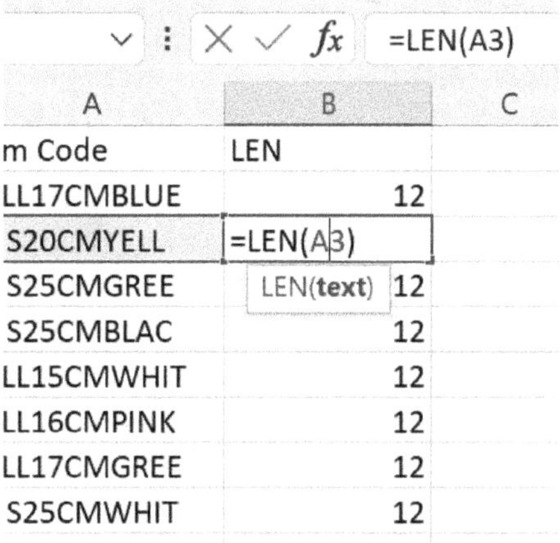

| | | fx | =LEN(A3) |

A	B	C
m Code	LEN	
LL17CMBLUE	12	
S20CMYELL	=LEN(A3)	
S25CMGREE	LEN(**text**) 12	
S25CMBLAC	12	
LL15CMWHIT	12	
LL16CMPINK	12	
LL17CMGREE	12	
S25CMWHIT	12	

Figure 6.22 – LEN function example

In the next section, we will go through the must-know date manipulation functions.

Date manipulation functions

Most business datasets have date fields because datestamps and timestamps are very important when recording activities for organizations. This makes it important for a data analyst and dashboard creator to be very proficient in manipulating dates in Excel.

The must-know date manipulation functions in Excel are as follows:

- TODAY
- DATE
- YEAR
- MONTH
- DAY
- EDATE
- EOMONTH
- WEEKNUM

The first of these date manipulation functions we will cover is TODAY.

TODAY

TODAY is an Excel function that returns the current date at all times (it uses the computer's date). It takes no arguments, so its syntax is TODAY(). The following screenshot shows using TODAY to do a countdown of the days to a planned activity:

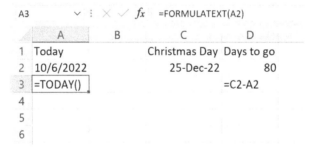

Figure 6.23 – TODAY function example

With TODAY, you can achieve a lot of dynamic date computations and countdowns. Next, we will cover another date manipulation function.

DATE

DATE is an Excel function that returns a date when supplied with the year, month, and day. Its syntax is DATE(year,month,day). It is very useful in recreating dates from partial date fields. The following screenshot shows an example of using DATE to create a date from the Year, Month, and Day fields:

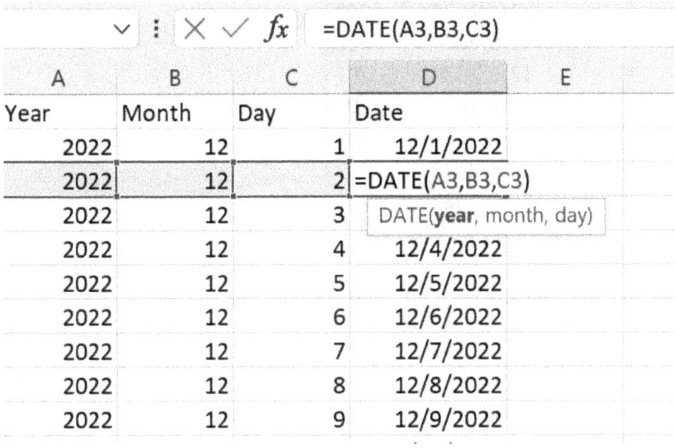

	A	B	C	D	E
	Year	Month	Day	Date	
	2022	12	1	12/1/2022	
	2022	12	2	=DATE(A3,B3,C3)	
	2022	12	3	DATE(**year**, month, day)	
	2022	12	4	12/4/2022	
	2022	12	5	12/5/2022	
	2022	12	6	12/6/2022	
	2022	12	7	12/7/2022	
	2022	12	8	12/8/2022	
	2022	12	9	12/9/2022	

fx =DATE(A3,B3,C3)

Figure 6.24 – DATE function example

DATE makes it easy to extract the same day and month in a different year, as well as other variants of a known date value. Now, let's cover another important date manipulation function.

YEAR

YEAR is an Excel function for extracting the year from a date. Its syntax is YEAR(date). It comes in very handy in cases where you need to have reports laid out by year or filtered by year and you only have a date field. A regular PivotTable often helps with automatically grouping date fields in such a way that you get the year without any formula. Unfortunately, the moment you use Power Pivot, that grouping feature is lost and you must create the year field yourself if you need it. The following screenshot shows the use of YEAR to extract the year from dates:

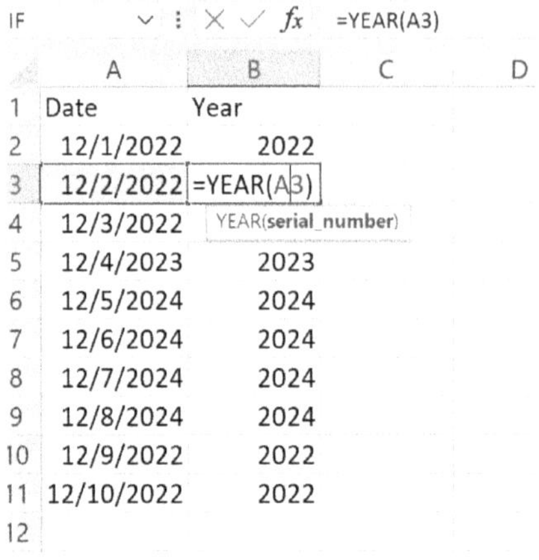

Figure 6.25 – YEAR function example

YEAR comes in handy for creating dynamic titles and computing date differences in years. We will now explore another date manipulation function.

MONTH

MONTH is an Excel function for extracting the month from a date in a numeric format. Its syntax is MONTH(date). The following screenshot shows an example of using MONTH to extract the month from dates:

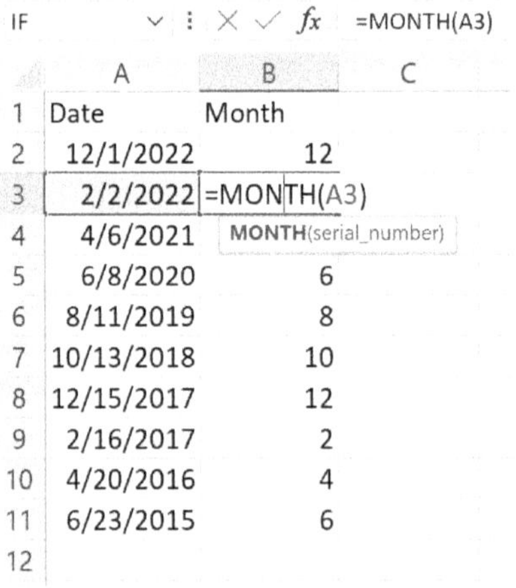

Figure 6.26 – MONTH function example

MONTH is a convenient way to extract months from given dates either as a standalone value or for use within another function. Next, we will explore the DAY function.

DAY

DAY is an Excel function for extracting the day from a date. Its syntax is DAY (date). The following screenshot shows an example of using DAY to extract the day from dates:

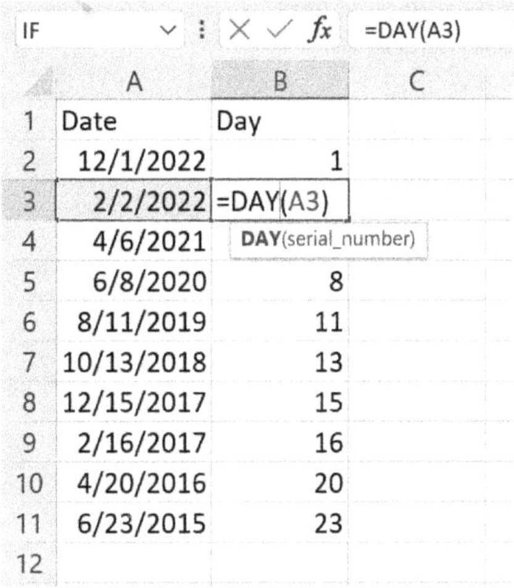

Figure 6.27 – DAY function example

DAY is a quick way to create dynamic texts that need to reflect the day within a date. Next, we will cover another date manipulation function.

EDATE

EDATE is an Excel function that adjusts a date backward or forward by a specified number of months. Its syntax is EDATE (date, months). The months must be specified in a numeric format and be positive to adjust the date forward or negative to adjust the date backward. The following screenshot shows an example of using EDATE to calculate subscription expiration dates:

∨ ⋮ ✕ ✓ *fx*	=EDATE(B3,C3)		

A	B	C	D	E
Customer	Last Payment Date	Subs. Months Paid For	Subs. Expiration Date	
C100123	05-Dec-2022	1	05-Jan-2023	
C100124	29-Nov-2022	1	=EDATE(B3,C3)	
C100125	28-Aug-2022	5	EDATE(start_date, **months**)	
C100126	11-Dec-2022	7	11-Jul-2023	
C100127	10-Nov-2022	1	10-Dec-2022	
C100128	30-Nov-2022	4	30-Mar-2023	
C100129	02-Sep-2022	2	02-Nov-2022	
C100130	29-Jun-2022	2	29-Aug-2022	
C100131	16-Jun-2022	1	16-Jul-2022	
C100132	03-Sep-2022	1	03-Oct-2022	
C100133	19-Oct-2022	7	19-May-2023	
C100134	11-Aug-2022	4	11-Dec-2022	
C100135	10-Oct-2022	6	10-Apr-2023	
C100136	28-Dec-2022	7	28-Jul-2023	
C100137	13-Jul-2022	6	13-Jan-2023	

Figure 6.28 – EDATE function example

You will notice that the outputs are exactly the supplied number of months ahead. This is useful for dealing with expiration date logic that involves validity in months. Now, let's look at the EOMONTH function.

EOMONTH

EOMONTH is very similar to EDATE, with the difference being that it returns the end-of-the-month date. It is an Excel function for getting the last day of the month for a provided date adjusted forward or backward by a specified number of months. It is useful for scenarios that involve activities that happen at the end or start of the month. To get the start of the month, you simply need to append "+1" to the EOMONTH formula. The following screenshot shows using EOMONTH to get the last day of the month:

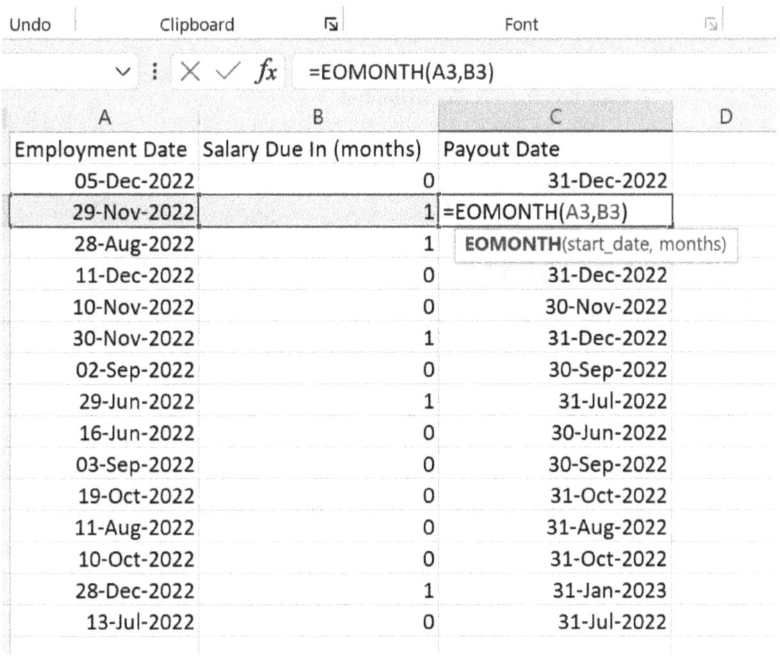

Employment Date	Salary Due In (months)	Payout Date
05-Dec-2022	0	31-Dec-2022
29-Nov-2022	1	=EOMONTH(A3,B3)
28-Aug-2022	1	
11-Dec-2022	0	31-Dec-2022
10-Nov-2022	0	30-Nov-2022
30-Nov-2022	1	31-Dec-2022
02-Sep-2022	0	30-Sep-2022
29-Jun-2022	1	31-Jul-2022
16-Jun-2022	0	30-Jun-2022
03-Sep-2022	0	30-Sep-2022
19-Oct-2022	0	31-Oct-2022
11-Aug-2022	0	31-Aug-2022
10-Oct-2022	0	31-Oct-2022
28-Dec-2022	1	31-Jan-2023
13-Jul-2022	0	31-Jul-2022

Figure 6.29 – EOMONTH function example

`EOMONTH` is slightly different from `EDATE` in that it always gives the last day of the month. This can be more beneficial for calculations that must reflect month-end periods. Next, we'll look at `WEEKNUM`.

WEEKNUM

`WEEKNUM` is an Excel function that returns the week of the year as a number. It can be useful for companies and sales units that have production plans and sales targets that are set weekly. Not all companies and sales teams use the regular calendar week numbering, but for those who do, `WEEKNUM` works perfectly. Its syntax is `WEEKNUM(date,weekstartday)`, where `weekstartday` is a number that indicates what day of the week marks the start of a new week. Excel gives a guiding popup for `weekstartday`. The following screenshot shows an example of using `WEEKNUM` to get the calendar week number for dates:

Figure 6.30 – WEEKNUM function example

With that, we have covered the must-know date manipulation functions. Next, we'll cover lookup functions.

Lookup and reference functions

Lookup functions in Excel are mostly for looking up values in a specified range and returning a related value. They are very useful for working between two tables or finding content related to a given value while reference functions are for manipulating cell references.

In this section, we will cover the following important lookup and reference functions in Legacy Excel:

- VLOOKUP

- HLOOKUP

- INDEX

- MATCH

- OFFSET

- INDIRECT

- CHOOSE

The first of these lookup and reference functions that we will cover is VLOOKUP.

VLOOKUP

VLOOKUP is an Excel function for looking up a value in a table and returning a related value in one of the table's columns. Its syntax is VLOOKUP(lookup_value,table,column_value_to_return,exact_or_approximate), where the value to look up is the first input, followed by the table to search in, then the column position of the value to return and, finally, whether to do an exact match (FALSE) or an approximate match (TRUE). You must ensure that the first column of the selected table is the one that contains the lookup value. The following screenshot shows an example of using VLOOKUP to get the location and account manager of a provided customer ID:

| UM | ⌄ ⋮ ✕ ✓ ƒx | =VLOOKUP(A2,A5:C24,2,FALSE) |

	A	B	C	D	E	F
	Customer ID	Location	Account Manager			
	C100012	New York	Adetosoye Chuku			
		=VLOOKUP(A2,A5:C24,2,FALSE)				
		VLOOKUP(lookup_value, table_array, col_index_num, [range_lookup])				
	Customer ID	Location	Account Manager			
	C100001	Frankfurt	Uwailomwan Akintunde			
	C100002	New York	Ibironke Abolanle			
	C100003	Pretoria	Efe Zoputa			
	C100004	Dubai	Uwailomwan Akintunde			
	C100005	Lagos	Ibironke Abolanle			
	C100006	Pretoria	Aduba Adesehinwa			
	C100007	Pretoria	Ibironke Abolanle			
	C100008	Lagos	Efe Zoputa			
	C100009	Valleta	Aduba Adesehinwa			
	C100010	Dubai	Adetosoye Chuku			
	C100011	Frankfurt	Uwailomwan Akintunde			
	C100012	New York	Adetosoye Chuku			
	C100013	New York	Aduba Adesehinwa			
	C100014	New York	Uwailomwan Akintunde			
	C100015	Dakar	Efe Zoputa			
	C100016	Tblisi	Uwailomwan Akintunde			
	C100017	New York	Adetosoye Chuku			
	C100018	Dakar	Adetosoye Chuku			
	C100019	Lagos	Adetosoye Chuku			

Figure 6.31 – VLOOKUP function example

VLOOKUP is a must-know Excel function, even though there are now newer Excel functions that can replicate what it does. It is still present in many company's existing reports, so it is essential that you are comfortable using it. We will now move on to another similar function, HLOOKUP.

HLOOKUP

HLOOKUP is an Excel function for looking up a value in a table and returning a related value in one of the table's rows. It's very much like VLOOKUP, with the major difference being that it searches across the first row of the selected table and returns a value on the same column but in a different row. Its syntax is HLOOKUP(lookup_value,table,row_value_to_return,exact_or_approximate), where the value to look up is the first input, followed by the table to search in, then the row position of the value to return and, finally, whether to do an exact match (FALSE) or an approximate match (TRUE). You must ensure that the first row of the selected table is the one that contains the lookup value. The following screenshot shows an example of using HLOOKUP to return the total sales for a desired month period:

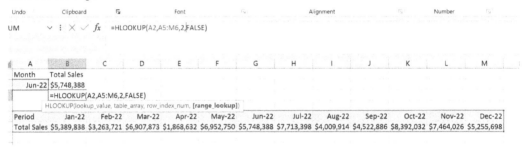

Figure 6.32 – HLOOKUP function example

Just like VLOOKUP, you must be very comfortable with using HLOOKUP so as not to struggle with working on existing reports that have this function within the report formulas. We'll cover another important function in the next section.

INDEX

INDEX is an Excel function that returns the cell at the interception of a specified row and column in a selected range. Its syntax is INDEX(table,row_number,column_number). There is a second, less-used syntax of the INDEX function: INDEX(reference,row_number,column_number,area). We will focus on the more commonly used first syntax here. The following screenshot shows an example of the first syntax being used to get what's on the fourth row and the third column of a table range:

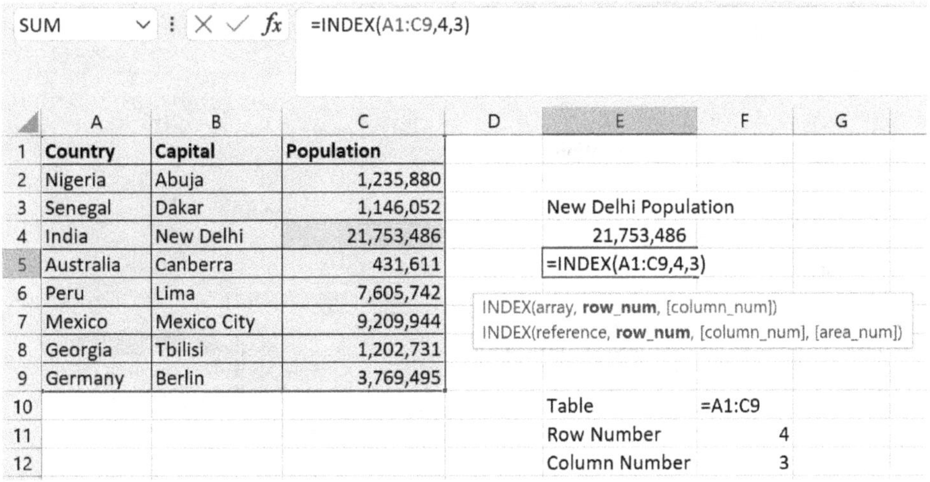

Figure 6.33 – INDEX function example

INDEX is a very powerful function that makes a lot of calculations possible when used in conjunction with other functions. You will come across it in many complex reports. Next, we'll look at the MATCH function.

MATCH

MATCH is an Excel function that gives the position of a lookup value within a specified array. Its syntax is MATCH(lookup_value,lookup_array,match_type), where lookup_value is the value whose position is to be determined in the supplied lookup array. match_type allows you to specify an exact match or an approximate match. The following screenshot shows an example of using MATCH to get the position of Peru in the **A1:A9** country range. The result could be supplied to INDEX to output related data on the returned row position. This is the rationale behind the popular use of INDEX and MATCH:

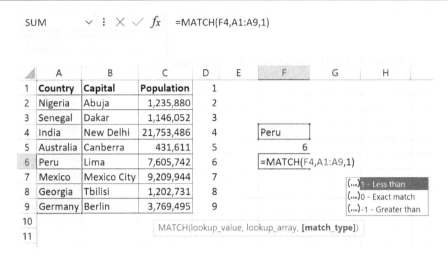

Figure 6.34 – MATCH function example

MATCH is often used together with INDEX to retrieve data from tables by providing a unique search item across the row and another unique search item across the column. Let's move on to the next function.

OFFSET

OFFSET is an Excel function that returns a range that is a specified amount of rows and columns away from a provided reference. Its syntax is OFFSET(reference,rows_away,columns_away,range_height,range_width). The following screenshot shows an example of using OFFSET to a range of one cell height and one cell width, but five rows below and one column after the **A1** cell reference:

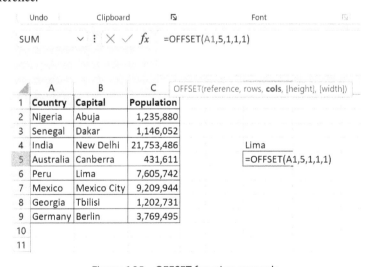

Figure 6.35 – OFFSET function example

OFFSET is a versatile function that allows you to achieve complex dynamic outcomes within your reports. It is not uncommon to find it in financial models and operations planning models. We will now explore another must-know function.

INDIRECT

INDIRECT is an Excel function for converting literal values into range references. Its syntax is INDIRECT(text,A1_orR1C1_style). It comes in handy occasionally when building very interactive dynamic dashboards in Excel and is the reason I have included it in this must-know list. The following screenshot shows an example of using INDIRECT to turn cell text into cell references:

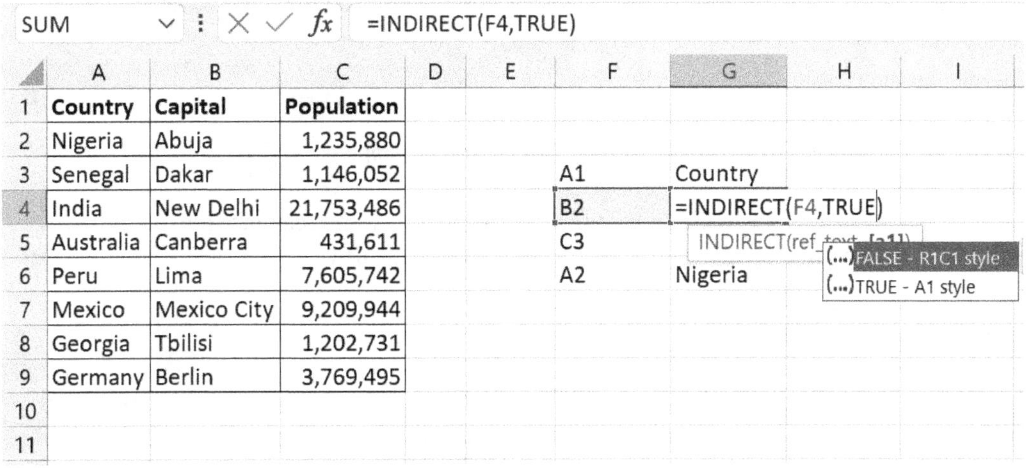

Figure 6.36 – INDIRECT function example

We will now explore another valuable function that eases the dynamic report creation process.

CHOOSE

CHOOSE is an Excel function for returning a value from a collection of values based on a position number. Its syntax is CHOOSE(position_number,value_at_position1, value_at_position2, ..). The following screenshot shows an example of using CHOOSE to set a growth rate based on one of many scenario options:

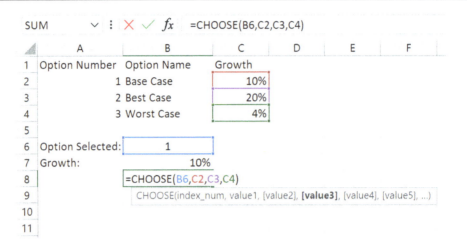

Figure 6.37 – CHOOSE function example

And with that, we have come to the end of the must-know lookup and reference functions. Attempt to try out the functions using the information and examples provided.

Summary

Functions are the bedrock of reports and dashboard creation in Excel. In this chapter, we covered the must-know Excel functions in Excel versions up until Excel 2019. This has laid an important foundation that we will build on in *Chapter 12, Best Practices for Real-World Dashboard Building*.

You are now knowledgeable about important math functions, logical functions, text manipulation functions, and lookup functions in Legacy Excel. In the next chapter, we will cover a new class of functions that are available in Excel 365: dynamic array functions and lambda functions. They make what used to require macros and complex processes possible in Excel. You will find them very interesting and useful in creating a modern interactive dashboard.

7
Dynamic Array Functions and Lambda Functions

Functions are a very important part of Excel and, recently, Microsoft has revamped the way functions work in Excel. In 2018, Microsoft introduced what it termed **dynamic array formulas**, which eliminated the need to use *Ctrl + Shift + Enter* for formulas that need to output values across multiple cells. It was an update of the formula engine in Excel to allow calculations to spill into as many cells as the output requires. In the Excel versions before this update, you needed to know how many cells and the dimensions (rows and columns) for formulas that output to multiple cells. Then, you would select the cells upfront, type in the formula, and use *Ctrl + Shift + Enter* to commit the formula. The formula couldn't spill beyond the initially selected cells.

The introduction of dynamic array formulas in Excel has made it possible to have formulas that can spill across cells without the need to use *Ctrl + Shift + Enter*. Also, they can shrink or expand across cells, which used to be impossible. Another great thing about dynamic array formulas is the introduction by Microsoft of a set of functions that output dynamic arrays. They are popularly referred to as **dynamic array functions**. We are going to explore these dynamic array functions, focusing primarily on the most versatile ones.

A more recent game-changing addition to Excel is a function called LAMBDA. LAMBDA is a function that allows you to create reusable custom functions in Excel right from the formula bar – no programming required. It enables a lot of interesting capabilities in Excel and powers some other new functions. We will cover the LAMBDA function and a family of functions that rely on it.

In this chapter, we will explore these new functions:

- Dynamic array functions
- Lambda functions

Dynamic array functions

There are over 22 dynamic array functions in Excel 365 and more are being added almost quarterly. We will, however, focus on the ones you can readily use in your reports and dashboards:

- UNIQUE
- FILTER
- SEQUENCE
- SORT
- SORTBY

Let's start with UNIQUE, which is a very popular dynamic array function.

UNIQUE

UNIQUE is the formula version of Excel's **Remove Duplicates** tool, which goes through a selection of Excel cells or tables and removes duplicate entries. It takes in a range and outputs a distinct version of that range. You can use it on a one-dimensional range – a list of values on a single row or single column. You can also use it on a table – a two-dimensional range. Unlike the **Remove Duplicates** tool, it is dynamically linked to the source range.

The function syntax is UNIQUE(array, [by_col], [exactly_once]). The array, as mentioned earlier, can be one-dimensional or two-dimensional. by_col is optional as the default of **FALSE** is set when you omit it in your formula. It simply means whether you want to extract a unique list or table by comparing columns or by comparing rows. exactly_once is also optional and set as **FALSE** if omitted; it asks if you want only records that occurred exactly once (ignoring records that occurred more than once).

In the following screenshot, we ignore **by_col** and **exactly_once** because we want to get unique records by comparing the row entries and we are not interested in just the values that occur only once. The formula extract is =UNIQUE(A2:A9):

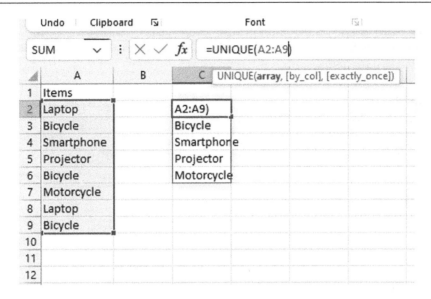

Figure 7.1 – UNIQUE to get a distinct list of items

If we need just the items that occur only once in the list, then we use the formula =UNIQUE(A2:A9,,TRUE). See the following screenshot for the implementation:

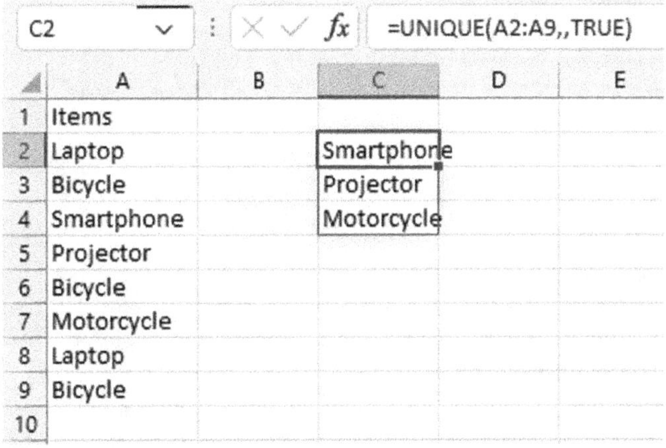

Figure 7.2 – UNIQUE with exactly_once set to TRUE

And if the list is a horizontal list, with items in separate columns on the same row, then we will need to set **by_col** to **TRUE**. See the following screenshot for an example of this. The formula extract is =UNIQUE(C12:J12,TRUE):

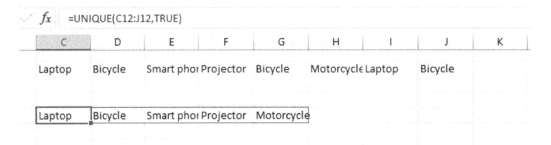

Figure 7.3 – UNIQUE to extract distinct items from a horizontal list

As the source range changes, the output from **UNIQUE** changes accordingly. This is one huge advantage it has over **Remove Duplicates**. And the good news doesn't end there; it can be used as an input to another formula. Instead of outputting to a cell directly, you can use it as a formula nested within another formula. As an example, this makes it possible to extract the count of distinct records by simply putting **UNIQUE** within a **COUNTA** function, as shown in the following screenshot. The formula extract is =COUNTA(UNIQUE(A2:A9)):

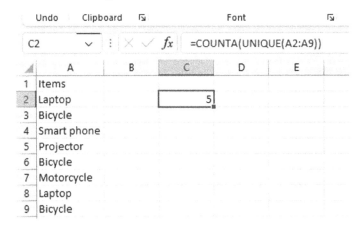

Figure 7.4 – Combining COUNTA and UNIQUE to get the count of distinct items

As we learn about the other dynamic array functions, keep in mind that they can be combined into one formula to achieve more than just one function can. We will now explore another function: FILTER.

FILTER

FILTER is the formula version of the **Filter** tool in Excel. It allows you to extract a filtered list or table from a range. Its syntax is FILTER(array,include,[if_empty]) where array is the range to apply the filter to, include is a logical operation to identify rows to return, and if_empty is what to return if nothing matches the criteria given. if_empty is optional. When omitted, the function will return a #CALC! error when no record is found that evaluates to TRUE for the logical operation in include.

In the following screenshot, we use FILTER to extract premium products from a table of both premium and regular products. The formula extract is =FILTER(A1:C17,B1:B17="Premium",""):

	A	B	C	D	E	F	G	H
1	Product	Category	Profit Margin					
2	BBQ Chicken	Premium	23%			BBQ Chicken	Premium	0.23
3	Hot Veggie	Premium	22%			Hot Veggie	Premium	0.22
4	Italiano	Premium	23%			Italiano	Premium	0.23
5	Pepperoni Suya	Premium	24%			Pepperoni Suya	Premium	0.24
6	Veggie Supreme	Premium	29%			Veggie Supreme	Premium	0.29
7	Hot Pepperoni Feast	Premium	26%			Hot Pepperoni Feast	Premium	0.26
8	Pepperoni Feast	Premium	23%			Pepperoni Feast	Premium	0.23
9	Meatzaa	Regular	18%					
10	Extravaganza	Regular	14%					
11	BBQ Philly Steak	Regular	20%					
12	Chicken Feast	Regular	20%					
13	Chicken Suya	Regular	20%					
14	Chicken Legend	Regular	13%					
15	Beef Suya	Regular	16%					
16	Margherita	Regular	15%					
17	Chicken Bali	Regular	17%					
18								
19								
20								
21								
22								

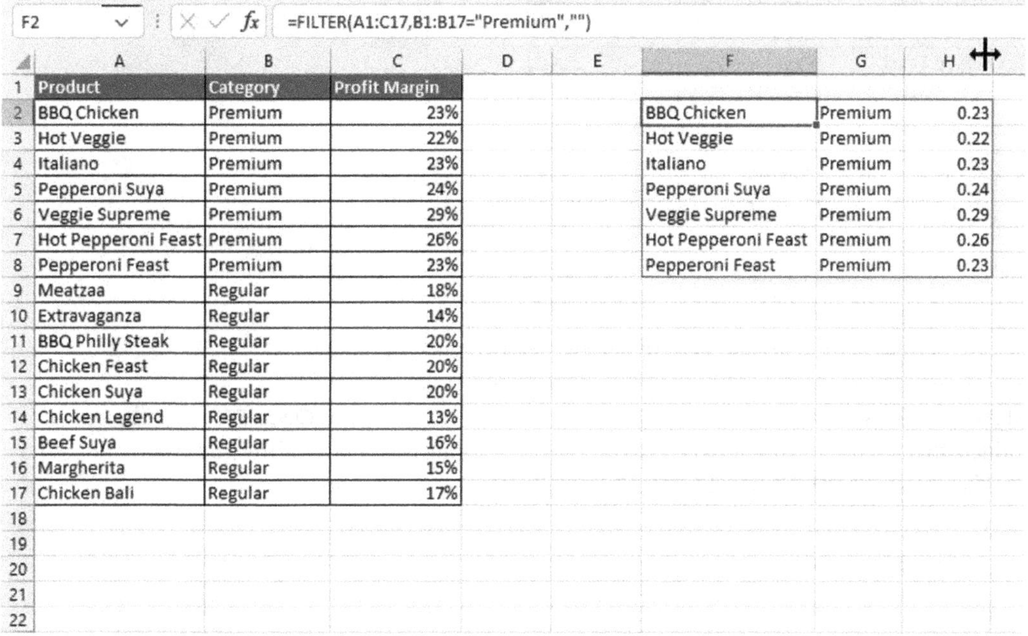

F2 — =FILTER(A1:C17,B1:B17="Premium","")

Figure 7.5 – FILTER to extract premium products

And if we need just the products and not the other columns (**category** and **profit margin**), we can specify a filter range that does not encompass the column the include condition works on. See the following screenshot for the implementation of this to extract just the product names. The formula extract is =FILTER(A1:A17,B1:B17="Premium",""). The filter range was set to just column A values while the include condition was set to column B values:

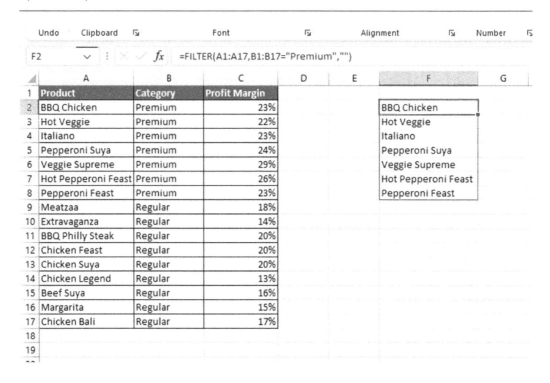

Figure 7.6 – FILTER to select product names only

Just like we did with UNIQUE, I can put the FILTER formula within COUNTA to get the count of products that are in the premium category. See the following screenshot of the implementation. The formula extract is =COUNTA(FILTER(A1:A17,B1:B17="Premium","")):

	A	B	C	D	E	F	G
	fx	=COUNTA(FILTER(A1:A17,B1:B17="Premium",""))					
1	Product	Category	Profit Margin				
2	BBQ Chicken	Premium	23%			7	
3	Hot Veggie	Premium	22%				
4	Italiano	Premium	23%				
5	Pepperoni Suya	Premium	24%				
6	Veggie Supreme	Premium	29%				
7	Hot Pepperoni Feast	Premium	26%				
8	Pepperoni Feast	Premium	23%				
9	Meatzaa	Regular	18%				
10	Extravaganza	Regular	14%				
11	BBQ Philly Steak	Regular	20%				
12	Chicken Feast	Regular	20%				
13	Chicken Suya	Regular	20%				
14	Chicken Legend	Regular	13%				
15	Beef Suya	Regular	16%				
16	Margarita	Regular	15%				
17	Chicken Bali	Regular	17%				

Figure 7.7 – FILTER within COUNTA to get the count of premium products

You might ask: why not use Excel's `Filter` tool? The answer is simple and is a great way to point out the advantage of using **FILTER** and other dynamic array functions. With **FILTER**, when we add a new record or modify an existing record within the selected range, the output changes instantly. As an illustration, we will change **Chicken Bali** (the last product) to be categorized as **Premium**. Notice how the `FILTER` formula output changes accordingly, in the following screenshot:

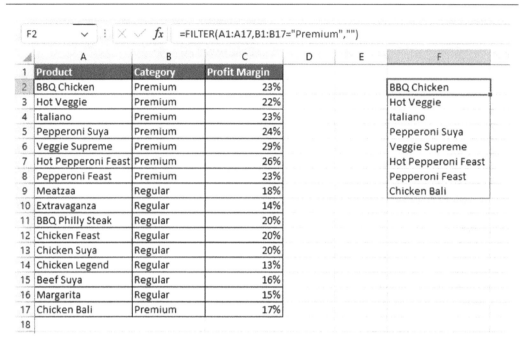

Figure 7.8 – Dynamic nature of the FILTER function

And COUNTA with **FILTER** within it also shows an updated output of **8**, as shown in the next screenshot:

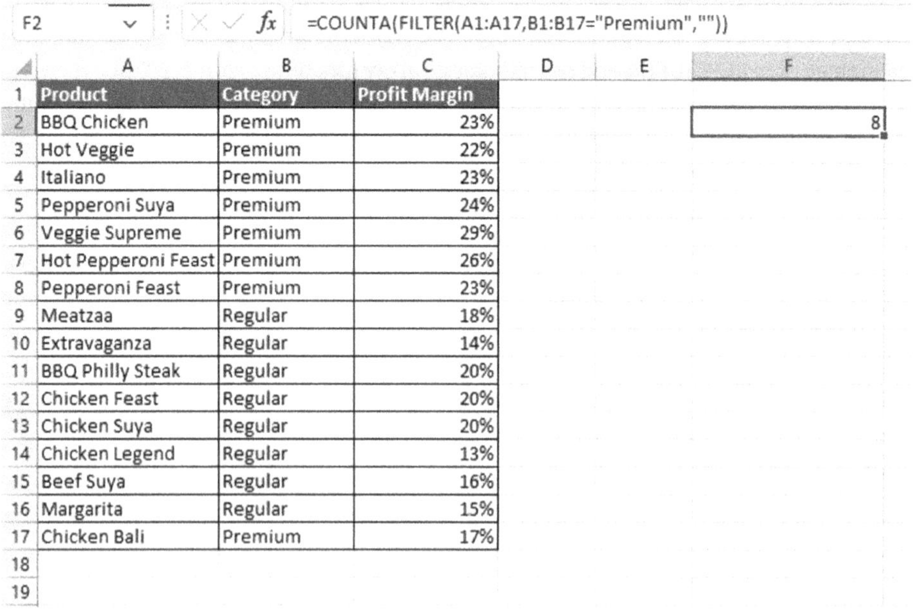

Figure 7.9 – COUNTA reflecting the updated table instantly

Now you know how **FILTER** works, we will go on to the next dynamic array function: **SEQUENCE**.

SEQUENCE

There are dynamic array functions that give the traditional Excel functions enhanced capabilities and SEQUENCE is one of those. SEQUENCE is simply a function that generates an array of numbers based on the number of rows, number of columns, starting value, and incremental value you provide. The function syntax is SEQUENCE (rows, [columns], [start], [step]).

In the example and the following screenshot, we use SEQUENCE to generate numbers across **10** rows and **1** column, starting from **100** and incremented by **1**. The formula extract is =SEQUENCE(10,1,100,1):

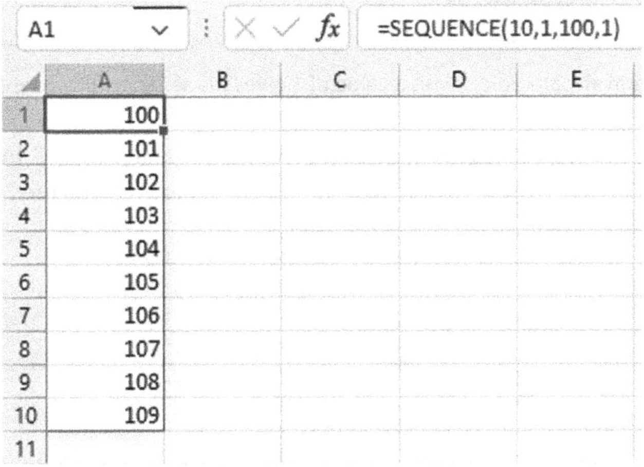

Figure 7.10 – SEQUENCE to generate a list of 10 numbers

SEQUENCE allows you to omit any of its parameters, but you must provide a value for either *rows* or *columns*. You can't omit both rows and columns. When you omit any of the parameters, a default value of **1** is used. So, we could have generated the same preceding list of records by using =SEQUENCE (10, , 100), as shown in the following screenshot:

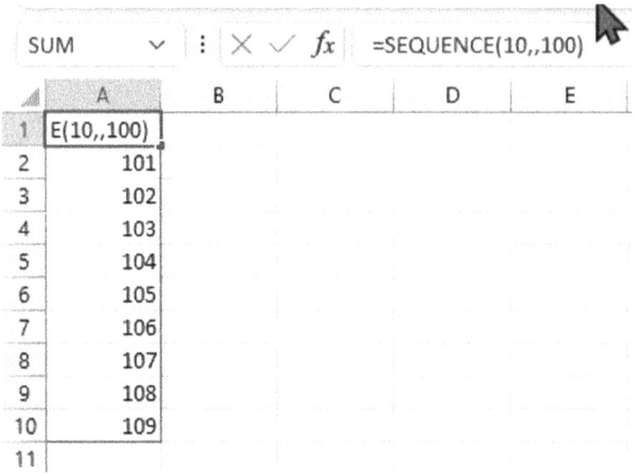

Figure 7.11 – Omitting all parameters with a value of 1 gives the same results as when not omitted

We can equally create columns of values by setting columns to greater than 1. In the example and the following screenshot, we create 5 records that start at **20** and are incremented by 5. The formula extract is =SEQUENCE(,5,20,5):

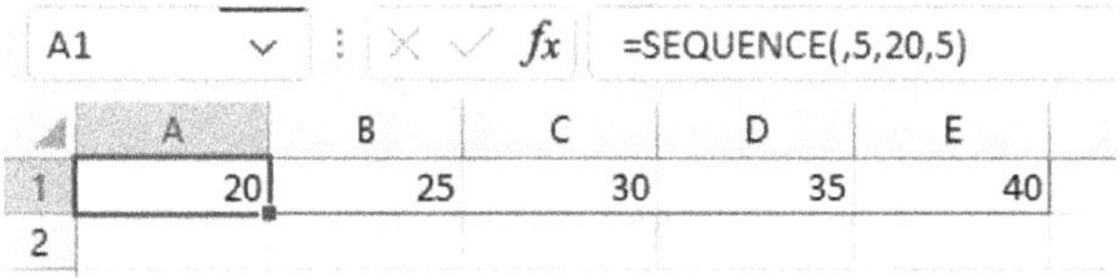

Figure 7.12 – SEQUENCE to create records across columns

The step parameter also accepts negative numbers to indicate a decreasing value array of numbers. In the example and the following screenshot, we create a list of 6 numbers that starts at **60** and decreases by 10. The formula extract is =SEQUENCE(6,,60,-10):

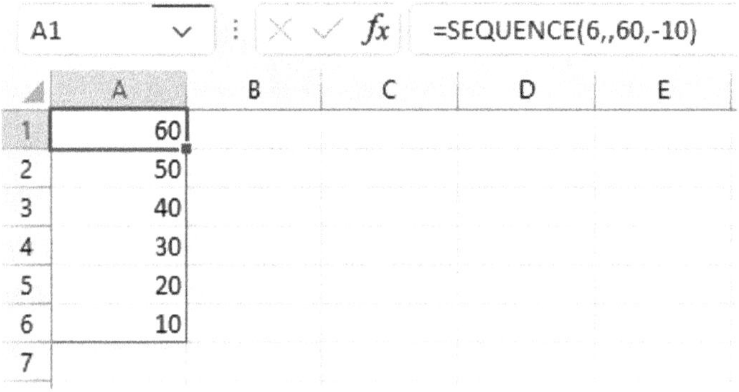

Figure 7.13 – SEQUENCE to generate a reducing value list of numbers

Where **SEQUENCE** shines most is when it is combined with other functions to achieve things that would have been otherwise difficult or require complex formulas. An example is to create a grouped list of numbers: 1-10, 11-20, 21-30, and so on. This can be easily achieved by concatenating two **SEQUENCE** functions with a hyphen in between. See the following screenshot for the implementation. The formula extract is `=SEQUENCE(10,,1,10)&" - "&SEQUENCE(10,,10,10)`:

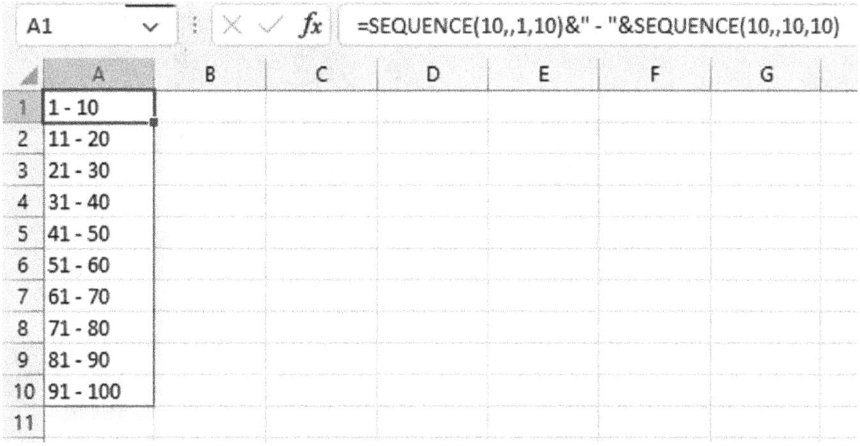

Figure 7.14 – Concatenating two SEQUENCE functions to generate a grouped list

We can also easily generate a series of consecutive dates using `SEQUENCE`. The example in the following screenshot shows how to generate a list of the next 7 days using the `SEQUENCE` and `TODAY` functions. The formula extract is `=SEQUENCE(7,,TODAY())`:

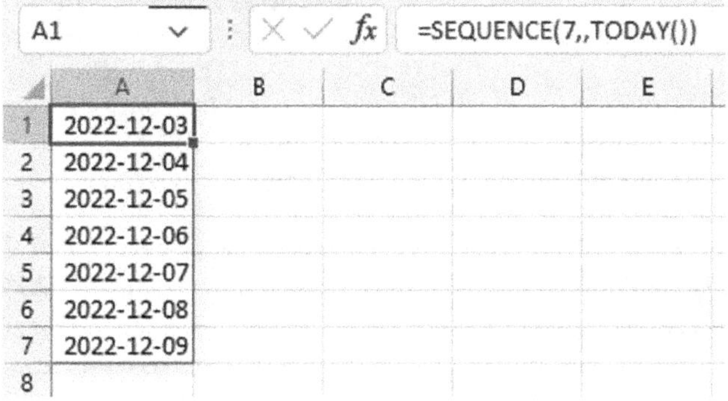

Figure 7.15 – Generating a list of dates using SEQUENCE and TODAY functions

One more interesting example is the use of SEQUENCE with CHAR to generate the values that are a mix of alphabet and numbers. In the following screenshot, we use SEQUENCE, INT, MOD, and CHAR functions to help a hotel generate a list of room numbers for their 10 rooms following the pattern of **101A**, **101B**, **102A**, **102B**, and so on. The formula extract is =INT(SEQUENCE(10,,101,0.5))&CHAR(65+MOD(SEQUENCE(10,,2),2)):

| A1 | | | | fx | =INT(SEQUENCE(10,,101,0.5))&CHAR(65+MOD(SEQUENCE(10,,2),2)) |

	A	B	C	D	E	F	G	H
1	101A			Alphabet	CHAR number			
2	101B			A	65			
3	102A			B	66			
4	102B							
5	103A							
6	103B							
7	104A							
8	104B							
9	105A							
10	105B							
11								
12								

Figure 7.16 – Combination of SEQUENCE, INT, MOD, and CHAR functions

If you are feeling dizzy from reading through the formula and trying to figure out how it works, you are not alone. I feel that way too when I look at long formulas that combine different functions. The trick to thinking through long complex formulas is to break them into parts and focus on one part at a time. The preceding formula has two major parts: one part is to generate the number portion and the other part is to generate the alphabet portion.

The part for the number portion has a **SEQUENCE** function that generates a series of numbers: {101;101.5;102;102.5;103;103.5;104;104.5;105;105.5}. These are then passed to INT to cut out the decimal part and output: {101;101;102;102;103;103;104;104;105;105}.

The part for the alphabet has a **SEQUENCE** function generating {2;3;4;5;6;7;8;9;10;11}. This is then passed into a modulus function, MOD, to convert it into {0;1;0;1;0;1;0;1;0;1}. Adding 65 to this gives a repeating set of 65 and 66, {65;66;65;66;65;66;65;66;65;66}, which corresponds to the character numbers for A and B. Passing that into the CHAR function converts the numbers into the letters A and B: {"A";"B";"A";"B";"A";"B";"A";"B";"A";"B"}.

Concatenating those two parts gives the final desired output, { "101A"; "101B"; "102A"; "10 2B"; "103A"; "103B"; "104A"; "104B"; "105A"; "105B" }, spilled across cells **A1** to **A10** as shown in the following screenshot:

	A	B	C	D	E	F	G	H	I
				fx	={"101A";"101B";"102A";"102B";"103A";"103B";"104A";"104B";"105A";"105B"}				
1	"105B"}			Alphabet	CHAR number				
2	101B			A	65				
3	102A			B	66				
4	102B								
5	103A								
6	103B								
7	104A								
8	104B								
9	105A								
10	105B								
11									
12									

Figure 7.17 – The final output spilling across cells A1 to A10

That wraps it up for our coverage of **SEQUENCE** and I hope you are getting cool ideas about interesting things to do with it. We will now move on to SORT.

SORT

SORT is the formula version of the **Sort** tool in Excel. It allows you to sort a range of values in an ordered way. The function syntax is SORT(array, [sort_index], [sort_order], [by_col]). The array represents the range of data you want to sort. [sort_index] is to set the column or row to sort by. If omitted, it defaults to 1. [sort_order] is to set the sort order to ascending (1) or descending order (-1). The default when omitted is 1. [by_col] is to indicate whether to sort by columns (TRUE) or by rows (FALSE). The default when omitted is FALSE.

We will work through an example that is a table of products with Product name, Category, Profit margin, and Price columns. Applying SORT to the range of data without providing sort_index, sort_order, and by_col results in the table being sorted by the first column in ascending order and by row. See the following screenshot for a demonstration. The formula extract is =SORT(A2:D17):

F2 | ⌄ | ⋮ | × ✓ | *fx*   =SORT(A2:D17)

▲	A	B	C	D	E	F	G	H	I
1	**Product**	**Category**	**Profit Margin**	**Price**					
2	BBQ Chicken	Premium	23%	$9.00		BBQ Chicken	Premium	0.23	9
3	Hot Veggie	Premium	22%	$15.00		BBQ Philly Steak	Regular	0.2	9
4	Italiano	Premium	23%	$9.00		Beef Suya	Regular	0.16	9
5	Pepperoni Suya	Premium	24%	$9.00		Chicken Bali	Premium	0.17	9
6	Veggie Supreme	Premium	29%	$12.00		Chicken Feast	Regular	0.2	12
7	Hot Pepperoni Feast	Premium	26%	$9.00		Chicken Legend	Regular	0.13	12
8	Pepperoni Feast	Premium	23%	$12.00		Chicken Suya	Regular	0.2	9
9	Meatzaa	Regular	18%	$9.00		Extravaganza	Regular	0.14	9
10	Extravaganza	Regular	14%	$9.00		Hot Pepperoni Feast	Premium	0.26	9
11	BBQ Philly Steak	Regular	20%	$9.00		Hot Veggie	Premium	0.22	15
12	Chicken Feast	Regular	20%	$12.00		Italiano	Premium	0.23	9
13	Chicken Suya	Regular	20%	$9.00		Margarita	Regular	0.15	9
14	Chicken Legend	Regular	13%	$12.00		Meatzaa	Regular	0.18	9
15	Beef Suya	Regular	16%	$9.00		Pepperoni Feast	Premium	0.23	12
16	Margarita	Regular	15%	$9.00		Pepperoni Suya	Premium	0.24	9
17	Chicken Bali	Premium	17%	$9.00		Veggie Supreme	Premium	0.29	12
18									

Figure 7.18 – SORT to arrange the products in ascending order

What if we wanted to sort by the price in ascending order? To achieve that, we need to provide the Price column as the sort_index. The final formula will read as =SORT(A2:D17,4) as prices are in the fourth column in the data range. The output is shown in the following screenshot:

F2 | ⌄ | ⋮ | × ✓ | *fx*   =SORT(A2:D17,4)

▲	A	B	C	D	E	F	G	H	I
1	**Product**	**Category**	**Profit Margin**	**Price**					
2	BBQ Chicken	Premium	23%	$9.00		BBQ Chicken	Premium	0.23	9
3	Hot Veggie	Premium	22%	$15.00		Italiano	Premium	0.23	9
4	Italiano	Premium	23%	$9.00		Pepperoni Suya	Premium	0.24	9
5	Pepperoni Suya	Premium	24%	$9.00		Hot Pepperoni Feast	Premium	0.26	9
6	Veggie Supreme	Premium	29%	$12.00		Meatzaa	Regular	0.18	9
7	Hot Pepperoni Feast	Premium	26%	$9.00		Extravaganza	Regular	0.14	9
8	Pepperoni Feast	Premium	23%	$12.00		BBQ Philly Steak	Regular	0.2	9
9	Meatzaa	Regular	18%	$9.00		Chicken Suya	Regular	0.2	9
10	Extravaganza	Regular	14%	$9.00		Beef Suya	Regular	0.16	9
11	BBQ Philly Steak	Regular	20%	$9.00		Margarita	Regular	0.15	9
12	Chicken Feast	Regular	20%	$12.00		Chicken Bali	Premium	0.17	9
13	Chicken Suya	Regular	20%	$9.00		Veggie Supreme	Premium	0.29	12
14	Chicken Legend	Regular	13%	$12.00		Pepperoni Feast	Premium	0.23	12
15	Beef Suya	Regular	16%	$9.00		Chicken Feast	Regular	0.2	12
16	Margarita	Regular	15%	$9.00		Chicken Legend	Regular	0.13	12
17	Chicken Bali	Premium	17%	$9.00		Hot Veggie	Premium	0.22	15
18									

Figure 7.19 – SORT by the fourth column (price)

It is also possible to sort on multiple columns at the same time. It may not be obvious by looking at the SORT options, but when you remember that you can put a function inside another function, then it becomes clear that we can sort by multiple columns. For illustration, we are going to sort the data by product and then by price. To achieve this, we put the sort-by-product formula inside a sort-by-price formula: =SORT(SORT(A2:D17),4).

| F2 | | | f_x | =SORT(SORT(A2:D17),4) | | | | |

	A	B	C	D	E	F	G	H	I
1	Product	Category	Profit Margin	Price					
2	BBQ Chicken	Premium	23%	$9.00		BBQ Chicken	Premium	0.23	9
3	Hot Veggie	Premium	22%	$15.00		BBQ Philly Steak	Regular	0.2	9
4	Italiano	Premium	23%	$9.00		Beef Suya	Regular	0.16	9
5	Pepperoni Suya	Premium	24%	$9.00		Chicken Bali	Premium	0.17	9
6	Veggie Supreme	Premium	29%	$12.00		Chicken Suya	Regular	0.2	9
7	Hot Pepperoni Feast	Premium	26%	$9.00		Extravaganza	Regular	0.14	9
8	Pepperoni Feast	Premium	23%	$12.00		Hot Pepperoni Feast	Premium	0.26	9
9	Meatzaa	Regular	18%	$9.00		Italiano	Premium	0.23	9
10	Extravaganza	Regular	14%	$9.00		Margarita	Regular	0.15	9
11	BBQ Philly Steak	Regular	20%	$9.00		Meatzaa	Regular	0.18	9
12	Chicken Feast	Regular	20%	$12.00		Pepperoni Suya	Premium	0.24	9
13	Chicken Suya	Regular	20%	$9.00		Chicken Feast	Regular	0.2	12
14	Chicken Legend	Regular	13%	$12.00		Chicken Legend	Regular	0.13	12
15	Beef Suya	Regular	16%	$9.00		Pepperoni Feast	Premium	0.23	12
16	Margarita	Regular	15%	$9.00		Veggie Supreme	Premium	0.29	12
17	Chicken Bali	Premium	17%	$9.00		Hot Veggie	Premium	0.22	15
18									

Figure 7.20 – Sorting by multiple columns at the same time

There will be situations where the data needs to be sorted column-wise. Take, for instance, a table showing sales by month but the months are not arranged in the usual calendar sequence. See the following screenshot for this type of data:

| I11 | | | f_x | | | | |

	A	B	C	D	E	F	G
1	Branch	Feb-22	Jun-22	Jan-22	Mar-22	May-22	Apr-22
2	Imo	₦2,521,764,800.00	₦2,922,241,900.00	₦2,591,742,600.00	₦2,013,994,900.00	₦3,014,428,300.00	₦4,994,515,700.00
3	Osun	₦3,080,572,127.00	₦3,151,982,550.00	₦2,333,094,114.00	₦2,195,287,135.00	₦2,964,466,474.00	₦2,858,954,963.00
4	Abia	₦821,123,500.00	₦4,544,916,100.00	₦1,297,498,300.00	₦1,175,454,800.00	₦2,265,644,000.00	₦967,327,400.00
5	Lagos	₦7,319,183,000.00	₦22,681,984,500.00	₦6,239,473,500.00	₦6,211,689,500.00	₦11,610,307,000.00	₦3,351,178,500.00
6	Kano	₦2,021,735,600.00	₦530,613,400.00	₦2,981,980,300.00	₦3,016,518,600.00	₦2,387,291,000.00	₦4,411,651,000.00
7	Ondo	₦1,690,422,800.00	₦4,925,747,700.00	₦716,222,900.00	₦4,362,953,800.00	₦4,300,936,900.00	₦977,876,300.00
8	Kogi	₦2,734,189,600.00	₦2,825,512,800.00	₦2,812,863,300.00	₦2,306,601,300.00	₦2,104,687,400.00	₦867,264,000.00
9	Benue	₦3,864,832,700.00	₦3,212,451,900.00	₦3,479,649,000.00	₦2,458,711,700.00	₦2,700,421,800.00	₦4,801,142,000.00
10	FCT	₦2,063,317,300.00	₦2,520,202,900.00	₦3,199,223,200.00	₦1,829,381,400.00	₦4,980,777,000.00	₦3,704,640,600.00
11	Ogun	₦2,586,000,100.00	₦3,200,451,900.00	₦3,434,714,900.00	₦3,907,557,600.00	₦2,265,022,600.00	₦1,642,410,200.00
12	Bayelsa	₦2,035,499,300.00	₦1,754,855,100.00	₦1,218,646,400.00	₦3,596,177,500.00	₦4,856,865,900.00	₦3,958,333,500.00
13	Rivers	₦4,860,256,800.00	₦4,459,705,200.00	₦2,423,028,900.00	₦4,148,808,900.00	₦4,882,684,300.00	₦859,719,700.00

Figure 7.21 – Branch sales value by months; months not well arranged

Getting the months sorted in the right order can be achieved with the SORT function. We only need to select the monthly sales data range and indicate that the sorting should be by column and not by row (which is the default). The formula to achieve this is =SORT(B1:G13,1,1,TRUE) and the following screenshot shows the outcome. Notice that the Branch column was omitted in the range selected. You can manually copy and paste it to the left of the SORT output:

B15   ⌄ ⋮ ✕ ✓ *fx* =SORT(B1:G13,1,1,TRUE)

	A	B	C	D	E	F	G
14							
15		Jan-22	Feb-22	Mar-22	Apr-22	May-22	Jun-22
16		₦ 2,591,742,600.00	₦ 2,521,764,800.00	₦ 2,013,994,900.00	₦ 4,994,515,700.00	₦ 3,014,428,300.00	₦ 2,922,241,900.00
17		₦ 2,333,094,114.00	₦ 3,080,572,127.00	₦ 2,195,287,135.00	₦ 2,858,954,963.00	₦ 2,964,466,474.00	₦ 3,151,982,550.00
18		₦ 1,297,498,300.00	₦ 821,123,500.00	₦ 1,175,454,800.00	₦ 967,327,400.00	₦ 2,265,644,000.00	₦ 4,544,916,100.00
19		₦ 6,239,473,500.00	₦ 7,319,183,000.00	₦ 6,211,689,500.00	₦ 3,351,178,500.00	₦ 11,610,307,000.00	₦ 22,681,984,500.00
20		₦ 2,981,980,300.00	₦ 2,021,735,600.00	₦ 3,016,518,600.00	₦ 4,411,651,000.00	₦ 2,387,291,000.00	₦ 530,613,400.00
21		₦ 716,222,900.00	₦ 1,690,422,800.00	₦ 4,362,953,800.00	₦ 977,876,300.00	₦ 4,300,936,900.00	₦ 4,925,747,700.00
22		₦ 2,812,863,300.00	₦ 2,734,189,600.00	₦ 2,306,601,300.00	₦ 867,264,000.00	₦ 2,104,687,400.00	₦ 2,825,512,800.00
23		₦ 3,479,649,000.00	₦ 3,864,832,700.00	₦ 2,458,711,700.00	₦ 4,801,142,000.00	₦ 2,700,421,800.00	₦ 3,212,451,900.00
24		₦ 3,199,223,200.00	₦ 2,063,317,300.00	₦ 1,829,381,400.00	₦ 3,704,640,600.00	₦ 4,980,777,000.00	₦ 2,520,202,900.00
25		₦ 3,434,714,900.00	₦ 2,586,000,100.00	₦ 3,907,557,600.00	₦ 1,642,410,200.00	₦ 2,265,022,600.00	₦ 3,200,451,900.00
26		₦ 1,218,646,400.00	₦ 2,035,499,300.00	₦ 3,596,177,500.00	₦ 3,958,333,500.00	₦ 4,856,865,900.00	₦ 1,754,855,100.00
27		₦ 2,423,028,900.00	₦ 4,860,256,800.00	₦ 4,148,808,900.00	₦ 859,719,700.00	₦ 4,882,684,300.00	₦ 4,459,705,200.00

Figure 7.22 – Sorting by column

Lastly, we can choose to sort the dates in descending order by changing sort_order to -1. The formula to achieve this is =SORT(B1:G13,1,-1,TRUE) and the following screenshot shows the outcome:

⌄ ⋮ ✕ ✓ *fx* =SORT(B1:G13,1,-1,TRUE)

B	C	D	E	F	G
Jun-22	May-22	Apr-22	Mar-22	Feb-22	Jan-22
₦ 2,922,241,900.00	₦ 3,014,428,300.00	₦ 4,994,515,700.00	₦ 2,013,994,900.00	₦ 2,521,764,800.00	₦ 2,591,742,600.00
₦ 3,151,982,550.00	₦ 2,964,466,474.00	₦ 2,858,954,963.00	₦ 2,195,287,135.00	₦ 3,080,572,127.00	₦ 2,333,094,114.00
₦ 4,544,916,100.00	₦ 2,265,644,000.00	₦ 967,327,400.00	₦ 1,175,454,800.00	₦ 821,123,500.00	₦ 1,297,498,300.00
₦ 22,681,984,500.00	₦ 11,610,307,000.00	₦ 3,351,178,500.00	₦ 6,211,689,500.00	₦ 7,319,183,000.00	₦ 6,239,473,500.00
₦ 530,613,400.00	₦ 2,387,291,000.00	₦ 4,411,651,000.00	₦ 3,016,518,600.00	₦ 2,021,735,600.00	₦ 2,981,980,300.00
₦ 4,925,747,700.00	₦ 4,300,936,900.00	₦ 977,876,300.00	₦ 4,362,953,800.00	₦ 1,690,422,800.00	₦ 716,222,900.00
₦ 2,825,512,800.00	₦ 2,104,687,400.00	₦ 867,264,000.00	₦ 2,306,601,300.00	₦ 2,734,189,600.00	₦ 2,812,863,300.00
₦ 3,212,451,900.00	₦ 2,700,421,800.00	₦ 4,801,142,000.00	₦ 2,458,711,700.00	₦ 3,864,832,700.00	₦ 3,479,649,000.00
₦ 2,520,202,900.00	₦ 4,980,777,000.00	₦ 3,704,640,600.00	₦ 1,829,381,400.00	₦ 2,063,317,300.00	₦ 3,199,223,200.00
₦ 3,200,451,900.00	₦ 2,265,022,600.00	₦ 1,642,410,200.00	₦ 3,907,557,600.00	₦ 2,586,000,100.00	₦ 3,434,714,900.00
₦ 1,754,855,100.00	₦ 4,856,865,900.00	₦ 3,958,333,500.00	₦ 3,596,177,500.00	₦ 2,035,499,300.00	₦ 1,218,646,400.00
₦ 4,459,705,200.00	₦ 4,882,684,300.00	₦ 859,719,700.00	₦ 4,148,808,900.00	₦ 4,860,256,800.00	₦ 2,423,028,900.00

Figure 7.23 – Setting the sort order to descending order

We have thoroughly examined the **SORT** function; we will now go on to the next dynamic array function: SORTBY.

SORTBY

You may wonder why there is a need for a **SORTBY** function if we already have a SORT function. Well, they are actually different and SORTBY solves a common need that SORT is unable to natively address. SORTBY is a function that allows you to sort a range using the order specified on another range and natively supports providing multiple columns for the sorting order. The function syntax is SORTBY(array,by_array1,[sort_order1],[by_array2],[sort_order2],..). The common need that SORTBY solves is the ability to select a range that does not include the sort_ by range. Take the sample data of products and their details we used for the SORT illustration. We constantly needed to specify the SORTBY column using an index (number) that identifies it within the selected range. For SORTBY, we can select just the Product column as our range to sort and select the Price column as our range to sort by. See the following screenshot for the implementation. The formula extract is =SORTBY(A2:A17,D2:D17):

Figure 7.24 – SORTBY to sort products by price

SORTBY also makes it very easy to sort by multiple columns. We can easily sort the complete products table by price and category. The formula to achieve that is =SORTBY(A2:D17,D2:D17,1,B2:B17,1) and the following screenshot shows the outcome:

| F2 | ⌄ : × ✓ *fx* | =SORTBY(A2:D17,D2:D17,1,B2:B17,1) |

▲	A	B	C	D	E	F	G	H	I
1	Product	Category	Profit Margin	Price					
2	BBQ Chicken	Premium	23%	$9.00		BBQ Chicken	Premium	0.23	9
3	Hot Veggie	Premium	22%	$15.00		Italiano	Premium	0.23	9
4	Italiano	Premium	23%	$9.00		Pepperoni Suya	Premium	0.24	9
5	Pepperoni Suya	Premium	24%	$9.00		Hot Pepperoni Feast	Premium	0.26	9
6	Veggie Supreme	Premium	29%	$12.00		Chicken Bali	Premium	0.17	9
7	Hot Pepperoni Feast	Premium	26%	$9.00		Meatzaa	Regular	0.18	9
8	Pepperoni Feast	Premium	23%	$12.00		Extravaganza	Regular	0.14	9
9	Meatzaa	Regular	18%	$9.00		BBQ Philly Steak	Regular	0.2	9
10	Extravaganza	Regular	14%	$9.00		Chicken Suya	Regular	0.2	9
11	BBQ Philly Steak	Regular	20%	$9.00		Beef Suya	Regular	0.16	9
12	Chicken Feast	Regular	20%	$12.00		Margarita	Regular	0.15	9
13	Chicken Suya	Regular	20%	$9.00		Veggie Supreme	Premium	0.29	12
14	Chicken Legend	Regular	13%	$12.00		Pepperoni Feast	Premium	0.23	12
15	Beef Suya	Regular	16%	$9.00		Chicken Feast	Regular	0.2	12
16	Margarita	Regular	15%	$9.00		Chicken Legend	Regular	0.13	12
17	Chicken Bali	Premium	17%	$9.00		Hot Veggie	Premium	0.22	15

Figure 7.25 – SORTBY to sort by multiple columns

Lastly, we can sort the products by category in ascending order and by price in descending order but output just the Product and Category columns. The formula to achieve this is =SORTBY(A2:B17,B2:B17,1,D2:D17,-1) and the following screenshot shows the output:

| F2 | ⌄ : × ✓ *fx* | =SORTBY(A2:B17,B2:B17,1,D2:D17,-1) |

▲	A	B	C	D	E	F	G
1	Product	Category	Profit Margin	Price			
2	BBQ Chicken	Premium	23%	$9.00		Hot Veggie	Premium
3	Hot Veggie	Premium	22%	$15.00		Veggie Supreme	Premium
4	Italiano	Premium	23%	$9.00		Pepperoni Feast	Premium
5	Pepperoni Suya	Premium	24%	$9.00		BBQ Chicken	Premium
6	Veggie Supreme	Premium	29%	$12.00		Italiano	Premium
7	Hot Pepperoni Feast	Premium	26%	$9.00		Pepperoni Suya	Premium
8	Pepperoni Feast	Premium	23%	$12.00		Hot Pepperoni Feast	Premium
9	Meatzaa	Regular	18%	$9.00		Chicken Bali	Premium
10	Extravaganza	Regular	14%	$9.00		Chicken Feast	Regular
11	BBQ Philly Steak	Regular	20%	$9.00		Chicken Legend	Regular
12	Chicken Feast	Regular	20%	$12.00		Meatzaa	Regular
13	Chicken Suya	Regular	20%	$9.00		Extravaganza	Regular
14	Chicken Legend	Regular	13%	$12.00		BBQ Philly Steak	Regular
15	Beef Suya	Regular	16%	$9.00		Chicken Suya	Regular
16	Margarita	Regular	15%	$9.00		Beef Suya	Regular
17	Chicken Bali	Premium	17%	$9.00		Margarita	Regular

Figure 7.26 – SORTBY to sort products by category in ascending order and by price in descending order

We have thoroughly examined **SORTBY** and seen how it is different from SORT. This wraps up our section on dynamic array functions. We will now move on to the next section, on Lambda functions.

Lambda functions

Microsoft created the Lambda function in Excel as a way for people to create user-defined functions without doing any programming, just by using the same Excel formulas they do within cells. In December 2020, when the Lambda function was released for Excel 365 and Excel on the web, many people saw it as a weak attempt to replicate the **Visual Basic for Applications** (**VBA**) user-defined functions and pointed out some limitations it has. Limitations such as it needs to be put in a named range to be able to call it like a proper function. But Microsoft was just getting started then and the Lambda function is just one of many functions it released to empower users to create truly powerful custom functions.

This section is all about Lambda and the functions that are built on it. Or, should I say, that require it. Altogether, I call them Lambda functions. We will be covering them individually, and they are as follows:

- LAMBDA
- BYCOL
- BYROW
- MAKEARRAY
- MAP
- REDUCE
- SCAN

Let's begin with the LAMBDA function itself. Understanding it makes it easier to understand the other functions that rely on it.

LAMBDA

LAMBDA is a function that allows Excel users to create their own functions, which are callable just like the in-built functions in Excel. The function syntax is LAMBDA([parameter1], [paramter2],..,calculation). The syntax looks backward as the optional parts come before the non-optional part. The calculation is a compulsory argument to provide while you specify zero, one, or more than one parameters as input for the calculation.

A simple illustration is a Lambda formula to calculate the area of a rectangle. We all know that the area of a rectangle is simply the length multiplied by the breadth. So we can put this in a Lambda function as =LAMBDA(length,breadth,length*breadth). Then, we have to call this formula and pass it the values for length and breadth. This is where people find Lambda different from all the other Excel functions. You have three general ways of calling Lambda:

- Pass the values as a suffix to the Lambda formula but within parentheses
- Call it as a function after saving the Lambda formula as a named range
- Call the formula within any function that requires a Lambda function

We will demonstrate the first and the second ways in the next paragraphs, while the third way is how all the other functions we will cover work. First, we start by passing the values as a suffix to the Lambda formula: =LAMBDA(length,breadth,length*breadth)(4,6).

See the implementation in the following screenshot:

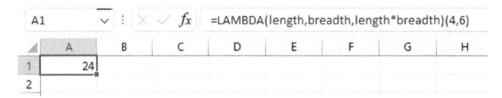

Figure 7.27 – Lambda entered directly into a cell alongside its parameter values

We'll now explore how to leverage a named range in making the LAMBDA a callable custom function. This requires saving =LAMBDA(length,breadth,length*breadth) as a named range. We will call it **Area** and the following screenshot shows the implementation:

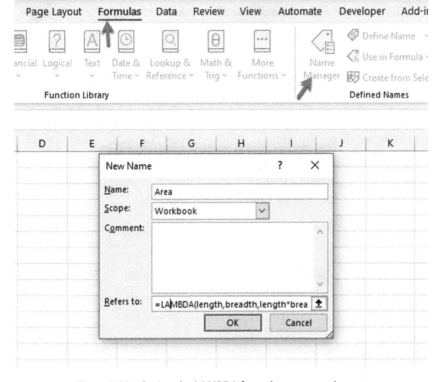

Figure 7.28 – Saving the LAMBDA formula as a named range

Now we can call the function, **Area**, anywhere in the workbook as we would the native Excel functions. See the example in the following screenshot of calling it with values of **10** for length and **5** for breadth. The formula extract is =Area(10,5):

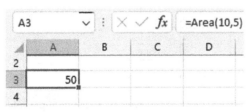

Figure 7.29 – Calling the LAMBDA function as a custom function

Try out the LAMBDA function for something else all by yourself and experience the joy of creating your very own custom function.

That brings us to the end for Lambda. We will now proceed to the next function: **BYCOL**.

BYCOL

BYCOL is a Lambda function that computes column-wise, applying a given Lambda formula across each column in a selected range. The syntax is BYCOL(array, LAMBDA_function).

We can run BYCOL to get average unit quantities and average unit prices from a daily sales table such as the one shown in the following figure. The formula extract is =BYCOL(B2:C17, LAMBDA(array, AVERAGE(array))):

F2				f_x	=BYCOL(B2:C17,LAMBDA(array,AVERAGE(array)))		

	A	B	C	D	E	F	G
1	Product	Quantity	Unit Price			Average Qty	Average Price
2	BBQ Chicken	8	$9.00			10.0625	10.125
3	Hot Veggie	8	$15.00				
4	Italiano	10	$9.00				
5	Pepperoni Suya	12	$9.00				
6	Veggie Supreme	10	$12.00				
7	Hot Pepperoni Feas	10	$9.00				
8	Pepperoni Feast	16	$12.00				
9	Meatzaa	9	$9.00				
10	Extravaganza	12	$9.00				
11	BBQ Philly Steak	5	$9.00				
12	Chicken Feast	12	$12.00				
13	Chicken Suya	15	$9.00				
14	Chicken Legend	12	$12.00				
15	Beef Suya	5	$9.00				
16	Margarita	9	$9.00				
17	Chicken Bali	8	$9.00				

Figure 7.30 – BYCOL to compute the average across multiple columns at once

BYCOL is that simple and makes your knowledge of Lambda more relevant as you make computations for entire tables that must result in a row of one result per column. We will now move on to the next Lambda function to cover: **BYROW**.

BYROW

BYROW is very much like the BYCOL function except that it computes each row of data in the supplied range. We can, then, define BYROW as a Lambda function that computes row-wise, applying a given Lambda formula across each row in a selected range. The syntax is BYROW(array,LAMBDA_function).

Running **BYROW** on the same product table we used for the BYCOL demonstration makes it possible for us to compute the sales amount (the quantity multiplied by the price) in one formula. The formula is =BYROW(B2:C17,LAMBDA(array,PRODUCT(array))).

The following screenshot illustrates the outcome of BYROW on the sales table for product-wise total sales computation:

	A	B	C	D	E	F	G
1	Product	Quantity	Unit Price				
2	BBQ Chicken	8	$9.00			72	
3	Hot Veggie	8	$15.00			120	
4	Italiano	10	$9.00			90	
5	Pepperoni Suya	12	$9.00			108	
6	Veggie Supreme	10	$12.00			120	
7	Hot Pepperoni Feas	10	$9.00			90	
8	Pepperoni Feast	16	$12.00			192	
9	Meatzaa	9	$9.00			81	
10	Extravaganza	12	$9.00			108	
11	BBQ Philly Steak	5	$9.00			45	
12	Chicken Feast	12	$12.00			144	
13	Chicken Suya	15	$9.00			135	
14	Chicken Legend	12	$12.00			144	
15	Beef Suya	5	$9.00			45	
16	Margarita	9	$9.00			81	
17	Chicken Bali	8	$9.00			72	

Cell reference: F2, formula: =BYROW(B2:C17,LAMBDA(array,PRODUCT(array)))

Figure 7.31 – BYROW to compute the sales amount for all products in one formula

That will be all for **BYROW**. We'll move on now to the next Lambda function: **MAKEARRAY**.

MAKEARRAY

MAKEARRAY is a Lambda function that generates an array of specified dimensions, based on a given LAMBDA formula. If all this sounds confusing, just think of it as a function that allows you to input the number of rows, the number of columns, and the formula that should work across those rows and columns. The function syntax is MAKEARRAY(rows,columns,LAMBDA(row,column,calculation)).

A simple example is a formula to generate a multiplication table:
`=MAKEARRAY(12,12,LAMBDA(row,column,row*column))`. You can read the formula as making an array of 12 rows and 12 columns, and for each combination of row and column, multiply the row value by the column value. The following screenshot shows the output:

A1				fx	=MAKEARRAY(12,12,LAMBDA(row,column,row*column))						
	A	B	C	D	E	F	G	H	I	J	K	L
1	1	2	3	4	5	6	7	8	9	10	11	12
2	2	4	6	8	10	12	14	16	18	20	22	24
3	3	6	9	12	15	18	21	24	27	30	33	36
4	4	8	12	16	20	24	28	32	36	40	44	48
5	5	10	15	20	25	30	35	40	45	50	55	60
6	6	12	18	24	30	36	42	48	54	60	66	72
7	7	14	21	28	35	42	49	56	63	70	77	84
8	8	16	24	32	40	48	56	64	72	80	88	96
9	9	18	27	36	45	54	63	72	81	90	99	108
10	10	20	30	40	50	60	70	80	90	100	110	120
11	11	22	33	44	55	66	77	88	99	110	121	132
12	12	24	36	48	60	72	84	96	108	120	132	144

Figure 7.32 – MAKEARRAY to generate a multiplication table

You can also make the Lambda formula within the MAKEARRAY reference other cells in the sheet for input. And you don't have to use the two parameters or even any of the parameters supplied to Lambda in the calculation. The following is an example of using MAKEARRAY to create 10 rows and 3 columns, with each column repeating a color name. Notice that we only used the `column` parameter in the Lambda calculation and we made reference to cells not part of the MAKEARRAY output cells. The formula extract is `=MAKEARRAY(10,3,LAMBDA(r,c,INDEX(F1:F3,c)))`:

A1			fx	=MAKEARRAY(10,3,LAMBDA(r,c,INDEX(F1:F3,c)))			
	A	B	C	D	E	F	G	H
1	Red	Green	Yellow			Red		
2	Red	Green	Yellow			Green		
3	Red	Green	Yellow			Yellow		
4	Red	Green	Yellow					
5	Red	Green	Yellow					
6	Red	Green	Yellow					
7	Red	Green	Yellow					
8	Red	Green	Yellow					
9	Red	Green	Yellow					
10	Red	Green	Yellow					
11								

Figure 7.33 – MAKEARRAY to generate columns of color names

That wraps up the coverage of MAKEARRAY. We will now move on to the next Lambda function: **MAP**.

MAP

MAP is a Lambda function that applies Lambda to every cell in a given range. The syntax is MAP(array1, [array2], ...LAMBDA(array, calculation)). A MAP formula to square every number in a supplied range is =MAP(A1:E8, LAMBDA(array, array^2)) and the output is shown in the following screenshot:

	A	B	C	D	E	F	G	H	I	J	K	L
								=MAP(A1:E8,LAMBDA(array,array^2))				
1	12	3	8	4	6			144	9	64	16	36
2	3	9	3	10	3			9	81	9	100	9
3	11	11	4	3	3			121	121	16	9	9
4	6	6	10	4	6			36	36	100	16	36
5	6	11	7	10	3			36	121	49	100	9
6	5	9	7	8	6			25	81	49	64	36
7	5	1	5	2	7			25	1	25	4	49
8	6	8	3	8	9			36	64	9	64	81
9												
10												

Figure 7.34 – MAP to square every value in a range

However, where many people find **MAP** useful is in carrying out a conditional check on the original values. Think of having a table of scores or KPI values and wanting to extract just the ones that meet a set benchmark. As an example, we will use MAP to extract values that are 5 and above from the same table used in the previous example. The formula extract is =MAP(A1:E8, LAMBDA(array, IF(array>=5, array, 0))):

	A	B	C	D	E	F	G	H	I	J	K	L
								=MAP(A1:E8,LAMBDA(array,IF(array>=5,array,0)))				
1	12	3	8	4	6			12	0	8	0	6
2	3	9	3	10	3			0	9	0	10	0
3	11	11	4	3	3			11	11	0	0	0
4	6	6	10	4	6			6	6	10	0	6
5	6	11	7	10	3			6	11	7	10	0
6	5	9	7	8	6			5	9	7	8	6
7	5	1	5	2	7			5	0	5	0	7
8	6	8	3	8	9			6	8	0	8	9

Figure 7.35 – MAP to extract values that meet a specific condition

And that ends our coverage of the MAP function. We'll move on to the next Lambda function: **REDUCE**.

REDUCE

REDUCE is a Lambda function that iterates through a provided range and carries out a calculation that outputs one value that is an accumulation of all the iterations. The syntax is REDUCE([initial_value], array, lambda(accumulator, value)), where accumulator is the result from the previous iteration and initial_value is the first value the accumulator is assigned at the start.

Using the same data we used for the MAP function demonstration, we can use **REDUCE** to compute the total of all the values by iterating through each value and adding up the numbers until the end. The formula to achieve this is =REDUCE(0,A1:E8,LAMBDA(a,v,a+v)) and the output is shown in the following screenshot:

	A	B	C	D	E	F	G	H
H1				=REDUCE(0,A1:E8,LAMBDA(a,v,a+v))				
1	12	3	8	4	6			251
2	3	9	3	10	3			
3	11	11	4	3	3			
4	6	6	10	4	6			
5	6	11	7	10	3			
6	5	9	7	8	6			
7	5	1	5	2	7			
8	6	8	3	8	9			
9								

Figure 7.36 – REDUCE to iterate over a range and total the values

And like we did with MAP, we can decide to sum up just values that are greater than or equal to 5. The formula is =REDUCE(0,A1:E8,LAMBDA(a,v,IF(v>=5,a+v,a))) and the output is shown in the following screenshot:

	A	B	C	D	E	F	G	H
H1				=REDUCE(0,A1:E8,LAMBDA(a,v,IF(v>=5,a+v,a)))				
1	12	3	8	4	6			212
2	3	9	3	10	3			
3	11	11	4	3	3			
4	6	6	10	4	6			
5	6	11	7	10	3			
6	5	9	7	8	6			
7	5	1	5	2	7			
8	6	8	3	8	9			

Figure 7.37 – REDUCE to sum all values that are equal to or greater than 5

And with that, we are done with **REDUCE** and will move on to the next Lambda function: SCAN.

SCAN

SCAN is a Lambda function that iterates through a provided range, carrying out a Lambda-based calculation and outputting the intermediate results. It is very much like REDUCE in syntax but instead of outputting one final answer, it outputs intermediate results. This makes it useful for calculations such as running totals. The function syntax is SCAN([initial_value], array, lambda(accumulator, value)).

Using **SCAN** on the same table of values as we did for REDUCE, the syntax is the same – only REDUCE is replaced by SCAN. For the total use case, SCAN gives us the running total. The formula extract is =SCAN(0,A1:E8,LAMBDA(a,v,a+v)) and the output is displayed in the following screenshot:

H1			fx	=SCAN(0,A1:E8,LAMBDA(a,v,a+v))							
	A	B	C	D	E	F	G	H	I	J	K	L
1	12	3	8	4	6			12	15	23	27	33
2	3	9	3	10	3			36	45	48	58	61
3	11	11	4	3	3			72	83	87	90	93
4	6	6	10	4	6			99	105	115	119	125
5	6	11	7	10	3			131	142	149	159	162
6	5	9	7	8	6			167	176	183	191	197
7	5	1	5	2	7			202	203	208	210	217
8	6	8	3	8	9			223	231	234	242	251

Figure 7.38 – SCAN to get the running total on a range

And for the total when the value is equal to or greater than 5, we get a running total that skips all values less than 5. The formula extract is =SCAN(0,A1:E8,LAMBDA(a,v,IF(v>=5,a+v,a))). The output is shown in the following screenshot:

H1			fx	=SCAN(0,A1:E8,LAMBDA(a,v,IF(v>=5,a+v,a)))							
	A	B	C	D	E	F	G	H	I	J	K	L
1	12	3	8	4	6			12	12	20	20	26
2	3	9	3	10	3			26	35	35	45	45
3	11	11	4	3	3			56	67	67	67	67
4	6	6	10	4	6			73	79	89	89	95
5	6	11	7	10	3			101	112	119	129	129
6	5	9	7	8	6			134	143	150	158	164
7	5	1	5	2	7			169	169	174	174	181
8	6	8	3	8	9			187	195	195	203	212

Figure 7.39 – SCAN to carry out a conditional running total

That wraps up the section on Lambda functions. You have now experienced their flexibility and unique syntax. You will find them useful in achieving very robust and fully automated dashboards. Just be aware that not all Excel users have Excel 365. For reports and dashboards that are to be consumed by members of your organization, it is important to verify the version of Excel everyone is using is Excel 365. Luckily, most companies deploy the same Excel version for all users.

Summary

This chapter has been a very interesting one as we covered some of the new types of functions in Excel. The dynamic array functions were game-changing when they were released. They made a lot of computations and reports easy that were previously only possible via VBA and a complex setup of a pivot table. Also, the formula engine update that came along with it, giving all formulas in Excel the ability to spill into multiple cells, was in itself a bigger deal than the new dynamic array functions. Now, we can use old formulas such as SUM and COUNTIF in a way that outputs into multiple cells. And more recently, another type of function has surfaced in Excel: Lambda functions. They allow Excel users to create custom functions and do things that used to be only possible with VBA or a dizzying cocktail of functions. On the surface, they look simple and are easily replaced by other existing functions, but when you leverage the custom function capabilities of Lambda and the dynamic array capabilities in Excel 365, you can achieve the seemingly impossible with these Lambda functions.

In the next chapter, we will cover Excel charts and take an in-depth look at the 19 natively available charts in Excel.

Part 3 – Getting the Visualization Right

This part completes the dashboard-building process. You'll get to understand the foundational data modeling and visual layout setup for dashboards, which is a critical aspect of building a dashboard.

This part has the following chapters:

- *Chapter 8, Getting Comfortable with the 19 Excel Charts*
- *Chapter 9, Non-Chart Visuals*
- *Chapter 10, Setting Up the Dashboard's Data Model*
- *Chapter 11, Perfecting the Dashboard*
- *Chapter 12, Best Practices for Real-World Dashboard Building*

Getting Comfortable with the 19 Excel Charts

Excel 365 has 19 chart types, and some of these charts were added as recently as six years ago. Charts are very important and form the core of most of the data visualization that happens within Excel. Building dashboards in Excel requires ample use of visualization tools, from charts to slicers and conditional formatting.

For over 20 years, Excel had no more than 11 chart types, but the number of charts has almost doubled in the last seven years. This is a reflection of the very important role charts now play in modern reports and dashboards. A lot of charts that used to be very difficult to create in Excel are now possible.

The goal of this chapter is to give you the requisite knowledge of the different charts within Excel, what each type is best used for, and how to create beautiful charts that powerfully present the insights of your reports or dashboards.

In this chapter, we will be covering all 19 chart types:

- Column chart
- Bar chart
- Line chart
- Area chart
- Pie chart
- Doughnut chart
- XY (scatter) chart
- Bubble chart
- Stock chart
- Surface chart
- Radar chart
- Treemap chart

- Sunburst chart
- Histogram chart
- Box and whisker chart
- Waterfall chart
- Funnel chart
- Filled map chart
- Combo chart

Column chart

The column chart is the most used chart type in Excel. It is a great visual representation of numerical values against a few categories or labels, depicting the numerical values with vertical bars against a horizontal axis. Think of showing sales value against regions, or expenses incurred against expense categories. As long as the categories to represent visually are not over a dozen, a column chart often works nicely. It has the dual advantage of being easy to create and easy to read. The following screenshot shows an example of a column chart showing sales across five regions:

Region	Sales
North America	$ 710,000,000
Europe	$ 489,000,000
Australia	$ 438,000,000
Asia	$ 684,000,000
Africa	$ 315,000,000

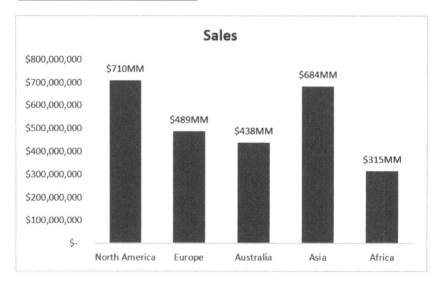

Figure 8.1 – Column chart showing company sales across five regions

Once you've decided to go with a column chart, based on your data and the insights you want to graphically present, the next important task is the design of the chart. A column chart can be created as a clustered column chart, a stacked column chart, or a 100% stacked column chart. Oftentimes, only one type will be appropriate to use, so you have to know when to use each type. See the following screenshot on how Excel presents the three chart types:

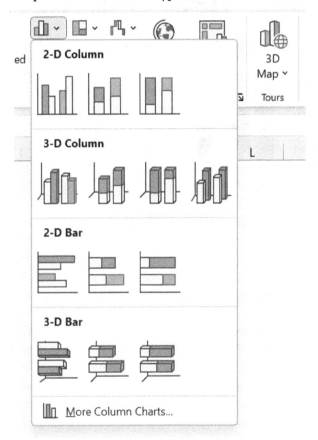

Figure 8.2 – Clustered, stacked, and 100% stacked column chart types

A clustered column chart shows every data point as a standalone bar and is the ideal choice for data series that have no breakdowns (usually just one set of labels against one set of values). *Figure 8.1* is an example of a data series with no breakdown. It is also a great choice for data series that show multiple data points for each label and that cannot be considered as breakdowns. The following screenshot is an example of sales and expenses by region. Since sales and expenses are not combinatory, they are better illustrated as standalone bars:

Region	Sales	Expenses
North America	$ 710,000,000	$ 641,131,716
Europe	$ 489,000,000	$ 148,236,925
Australia	$ 438,000,000	$ 155,322,744
Asia	$ 684,000,000	$ 184,866,041
Africa	$ 315,000,000	$ 234,567,373

Figure 8.3 – Sales and expenses clustered column chart

A clustered column chart can also be used for series that have breakdowns – an example is sales broken down by month across five different regions. See *Figure 8.4* for such an example, plotted on a clustered column chart:

Region	Jan-24	Feb-24	Mar-24
North America	$ 710,000,000	$ 843,092,165	$ 438,589,880
Europe	$ 489,000,000	$ 237,092,159	$ 375,443,219
Australia	$ 438,000,000	$ 234,365,723	$ 259,189,603
Asia	$ 684,000,000	$ 308,983,322	$ 870,097,458
Africa	$ 315,000,000	$ 114,943,205	$ 340,448,317

Figure 8.4 – Monthly sales by region displayed as a clustered column chart

A stacked column chart is specifically for data series that have breakdowns. It allows the report user to see the total value and the breakdown at the same time. *Figure 8.5* shows the stack column chart for the same monthly sales by region data:

Region	Jan-24	Feb-24	Mar-24
North America	$ 710,000,000	$ 843,092,165	$ 438,589,880
Europe	$ 489,000,000	$ 237,092,159	$ 375,443,219
Australia	$ 438,000,000	$ 234,365,723	$ 259,189,603
Asia	$ 684,000,000	$ 308,983,322	$ 870,097,458
Africa	$ 315,000,000	$ 114,943,205	$ 340,448,317

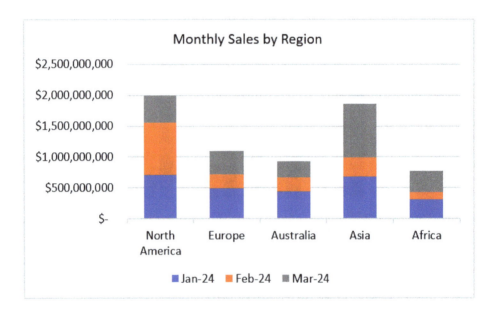

Figure 8.5 – Monthly sales by region displayed on a stacked column chart

A 100% stacked column chart is a variant of the stacked column chart that shows relative contribution rather than absolute values. It always displays a bar that is pegged at 100% but is divided into segments that reflect the relative contributions of the breakdown categories to the overall value for each label. It is often used as a substitute for pie charts and doughnut charts when multiple series must be displayed in one chart. *Figure 8.6* shows a 100% stacked column chart with the sales for the first three months of the year by region for a company:

Region	Jan-24	Feb-24	Mar-24
North Ame	$710,000,000	$843,092,165	$438,589,880
Europe	$489,000,000	$237,092,159	$375,443,219
Australia	$438,000,000	$234,365,723	$259,189,603
Asia	$684,000,000	$308,983,322	$870,097,458
Africa	$315,000,000	$114,943,205	$340,448,317

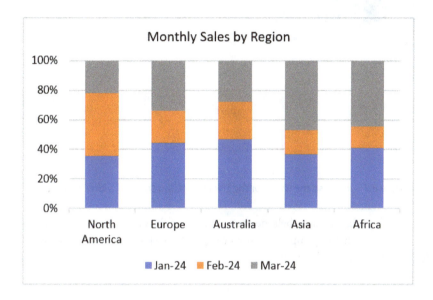

Figure 8.6 – Example of a 100% stacked column chart

Other charts that have these three options are line charts and bar charts. We won't repeat these explanations for them but keep in mind that they also have these clustered, stacked, and 100% stacked options.

You should always improve the look of the default chart that comes up when you insert the column chart in Excel. There are a few tricks to easily enhance the default look:

1. Increase the width of the bars by right-clicking on one of the bars, selecting **Format Data Series**, and setting **Gap Width** to 100%. See the following screenshot for an illustration of the steps:

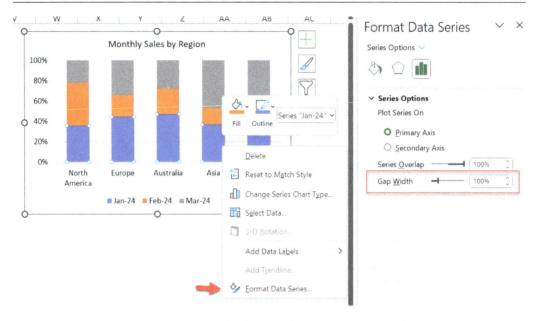

Figure 8.7 – Increase the width of the bars by setting the gap width to 100%

2. If you can neatly add the data labels, do that and turn off the gridlines. The options are accessible via the green plus that pops up in the upper right of the chart when the chart is selected. See the following screenshot for an illustration:

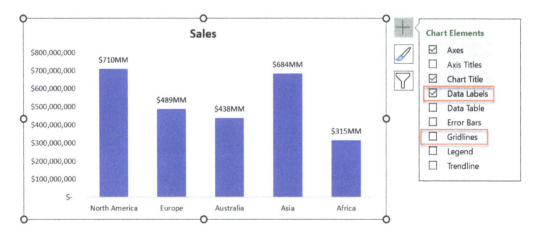

Figure 8.8 – Turning on data labels and turning off gridlines

3. Change the default colors to better ones or ones that align with the company's brand. You can use external sites, such as coolors.co, to get beautiful matching colors.

And with that, we have come to the end of the section on column charts. Do remember that it is the most used chart in Excel and it's very important that you are comfortable creating it.

Bar chart

A bar chart is a variant of a column chart – same use case and same design options. The main difference is that a bar chart has horizontal bars while a column chart has vertical bars. Bar charts can be a more user-friendly chart to use when you have long axis labels and making them show in the horizontal orientation is far better than having them slant at an angle. In *Figure 8.9*, you'll see how a bar chart handles long axis labels compared to how a column chart handles the same in *Figure 8.10*:

Figure 8.9 – Good handling of long axis labels by a bar chart

The handling of the same long axis label by a column chart is shown as follows. Do, however, note that if the width of the column chart is made wider, it may eventually display the labels horizontally as preferred:

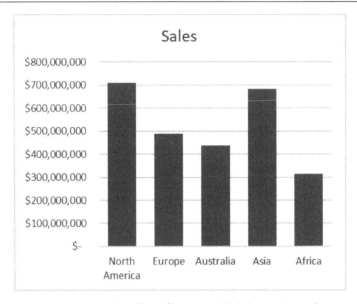

Figure 8.10 – Poor handling of long axis labels by a column chart

Another advantage of a bar chart is that for instances when you want to use an icon or image in the bars, it may look more natural to stack the images horizontally as a bar chart would do rather than vertically as a column chart would do.

To demonstrate this difference, we are going to learn how to use icons or images in the bars for both column charts and bar charts. The first step is to get the image to be used. We will use the icons that are accessible from within Microsoft Excel. All you need to do is go to the **Insert** menu and click on **Icons**, as shown in *Figure 8.11*:

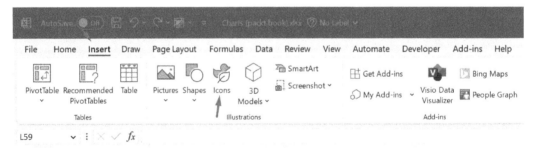

Figure 8.11 – Access icons within Microsoft Excel

Once the search window for icons comes up, type bags so we can grab a bag icon, assuming the sales we are reporting are for a company that retails bags. Select one of the icons and hit **Insert (1)** in the bottom right, as shown in *Figure 8.12*:

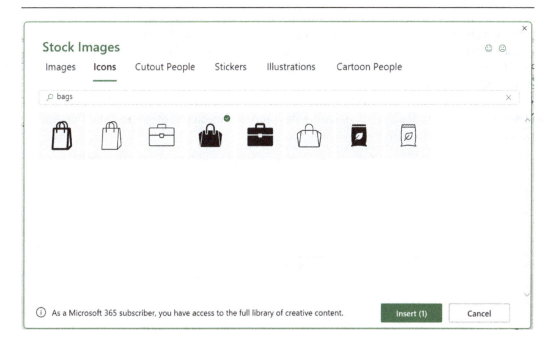

Figure 8.12 – Inserting an icon in Excel

We now have an icon we will use in place of the solid color bars that come by default when we create column and bar charts. Select the icon, right-click on it, and set its fill color to purple, as shown in *Figure 8.13*:

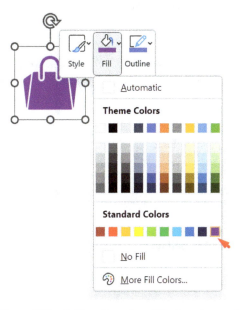

Figure 8.13 – Setting the color of the icon to purple

All that is left is to right-click on the icon and copy (you can also use *Ctrl + C* to do the copying), then select any of the chart bars and paste. That will instantly replace the solid bars with the icon or image copied (works also for pictures, not just icons). The default layout will have the icon stretched; you can easily adjust the settings to one that stacks multiple copies of the icon, which often is better. You achieve that by right-clicking on the bar, selecting **Format Data Series**, expanding the **Fill** options, and setting the layout to **Stack**. You can see the steps and the outcome in the following screenshot:

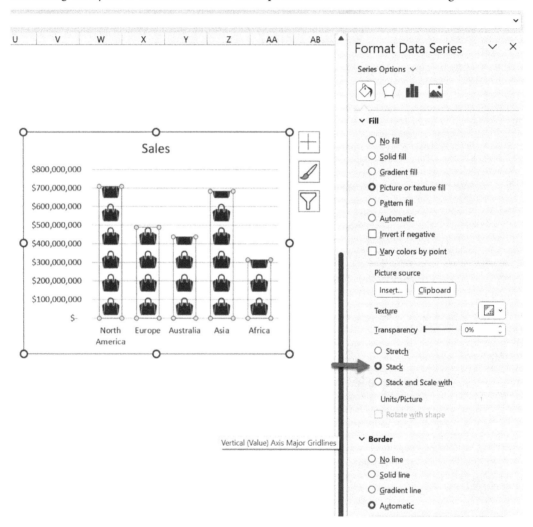

Figure 8.14 – Setting the icons to the stack layout

Now that you know how to create column and bar charts that use icons or images in place of the solid color fill for the bars, we are going to see how the bar chart looks compared to the column chart for the same icon fill. *Figure 8.15* shows the comparison:

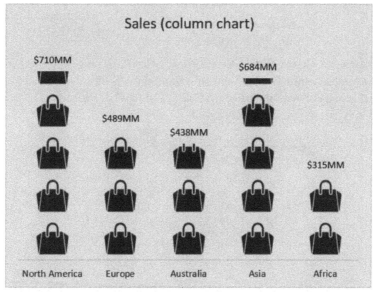

Figure 8.15 – Column chart versus bar chart for icon/image fill

You'll likely agree with me that the bar chart looks better than the column chart. Besides those cosmetic differences, column and bar charts are the same.

We will now go on to the next chart type.

Line chart

A line chart shows trends – how a metric performs over a date/time range. It is, perhaps, the second most used chart after the column chart. It's the same process you're already familiar with for creating column and bar charts. It also has the clustered, stacked, and 100% stacked options. *Figure 8.16* shows an example of a line chart to visualize yearly sales for a company:

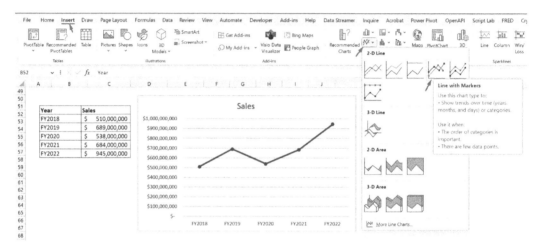

Figure 8.16 – Line chart of yearly sales

You will notice that, in addition to a plain line chart option, there's a **Line with Markers** option. We have selected the clustered line with markers option for the chart in *Figure 8.16*.

Something to note about the line chart is that the trendline chart element display option it has can be more relevant than in the column and bar charts. Trendlines are meaningful for seeing the general trend of performance over time, so it is naturally relevant for line charts that already show the performance of a metric over time. For column and bar charts, the trendlines are not always meaningful when you have charts plotting non-time series data. In *Figure 8.17*, you'll see the trendline enabled for a line chart:

Figure 8.17 – Line chart with trendline enabled

Line charts are also an excellent way to show the comparison between two related metrics. An example is showing sales and corresponding expenses over the years. Unlike a column and bar chart, both the relative performance and trend are instantly visible to the user in one chart. See *Figure 8.18* for such an example:

Year	Sales	Expenses
FY2018	$ 510,000,000	$ 275,000,000
FY2019	$ 689,000,000	$ 190,000,000
FY2020	$ 538,000,000	$ 238,000,000
FY2021	$ 684,000,000	$ 232,000,000
FY2022	$ 945,000,000	$ 362,000,000

Figure 8.18 – Line chart to show sales and expenses over a time period

Lastly, you would want to be careful using stacked and 100% stacked line charts as they can be misleading and difficult to read properly for report users. See *Figure 8.19* for a stacked chart of the same data used for *Figure 8.18*. Notice that it makes the expenses look higher than the sales, which is not correct:

Year	Sales	Expenses
FY2018	$ 510,000,000	$ 275,000,000
FY2019	$ 689,000,000	$ 190,000,000
FY2020	$ 538,000,000	$ 238,000,000
FY2021	$ 684,000,000	$ 232,000,000
FY2022	$ 945,000,000	$ 362,000,000

Figure 8.19 – Stacked line chart

A line chart shares a lot of options and design settings with column and bar charts, so we will not be repeating those settings options to prevent the book from becoming too wordy and tiresome to read. We will now go on to the next chart.

Area chart

An area chart is essentially a line chart with the section below the line shaded or color-filled. This can be very useful when you want to emphasize both the absolute value of a time series and the trend pattern. The distinct fill below the line gives it a peak-and-trough design that makes it easy for users to recognize the absolute performance alongside the trend. The following screenshot shows an area chart for the same yearly sales data we plotted a line chart on earlier:

Year	Sales
FY2018	$ 510,000,000
FY2019	$ 689,000,000
FY2020	$ 538,000,000
FY2021	$ 684,000,000
FY2022	$ 945,000,000

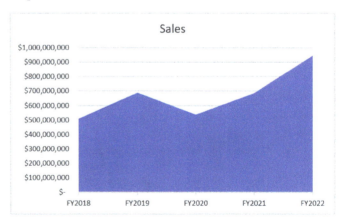

Figure 8.20 – Area chart of sales over a period

Things can be a bit tricky with using area charts for two or more metrics. See *Figure 8.21* of the area chart of sales and expenses. Notice that the user could be confused about the actual value of sales and likely interpret it wrongly as it is stacked on the expense chart:

Year	Sales	Expenses
FY2018	$ 510,000,000	$ 275,000,000
FY2019	$ 689,000,000	$ 190,000,000
FY2020	$ 538,000,000	$ 238,000,000
FY2021	$ 684,000,000	$ 232,000,000
FY2022	$ 945,000,000	$ 362,000,000

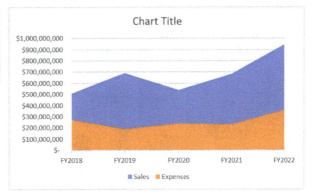

Figure 8.21 – Area chart of sales and expenses

We will move on, now, to another chart.

Pie chart

A pie chart is a chart used to show the relative (often percentage-wise) breakdown of a measure by related categories. An example is a pie chart of sales broken down by contributing regions, as shown in the following screenshot:

Region	Sales
North America	$ 710,000,000
Europe	$ 489,000,000
Australia	$ 438,000,000
Asia	$ 684,000,000
Africa	$ 315,000,000

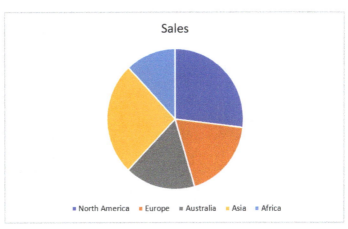

Figure 8.22 – Pie chart of sales by region

An obvious problem with the pie chart is that the default design you get from Excel is not user-friendly. It has two major problems: it gives no clear indication of the values of each category and you have to match the colors to the categories. However, there is a quick fix. Select the chart, go to **Chart Design**, click on **Quick Layout**, and select **Layout 1**. The outcome is shown in *Figure 8.23*. Notice that the two issues mentioned earlier with the default chart have been addressed in this layout choice. The values are visible and the categories have their names displayed on their pie piece:

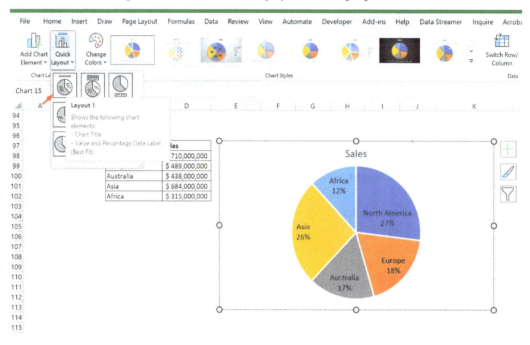

Figure 8.23 – Pie chart showing quick layout improvement

Pie charts, when done right, are very easy to interpret by users and can be an excellent way to convene insights about the relative contribution of segments to an important metric. You may have come across self-proclaimed visualizations experts who advise against ever using a pie chart. As a business-supporting data analyst, you should care more about your report users than possible criticism from peers. There will be numerous occasions when a pie chart will be the best chart for giving insights to the user. Personally, I find that when creating charts and analyses that will be printed and circulated to an unsophisticated audience, pie charts are a more engaging way to show actionable insights relating to contributions to a measure. In educating the general public on the importance of personal hygiene, a pie chart of the ratio of hospital admissions due to hygiene-negligence-related versus non-hygiene-negligence-related admissions is preferable to using a column chart or another non-pie family of charts.

Lastly, pie charts cannot show more than one set of relative contributions. If you need to show sales broken down by region for multiple years or any dataset with multiple sets of breakdowns, you either create a pie chart per breakdown set or use a 100% stacked column/bar chart. An example of using a pie chart for multiple sets of breakdowns follows. In the following screenshot, notice how the resulting pie chart does not capture all the sets of periods:

Region	2021 Sales	2022 Sales	2023 Sales
North America	$ 710,000,000	$ 755,000,000	$ 839,000,000
Europe	$ 489,000,000	$ 762,000,000	$ 551,000,000
Australia	$ 438,000,000	$ 700,000,000	$ 560,000,000
Asia	$ 684,000,000	$ 531,000,000	$ 755,000,000
Africa	$ 315,000,000	$ 761,000,000	$ 667,000,000

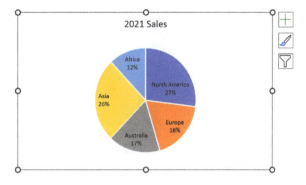

Figure 8.24 – Pie chart showing multiple sets of breakdowns

When we use a 100% stacked column chart, we get a more meaningful outcome that captures all the sets of breakdowns. See the following screenshot for the 100% stacked column chart outcome:

Region	2021 Sales	2022 Sales	2023 Sales
North America	$ 710,000,000	$ 755,000,000	$ 839,000,000
Europe	$ 489,000,000	$ 762,000,000	$ 551,000,000
Australia	$ 438,000,000	$ 700,000,000	$ 560,000,000
Asia	$ 684,000,000	$ 531,000,000	$ 755,000,000
Africa	$ 315,000,000	$ 761,000,000	$ 667,000,000

Figure 8.25 – 100% stacked column chart

We will now go on to the next chart.

Doughnut chart

A doughnut chart is like a pie chart with a big hole in the center. So, it is technically the same chart with applicable settings. The following screenshot is a doughnut chart of the same regional sales data used to demonstrate a pie chart:

Region	Sales
North America	$ 710,000,000
Europe	$ 489,000,000
Australia	$ 438,000,000
Asia	$ 684,000,000
Africa	$ 315,000,000

Figure 8.26 – Doughnut chart showing regional sales

Just like the pie chart, the default doughnut chart suffers some usability issues: no visible values for the categories and a color matching task. We can fix the issue by setting the layout to **Layout 1** as we did for the pie chart. See *Figure 8.27* for the outcome:

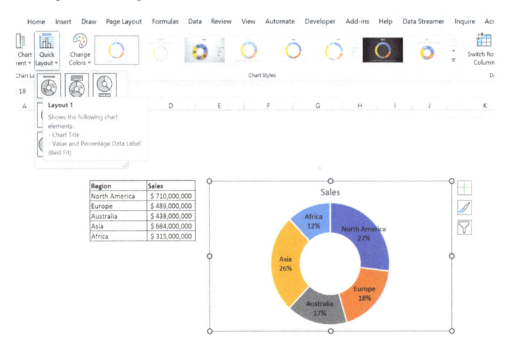

Figure 8.27 – Changing the default layout of the doughnut chart

Every other point we covered about the pie chart also applies to the doughnut chart. So, we will move on to the next chart.

XY (scatter) chart

The XY (scatter) chart, which we will begin to refer to as a scatter chart, is a relationship plot chart. It plots the relationship between two variables: the independent (X) variable and the dependent (Y) variable. A scatter chart is more popular in the research and academic space than in the business domain because most business users are looking for the performance of known metrics rather than trying to find the relationship between two metrics. So, you have to be careful when using this chart in the business domain: you should be able to confirm that the report users don't have a well-established interpretation of the relationship between the metrics and that there is business value in showing how the two metrics are related.

One more important thing to note when using a scatter chart is that it is a values-only chart, meaning the horizontal axis is not used to display labels but numerical values. You should never use a scatter chart to plot values against labels. If you have some values against years, even though years are numbers, you are not expected to create a scatter chart with years, dates, time, phone numbers, postal code numbers, or any identifier number as one of the axes. For those, use a line chart. A scatter chart is strictly for numerical values on both the vertical and horizontal axes.

Now that you are clear as to the type of data to use in a scatter chart, we will proceed to build the chart in Excel. An easy rule of thumb is to put the independent variable (X) series to the left of the dependent variable (Y) series, that is, make the X series come before the Y series in your table.

Figure 8.28 shows a scatter chart of ice cream sales against temperature. Notice how easy it is to see the relatedness between ice cream sales and the temperature on a given day:

Temperature (°C)	Ice Cream Sales
15	349
28	660
2	91
28	667
17	417
6	176
28	660
21	512
26	615
3	88
4	140
28	672
12	283
23	537
29	693
8	210
6	151
11	255
15	370
17	417
17	410
20	509
29	715
27	665
29	716
29	702
3	112
24	586
27	636
27	668
5	138

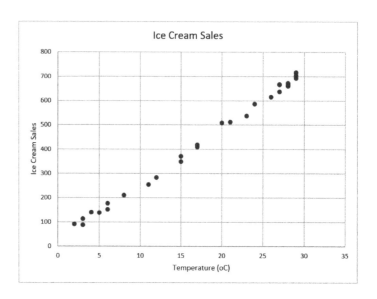

Figure 8.28 – Scatter chart of ice cream sales against temperature

You have many options of how you want the scatter chart to be displayed: dotted plot, straight line plot, curved line plot, or with markers. The options are shown in the following screenshot:

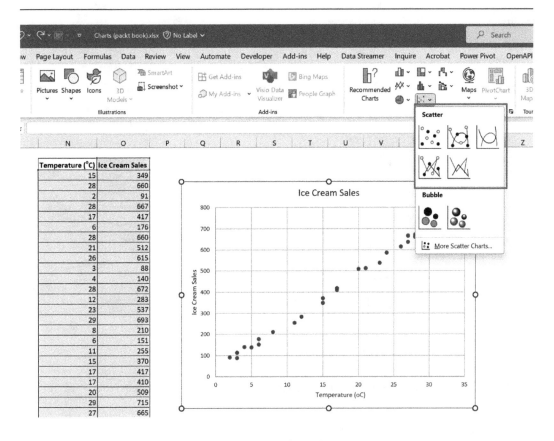

Figure 8.29 – Scatter chart plot options

Lastly, you can enable a trend line and display the equation that explains the relationship between the two variables. See *Figure 8.30* for this:

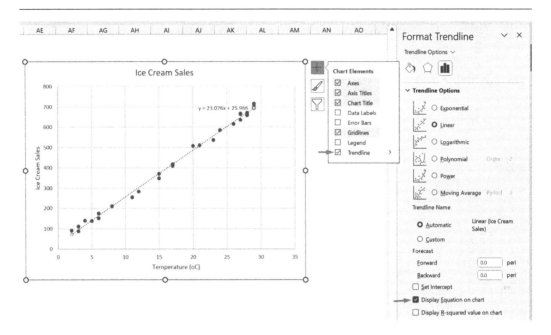

Figure 8.30 – Enabling a trendline on a scatter chart

With that, we conclude the section on scatter charts and move on to the next chart.

Bubble chart

A bubble chart is actually an XY (scatter) chart with a variable size dot marker. Some even consider it as an XYZ chart, which helps you visualize the relationship between three different variables.

Just like a scatter chart, you can only plot true numerical values and it is best to have them arranged as an X series before the Y series before the third (Z) series. The following screenshot shows a bubble chart for ice cream sales against temperature, and is inclusive of a third series, average order quantity:

Temperature (°C)	Ice Cream Sales	Average Order Quanity
15	349	2
28	660	1
2	91	5
12	321	3
17	417	2
6	176	4
28	660	1
21	512	2
26	615	1
3	88	5

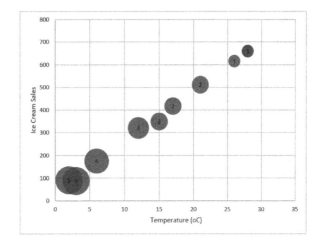

Figure 8.31 – Bubble chart of ice cream sales and order size by temperature

The major concern with a bubble chart is whether the audience will understand the interpretation easily. If you have an unsophisticated audience and you won't be there to explain the charts to them, you might want to use another easier-to-read chart.

And that's it about bubble charts; they are very much like scatter charts, so all we mentioned about scatter charts also applies: trendline and use only with numerical values. We will now go on to the next chart.

Stock chart

A stock chart is a niche chart in Excel and is mostly useful for displaying the price movement summary of financial market securities. It requires a strict table structure and may not be easy to read for those not accustomed to it.

Stock charts accept a four-table structure:

- **High-Low-Close**
- **Open-High-Low-Close**
- **Volume-High-Low-Close**
- **Volume-Open-High-Low-Close**

Figure 8.32 shows a stock chart with the **Open-High-Low-Close** table structure. The bars can be set to different colors:

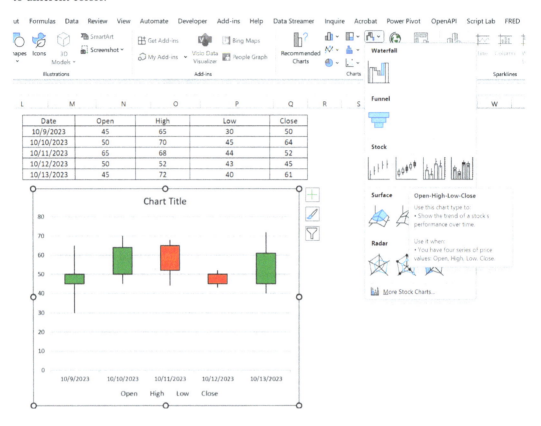

Figure 8.32 – Stock chart for the Open-High-Low-Close data series

We will move now to the next chart.

Surface chart

A surface chart is another niche chart used mostly in the research and academia domain. It is used to plot the relationship between two independent variables and one dependent variable. *Figure 8.33* shows sample data and the corresponding surface chart plot:

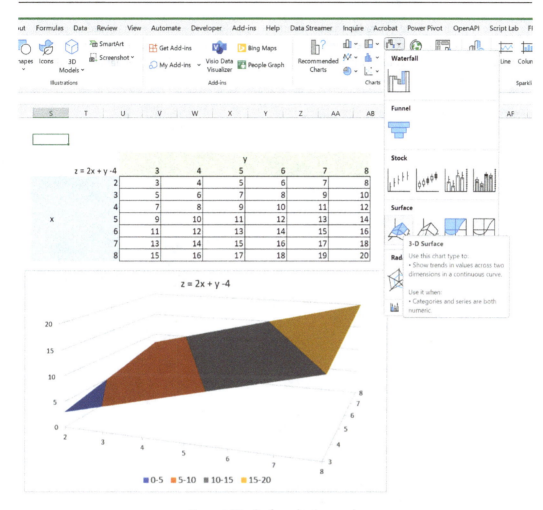

Figure 8.33 – Surface chart example

It is seldom used in the business domain and can be very difficult to interpret. Personally, I have only had to use it for visualizing a heuristic algorithm for academic purposes. It is predominantly used in the research and academic domain for visualizing three-dimensional relationships.

We will move on to the next chart.

Radar chart

A radar chart is a chart used for comparing different items across multiple range-bound numerical criteria. It is also known as a spider chart because of the weblike form it has. It is a very useful chart for decision-making, based on known criteria, with scores assigned to the items compared across each criterion.

An example of a relevant use of a radar chart is a comparison of two or more vendors based on criteria, such as quality of service, cost of service, support offering, and years of experience. A radar chart is perfectly suited for such comparisons, and the following screenshots show us what it looks like:

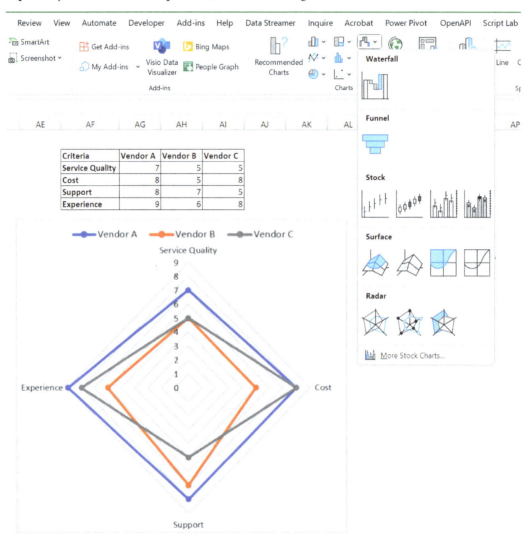

Figure 8.34 – Radar chart for vendor comparison

You will, however, want to be careful that you do not confuse the report users. If you sense that your report users will struggle to get the insights presented by the radar chart, you can switch to the more familiar column or bar chart to convene the same insights.

We will go on to explore the next chart.

Treemap chart

A treemap chart is a hierarchical chart that is relatively new in Excel. It can be used in place of a clustered column chart for just one set of values for a metric. It always arranges the category values in descending order. It also has the advantage of being space-optimal, adjusting very well to size changes. The following screenshot is an example of a treemap showing regional sales:

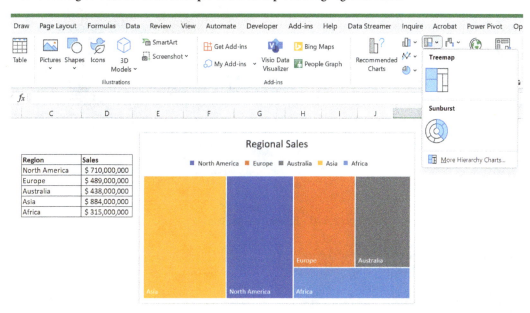

Figure 8.35 – Treemap chart of regional sales

Notice that the arrangement of the category values in the chart is in descending order and not in their natural order in the source table. That can be useful in a dashboard of changing data values, as it will always rearrange the category values in descending order.

Lastly, if we reduced the width of the chart, it would reshape its entire plot to make good use of the new size dimensions assigned to it. See the following screenshot for this size adjustment:

Region	Sales
North America	$ 710,000,000
Europe	$ 489,000,000
Australia	$ 438,000,000
Asia	$ 884,000,000
Africa	$ 315,000,000

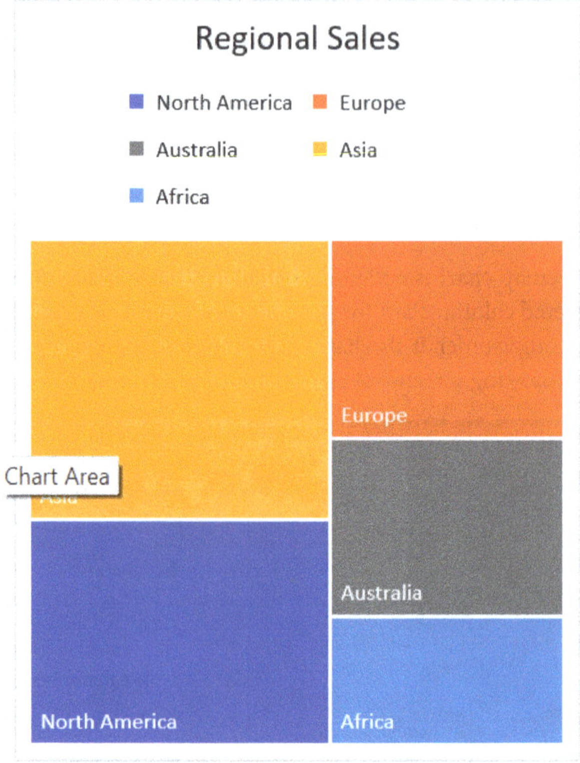

Figure 8.36 – Resized treemap chart

With that, we have come to the end of the treemap chart and will go on to the next chart.

Sunburst chart

Sunburst is another hierarchical chart, like the treemap chart, but it is meant to replace pie charts in some situations. Its hierarchical behavior and the ability to show multiple levels of granularity make it well suited for data that has two or more detail levels.

An example is to visualize sales by region broken down into constituent countries. See the following screenshot as an example:

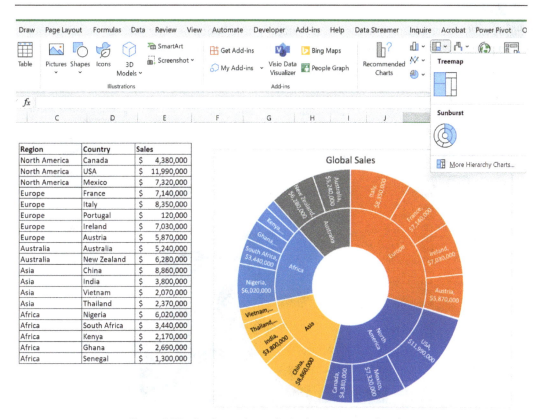

Figure 8.37 – Sunburst chart of sales by country and region

Notice how the regions and countries are not arranged in the same order as in the table; the largest values appear first. It also shows the regional level and then the country level in the same plot.

And that is it for the sunburst chart; we will move on to the next chart.

Histogram chart

The histogram chart is a niche chart mostly used to visualize the distribution of a set of values. If you have income data of over 200,000 people in your market catchment area, you might want to plot a histogram chart on the data to see the income brackets most people fall into. So, if you have sales data for the last quarter and you are trying to help the business set an appropriate order volume at which a discount promotion should kick in, a histogram will come in handy by showing you what that order volume target should be.

In *Figure 8.38*, we see a histogram used to visualize the distribution of order value across sales made within a particular period. This can be useful for a business to understand customers' purchase patterns:

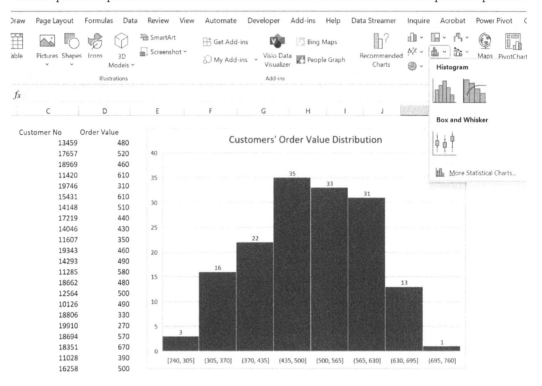

Figure 8.38 – Histogram to show sales order value distribution

That will be it for histograms; we will move on to the next chart.

Box and whisker chart

The box and whisker chart is a niche chart for visualizing statistical measures of central tendency – mean, median, outliers, and quartiles. This can be very difficult to read for an audience not accustomed to the chart and the measures, but in an academic or research environment, it may be the only way to convey all those vital details in one plot.

The following screenshot shows a box and whisker chart plot of a daily series of sales order values showing the outliers, mean, median, and quartiles. It can be a very rich source of insights for a statistician when describing order patterns:

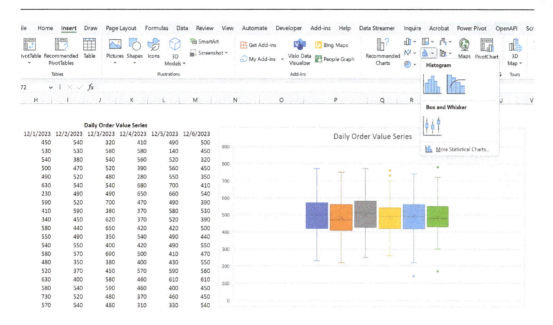

Figure 8.39 – Box and whisker chart of daily order values

That brings us to the end of the box and whisker chart; we will move on to the next chart.

Waterfall chart

A waterfall chart is a movement visualization chart, used very frequently in the finance domain to show cash flow or asset value movement from a period start to a period end. It is easy to read and can be the best way to present insights that involve showing a period start value, value changes, and a period end value.

Figure 8.40 is an example of a waterfall chart, showing a company's annual cash flow position inclusive of monthly movements:

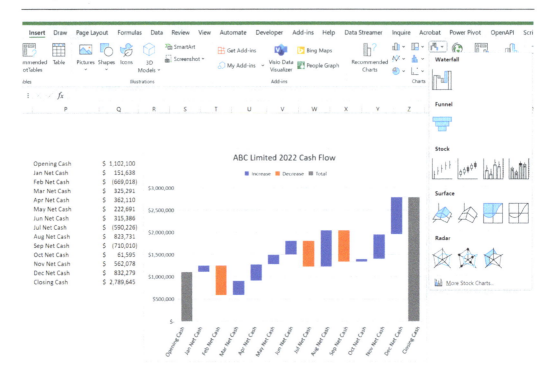

Figure 8.40 – Waterfall chart to show cash flow movements

One thing that you need to set every time you create a waterfall chart is the opening and closing bars differently from the movement bars. It is very easy to do. Just click twice on the opening or closing bar, right-click, pick **Format Data Point**, and then tick **Set as total**. See *Figure 8.41* for an illustration of the steps:

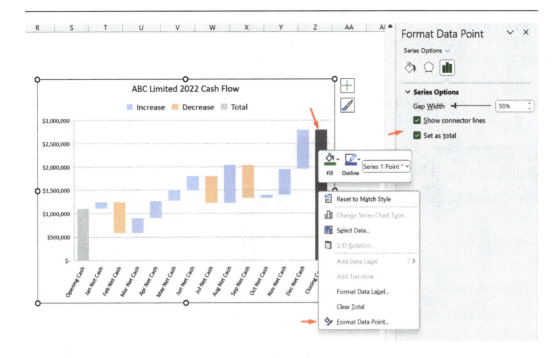

Figure 8.41 – Setting the opening and closing bars in a waterfall chart

With that, we have come to the end of the waterfall chart and will move on to the next chart type.

Funnel chart

A funnel chart is a niche chart showing the linearly linked stage performance for a metric. A classic example is the use of a funnel chart by marketing teams to show sales funnel conversion performance.

Figure 8.42 is an example of a funnel chart showing the sales conversion for a multi-stage marketing campaign:

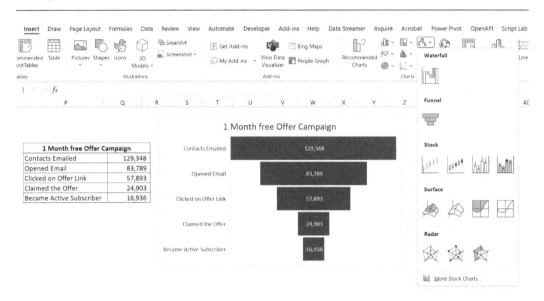

Figure 8.42 – Funnel chart showing the performance of an email marketing campaign

Funnel charts are easy to create and easy to understand even for non-sophisticated users. The trick is to ensure that you are using it to show insights about linked processes where each process will always have a value that is not greater than its preceding process.

That brings us to the end of funnel charts. We will move on to another chart.

Filled map chart

A filled map chart is a map chart that carves out the coverage areas of each geographical location supplied and uses a dark-to-light color fill to present the values for each location. It is a good chart to use for location-based data as it adds the geographical positioning insight that is lost when other chart types are used.

Figure 8.43 is an example of a filled map chart showing the sales for a retail company across different Canadian provinces:

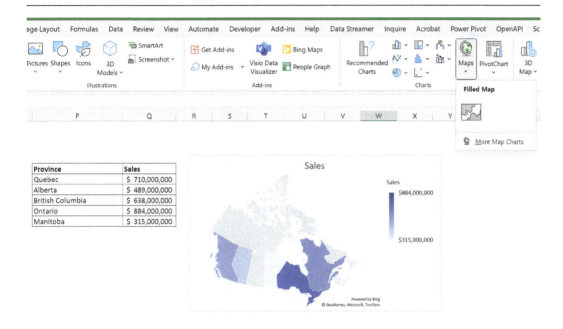

Figure 8.43 – Sales by province on a filled map chart

That wraps it up for the filled map chart. We will move on to the last chart type.

Combo chart

A combo chart is a combination of more than one chart type, and it is usually one of the following combinations:

- Line and column charts combination

- Line and bar charts combination

- Area and column charts combination

- Area and bar charts combination

- Any combination of line, bar, column, and area charts

Combo charts are useful for showing multiple insights without needing to plot two separate charts. You could combine a column chart of monthly sales with a line chart of profit margin. This ensures the user focuses on the whole message intended.

Figure 8.44 shows a combo chart of annual sales and operating profit margin:

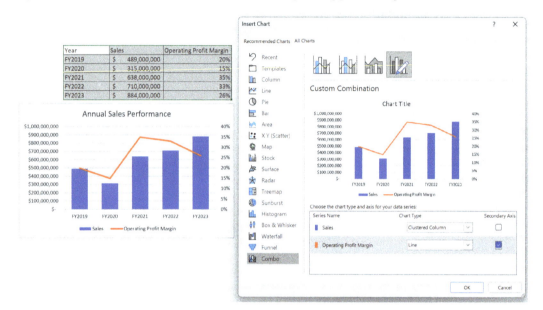

Figure 8.44 – Combo chart

Combo charts require that you specify which chart type each data series is plotted as and also indicate the primary axis or secondary axis. With that, we have come to the end of combo charts.

Summary

This chapter has been a fairly long one, as we have covered all 19 chart types you will come across in modern Excel versions. It is a commendable feat to master all 19 charts but it is not recommended to use them all in your report creation. The first four charts we covered are going to be your go-to charts: column chart, bar chart, line chart, and pie chart. They are versatile and easy to interpret by all classes of users. Then, a few charts are great to try out occasionally: filled map chart, sunburst chart, area chart, waterfall chart, treemap chart, and funnel chart. The rest must be used, if ever, with a great deal of caution as they can prove unreadable for untrained audiences.

The biggest takeaway we want you to have from this chapter is that charts are extremely important in modern-day reports and dashboard creation. You have to be good at selecting the right charts and ensuring the design looks good.

In the next chapter, we will cover non-chart visuals. You will be amazed by how many insightful visualizations you can include in your reports by using elements that are not charts.

9

Non-Chart Visuals

Most people think only of charts when it comes to visualizations in Excel. Charts are not the only tool for creating visualizations in Excel, as there are over six other tools that help you visualize data in Excel.

In this chapter, we will explore these non-chart visuals. Some can be dynamically linked to values in Excel sheets. A few are multi-functional and are not primarily seen as visualization tools. We will do an exploration of these tools and get you comfortable with creatively using them in your reports and dashboards.

The main broad categories we will explore in this chapter are as follows:

- Conditional Formatting
- Shapes
- SmartArt
- Sparkline
- Images
- Symbols

More importantly, we will need to draw on some creativity. Even boring text can be used to create visuals as evidenced by the following text terminal image of the first Power BI logo:

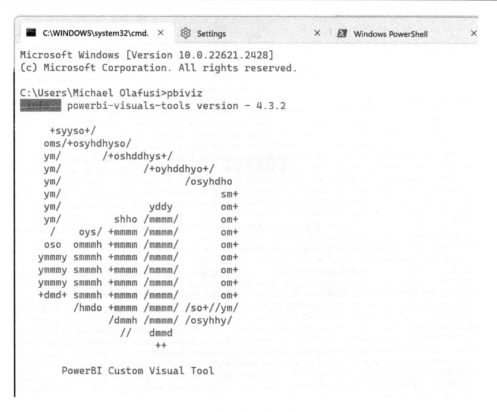

Figure 9.1 – Text used to draw the old Power BI logo

We will start with the first and likely the most important on our list: conditional formatting.

Conditional formatting

Conditional formatting is the use of logical rules to set the format for a cell or range of cells in Excel. With conditional formatting, you can set the cell value display format, font settings, border settings, and fill settings.

The following screenshot shows the format settings pane for the cell value. Notice that you can set the display for number, date, and text values:

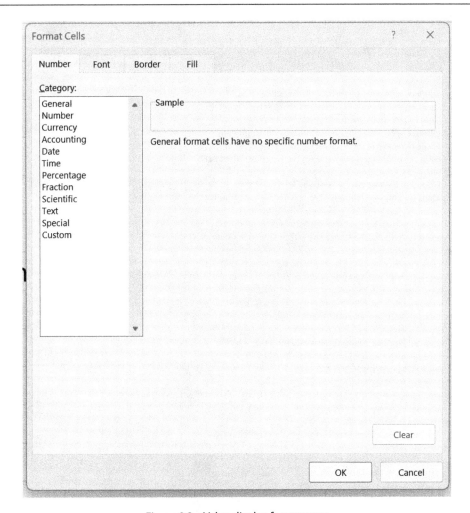

Figure 9.2 – Value display format pane

From the **Font** settings pane, you can set the **Font** type, **Font style**, **Size**, **Color**, **Underline**, **Strikethrough**, **Superscript**, and **Subscript**. See the following screenshot for the **Font** settings pane:

Figure 9.3 – Font settings pane

There are also border settings that make it possible to create dynamically expanding or contracting borders, and different border types based on cell values. The following screenshot shows the **Border** settings pane:

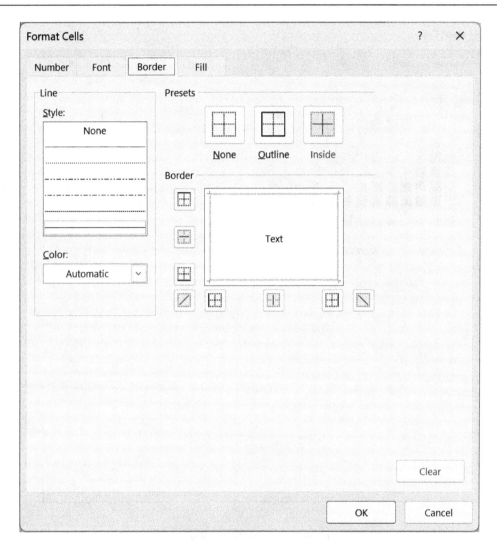

Figure 9.4 – Border settings pane

And, lastly, there's the **Fill** settings pane, which is the most used pane. It allows you to set the cell fill color, fill effects, and shading pattern. The following screenshot shows the **Fill** settings pane:

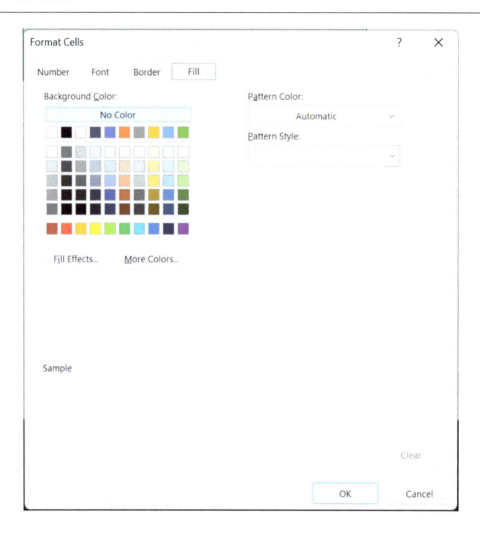

Figure 9.5 – Fill settings pane

When using **Conditional Formatting**, you are presented with five categories of preset configurations:

- **Highlight Cells Rules**
- **Top/Bottom Rules**
- **Data Bars**
- **Color Scales**
- **Icon Sets**

The following screenshot shows the in-Excel listing of these presets:

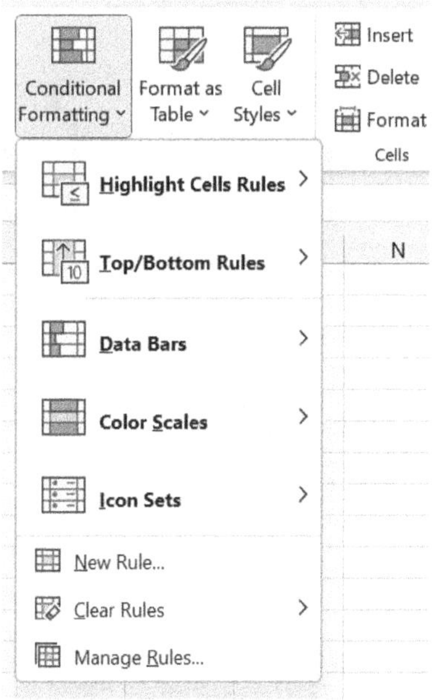

Figure 9.6 – The Conditional Formatting presets

We are going to now cover these presets, starting with **Highlight Cells Rules**.

Highlight Cells Rules

This preset allows you to easily set formatting rules that kick in when a cell contains values that meet a comparison condition to a specified value. It also helps set formats to highlight duplicate or unique values. Using this preset, you can set up the following comparison logic:

- Greater than a specified value
- Greater than or equal to a specified value
- Less than a specified value
- Less than or equal to a specified value
- Between a specified range
- Equal to a specified value
- Not equal to a specified value
- Text that contains a specific string
- Dates that match a specified date or occur within a specified range
- Highlight duplicate or unique values

As an example, we will set up a conditional format on a sales table using the **Highlight Cells Rules** preset to change the cell fill color to green for sales amounts higher than $900. The following screenshot shows the sales table we will set the rule on:

	A	B	C
1	Customer ID	Sales ID	Sales Amount
2	10118	971249	875.14
3	10183	971454	1436.13
4	10167	972196	880.61
5	10073	974896	732.03
6	10164	976540	1300.23
7	10075	978006	1054.47
8	10066	980778	1209.86
9	10067	981463	1148.94
10	10168	982237	1989.98
11	10195	983363	1527.28
12	10208	983859	592.72
13	10206	986198	1157.4
14	10186	989232	1120.7
15			

Figure 9.7 – Sample sales table

To set conditional formatting, select the sales amount values, click on **Conditional Formatting**, click on **Highlight Cells Rules**, and then click on **Greater Than**. Then type 900 into the input field and set the color that should show for values that meet the condition. See the following screenshot for an illustration of the steps:

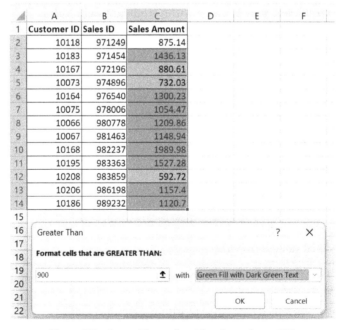

Figure 9.8 – Formatting cells with values above 900

We will now explore the **Top/Bottom Rules** preset.

Top/Bottom Rules

This preset allows you to easily highlight cells whose values have a specified relative performance to all the selected cells. It can be used to highlight cells with the following features:

- Top specified values (e.g., top 10 values)
- Values that rank in the top specified percentage (e.g., top 10%)
- Bottom specified values (e.g., bottom 10 values)
- Values that rank in the bottom specified percentage (e.g., bottom 10%)
- Values that are above the average
- Values that are below the average

See the following screenshot for the listing of these conditions:

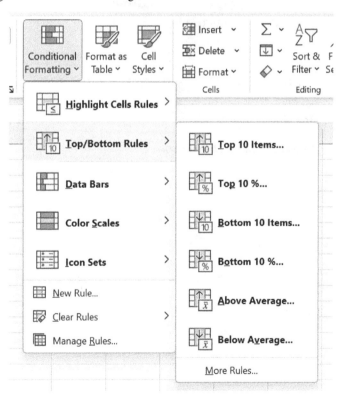

Figure 9.9 – Top/Bottom Rules

Using the same sales amount table in *Figure 9.7*, we can set a conditional format to highlight sales in the top 30%. Again, we select the sales amount cells, click on **Conditional Formatting**, click on **Top/Bottom Rules**, and then click on **Top 10 %**. In the window that comes up, we set it to the top 30% and specify the format desired. See the following screenshot for the result:

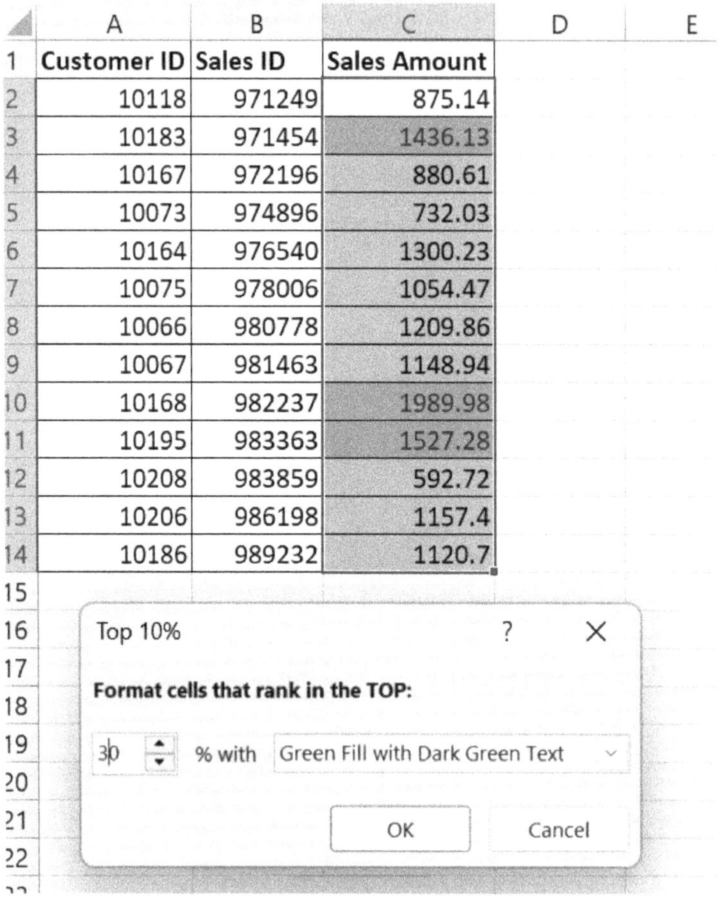

	A	B	C	D	E
1	Customer ID	Sales ID	Sales Amount		
2	10118	971249	875.14		
3	10183	971454	1436.13		
4	10167	972196	880.61		
5	10073	974896	732.03		
6	10164	976540	1300.23		
7	10075	978006	1054.47		
8	10066	980778	1209.86		
9	10067	981463	1148.94		
10	10168	982237	1989.98		
11	10195	983363	1527.28		
12	10208	983859	592.72		
13	10206	986198	1157.4		
14	10186	989232	1120.7		

Top 10%   ?   ✕

Format cells that rank in the TOP:

30   % with   Green Fill with Dark Green Text   ∨

OK   Cancel

Figure 9.10 – Highlighting the top 30% of sales

We will now explore data bars.

Data bars

Data bars are horizontal in-cell bars that reflect the value of a cell relative to a set range. There are two general options for data bars in Excel: **Gradient Fill** and **Solid Fill**. See the following screenshot showing the two options:

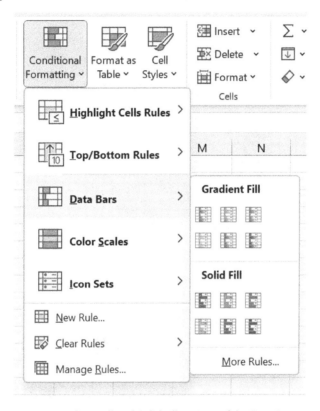

Figure 9.11 – Gradient Fill and Solid Fill options of the Data Bars preset

When applied, data bars, by default, use a range that is inferred from the selected range. Usually, the cell with the largest value in the range will have a bar that fills its entire cell. See the following screenshot for an example:

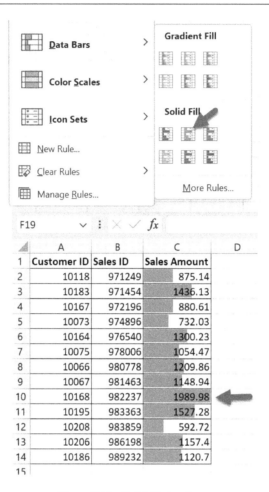

Figure 9.12 – Solid fill data bars

It is possible to change this default setting and input a different range for the data bars. All you need to do is click on **More Rules** if applying the data bars for the first time or **Manage Rules** if editing an applied data bar. See the following screenshot, which shows how to edit the range settings. Notice that you can also set other options such as the fill type, border, bar direction, and fill color:

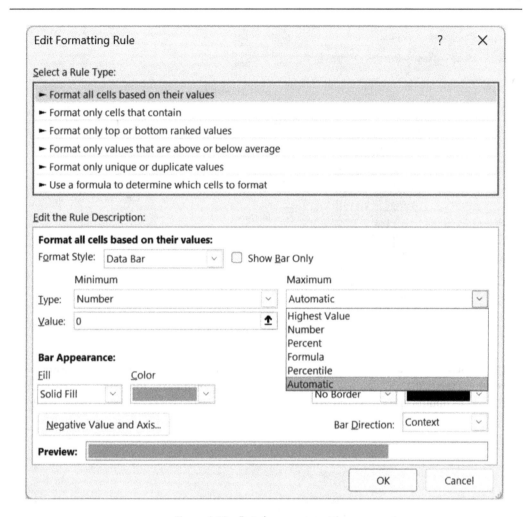

Figure 9.13 – Data bars range settings

We will move on to the fourth conditional formatting preset category.

Color scales

Color scales are a preset of cell-based heat maps. The most common color combinations are green, yellow, and red. Unlike the highlight cells rules, the colors defined in color scales form a spectrum that blends the selected colors. The following screenshot shows an example using the green–yellow–red color scale:

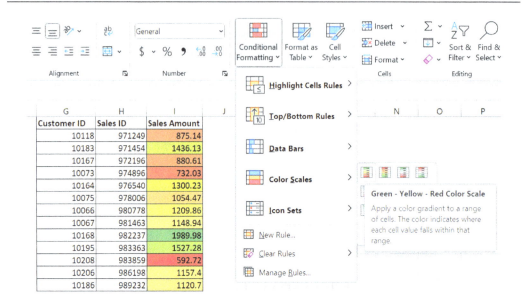

Figure 9.14 – Conditional Formatting | Color Scales

Once you've selected the color scale type you want, you will need to go to the settings to ensure that it is working exactly the way you want. The default setting, shown in the following screenshot, of inferring the minimum and maximum values for the color spectrum is not what you always want:

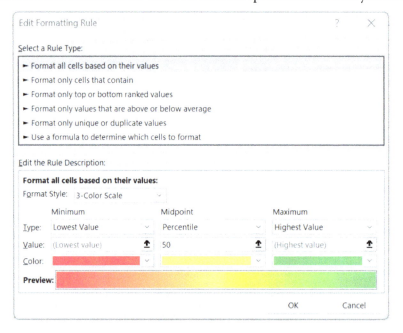

Figure 9.15 – Default settings for color scales

You can set the minimum value, midpoint, and maximum value to whatever will reliably capture the insights you want to show. The next screenshot is an example of setting the minimum to 100 (assuming that no order value can be less than 100), setting the midpoint to 500 (if that reflects the business average order value), and letting the maximum be inferred from the dataset:

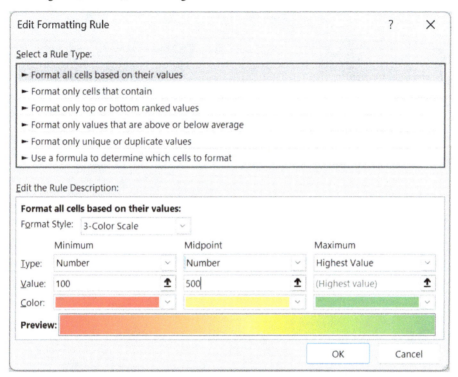

Figure 9.16 – Custom settings for color scales

You can also change the color sets to whatever you want. Just be aware that people typically interpret green and blue as positive, yellow as needing attention, and red as negative. Hence, it can be more impactful to stick to popular color sets such as green, yellow, and red.

We will now move on to the last preset category.

Icon sets

Icon sets are a preset category that houses different icon-based indicators. You can select directional or arrow-shaped icons, basic geometric shape icons, grading or flag icons, and rating icons. See the next screenshot for what these icon options look like:

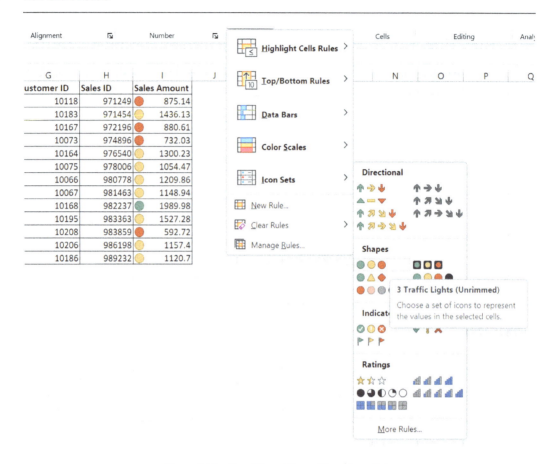

Figure 9.17 – Conditional Formatting | Icon Sets

Just like color scales, the default settings often need to be changed to a setting that properly reflects the conditions to be captured. In the following screenshot, we will set the icon to show a green icon for order values above 800, a yellow icon for order values between 500 and 800, and a red icon for order values less than 500:

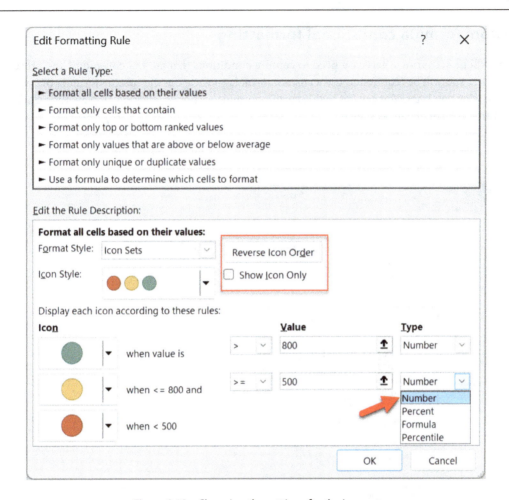

Figure 9.18 – Changing the settings for the icon set

Notice that **Type** is set to **Number**, as the default of **Percent** means it will infer from the dataset. You can also reverse the icon order if you want a red icon to show for the upper range of records and green for the bottom range. This is common for negative business-impacting metrics – customer returns, expenses, failure counts, hazards, and so on. If you prefer, you can display only the icons and make the values not show. This can be useful in some dashboards where you want the focus to be on the performance category rather than on the actual values.

With that, we have come to the end of the preset categories. We will now explore the custom formula-based conditional formatting that allows you to do a lot more than the presets we covered.

Custom formula conditional formatting

There will be scenarios where you need to capture conditions that are not covered by the preset categories. You will be required to use a custom formula to write out the specific formula that will achieve what you want. You can get to this custom formula section by clicking on **New Rule** under **Conditional Formatting**, as shown in the following screenshot:

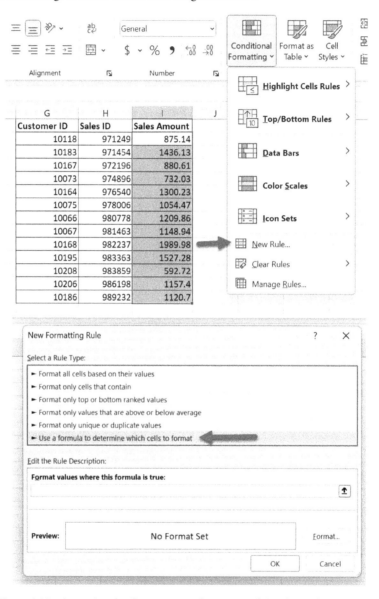

Figure 9.19 – Accessing the Custom Formula section of Conditional Formatting

There are three basic and important steps to setting up a custom formula conditional formatting, and they are as follows:

1. Select the range of cells you want to apply the conditional formatting on.
2. Take note of the active cell (which will be indicated in the name box).
3. Set the formula and the formatting that will be applied when the formula evaluates to TRUE or a non-zero number.

Notice that in the third step, I mentioned TRUE or a non-zero number, and that is because conditional formatting kicks in not just for logical formulas that evaluate to TRUE and FALSE, but also when you put in any formula that gives a non-zero number result.

To demonstrate these three steps, we will set up conditional formatting to highlight sales record rows where the customer has made some payments (the Payment Made column having a greater than 0 value). The following screenshot shows the sample sales data table we will use for the demonstration:

Customer ID	Sales ID	Sales Amount	Payment Made
10118	971249	875.14	875.14
10183	971454	1436.13	0
10167	972196	880.61	500
10073	974896	732.03	732.03
10164	976540	1300.23	0
10075	978006	1054.47	1054.47
10066	980778	1209.86	400
10067	981463	1148.94	1148.94
10168	982237	1989.98	1989.98
10195	983363	1527.28	625
10208	983859	592.72	592.72
10206	986198	1157.4	0
10186	989232	1120.7	1120.7

Figure 9.20 – The sample sales data with the Payment Made column

The first step is to select the entire records range (not just the Payment Made column) since we want to highlight all the column values for the rows with above 0 Payment Made values.

The second step is to take note of the active cell; this is the cell we started our selection from. Most times, it is the first cell in our selection as we tend to select a range from the upper left to the lower right. But if you selected from the upper right, lower right, or lower left, it won't be the first cell in the selection range. The easiest way to spot it is to look in the name box beside the formula bar.

The following screenshot shows us highlighting the table and taking note of the active cell:

	Customer ID	Sales ID	Sales Amount	Payment Made
1	Customer ID	Sales ID	Sales Amount	Payment Made
2	10118	971249	875.14	875.14
3	10183	971454	1436.13	0
4	10167	972196	880.61	500
5	10073	974896	732.03	732.03
6	10164	976540	1300.23	0
7	10075	978006	1054.47	1054.47
8	10066	980778	1209.86	400
9	10067	981463	1148.94	1148.94
10	10168	982237	1989.98	1989.98
11	10195	983363	1527.28	625
12	10208	983859	592.72	592.72
13	10206	986198	1157.4	0
14	10186	989232	1120.7	1120.7
15				

Figure 9.21 – Records selection before inputting the custom formula

The next step will be to go to **Conditional Formatting | New Rule** and pick **Use a formula to determine which cells to format**. Remember that we need to input a formula that factors in our active cell and evaluates to TRUE or a non-zero number. In addition, we must ensure that we adjust the default absolute referencing that comes up when we pick a cell within the formula box.

In this example, we want the formula to check that the active cell record's Payment Made value (cell J2) is greater than 0, and we want the formula to change row-wise, picking the correct Payment Made values for each record row, but it should not change column-wise as only the Payment Made column should be checked. This means we will input =$J2 >0 in the formula box and then set the format to a fill color of light green or whatever format you prefer. See the following screenshot for the setting and result:

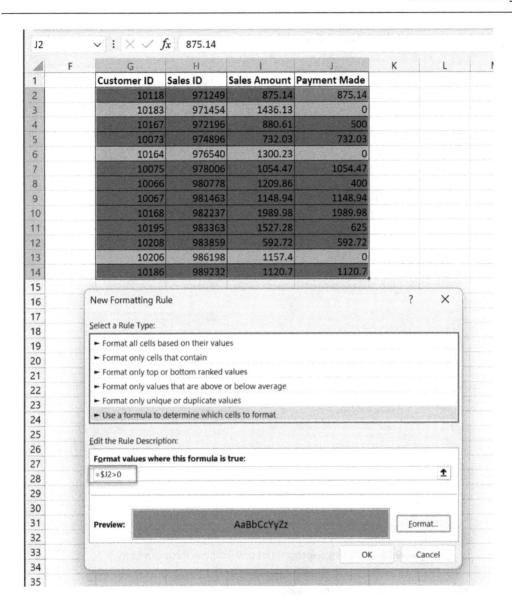

Figure 9.22 – The custom formula and fill setting

Lastly, I will prove that we could have started our table selection from a different cell and that we could have used a different formula that evaluates to a non-zero number (not just a TRUE value). I will start the records selection from the lower left, cell G14. And in the formula box, I will simply input =$J14. And since any numeric value different from 0 will make the conditional formatting kick in, this will achieve the same result as our previous formula that did a greater than 0 check.

The following screenshot shows the results:

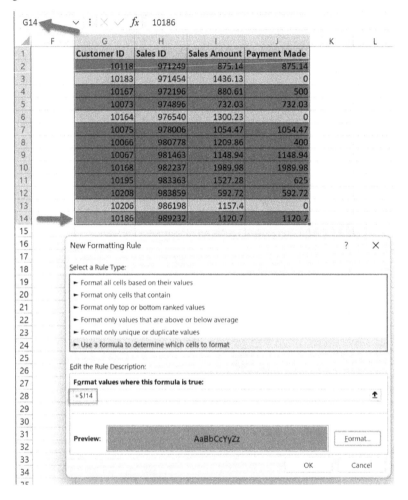

Figure 9.23 – Different selection start and a different custom formula

With that, we have come to the end of conditional formatting. We will now go on to the next non-chart visual tool.

Shapes

Shapes can be found under the **Insert** menu in Excel. They are another interesting way to visually present insights in Excel. Shapes have been in Excel for decades and are currently broadly categorized as lines, rectangles, basic shapes, block arrows, equation shapes, flowcharts, stars and banners, and callouts. The following screenshot shows the categories:

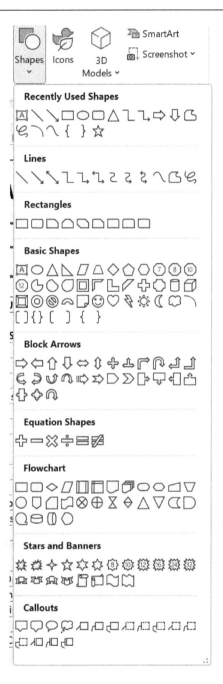

Figure 9.24 – Shape categories in Excel

There are two general ways of using shapes for visualization in Excel. The first is to have the shape linked to a cell, and the second is to use the shape to organize other objects to achieve a visually engaging outlook.

We will demonstrate how to link a shape to a cell so that the shape reflects the value in that cell. We start by inserting a rectangle, changing the default fill color and outline to a more visually pleasing one, and positioning it where we want. Then we click on the shape, click inside the formula bar, hit = on the keyboard, and select the cell we have to link the shape to. The following screenshot illustrates the process:

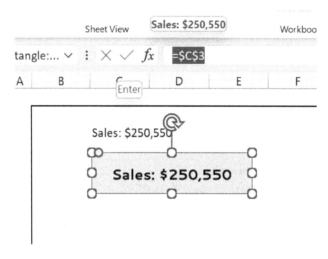

Figure 9.25 – Shape linked to a cell

For the second general use of shapes, we will set up two sales tables showing regional sales for a company that operates in North America and Europe. Using rectangular shapes, we turn the boring tables into a more visually engaging report. We put the rectangular shapes over the tables, set their fill color as **No Fill**, set the outline weight to 3, set the outline color to a nice light blue (color hex #ACECF7), and put two corner-shaped rectangles above the tables for the titles. See the outcome in the following screenshot:

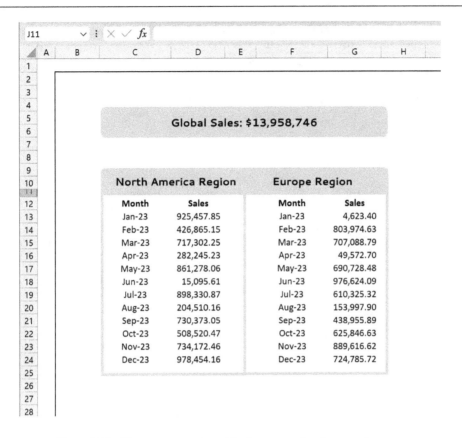

Figure 9.26 – Shapes to organize tables in a more visually engaging way

With that, we have come to the end of the section on shapes. We will now go on to SmartArt.

SmartArt

SmartArt is also housed in the **Insert** menu, in the same section as shapes. It is mostly used for text descriptions of processes and relationships. The following screenshot shows the categories of SmartArt within Excel:

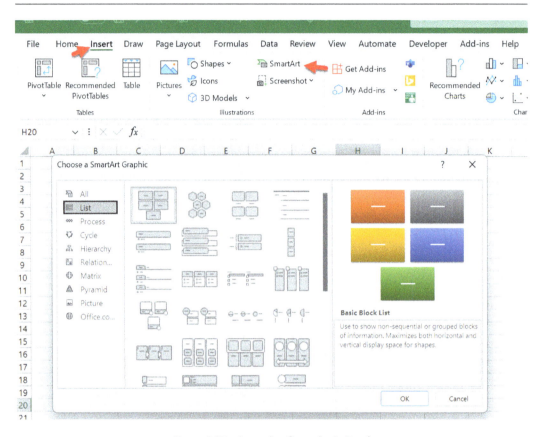

Figure 9.27 – Accessing SmartArt in Excel

A common use of SmartArt is to illustrate an organogram or an escalation matrix. The following figure is an example of using a SmartArt Pyramid to visually present information on a company's support levels (L0, L1, L2, and L3) tickets:

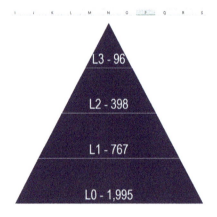

Figure 9.28 – SmartArt to indicate support level tickets treated

I have used SmartArt to create elaborate infographics that tell a much more visually engaging and coherent story than a block of text beside a chart can do. However, SmartArt content cannot be dynamically linked to cells as we have shown for shapes. This can be a limiting factor when you have dynamic text being generated in a cell and want it displayed on the SmartArt. But for static texts that depict relationships and processes, you will find SmartArt a good tool to use to visualize them.

We are now done with SmartArt and will move on to sparklines.

Sparkline

A sparkline is a one-cell chart. It gives the option of a line, column, and a win/loss chart. The chart size is always constrained to the size of the housing cell. The line option is great for depicting values over time (trends). The column option is great for highlighting individual performance. The win/loss option is best suited for depicting three states: positive, zero, and negative.

To create a sparkline, you select the numeric values to plot (ensure you do not include the labels), go to the **Insert** menu, and pick the type of sparkline you want. A dialog box will come up asking you to specify the cell/location to put the sparkline. The following screenshot shows an example of a line sparkline for a monthly sales trend:

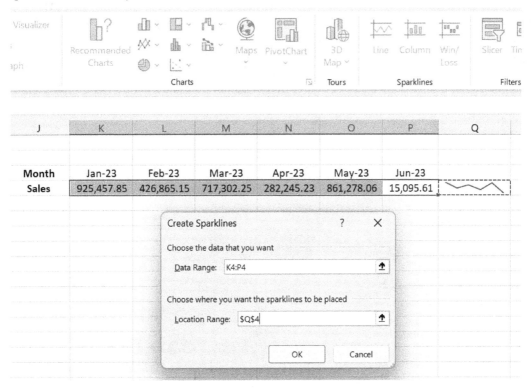

Figure 9.29 – Creating a sparkline in Excel

The column sparkline would be great for sales by regional data. The separate bars for each region make it more appropriate than a line sparkline that puts a line through all the regions. Also, if the regions have targets, showing the variance as a win/loss sparkline will be insightful. The following screenshot shows these two sparklines:

Figure 9.30 – Column sparkline and win/loss sparkline

With that, we have come to the end of the section on sparklines; we will now move on to images.

Images

You can creatively use images in Excel beyond just inserting them as static pictures. One popular visualization use of images in Excel is when you copy a range and paste it as a linked picture. This makes a lot of interesting things possible for a dashboard builder in Excel. To achieve this, we will set up a richly formatted cell that has an underlying formula and we will then copy this cell and paste it as a linked picture. Whenever the cell changes, both in format and value, the image from the linked picture will also change. This makes it possible to put these dynamic images on a chart, on a shape, or sized perfectly within a dashboard. The following screenshot is an illustration of this:

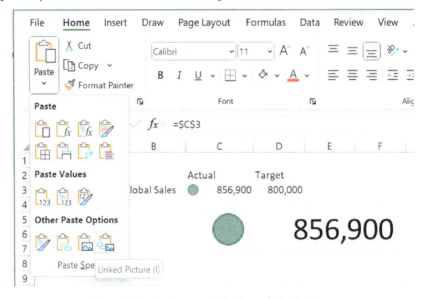

Figure 9.31 – Pasting copied cell as a linked picture

Another interesting use of images as a visualization tool in Excel is to have them replace the regular bars in a column and bar chart. All one needs to do is copy the image, select the bar on a bar or column chart, and hit *Ctrl + V* to paste the copied image. This will replace the bar with the image copied. Right-click on the bar, click on **Format Data Series**, and set the **Fill** value to **Stack**. See the following screenshot for illustration:

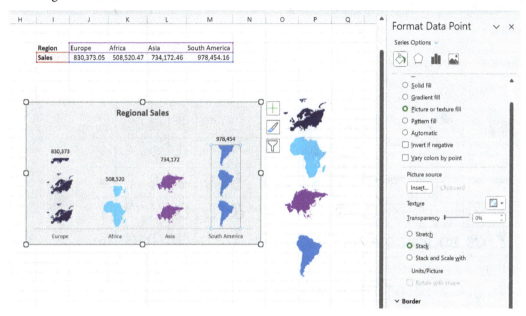

Figure 9.32 – Using an image as a bar in a chart

That brings us to the end of the section on images. We will now move on to the last category of non-chart visuals.

Symbols

Excel has a nice collection of symbols and special characters that can be very useful for applying a visual marker to your data and report. Need a checkmark? Need a cancel mark? Need a timer icon? Need each of them to automatically show up depending on the value in a cell? That is what symbols make possible. To access these symbols, all you need to do is go to the **Insert** menu and click on **Symbols**, as shown in the following screenshot:

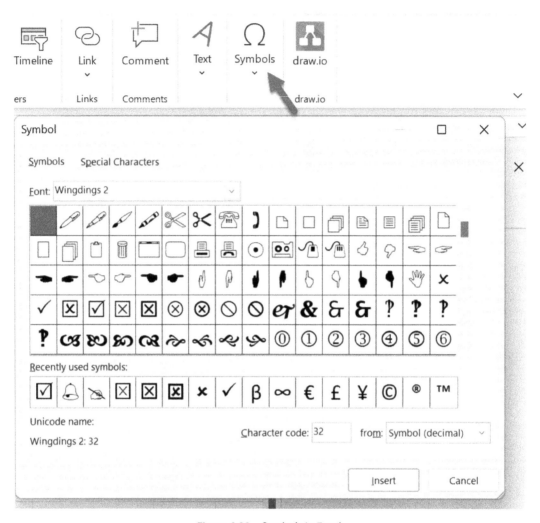

Figure 9.33 – Symbols in Excel

Beneath the symbol icons are font types such as Wingdings, Wingdings 2, Wingdings 3, Webdings, Bookshelf Symbol 7, and Marlett. If you select a symbol, you will see both its font type and character code. With those two details, you can create the symbol within a formula and use it to dynamically highlight scenarios.

The following screenshot highlights where to get the font type and character code details:

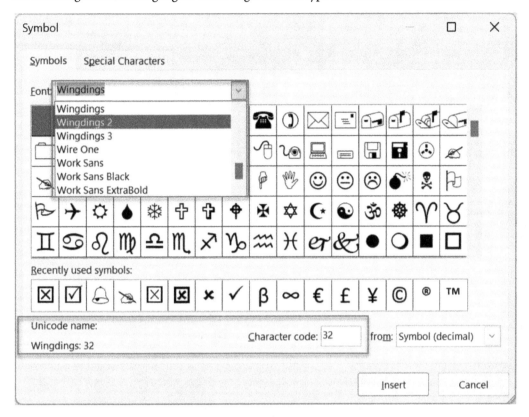

Figure 9.34 – Getting the font and character code

The following screenshot shows an example of using a checkmark of the Wingdings 2 font and alphabet R to highlight the months that targets were met while using a cancel mark of Wingdings 2 font and alphabet T to highlight the months when sales were below target. Notice that I included a conditional format:

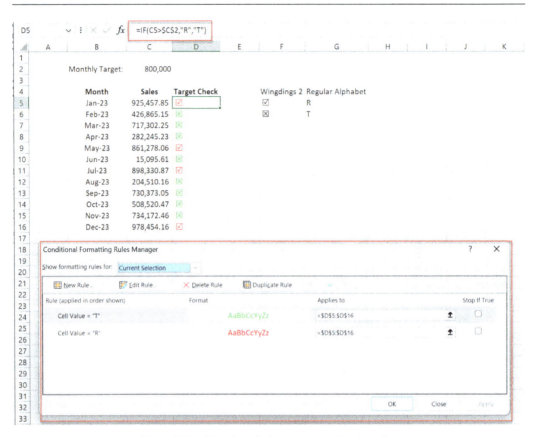

Figure 9.35 – Use of symbols to create a visual marker

With that, we have come to the end of the section on symbols.

I hope you have learned a lot of interesting ways you can visualize data within Excel without using a chart. These methods do not replace charts nor should they be construed as alternatives to charts. They are complementary visualization tools that should be used alongside charts for a professional dashboard.

Summary

In this chapter, you have learned how to use conditional formatting, shapes, SmartArt, sparklines, images, and symbols as visualization tools. They are all important tools in a competent dashboard builder's toolbox, and you will see your reports look more professional as you put them to use.

This chapter on non-chart visuals brings us closer to the end of this book on *Building Interactive Dashboards in M365 Excel & Excel 2021*. We have covered all the technical pieces that go into a dashboard in Excel. In the next and last three chapters, we will combine all we have learned so far to set up a dashboard layout, perfect the data model behind the dashboard, and complete a company-wide dashboard for a retail company. Exciting, right?

In the next chapter, we will begin the end of our journey by going through how to set up a dashboard layout. See you in the next chapter!

10

Setting Up the Dashboard's Data Model

Congratulations on making it this far in this book. We have now gotten to the hands-on section, where we will begin working on creating actual dashboards from scratch by combining everything we have learned so far.

This chapter is the first of three chapters that will walk you through building a dashboard from scratch. We will introduce the fictitious company we are going to work on, connect to the company's data, and start the data modeling process.

Here's a breakdown of what we will cover:

- Adventure Works Cycle Limited
- Building business-relevant dashboards
- Data transformation in Power Query

Buckle up as we embark on this interesting dashboard creation journey. Ensure you follow along so that you fully grasp everything we cover.

We will start by introducing to you the fictitious company we are going to build management dashboards for.

Adventure Works Cycle Limited

The company we will be building dashboards for is called **Adventure Works Cycle Limited**. For both your and my convenience, we will simply refer to the company as **Adventure Works**. The company is a bicycle manufacturer with its head office in the USA and a manufacturing plant in Mexico. In addition to selling bicycles, the company also sells bicycle components, cycling apparel, and bicycle accessories.

The company has customers spread across the globe – individual customers who shop via its online store and corporate stores who place orders directly via their assigned account managers or the enterprise sales platform. To be operationally efficient, the company has partnered with different vendors to supply it with the raw materials and intermediate products it needs to manufacture its final products.

The company has a Microsoft Dynamics **Enterprise Resource Planning** (**ERP**) application that is set up to manage the company's activities across its functional units. The company's data is stored on an enterprise database and we have been given access to that data. For our practice, we will use an exported copy of the company's ERP data that captures business data across the **human resources** (**HR**) department, production department, and sales department. You can access this data at `https://github.com/PacktPublishing/Building-Interactive-Dashboards-in-Microsoft-365-Excel/tree/main/AdventureWorksDataset`.

You will notice that the data tables have a naming pattern of two words – for example, `HumanResources Department.csv`. The first word denotes the schema and the second word denotes the actual table name. A schema, in this context, is a database term for a logical group of related tables and storage entities. However, since we will be dealing with the exported copy of the data, which is stored as an easy-to-use flat file, we will only need these groupings for reference.

The following figure shows the different original logical groupings (schemas) within the Adventure Works database:

Figure 10.1 – Adventure Works schemas

To ease you into the value we will be creating for the company's management via the dashboards we will build, I will walk you through the different schemas and the tables we will use for our dashboards. We will start with the HR schema.

HR schema

The HR schema contains the following tables:

- **Department**: This contains a list of the 16 departments in the company, the department identifier number, and the business groups the departments belong to.

- **Employee**: This holds the records of each employee in the company, including their birth date, gender, hire date, remuneration type, sick leave entitlement, and vacation entitlement.

- **EmployeeDepartmentHistory**: This is a fairly small table that maps employees to their respective departments and their assigned shift identifiers.

- **EmployeePayHistory**: This contains the records of each employee's per-hour pay and how many times they were paid per month.

- **JobCandidate**: This contains information about job candidates resumes. We will not be using this table in our dashboard because it has too few records and little actionable data.

- **Shift**: This contains the details of the three shift identifiers, essentially mapping them to day, evening, and night shifts.

One of the final dashboards that we will build will be centered on these tables to show some interesting and management actionable insights on the company's staff diversity, pay scale, and staff benefits. For now, we will move on to the sales schema.

Sales schema

The sales schema includes the following tables:

- **CountryRegionCurrency**: This contains records of the 109 countries the company makes sales in and each country's currency code.

- **CreditCard**: This table holds the credit card details of the online buyers to ease repurchase. Nowadays, it is not recommended to save customer credit card details in clear text. They should be encrypted and made difficult to access.

- **Currency**: This table holds the currency codes and the full name of the currencies. It will have to be linked to **CountryRegionCurrency** to get the countries for the currencies.

- **CurrencyRate**: This table holds daily currency conversion rates from USD to all sales currencies.

- **Customer**: This table holds the company's customer details and helps with matching sales to regions, stores, and individuals.

- **PersonCreditCard**: This table maps the credit card details in the **CreditCard** table to the customer/owner.

- **SalesOrderDetail**: This table holds the item-wise record of sales and shows the product, unit price, applied discount, quantity, and sales amount.

- **SalesOrderHeader**: This table contains order-wise records that show the order date, shipping date, customer, salesperson, order value, and if the order was an online store order.

- **SalesOrderHeaderSalesReason**: This table contains sales orders related to the sales campaign type (sales reason) that generated the sales order.

- **SalesPerson**: This table holds the records of sales representatives across different regions, the yearly sales target, the bonus that kicks in when the target is met, the sales commission percentage, and their sales performance.

- **SalesPersonQuotaHistory**: This table holds historical sales targets (quota) over the years for the sales representatives.

- **SalesReason**: This table holds the different types of sales campaigns and their sales reason ID.

- **SalesTaxRate**: This table holds the different applicable sales taxes.

- **SalesTerritory**: This table contains the different sales territories, the regions they fall under, the territory ID, and sales performance.

- **SalesTerritoryHistory**: This table holds the historical mapping of sales representatives to territories. This is useful for analyzing sales by territory and sales representative; this makes it possible to know who was in charge of which territory at any date period.

- **ShoppingCartItem**: This table contains records of customers' unsubmitted online orders.

- **SpecialOffer**: This table contains details of ongoing special sales offers, the sales discount rates, and eligibility criteria.

- **SpecialOfferProduct**: This table holds the records of products eligible for the special offers and the special offers they are eligible for.

- **Store**: This table holds the records of the stores and resellers who can directly place orders with the company without using the online sales platform that is aimed at individuals and non-resellers. It holds the details of the sales representative managing the accounts of the stores.

Now that we have covered the 19 tables in the sales schema, we will move on to the purchasing schema.

Purchasing schema

The purchasing schema of tables includes the following:

- **ProductVendor**: This table holds the records of the different products, the approved suppliers/vendors, supply lead time, cost price, last time the vendor was used, minimum order size, and maximum order size.

- **PurchaseOrderDetail**: This table holds item-wise records of purchase orders placed with vendors showing the products ordered, quantities per product, unit price, and total amount, but does not contain details of the vendor the order was placed with and who placed the order.

- **PurchaseOrderHeader**: This table holds the order-wise records of purchase orders with details of the vendor the order was placed with and the employee who placed the order.

- **ShipMethod**: This table contains the different shipping methods and associated costs.

- **Vendor**: This table holds records of the vendors – their entity ID, name, creditworthiness rating, preferred vendor status, and active flag.

That's it for the purchasing schema! It doesn't have as many tables as the sales schema. Next, we will move on to the production schema, which has the most number of tables.

Production schema

The production schema consists of the following tables:

- **Culture**: This table holds regional or locale settings. It's not going to be useful for our analysis project.

- **Document**: This table holds the navigation settings for different documentation files and pages on the enterprise application. It is not going to be useful for our analysis project.

- **Illustration**: This table holds some visual documentation links for backend use on the enterprise application. It is not going to be useful for our analysis project.

- **Location**: This table contains records of the different factory locations.

- **Product**: This table holds the records of all the company's products, both final/finished goods and raw materials.

- **ProductCategory**: This table contains the records of four different major types of products the company produces.

- **ProductCostHistory**: This table holds the records of the cost price history of the company's products.

- **ProductDescription**: This table contains the records of product description identifiers and the corresponding description text. It is linked to the **Product** table via the **ProductModelProductDescriptionCulture** table.

- **ProductDocument**: This table holds the page navigation details for some products' documentation. We won't be needing it for any analytical work.

- **ProductInventory**: This table contains the records of current inventory stock position by products, warehouse location, shelf, bin, and quantity in stock.

- **ProductListPriceHistory**: This table contains the records of price changes for products, which is useful for accurate reporting when translating quantities into values over a date period.

- **ProductModel**: This table holds the details of the different product models, their model IDs, and catalog.

- **ProductModelIllustration**: This table contains the records of product model IDs and their illustration IDs. We won't be using this table for any analytical work.

- **ProductModelProductDescriptionCulture**: This table links the **ProductModel** table to the **ProductDescription** table.

- **ProductPhoto**: This table holds the filenames of the thumbnails and full images of the products. This is not going to be relevant to our analytical work.

- **ProductProductPhoto**: This table holds the records of the product ID and the corresponding product photo ID. We won't be using this table for our dashboard building.

- **ProductReview**: This table contains customer reviews of the products the company sells.

- **ProductSubcategory**: This table holds the mapping of product subcategories to product categories and shows the names of the subcategories. This is useful for category-based sales and production analysis.

- **ScrapReason**: This table holds the different product scrap reasons and the corresponding reason ID.

- **TransactionHistory**: This table holds a record of the product procurement transaction history at an item level and actual cost price.

- **TransactionHistoryArchive**: This table holds records of archived transactions.

- **UnitMeasure**: This table contains different product measurement unit codes and names. Examples are BTL – Bottle, CTN – Container, GAL – Gallon, and PAK – Pack.

- **WorkOrder**: This table holds records of work orders by associated product.

- **WorkOrderRouting**: This table contains records of work orders by associated product, factory location, and operation sequence.

With that, we have covered the numerous tables in the production schema. Now, we will move on to a related schema – person.

Person schema

The person schema holds the tables of customers, vendors, and employees of the company. The individual tables are as follows:

- **Address**: This table holds the customers' addresses and an assigned address identifier number. This provides a unified address table that other tables can refer to and acts like a customer address master list.

- **AddressType**: This table holds the different address types – billing, home, office, shipping, and so on.

- **BusinessEntity**: This table contains the master list of the company's employees, vendors, and customers.

- **BusinessEntityAddress**: This table maps the records in the **BusinessEntity** table to their addresses in the **Address** table using identifier fields.

- **BusinessEntityContact**: This table maps the vendors and customers in **BusinessEntity** to their representatives or staff within the **Persons** table and their role in the **ContactType** table.

- **ContactType**: This table holds a record of all the different contact types as roles. The roles range from the owner of the corporate entity to sales representative.

- **ContactRegion**: This table holds the records of the countries across which the company has dealings with customers, vendors, and employees.

- **EmailAddress**: This table holds the email addresses of the employees, vendors, and customers. The external people have been mapped to internal email addresses.

- **Password**: This table holds the email login passwords in an encrypted format.

- **Person**: This table holds the names and basic details of the customers' representatives, vendors' representatives, and employees.

- **PersonPhone**: This table contains the phone numbers of the customers, vendors, and employees.

- **PhoneNumberType**: This table holds the three different types of phone numbers – cell, home, and work.

- **StateProvince**: This table holds the records of the 181 states and provinces where the company has staff, vendors, or customers.

That brings us to the end of the tables in the person schema, which is the last of the schemas in the Adventure Works dataset.

We have provided a thorough overview of the company, Adventure Works, and the different data tables within its business database that we are going to need to build some business-relevant dashboards for.

In the next section, we will talk about the different dashboards we are going to build.

Building business-relevant dashboards

We will be building dashboards to support three key departments of Adventure Works. We will help the sales department keep track of sales by product, by region, by sales representative, and by product category. We will also help the production department keep track of production metrics, warehouse utilization, suppliers, raw materials procurement, and production costs. Lastly, we will help the HR department keep track of different HR metrics and the diversity of the company's employees.

Data transformation in Power Query

The first step in setting up the data model is to download the necessary Adventure Works data files. You can access the files at `https://github.com/PacktPublishing/Building-Interactive-Dashboards-in-Microsoft-365-Excel/tree/main/AdventureWorksDataset`, as shown in the following screenshot:

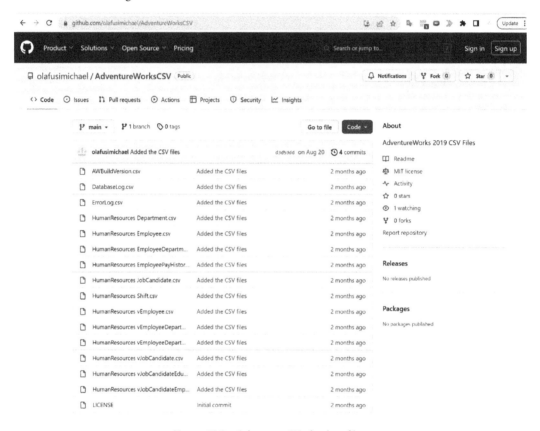

Figure 10.2 – Adventure Works data files

An easy way to download all the data files at once is to click on the green **Code** button at the top right of the web page and click the **Download ZIP** button, as shown in the following screenshot:

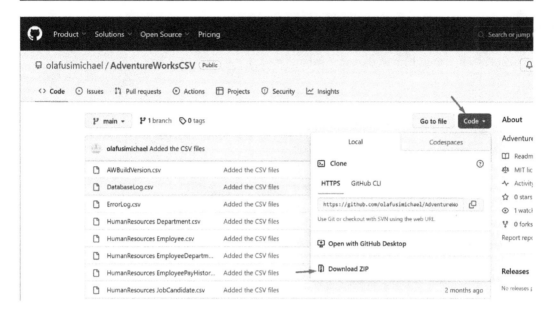

Figure 10.3 – Downloading the data files

After downloading the zipped folder, unzip it to extract the data files, as shown in the following screenshot:

Figure 10.4 – Extracting the data files from the zipped folder

These data files are **comma-separated values (CSV)** files of the datasets of Adventure Works. They are the very files we will use for our dashboard creation. The following screenshot shows a snapshot of the files as you'll find them in the extracted folder:

Name	Date modified	Type	Size
⌄ Earlier this year			
AWBuildVersion.csv	8/20/2023 3:34 PM	Microsoft Excel Comma Separated Values File	1 KB
DatabaseLog.csv	8/20/2023 3:34 PM	Microsoft Excel Comma Separated Values File	2,539 KB
ErrorLog.csv	8/20/2023 3:34 PM	Microsoft Excel Comma Separated Values File	0 KB
HumanResources Department.csv	8/20/2023 3:34 PM	Microsoft Excel Comma Separated Values File	2 KB
HumanResources Employee.csv	8/20/2023 3:34 PM	Microsoft Excel Comma Separated Values File	63 KB
HumanResources EmployeeDepartmentHistory.csv	8/20/2023 3:34 PM	Microsoft Excel Comma Separated Values File	17 KB
HumanResources EmployeePayHistory.csv	8/20/2023 3:34 PM	Microsoft Excel Comma Separated Values File	19 KB
HumanResources JobCandidate.csv	8/20/2023 3:34 PM	Microsoft Excel Comma Separated Values File	63 KB
HumanResources Shift.csv	8/20/2023 3:34 PM	Microsoft Excel Comma Separated Values File	1 KB
HumanResources vEmployee.csv	8/20/2023 3:34 PM	Microsoft Excel Comma Separated Values File	54 KB
HumanResources vEmployeeDepartment.csv	8/20/2023 3:34 PM	Microsoft Excel Comma Separated Values File	34 KB
HumanResources vEmployeeDepartmentHistory.csv	8/20/2023 3:34 PM	Microsoft Excel Comma Separated Values File	30 KB
HumanResources vJobCandidate.csv	8/20/2023 3:34 PM	Microsoft Excel Comma Separated Values File	12 KB
HumanResources vJobCandidateEducation.csv	8/20/2023 3:34 PM	Microsoft Excel Comma Separated Values File	4 KB
HumanResources vJobCandidateEmployment.csv	8/20/2023 3:34 PM	Microsoft Excel Comma Separated Values File	18 KB
LICENSE	8/20/2023 3:34 PM	File	2 KB
Person Address.csv	8/20/2023 3:34 PM	Microsoft Excel Comma Separated Values File	3,050 KB
Person AddressType.csv	8/20/2023 3:34 PM	Microsoft Excel Comma Separated Values File	1 KB
Person BusinessEntity.csv	8/20/2023 3:34 PM	Microsoft Excel Comma Separated Values File	1,410 KB
Person BusinessEntityAddress.csv	8/20/2023 3:34 PM	Microsoft Excel Comma Separated Values File	1,483 KB
Person BusinessEntityContact.csv	8/20/2023 3:34 PM	Microsoft Excel Comma Separated Values File	68 KB

Figure 10.5 – The extracted CSV data files

We are going to load related tables into one Excel file for each type of dashboard we are building. You might be wondering if that would not greatly slow down Excel. Your concern is valid. This, however, is an opportunity to explain to you the amazing improvement Microsoft has made to how data is stored within Excel when you leverage the data model. At the core of the data model in Excel are Power Query and Power Pivot. The data you bring into Excel via Power Query and work on in Power Query is stored in a highly compressed and performance-optimized format powered by the Vertipaq engine. The advantage of this is that we can bring in all these tables for our modeling work and not experience significant performance degradation. However, the moment we load all these data into Excel sheets, we lose that advantage. So, we will aim to expose the data via a pivot table to Excel sheets.

We will start with the HR dashboard data model and load the following CSV files:

- `HumanResources Department`
- `HumanResources Employee`
- `HumanResources EmployeeDepartmentHistory`
- `HumanResources EmployeePayHistory`
- `HumanResources Shift`
- `Person Person`
- `Person BusinessEntityAddress`
- `Person Address`
- `Person StateProvince`
- `Person CountryRegion`

Did you notice that we skipped the `HumanResources JobCandidate` table and included two tables from the **person** schema? The `HumanResources JobCandidate` table holds data that is not relevant to our analysis as it just contains 13 rows of a few job application details.

We needed the `Person Person` table to get the employee names and the `Person StateProvince` table to get the employee state of residency. The `Person CountryRegion` table helps us map the state of residency to the country of residence.

To bring in the CSV files, go to the **Data** menu and choose **Get Data | From File | From Text/CSV**. This is illustrated in the following screenshot:

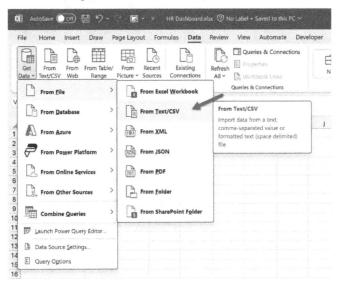

Figure 10.6 – Bringing CSV files into the Excel data model

This will bring up a file explorer requesting you to select the CSV file to import. Sadly, you can't select all the CSV files at once. You have to pick and load one file at a time. We will start with the first, `HumanResources Department.csv`.

On selecting this CSV file, you will be presented with a preview screen that has the option to load or transform the data. Picking **Load** will pull the data through the data model and straight into a dedicated Excel sheet. Based on what I explained some paragraphs ago, we want to leverage the performance benefits that come with keeping most of our data at the data model level and loading as little data as possible into the Excel sheets. This means that we will select the **Transform Data** option. See the following screenshot for this step:

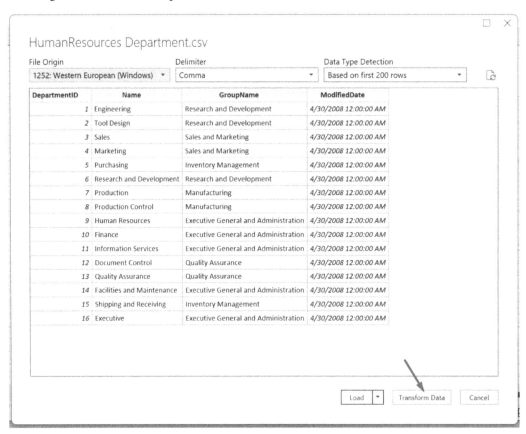

Figure 10.7 – Selecting the Transform Data option

Clicking on **Transform Data** presents a Power Query window showing the selected CSV file data loaded in as a table. See the following screenshot for the `HumanResources Department.csv` table we just imported:

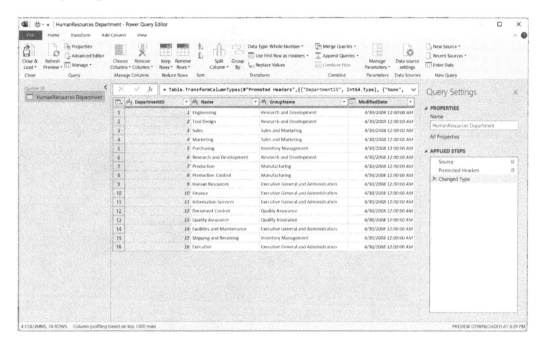

Figure 10.8 – An overview of the Power Query window

We will have to repeat these steps for the remaining tables with just one minor step difference: rather than doing the file imports from within Excel's **Data** menu, we will import them from Power Query's **New Source** tool. All that is required is to go to the **Home** menu, choose **New Source** from the far right, select **File**, and then select **Text/CSV**. See the following screenshot:

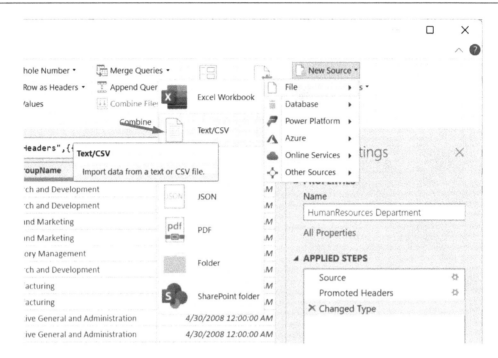

Figure 10.9 – Importing a CSV file into Power Query

Every other step after that is the same as what we followed to bring in the first file. By the time you are done importing the other nine files, you will have a Power Query window that looks very much like the one shown in the following screenshot:

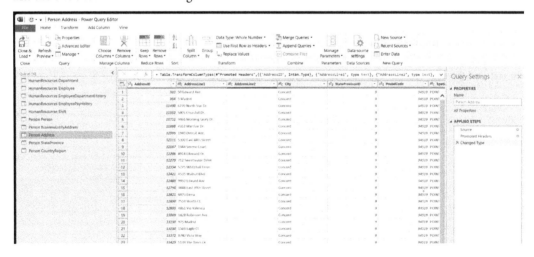

Figure 10.10 – An overview of all the required CSV files loaded into Power Query

To keep our tables performance-tuned, we are going to remove columns that we do not need. Two columns top that list: **ModifiedDate** and **rowguid**. So, go through the tables one by one and delete those columns. Some tables have just the **ModifiedDate** column and no **rowguid** column. For those, delete the **ModifiedDate** column. We are deleting them because they are database-autogenerated fields that hold no reporting benefits. The following screenshot shows the process of deleting the **ModifiedDate** and **rowguid** columns in the **HumanResources Employee** table:

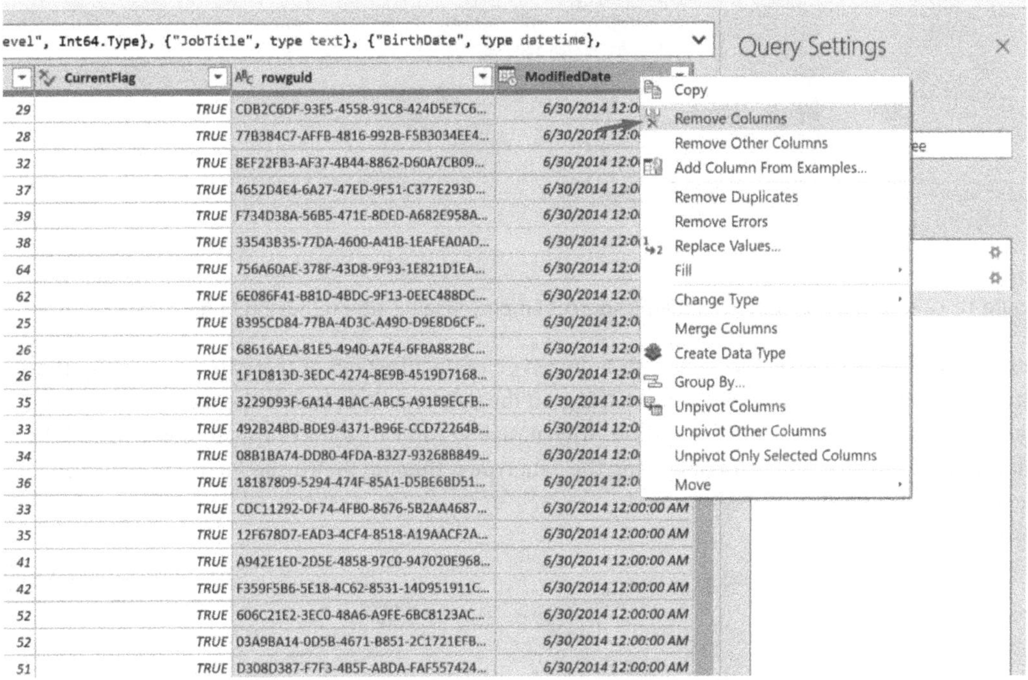

Figure 10.11 – Deleting the ModifiedDate and rowguid columns

We will now go to table-specific transformations. In the **HumanResources Employee** table, we will delete the following additional columns: **NationalIDNumber**, **LoginID**, and **OrganizationNode**. When you are done, the final table should look as follows:

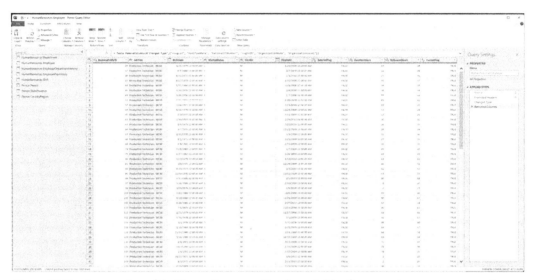

Figure 10.12 – An overview of the HumanResources Employee table after removing unnecessary columns

Next, we will set all the date columns to a data type of date instead of the datetime setting they currently have. You can achieve this by clicking on the data type icon beside the column name, and making the change one column at a time. Alternatively, you can achieve this by selecting all the columns to make this change for and using the data type setting on the **Home** menu, as displayed in the following screenshot:

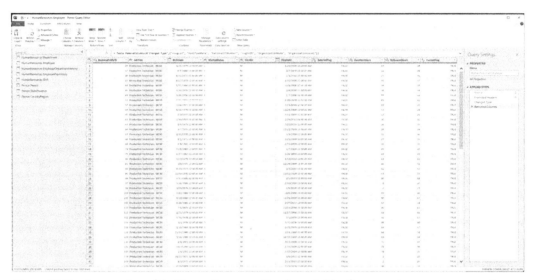

Figure 10.13 – An overview of the Data Type setting under the Home menu

Next, we'll carry out a similar date column transformation on **HumanResources EmployeeDepartmentHistory**. Set the **StartDate** and **EndDate** values to a date data type. The final table should look like the one shown in the following screenshot. If you get an error for the **EndDate** column, set it to **DateTime** first and then to **Date**:

| fx | = Table.TransformColumnTypes(#"Changed Type2",{{"StartDate", type date}, {"EndDate", type date}}) |

BusinessEntityID	DepartmentID	ShiftID	StartDate	EndDate
255	254	5	1	1/4/2010	null
256	255	5	1	1/11/2010	null
257	256	5	1	1/23/2010	null
258	257	5	1	1/27/2010	null
259	258	5	1	1/31/2010	null
260	259	5	1	3/9/2010	null
261	260	5	1	12/6/2010	null
262	261	5	1	12/25/2010	null
263	262	10	1	1/12/2009	null
264	263	11	1	12/11/2008	null
265	264	11	1	2/4/2009	null
266	266	11	1	2/23/2009	null
267	267	11	1	2/16/2009	null
268	268	11	1	2/3/2009	null
269	269	11	1	1/11/2009	null
270	270	11	1	1/17/2009	null
271	271	11	1	1/22/2009	null
272	272	11	1	12/23/2008	null
273	273	3	1	2/15/2011	null
274	274	3	1	1/4/2011	null
275	275	3	1	5/31/2011	null
276	276	3	1	5/31/2011	null
277	277	3	1	5/31/2011	null
278	278	3	1	5/31/2011	null
279	279	3	1	5/31/2011	null
280	280	3	1	5/31/2011	null
281	281	3	1	5/31/2011	null
282	282	3	1	5/31/2011	null
283	283	3	1	5/31/2011	null
284	284	3	1	9/30/2012	null
285	285	3	1	3/14/2013	null
286	286	3	1	5/30/2013	null
287	287	3	1	4/16/2012	null
288	288	3	1	5/30/2013	null
289	289	3	1	5/30/2012	null
290	290	3	1	5/30/2012	null
291	4	1	1	12/5/2007	5/30/2010
292	16	5	1	12/20/2007	7/14/2009
293	224	7	1	1/7/2009	8/31/2011
294	234	10	1	1/31/2009	11/13/2013
295	250	4	1	2/25/2011	7/30/2011
296	250	13	1	7/31/2011	7/14/2012

Figure 10.14 – An overview of the HumanResources EmployeeDepartmentHistory transformed table

Moving on to the **HumanResources EmployeePayHistory** table, set **RateChangeDate** to a date data type and check that the final table looks like the one shown in the following screenshot:

	1²₃ BusinessEntityID	RateChangeDate	1.2 Rate	1²₃ PayFrequency
1	1	1/14/2009	125.5	2
2	2	1/31/2008	63.4615	2
3	3	11/11/2007	43.2692	2
4	5	1/6/2008	32.6923	2
5	6	1/24/2008	32.6923	2
6	7	2/8/2009	50.4808	2
7	8	12/29/2008	40.8654	2
8	9	1/16/2009	40.8654	2
9	10	5/3/2009	42.4808	2
10	11	12/5/2010	28.8462	2
11	12	12/11/2007	25	2
12	13	12/23/2010	25	2
13	14	12/30/2010	36.0577	2

`= Table.TransformColumnTypes(#"Removed Columns",{{"RateChangeDate", type date}})`

Figure 10.15 – The HumanResources EmployeePayHistory transformed table

For the **HumanResources Shift** table, we set the **StartTime** and **EndTime** columns to the time data type. The transformed table should be similar to the one shown in the following screenshot:

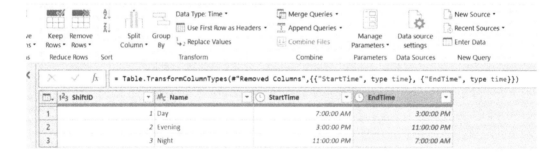

`= Table.TransformColumnTypes(#"Removed Columns",{{"StartTime", type time}, {"EndTime", type time}})`

	1²₃ ShiftID	A⁶C Name	StartTime	EndTime
1	1	Day	7:00:00 AM	3:00:00 PM
2	2	Evening	3:00:00 PM	11:00:00 PM
3	3	Night	11:00:00 PM	7:00:00 AM

Figure 10.16 – The transformed HumanResources Shift table

Moving on to the **Person Person** table, delete the **NameStyle**, **AdditionalContact**, and **Demographics** columns. The final table should look similar to the one shown in the following screenshot:

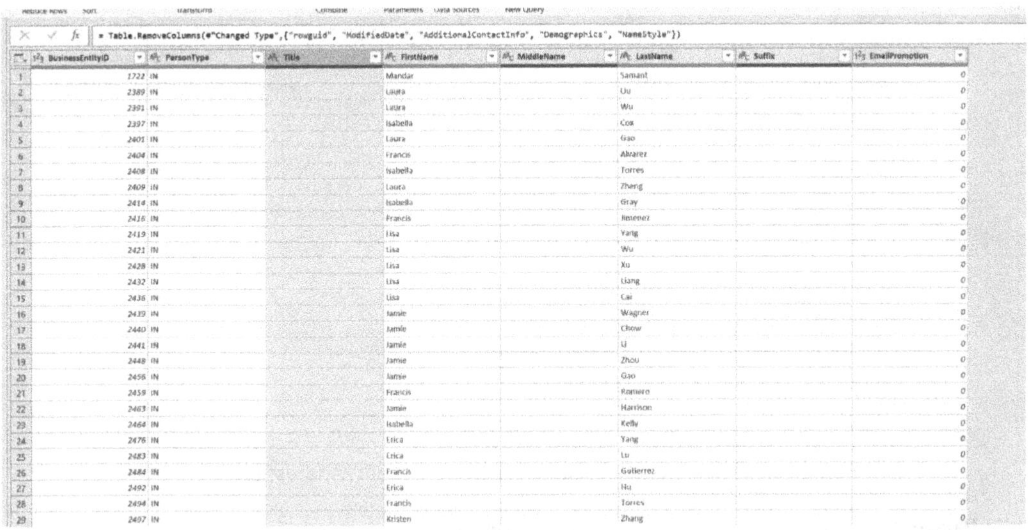

Figure 10.17 – An overview of the transformed Person Person table

For the **Person BusinessEntityAddress** table, before removing the unneeded columns, we will remove duplicate records in the **BusinessEntityID** column as we are not interested in mapping multiple entities to the same address. Depending on the type of dimensions (reporting categories) we want to present in our dashboard, this might cause data loss and is not always recommended. However, for our HR dashboard, we can safely proceed with doing this and show one of the common data transformation steps you will often do – removing duplicates. To achieve this, right-click on the **BusinessEntityID** column and select **Remove Duplicates**. Then, you can proceed to remove the **rowguid** and **ModifiedDate** columns. The final table will look similar to the one shown in the following screenshot:

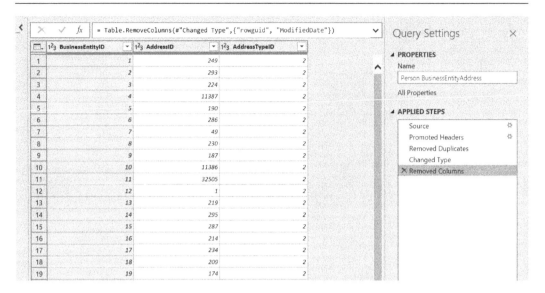

Figure 10.18 – The transformed Person BusinessEntityAddress table

In the **Person Address** table, we will delete the **SpatialLocation** column as we won't be needing it for our dashboard building. The final table will look like the one shown in the following screenshot:

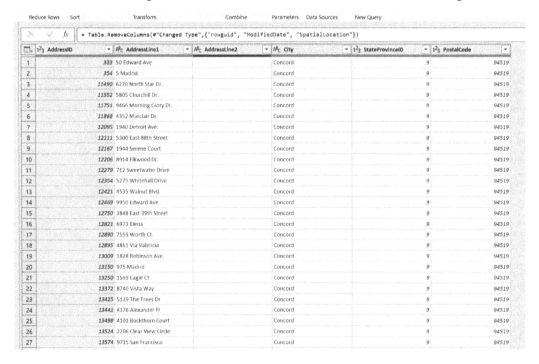

Figure 10.19 – An overview of the transformed Person Address table

For the remaining two tables, **Person StateProvince** and **Person CountryRegion**, we will simply remove the **rowguid** and **ModifiedDate** columns. That will conclude the table-specific transformations.

The next step is to hit **Close & Load To…** under the **Home** menu. This will allow us to pull in the transformed tables into Power Pivot for more data modeling steps. See the following screenshot:

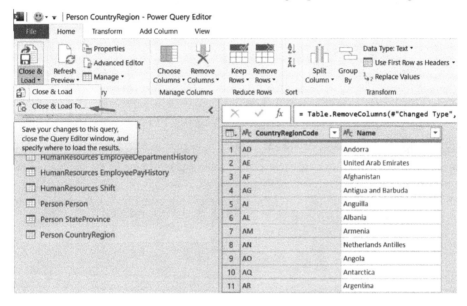

Figure 10.20 – The Close & Load To… option under the Home menu

In the dialog box that appears, set the option to **Only Create Connection** and tick the option to add to the data model, as shown in the following screenshot:

Figure 10.21 – Loading the data into Power Pivot

Once the loading process has completed, click on **Manage Data Model** in the **Data** menu, as shown in the following screenshot:

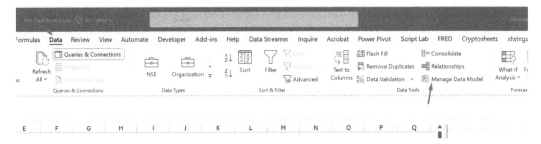

Figure 10.22 – Accessing the data model

This will launch the **Power Pivot for Excel** window. All the tables we loaded will be displayed at the bottom as separate tabs. The content of each selected table will be shown in the main window area below the menu section. One of the most important steps we must do is set up the logical relationships between the tables. We will begin that process by clicking on **Diagram View** under the **Home** menu, as illustrated in the following screenshot:

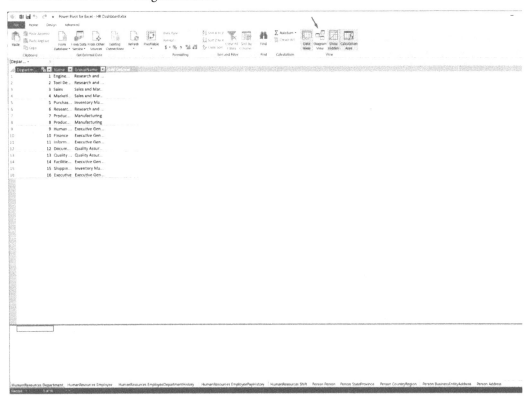

Figure 10.23 – An overview of accessing Diagram View in Power Query

We will proceed to create the following relationships:

- The **BusinessEntityID** column from **HumanResources EmployeeDepartmentHistory** mapped to the **BusinessEntityID** column from **Person Person**

- The **BusinessEntityID** column from **HumanResources Employee** mapped to the **BusinessEntityID** column from **Person BusinessEntityAddress**

- The **BusinessEntityID** column from **HumanResources Employee** mapped to the **BusinessEntityID** column from **HumanResources EmployeeDepartmentHistory**

- The **DepartmentID** column from **HumanResources EmployeeDepartmentHistory** mapped to the **DepartmentID** column from **HumanResources Department**

- The **ShiftID** column from **HumanResources EmployeeDepartmentHistory** mapped to the **ShiftID** column from **HumanResources Shift**

- The **BusinessEntityID** column from **HumanResources EmployeePayHistory** mapped to the **BusinessEntityID** column from **Person Person**

- The **StateProvinceID** column from **Person Address** mapped to the **StateProvinceID** column from **Person StateProvince**

- The **AddressID** column from **Person BusinessEntityAddress** mapped to the **AddressID** column from **Person Address**

- The **BusinessEntityID** column from **Person BusinessEntityAddress** mapped to the **BusinessEntityID** column from **HumanResources Employee**

- The **CountryRegionCode** column from **Person StateProvince** mapped to the **CountryRegionCode** column from Person **CountryRegion**

There are two general ways to create these relationships. The easiest is to drag a related column from one table to the related column on the other table. This will instantly create the relationship, as shown in the following screenshot:

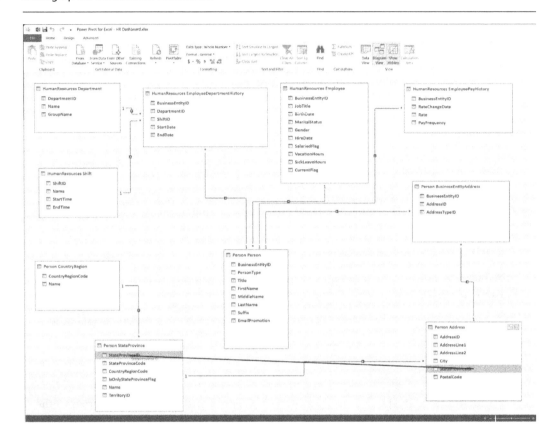

Figure 10.24 – An overview of dragging one column over another to create a relationship

The second approach is to use the **Manage Relationships** tool under the **Design** menu. It has a **Create** button that lets you select the columns to relate across any two selected tables. You should always pick the many-side table (the table where the relating column has repeated entries) first and the one-side table (the table where the relating column only has unique entries). This ensures that the relationship comes out right all the time. The following screenshot shows how it works:

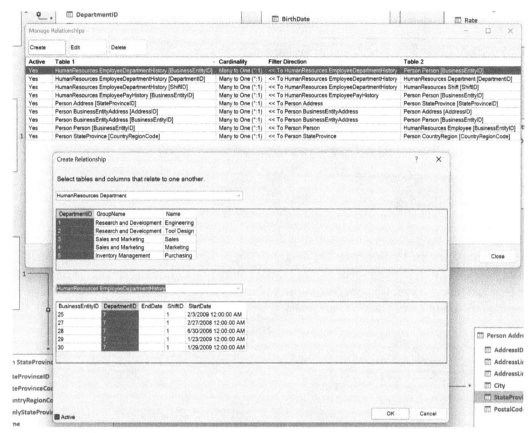

Figure 10.25 – An overview of using the Manage Relationships tool to create relationships

With the relationships completed, we are done with the preparatory data model for the HR dashboard. Save the current Excel file with all the work done as HR Dashboard.xlsx. For now, you can close it. We will reuse it in the next chapter:

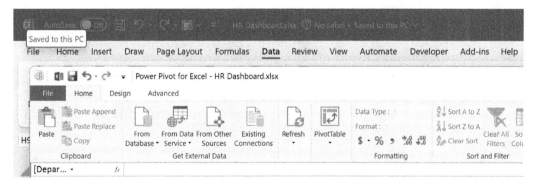

Figure 10.26 – Saving the Excel file as HR Dashboard

We will replicate most of what we've done here for the sales dashboard.

For the sales dashboard, we need to import the following tables:

- `Sales Customer`
- `Sales SalesOrderDetail`
- `Sales SalesOrderHeader`
- `Sales SalesOrderHeaderSalesReason`
- `Sales SalesReason`
- `Sales SalesTerritory`
- `Sales Store`

Then, we must delete the **ModifiedDate** and **rowguid** columns from all the tables. Set all date columns to date data type. Delete the **Comment** column from the **Sales SalesOrderHeader** table. Then, delete the **Demographics** column from the **Sales Store** table. With those edits, we are almost done in the **Power Query** window, which should look similar to what I have in the following screenshot:

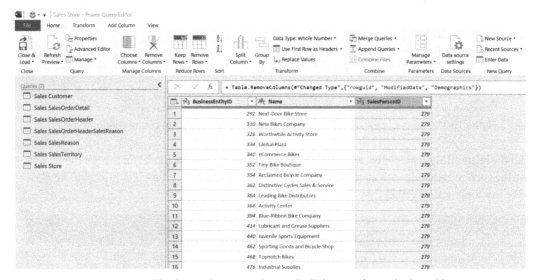

Figure 10.27 – The Power Query window with all the transformed sales tables

There is one special transformation we will need to carry out on the **Sales SalesOrderHeaderSalesReason** table: we will combine all the sales reasons in a comma-separated entry per sales order so that we have distinct sales orders and all the sales reasons are combined into one comma-separated list. Then, we will split the list into separate columns of sales reasons. This will allow us to interact with the autogenerated Power Query codes, modifying them when we need some more customization than what the menus have a button for.

To achieve this, change the **SalesReasonID** column data type to text, then right-click on the column and select **Group By**. Set the **New column name** field to `SalesReasonIDs`, set **Operation** to **Sum**, and set **Column** to **SalesReasonID**, as shown in the following screenshot:

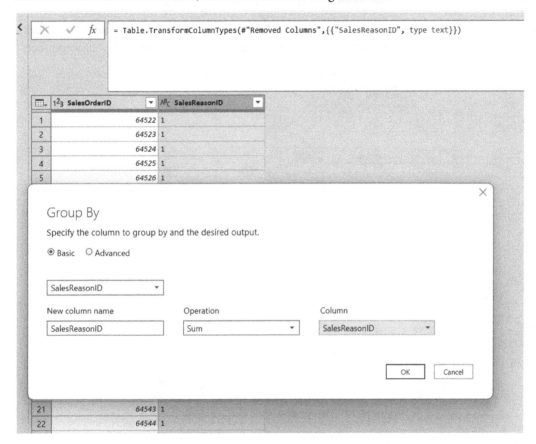

Figure 10.28 – The Group By window in Power Query

You might notice an error within the table, but don't worry about it – we will fix it by customizing the Power Query-generated code to achieve our unique need of combining the sales reasons rather than summing them.

The code for the step we've just concluded will look very much like this:

```
Table.Group(#"Changed Type1", {"SalesReasonID"}, {{"SalesReasonID.1",
each List.Sum([SalesReasonID]), type nullable text}})
```

Change the last part from summation to text combination by editing the code so that it looks as follows:

```
Table.Group(#"Changed Type1", {"SalesOrderID"}, {{"SalesReasonIDs",
each Text.Combine([SalesReasonID],","), type nullable text}})
```

Here, `Text.Combine([SalesReasonID],",")` indicates that all sales reasons for the sales order should be combined with a comma separation. The outcome is shown in the following screenshot:

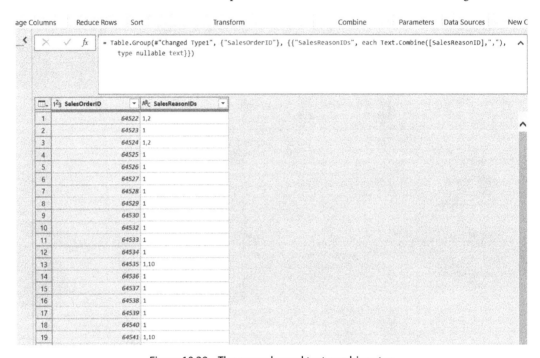

Figure 10.29 – The group by and text combine step

With that done, we can simply right-click on the **SalesReasonIDs** column and split the column by delimiter, as shown in the following screenshot:

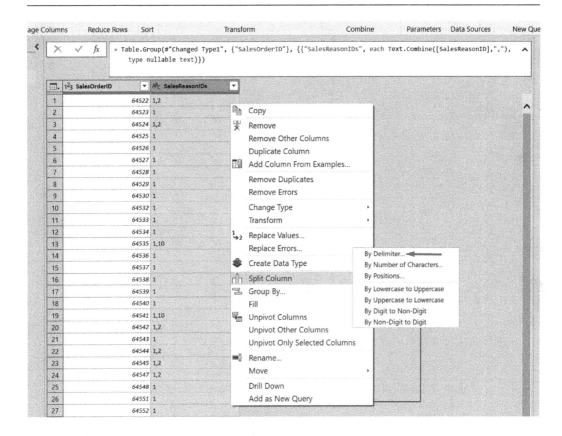

Figure 10.30 – Split Column

Set the delimiter to a comma, then change the data type of the split columns to a whole number. That will complete the special transformation, with the final table looking like what's shown in the following screenshot:

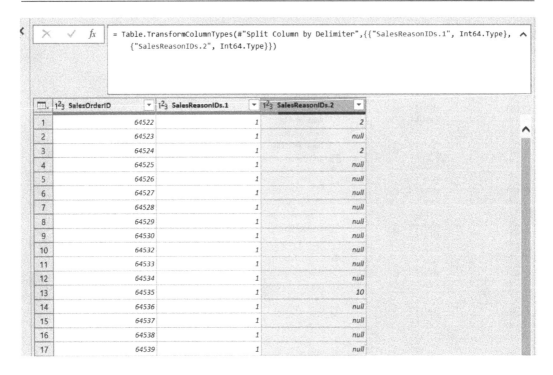

Figure 10.31 – Final transformed Sales SalesOrderHeaderSalesReason table

Then, like we did for the HR dashboard, close and load the Power Query tables to connection only and data model settings. You will notice the **Queries & Connections** pane on the right showing you the number of rows that have been loaded, as shown in the following screenshot:

Figure 10.32 – The Queries & Connections pane

Head over to **Manage Data Model** under the **Data** menu. Then, create the following relationships:

- The **StoreID** column from **Sales Customer** mapped to the **BusinessEntityID** column from **Sales Store**

- The **TerritoryID** column from **Sales Customer** mapped to the **TerritoryID** column from **Sales SalesTerritory**

- The **SalesOrderID** column from **Sales SalesOrderDetail** mapped to the **SalesOrderID** column from **Sales SalesOrderHeader**

- The **CustomerID** column from **Sales SalesOrderHeader** mapped to the **CustomerID** column from **Sales Customer**

- The **SalesOrderID** column from **Sales SalesOrderHeaderSalesReason** mapped to the SalesOrderID column from **Sales SalesOrderHeader**

- The **SalesReasonID** column from **Sales SalesOrderHeaderSalesReason** mapped to the **SalesReasonIDs.1** column from **Sales SalesReason**

The resulting relationship schema will look like the one shown in the following screenshot:

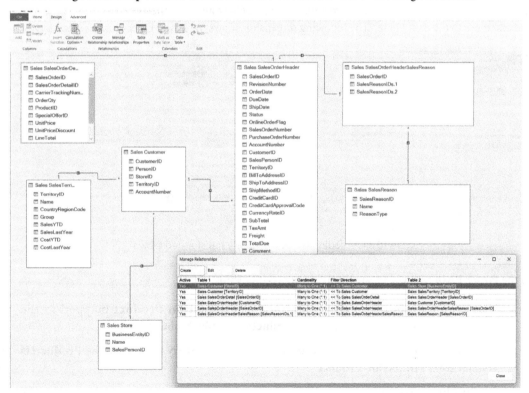

Figure 10.33 – An overview of sales dashboard tables relationships

Save this Excel file as `Sales Dashboard.xlsx`.

Finally, we will create the data model for the last dashboard. We will call it `Supply Chain Dashboard`. We'll import the following tables into Power Query in a new Excel file:

- `Production Product`
- `Production ProductCategory`
- `Production ProductInventory`
- `Production ProductSubcategory`
- `Purchasing ProductVendor`
- `Purchasing PurchaseOrderDetail`
- `Purchasing PurchaseOrderHeader`
- `Purchasing Vendor`
- `Production Location`

After importing these tables into Power Query, we must delete all the **ModifiedDate** and **rowguid** columns. Change all the date columns to date data types. Close and load the tables to connection only and add them to the data model. The following screenshot shows the Power Query transformed tables:

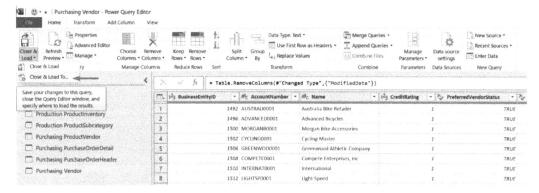

Figure 10.34 – Loading the Power Query transformed tables

In the **Power Pivot** window, create the following relationships:

- The **ProductSubcategoryID** column from **Production Product** mapped to the **ProductSubCategoryID** column from **Production ProductSubCategory**
- The **ProductID** column from **Production ProductInventory** mapped to the **ProductID** column **from Production Product**
- The **ProductCategoryID** column from **Production ProductSubcategory** mapped to the **ProductCategoryID** column from **Production ProductCategory**

- The **ProductID** column from **Purchasing ProductVendor** mapped to the **ProductID** column from **Production Product**

- The **ProductID** column from **Purchasing PurchaseOrderDetail** mapped to the **ProductID** column from **Production Product**

- The **PurchaseOrderID** column from **Purchasing PurchaseOrderDetail** mapped to the **PurchaseOrderID** column from **Purchasing PurchaseOrderHeader**

- The **VendorID** column from **Purchasing PurchaseOrderHeader** mapped to the **BusinessEntityID** column from **Purchasing Vendor**

- The **Location** column from **Production ProductInventory** mapped to the **Location** column from **Production Location**.

The final relationship schema will look like what's shown in the following screenshot:

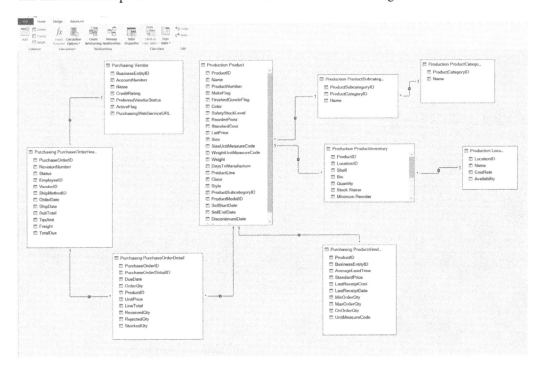

Figure 10.35 – An overview of supply Chain Dashboard table relationships

All that's left is to save the file as `Supply Chain Dashboard`. You can close it too as we will pick it up in *Chapter 11, Perfecting the Dashboard.*

And with that, we have come to the end of creating the data model for our Adventure Works company dashboards.

Summary

In this chapter, I walked you through the demo company we are building business-wide dashboards for – Adventure Works Cycle Limited. Together, we examined the company's line of business and its database tables. We identified the different business units within the company and what types of data the database tables hold.

Lastly, we created data models for the HR dashboard, sales dashboard, and supply chain dashboard. This gave us a chance to put to use the learning we covered on Power Query.

In the next chapter, we will build on our data models and take one of the two giant steps left to servicing the management of Adventure Works with the management decision-driving dashboard they need.

See you in the next chapter!

11

Perfecting the Dashboard

Great job on the progress you have made so far. In the previous chapter, we were introduced to **Adventure Works Cycle Limited** (**AWCL**) and explored the company's dataset across human resources, sales, production, and procurement. We built a data model and put into practice our Power Query knowledge in ingesting and transforming data.

In this chapter, we will build on that progress and build three dashboards, putting to use our knowledge of data visualization tools, such as charts, slicers, and shapes, to create interactive and visually engaging dashboards.

Here's a breakdown of what we will cover in this chapter:

- Building the **human resources** (**HR**) manpower dashboard
- Building the sales performance dashboard
- Building the supply chain inventory dashboard

This is going to be a very exciting chapter as we put together all we have learned from the previous chapters to achieve beautiful and neatly developed dashboards. We will not be creating any hidden sheet that will house intermediate calculations, as you probably would have come across in Excel dashboards built years before we had a data model in Excel.

Building the HR manpower dashboard

We will pick up from where we left off in the previous chapter when we built the data model, like the one in the following screenshot:

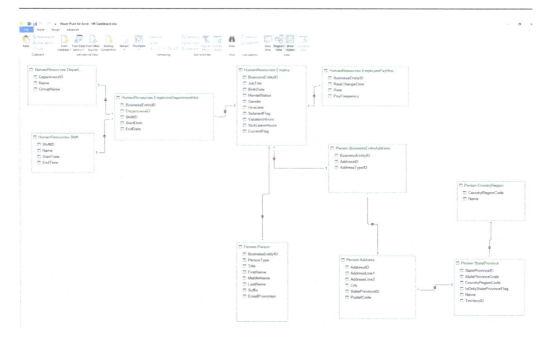

Figure 11.1 – An overview of the HR dashboard data model

We are going to build an HR manpower dashboard that will look like the one in the following screenshot:

Figure 11.2 – An overview of a snapshot of the dashboard to be built

To build this dashboard, we will use the following components in Excel:

- A PivotTable to generate the interactive tables
- A PivotChart to create two column charts in the dashboard
- Insert a picture to add the company logo
- Shapes and icons to create single-value cards at the top of the dashboard

By the time we have finished building the dashboard, you will get to experience the power that having a proper data model puts in your hands, building beautiful interactive dashboards without using complex formulas or creating helper calculation sheets.

Inserting PivotTables

We start by using the Excel file we created for the HR dashboard in the previous chapter. It has a complete data model. If you did not follow along in the previous chapter, you can download the file and other files from the book's GitHub folder at `https://github.com/PacktPublishing/Building-Interactive-Dashboards-in-Microsoft-365-Excel`. The data model files are in the folder bearing that same name, and for now, we will work on `HR Dashboard Data Model.xslx`, as indicated in the following screenshot:

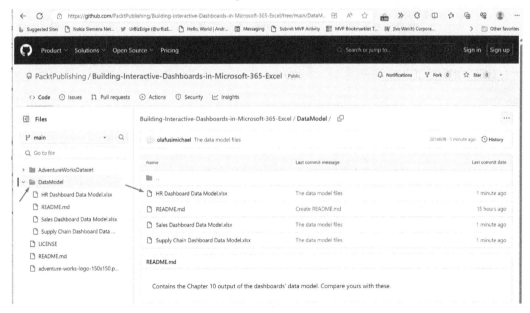

Figure 11.3 – The DataModel folder

The steps to insert PivotTables are as follows:

1. On opening the `HR Dashboard Data Model.xslx` file, go to the **Data** menu and click on **Manage Data Model**. This will launch the **Power Pivot** window.

2. To insert a PivotTable, click on **PivotTable** under the **Home** menu and select **PivotTable**. In the dialog box that appears, select **Existing Worksheet** and set the cell to B9, as shown in the following screenshot:

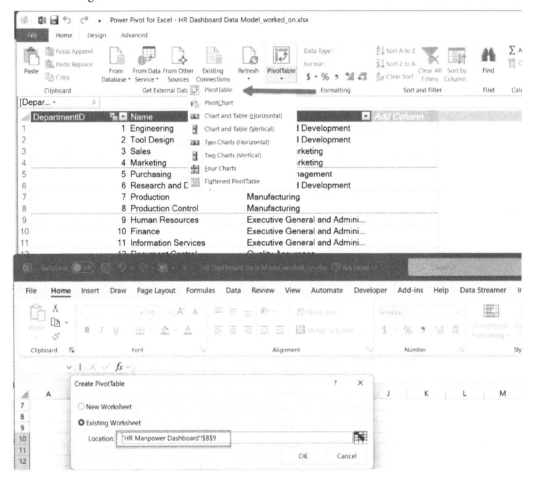

Figure 11.4 – Inserting a PivotTable from the Power Pivot window

3. In the PivotTable that comes up, place **EndDate** from the `HumanResources EmployeeDepartmentHistory` table into **Filters**, allowing us to set **EndDate** to blank and capture only active staff.

4. We then place **Name** from the `HumanResources Department` table into **Rows** to get the department list in the row-wise format.

5. We also place **Name** from the `HumanResources Shift` table to get the shift categories to show column-wise.

6. Lastly, we place **BusinessEntityID** from the `HumanResources EmployeeDepartmentHistory` table into **Values**, setting its calculation to a distinct count. This will get us a distinct count of staff across the departments and by the shift they run. The final PivotTable should look like the one in the following screenshot:

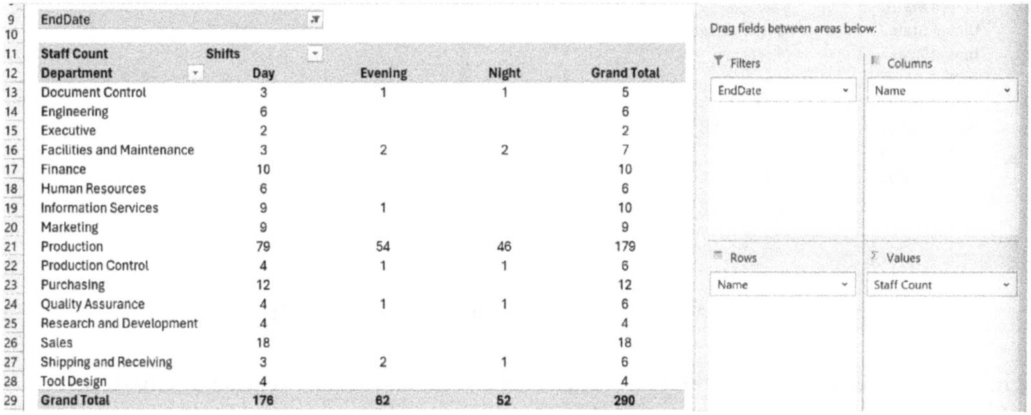

	Staff Count	Shifts						
9	EndDate						Drag fields between areas below:	
11	**Staff Count**	**Shifts**						
12	**Department**	**Day**	**Evening**	**Night**	**Grand Total**			
13	Document Control	3	1	1	5			
14	Engineering	6			6			
15	Executive	2			2			
16	Facilities and Maintenance	3	2	2	7			
17	Finance	10			10			
18	Human Resources	6			6			
19	Information Services	9	1		10			
20	Marketing	9			9			
21	Production	79	54	46	179			
22	Production Control	4	1	1	6			
23	Purchasing	12			12			
24	Quality Assurance	4	1	1	6			
25	Research and Development	4			4			
26	Sales	18			18			
27	Shipping and Receiving	3	2	1	6			
28	Tool Design	4			4			
29	**Grand Total**	**176**	**62**	**52**	**290**			

Drag fields between areas below:

- **Filters**: EndDate
- **Columns**: Name
- **Rows**: Name
- **Values**: Staff Count

Figure 11.5 – A PivotTable of Staff Count by Department and Shifts

We will then insert one more PivotTable by following the following steps:

1. Go to the **Data** menu and click on **Manage Data Model** to launch the **Power Pivot** window.

2. Insert another PivotTable but set it to display on cell `B31`. And for this, place **Name** from the `Person CountryRegion` table into **Rows** to get a row-wise list of the countries the company has staff in.

3. We, again, place **Name** from the **Person StateProvince** table in **Rows** in order to see a breakdown by state. Lastly, place **BusinessEntityID** from the `HumanResources EmployeeDepartmentHistory` table into **Values**, and set its calculation to a distinct count.

4. Next, improve the formatting by going to the **Design** menu on the far right, click on **Report Layout**, and set it to **Show in Tabular Form**. Then, click on **Subtotals** and set it to **Do Not Show Subtotals**.

5. To make the report easy to read, rename the column headers **Country** and **State** by simply typing over the current default name in the header cells. The final PivotTable will look very much like the one in the following screenshot:

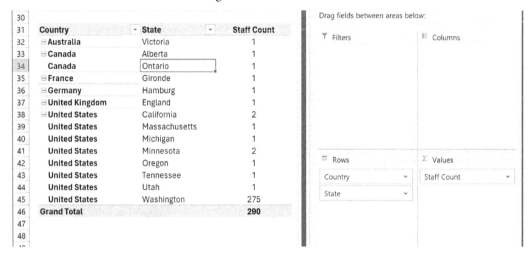

Figure 11.6 – A PivotTable of Staff Count by Country and State

We have now finished setting up the PivotTables in our dashboard. Now, we will move on to setting up the PivotCharts.

Inserting PivotCharts

The steps to insert PivotCharts are very similar to what we did for the PivotTables. We will insert two PivotCharts, related to the PivotTables we created, and place them right beside the PivotTables. This will provide a visual illustration of the insights.

Again, go to **Data | Manage Data Model** to bring up Power Pivot. This time, pick **PivotChart** instead of **PivotTable** and set the location to cell G9. Place **Name** from HumanResources Department in **Axis (Categories)** so that the departments will show as horizontal axis categories on a column chart. Then, place **BusinessEntityID** from the HumanResources EmployeeDepartmentHistory table into **Values** and set the calculation to a distinct count.

Finally, improve the look of the column chart by removing the gridlines, adding data labels, removing the vertical axis, and adding a chart title. The final chart will look like the one in the following screenshot:

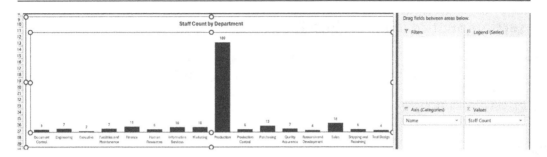

Figure 11.7 – An overview of a PivotChart of Staff Count by Department

Next, insert a similar PivotChart in cell E31 for the staff count by state and county by following the same steps, but instead, place **Name** from the Person StateProvince table in **Axis (Categories)** and **Name** from the Person CountryRegion table in **Axis (Categories)**. Then, place **BusinessEntityID** from the HumanResources EmployeeDepartmentHistory table into **Values** and set the calculation to a distinct count. The final column chart will look very much like the one in the following screenshot:

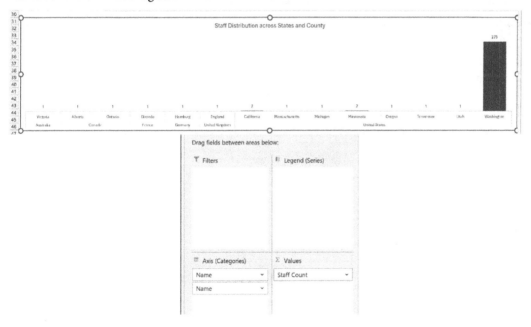

Figure 11.8 – An overview of a PivotChart of staff count by state and county

Now that we have finished with the PivotCharts, we will move on to the other components of our dashboard.

Inserting picture, shapes, and icons

The final components of our HR manpower dashboard are shapes, icons, and the company logo (which you will find in the resource folder: `https://github.com/PacktPublishing/Building-Interactive-Dashboards-in-Microsoft-365-Excel`). Ultimately, we will have a setup that looks very much like the following screenshot:

Figure 11.9 – The final setup for the logo, shapes, and icons

Note that there are three PivotTables in the preceding screenshot; they are instrumental in providing the values that will be reflected in the rounded-corner rectangles.

Start by placing the company logo to the upper left of the Excel sheet. Then, insert a PivotTable in cell C2, place **Gender** from the `HumanResources Employee` table into **Columns** and **BusinessEntityID** from the same `HumanResources Employee` table into **Values**. Set the calculation for **BusinessEntityID** as a distinct count. Also, because we will need to create a pie chart of the female/male staff ratio, amend the cells right below the PivotTable values to reference those values. The result will look very much like the following screenshot:

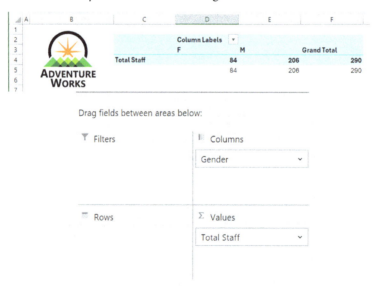

Figure 11.10 – A staff count by gender PivotTable

We will add two more PivotTables, showing the staff count by marital status and `SalariedFlag`. All these fields are in the `HumanResources Employee` table. The result will be similar to what's shown in the following screenshot:

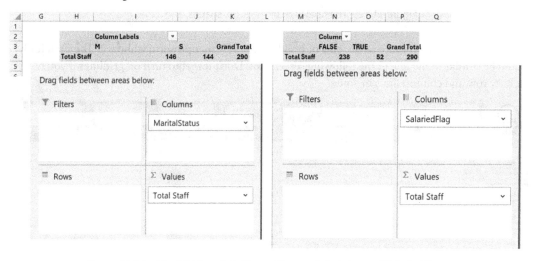

Figure 11.11 – PivotTables of staff count by marital status and SalariedFlag

Insert six rounded-corner rectangles, one regular rectangle, an icon of a woman, and another icon of a man. Link the rectangles to values in the already created PivotTable. Do this in the following order: the total staff count, the female staff count, the male staff count, the married staff count, the single staff count, the `SalariedFlag TRUE` staff count, and the `SalariedFlag FALSE` staff count. Set the shape value display format to be center aligned for both vertical and horizontal alignment. Put a textbox under each rectangle to serve as the label for the value in the rectangle. You can simply type out the metric that the rectangle above displays the value of.

Place the woman icon on top of the rectangle showing the female staff count, to the left of the displayed value. Do likewise for the man icon and the rectangle showing the male staff count.

Create a pie chart of the female staff and male staff, using the cells below that first PivotTable that reference the values. Remove the chart title, legend, and outer outline. Duplicate the chart. Set the color of the female pie to orange and the male pie to white for the first chart. Set the color of the female pie to white and the male pie to blue for the other. Place the charts on the rectangles for the female and male staff count, ensuring the one with the female pie colored orange is on the female staff count rectangle.

Set the color of the regular rectangle to blue, and set its size to be big enough to provide a background for all the six rounded-corner rectangles. Place all the rounded-corner rectangles on the regular rectangle, space them equally, and set their background to white and their font color to black. Select all the elements and group them together by right-clicking and selecting **Group**. Place the grouped elements on top of the PivotTables just created. The result will look like the one in the following screenshot:

Figure 11.12 – The final look of the logo, shapes, and icons

And with that, we have come to the end of building the HR manpower dashboard. The final look should be similar to the one in the following screenshot. Don't forget to turn off gridlines if you have the busy row and column lines in yours.

Figure 11.13 – An overview of the final HR manpower dashboard

We will now move on to the sales performance dashboard.

Building the sales performance dashboard

We will build on the data model we created in the previous chapter for the sales dashboard, and you can see what it looks like in the following screenshot:

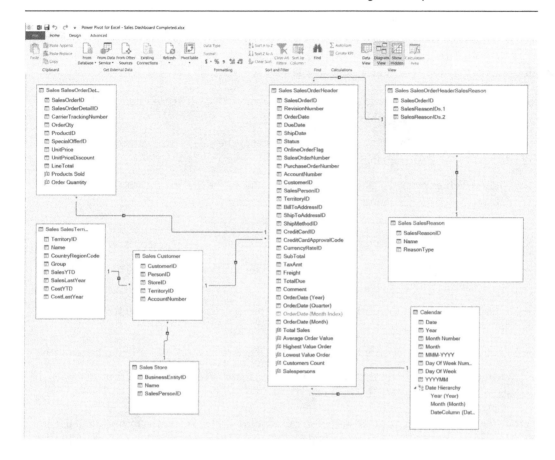

Figure 11.14 – An overview of the sales dashboard data model

We will take the steps we followed in creating the HR dashboard – inserting PivotTables, inserting PivotCharts, and inserting illustrations (pictures and shapes). However, in addition to those steps, we will insert slicers, insert a timeline, and create calculation measures. So, this will involve more steps than the HR dashboard, and you will enjoy taking these new steps, as they will empower you with the knowledge to create very robust dashboards that meet business decision makers' needs.

We will start by creating the calculation measures.

Creating measures

Measures are formulas you create within a table in Power Pivot to output one result for the entire table. They are typically an aggregation calculation, a formula that gives a summarized metric. Common examples utilize functions such as sum, count, average, and distinctcount.

The measures we are going to create will be within two different tables – six measures in the `Sales SalesOrderHeader` table and two measures in the `Sales SalesOrderDetail` table. A list with a short description of each measure is as follows:

- **Total Sales**: To compute the sum of the sales value (`TotalDue`) field in the `Sales SalesOrderHeader` table
- **Average Order Value**: To compute the average of the sales order values in the `Sales SalesOrderHeader` table
- **Highest Value Order**: To get the largest order value in the `Sales SalesOrderHeader` table (actually, you can give the measures whatever name you prefer if you feel a different name would read better)
- **Lowest Value Order**: To get the smallest order value in the `Sales SalesOrderHeader` table
- **Customers Count**: To get the distinct count of customers who placed orders in the `Sales SalesOrderHeader` table
- **Salespersons**: To get the distinct count of salespersons who generated all the orders in the `Sales SalesOrderHeader` table
- **Products Sold**: To get the distinct count of products sold in the `Sales SalesOrderDetail` table
- **Order Quantity**: To get the total quantities ordered across all products in the `Sales SalesOrderDetail` table

To create the measures, first go to the host (also called home) table to enter the measure and use any of the cells in the unnumbered rows at the bottom of the table. Then, type in the cell in the following format – `MeasureName := Formula`.

Using that approach for the `Sales SalesOrderHeader` table, you create the following measures:

- `Total Sales := SUM('Sales SalesOrderHeader'[TotalDue])`
- `Average Order Value := [Total Sales]/COUNT('Sales SalesOrderHeader'[SalesOrderNumber])`
- `Highest Value Order := MAX('Sales SalesOrderHeader'[TotalDue])`
- `Lowest Value Order := MIN('Sales SalesOrderHeader'[TotalDue])`
- `Customers Count := DISTINCTCOUNTNOBLANK('Sales SalesOrderHeader'[CustomerID])`
- `Salespersons := DISTINCTCOUNTNOBLANK('Sales SalesOrderHeader'[SalesPersonID])`

The following screenshot shows what these measures end up looking like when created:

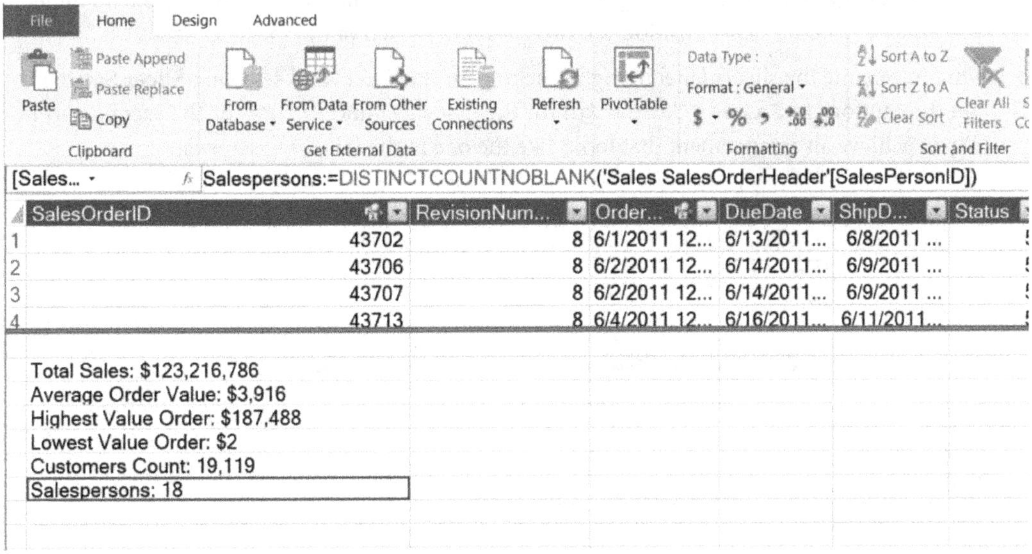

Figure 11.15 – The SalesOrderHeader table measures

Finally, we create the two measures for the `Sales SalesOrderDetail` table:

- `Products Sold := DISTINCTCOUNTNOBLANK('Sales SalesOrderDetail'[ProductID])`

- `Order Quantity := SUM('Sales SalesOrderDetail'[OrderQty])`

And with that, we are done writing the measures we will need to build our sales performance dashboard. We will move on now to adding the slicers and timeline.

Inserting slicers and timelines

Slicers and timelines are more interactive shape versions of filters. They come with a default rectangle shape that can be resized and formatted to create different visual styles. However, at their core, they have the same effect as a filter does on a report – allowing the report to reflect only a desired section of the full underlying data. Let's go through the steps:

1. First, insert a PivotTable in cell `C10` of the sales dashboard sheet, then right-click on any field you want to use for a slicer or timeline, and click on **Add as Slicer** or **Add as Timeline**. Note that the **Add as Timeline** option will only appear for date or time fields.

2. Create one timeline and two slicers. For the timeline, right-click on the `Date` field under the `Calendar` table, and select **Add as Timeline**. Place the timeline shape at the top of the sheet, and set the periodicity in the upper-right corner to **QUARTERS**.

3. Next, we create the two slicers by right-clicking on the Name field under the Sales SalesReason table and selecting **Add as Slicer**. Then, do likewise for the Name field under the Sales Store table. Position the two slicers to the left of the sheet.

4. Finally, rename the slicers label by right-clicking on the slicers and selecting **Slicer Settings**. Set the captions to Sales Campaign for the first slicer and Store for the second slicer. Try to achieve an arrangement that looks like the one in the following screenshot:

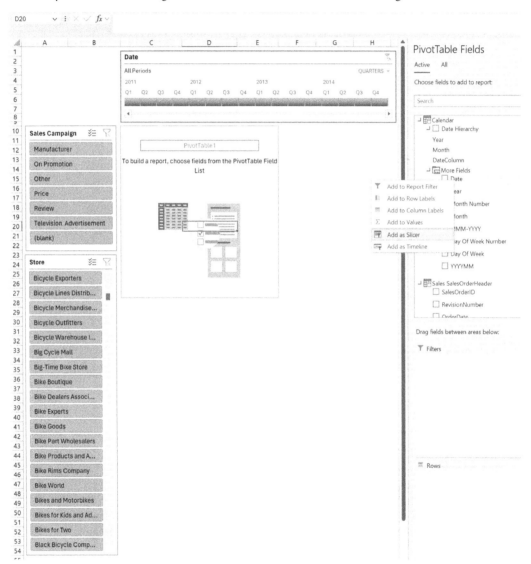

Figure 11.16 – Inserting the timeline and slicers

We are now done with the timeline and slicers, and we will move on to adding a PivotTable and a PivotChart.

Inserting a PivotTable and a PivotChart

We will add one giant PivotTable and a giant PivotChart right beside it. Start by using the PivotTable we added to cell `C10`, enabling us to create the timeline. Place the `Year` and `MMM-YYYY` fields under the `Calendar` table into **Rows**. Then, put one our measures, **Total Sales**, into **Values**. Finally, place **Name** under the `Sales SalesTerritory` table into **Columns**.

The resulting PivotTable will reflect sales over the months and years across the different sales territories, and it will look similar to the one in the following screenshot:

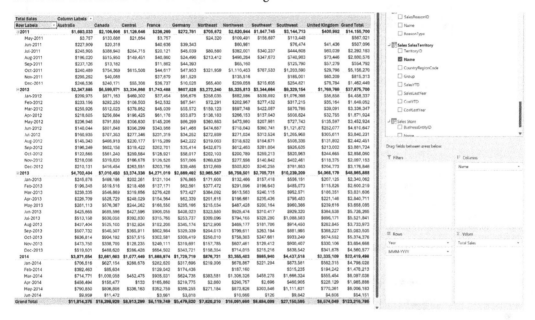

Figure 11.17 – A sales by territories PivotTable

With the PivotTable done, we will now move on to the PivotChart that we will insert in cell `P10`. Place `OrderDate` from the `Sales SalesOrderHeader` table in **Axis (Categories)**, and you will see that, suddenly, four fields appear in there – `OrderDate (Year)`, `OrderDate (Quarter)`, `OrderDate (Month)`, and `OrderDate`. This happens a lot with date fields and can be a good thing, as it helps you to have ready-to-use groups that can be more meaningful than just showing day-by-day categories in the chart. Also, in our case, we are going to need these additional auto-generated fields. In fact, you will have to remove the actual `OrderDate` field from **Axis (Categories)** and leave the auto-generated ones – `OrderDate (Year)`, `OrderDate (Quarter)`, and `OrderDate (Month)`.

Finally, place the **Total Sales** measure into **Values**. Technically, we have made the PivotChart we want. However, as usual, we need to improve the look and design. Start by right-clicking on the PivotChart and selecting **Change Chart Type**. Set the chart type to a clustered bar chart. Turn off the field buttons, the gridlines, and legend. Size the chart to be same height as the PivotTable. You should now have a PivotChart that looks like the one in the following screenshot:

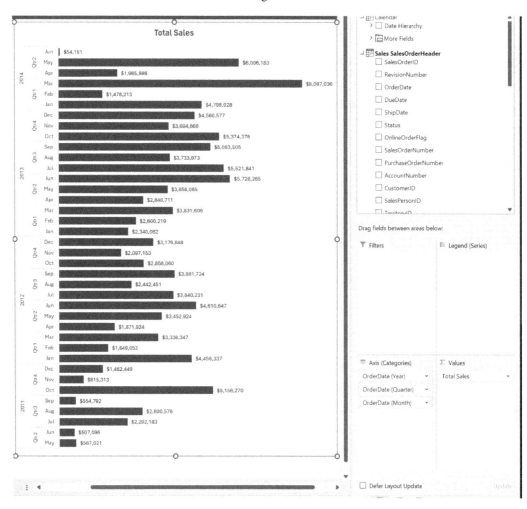

Figure 11.18 – An overview of a PivotChart of total sales by date period

Now that we have built the required PivotTable and PivotChart, we will move on the shapes and picture.

Inserting shapes and a picture

We will again insert the company logo and place it in the upper-left corner of the sheet, as we did for the HR manpower dashboard. This helps us to achieve a consistent branding across the dashboards. With the slicer positioned on the right, you will have a setup like the one in the following screenshot:

Figure 11.19 – An overview of the logo and slicer placement

We will put to use some of the measures we earlier created, placing them within the newly inserted PivotTable. In the cell J3, insert a PivotTable and place the **Total Sales** measure in **Values**. Insert another PivotTable in the cell L3 and place **Order Quantity** in **Values**. Likewise in cell N3, insert a PivotTable and place **Products Sold** in **Values**. In cell P3, insert one more PivotTable and place **Customers Count** in **Values**. Lastly, in cell R3, insert a final PivotTable and place **Salespersons** in **Values**. The result will look like the following screenshot:

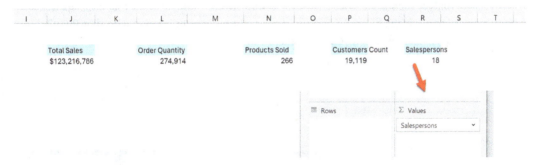

Figure 11.20 – The PivotTables to feed display values to the shapes

With the PivotTables now in place, we will add one large regular rectangle shape and five small rounded-corner rectangle shapes. Also, as we did for the HR manpower dashboard, we would like to add shapes to the values in the created PivotTables, using textboxes to add labels underneath the small shapes. Place the shapes and the labels on top of the big rectangle shape, and try to size them visually, like in the following screenshot:

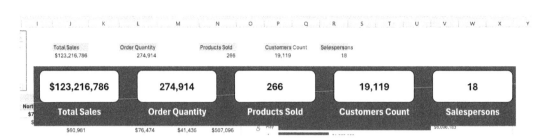

Figure 11.21 – The shapes' design and arrangement

Now, we are left with one critical step that we will address in the next section on filter and slicer connections.

Connecting slicers to the PivotTables and PivotCharts

You will have noticed that using slicers to make a selection of what to display in the dashboard is not working correctly. Each slicer seems to control just one table. In particular, the PivotTables we created to display values on the shapes are completely unaffected by the slicer selections. We will fix that now.

All we have to do is to properly set the filter connections between the PivotTables/PivotCharts and the slicers/timeline. We achieve this by clicking within each PivotTable and PivotChart, clicking on the **PivotTable Analyze** menu, and selecting **Filter Connections**. In the window that pops up, tick all the filters you see to allow the filters behind the slicer and timelines to interact with that PivotTable or PivotChart. See an example in the following screenshot:

Figure 11.22 – Setting the slicers and timeline to interact with a PivotTable

And with that final step, the sales performance dashboard is complete and should look similar to what's in the following screenshot:

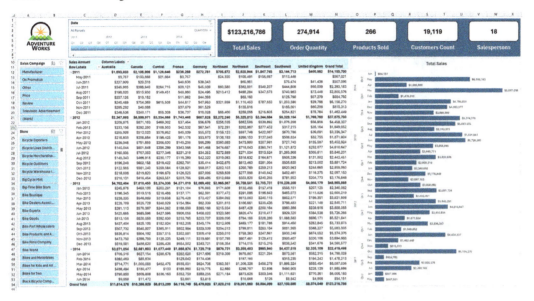

Figure 11.23 – An overview of the completed sales performance dashboard

We will now move on to the last dashboard – the supply chain inventory dashboard.

Building the supply chain inventory dashboard

We will reuse the steps and what we learned from building the other two dashboards, so I won't do an elaborate repetition of what I already explained in previous paragraphs. The data model for the supply chain dashboard we built in the previous chapter is shown in the following screenshot:

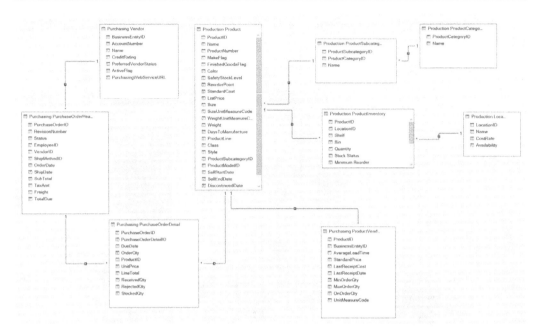

Figure 11.24 – An overview of the supply chain dashboard data model

To achieve the dashboard we want, we will start by creating seven measures – six in the `Production Product Inventory` table and one in the `Production Product` table. The measures are listed as follows:

- `Products:=DISTINCTCOUNTNOBLANK('Production ProductInventory'[ProductID])` to get the total count of products in the company's warehouses

- `In Stock:=CALCULATE(DISTINCTCOUNTNOBLANK('Production ProductInventory'[ProductID]),'Production ProductInventory'[Stock Status]="In Stock")` to get the count of products that are in stock above their reorder quantity level

- `Out of Stock:=CALCULATE(DISTINCTCOUNTNOBLANK('Production ProductInventory'[ProductID]),'Production ProductInventory'[Stock Status]="Out of Stock")` to get the count of products that are below their safety stock quantity level

- `Low Stock:=CALCULATE(DISTINCTCOUNTNOBLANK('Production ProductInventory'[ProductID]),'Production ProductInventory'[Stock Status]="Low Stock")` to get the count of products that are at a quantity level that is below the reorder quantity level but above the safety stock quantity level

- `Raw Materials:=CALCULATE(DISTINCTCOUNTNOBLANK('Production ProductInventory'[ProductID]),FILTER('Production Product','Production Product'[FinishedGoodsFlag]=FALSE()))` to get the distinct count of raw materials in the warehouses

- `Finished Goods:=CALCULATE(DISTINCTCOUNTNOBLANK('Production ProductInventory'[ProductID]),FILTER('Production Product','Production Product'[FinishedGoodsFlag]=TRUE()))` to get the distinct count of finished goods in the warehouses

- `Product Count:=DISTINCTCOUNT('Production Product'[ProductID])` to get the total number of products in the products table

With these measures set up, we can proceed to insert the PivotTables and PivotChart needed for the dashboard. We will start by inserting two slicers. The easiest way to do this is to insert a PivotTable in cell C9. Right-click on **Name** under `Production ProductCategory` and select **Add as Slicer**. Position the slicer to the left of the PivotTable. That's just one out of the two slicers we need to create. For the second slicer, click again within the PivotTable, right-click on **Name** under `Production ProductSubcategory`, and select **Add as Slicer**. The final look should be similar to the one in the following screenshot:

Figure 11.25 – The slicers for Product Categories and Subcategories

We will then complete the PivotTable setup by placing **Name** from the `Production Location` table into **Rows**, and then we place the **In Stock**, **Out of Stock**, **Low Stock**, and **Total Products** measures into **Values**. Then, we insert a second PivotTable in cell `C25`, placing **Class** and **ProductLine** from the `Production Product` table. In addition, we place **In Stock**, **Low Stock**, and **Out of Stock** in **Values**. For a better formatted table, set the table layout under the **Design** menu to a tabular form. The resulting look will be similar to the following screenshot:

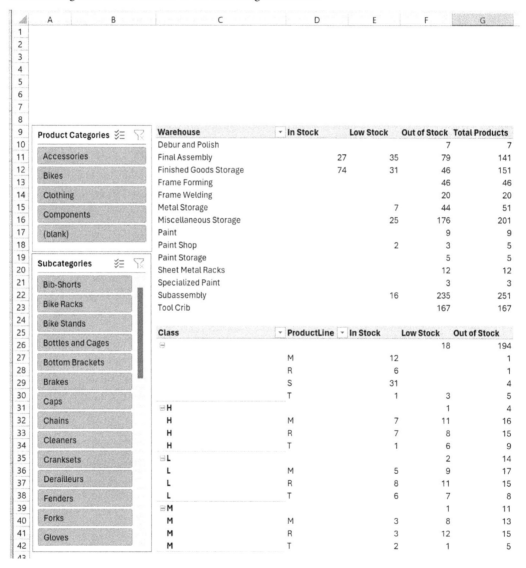

Figure 11.26 – The inventory level PivotTables

We then insert a PivotChart of the stock levels by warehouse. This is achieved by placing **Name** from `Production Product` into **Axis (Categories)** and placing the **In Stock**, **Low Stock**, and **Out of Stock** measures in **Values**. Change the chart type to a stacked bar chart. The resulting chart will look similar to the following screenshot:

Figure 11.27 – An overview of a PivotChart of the inventory level by warehouse

Finally, we insert the company logo in the upper-left corner and build the shapes as we did for the other two dashboards. We will use the shapes to present the total numbers of warehouses, the distinct count of stocked products, the distinct count of finished goods, the distinct count of raw materials, the products in stock, the count of products that are low in stock, and the count of products that are out of stock. We achieve this by creating a PivotTable and placing **Name** from `Production Location` (setting the calculation to a distinct count), **Products**, **Finished Goods**, **Raw Materials**, **In Stock**, **Low Stock**, and **Out of Stock** in **Values**. See the following screenshot for an illustration of this:

Figure 11.28 – An overview of inserting the logo and shapes

What is now left to complete our supply chain inventory dashboard is to connect the PivotTables and PivotChart to the slicers. This will enable them to dynamically update as selections are made on the slicers. If you have forgotten how we achieve this, select each PivotTable/PivotChart, and under the

PivotTable Analyze menu, click on **Filter Connections**. Then, tick all the filters listed in the window that pops up.

Finally, we should have a dashboard that looks like the one in the following screenshot:

Figure 11.29 – An overview of the final supply chain inventory dashboard

Congratulations on the work done so far! If you did not follow along, this is an opportunity to pause and attempt to replicate all we have done so far before proceeding to the chapter summary.

Summary

This has been an exciting and fully hands-on chapter. I hope you practiced the dashboard building by yourself and are now brimming with confidence in your dashboard-building skills.

Together, we have built three different dashboards and used all the common tools (PivotTables, PivotCharts, slicers, shapes, and icons) that you'll end up using as you build real-world, business-relevant dashboards.

The next chapter is the last one in this book and will cover the best practices to follow in carrying out real-world dashboard-building tasks.

Again, congratulations on making it this far, and see you in the next chapter!

12

Best Practices for Real-World Dashboard Building

Congratulations on making it to the last chapter. By now, you should be eager to deploy your newly acquired skills in the real world. But before you unleash your skills in the corporate world, we have to equip you with the best practices that will help you deliver professional, high-quality work.

The chapter breakdown is as follows:

- Gathering the dashboard requirements
- An overview of different data professionals
- Advantages and limitations of Excel dashboards

You will want to pay very good attention to everything covered in this chapter as your success in the corporate world depends on understanding all the points we will address.

Gathering the dashboard requirements

Your role as a data analyst is usually to support business managers with reporting and analysis that will be used for decision-making. You will typically encounter three categories of dashboards to build:

- Existing established analysis dashboards
- Newly established analysis dashboards
- Ad hoc analysis dashboards

We will go through the three categories and how to handle gathering requirements for them.

Existing established analysis dashboards

The first category comprises dashboards that capture existing standardized analyses that are already in use in the company. This could be monthly financial analyses or monthly sales analyses that have been carried out in one form or another in the company for years already. You are now being given the lofty task of recreating those analyses as a modern dashboard in Excel.

The key characteristics that distinguish this category are that the analyses are being done already and have an established structure. By structure, we mean the metrics to present them are well-known, and the required visual layout is known. As a data analyst, you should request past copies of the analyses. If they are done monthly, you could request the last three months' copies. And if they are done quarterly or yearly, you could request the most recent one.

Your work will be much easier now that you have a historical copy. You will then proceed with confirming how much of the historical presentation they want to keep and what minor changes they want you to incorporate in the dashboard replica you will build. Usually, the copy you will be given will be a static report that does not have dynamic slicers and filters. However, as we have learned, a dashboard must be dynamic and able to allow new data records in the underlying data sources. This is typically the advantage that creating a dashboard version of analyses will give business managers.

You will then proceed with requesting the primary sources of the data for the analyses. You don't want to connect to static file exports, and you don't want to connect to another report if you can connect directly to the primary source of the data. This is often the most difficult part of a real-world dashboard-building process. Oftentimes, existing reports the company wants you to recreate as a dashboard are built from manual user entries, static file exports, and other error-prone reports. You must repeatedly ask for the original data source for every set of data you are provided with. The following flowchart illustrates the decision process:

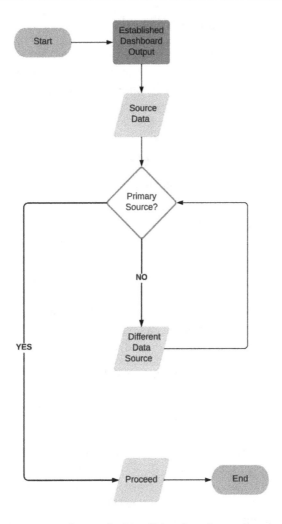

Figure 12.1 – Process for identifying the primary data source

Armed with the old copies of the reports to recreate as a dashboard and the primary data source, you can then proceed with deploying your dashboard-building skills. When you are done, you can set your filter or slicer to mirror the periods in the static reports you were provided with to validate the accuracy of your dashboard. If you notice any discrepancies, you will want to go through your transformations and data model to ensure you did all the necessary transformations, relationships, and measures.

Your dashboard will allow the business managers to now have interactive analyses that do not need to be rebuilt monthly, quarterly, or yearly. With just a refresh of the datasets and by setting the filters or slicers, they can have the analyses and charts for any period they want. We will now move on to the second category.

Newly established analysis dashboards

Occasionally, business managers come up with new ideas for analysis they want to see daily or monthly. And as we now know, a dashboard is excellent for such recurrent analysis. Unlike the first category we just explained, this category involves no existing versions you can be provided with. You will have to do more work to figure out exactly the metrics to present and the visual layout. On the surface, this should be easy. Unfortunately, business managers who are not familiar with the features of Excel and how data analysis works for recurrent analysis will either give you vague explanations of what they want or give you requirements that are impossible to execute in Excel.

You have to guide business managers to translate their expectations into what is possible in Excel. The trouble doesn't end there. You may also find that since it involves analysis that has never been done before, the business may not have some of the data you need to carry out the requested analysis.

For this dashboard category, you should plan to spend more time establishing the feasibility of building the dashboard. You will start with translating the original dashboard request into one that is possible in Excel. This means eliminating requests such as the ability to open it on a mobile phone or the inclusion of a decomposition tree. It would also work in your favor if you could do a basic wireframe to illustrate the metric that would be presented, the filters, the slicers, the tables, and the charts. This helps to eliminate an expectation mismatch; you and the business manager would be on the same page as regards what the final dashboard would have and look like.

With the output decided on, you will begin another potentially difficult journey. One of establishing that all the data needed to achieve the output analysis exists and locating the primary source. When you encounter situations where data is unavailable, you will propose to the business to begin gathering that data or that they drop metrics that depend on the data.

Finally, when you are done with the dashboard, do not be surprised if the business manager suddenly gets new ideas to incorporate into the dashboard. The reward of creating a useful dashboard is unending revisions. If you are a consultant, you had better be on an hourly rate or you might be in for a very difficult experience. And if you are a full-time employee, try to get a business analyst or project manager between you and the dashboard owner.

Ad hoc analysis dashboards

Eventually, you will be asked to build dashboards for one-off analysis, which no one needs to see again because it's to address a one-time, uncommon need.

As a data analyst, you must be able to judge what is worth the time and effort, and what is best created as an interactive or static report from a convenient data source. Most ad hoc analyses should not be built as a dashboard with the rigor of searching for primary data sources and refresh capability.

This is a category where you can leverage the ignorance of most business managers on the hard requirements of dashboards to be connected to primary data sources with refresh capability. Many business managers consider every report that looks beautiful with modern-looking charts to be a dashboard. If the dashboard-requesting manager is in that category, you may skip explaining to them that ad hoc analyses are not worth the stress of dashboards. Just give them a beautiful report from the most convenient data source you can access.

As a rule, dashboards should be created for recurrent analysis and ongoing business needs. Never go through the stress of searching for a refresh-capable primary data source, creating elaborate data models, and using Power Pivot if all your work will be discarded after one use.

The only time a case can be made for an ad hoc, one-time-use, analysis dashboard is if it's meant to be a proof-of-concept dashboard – something built to convince business managers to migrate recurrent analyses to proper refresh-enabled dashboards. So, as a consultant or job seeker, you can go ahead to build these types of dashboards so that you can get the chance and reward of building proper ones.

We will move on to detailing the other data professionals you will have to work with as a data analyst. Not all companies will have these roles, but you need to be aware of them. Many big organizations have these roles.

An overview of different data professionals

I had to be careful with the section title, using "An overview of *different* data professionals" instead of "An overview of *all* data professionals" because there is no universally agreed upon list of data professionals. However, there are some well-accepted roles that I believe you will come across frequently:

- Data analyst
- Business intelligence (BI) analyst
- Data engineer
- Data scientist
- Database administrator

We will begin to examine each role and I must state that the explanations I give are not exhaustive or to be taken as authoritative. You should take them as my attempt to give a bird's-eye view of what each role is about.

Data analyst

Twenty years ago, all data professionals fell into two broad categories – data analysts and database administrators. Data analysts are business units supporting professionals building reports and dashboards. In large organizations, you would come across HR professionals posted to different business units to provide tailored HR services to those business units. It is the same for data analysts. They are business partners – using their data analysis skills and interactions with business teams to understand and fulfill their reporting needs.

I started my career in this domain 13 years ago as a data analyst working for a large telecommunications company. My line manager was the head of the continent's operations, and I was creating reports and dashboards that tracked operations across 10 countries.

What has stayed the same about the data analyst role over the decades, even as new roles emerge and people stuff their resumes with keywords that reflect all sorts of roles, is that the data analyst is primarily a business-supporting role and not a technology role. The data analyst needs to understand the business needs and be closer to the business managers who rely on the reports than they need to be to technology. This often means that a data analyst today might still be using Excel more than all the new technology products that are now available. In the choice between the shiny new tool that business managers will struggle to use and old, familiar Excel, Excel wins.

A data analyst should not be a single-tool person. The industry expects a data analyst to be proficient in Excel, SQL, and a **business intelligence** (**BI**) tool. The core though, will be the tool the business users and managers adopt. A data analyst can be instrumental in recommending and training the report users, but the final choice of tool lies with the business team.

Business intelligence analyst

The BI analyst role is also a business-supporting role, but the focus is more on report automation and it is technology-heavy. Unlike the data analyst, a BI analyst must use a BI tool even if the business team has a different preference. Common BI tools are Power BI, Tableau, Qlik Sense, QuickSight, MicroStrategy, Looker, Domo, and Sisense.

The BI analyst recently became a standalone role. It used to be merged with a data analyst role or a database administrator role, depending on the tool used. About 10 years ago, you were either a data analyst using one of the heaven-promising, budget-draining, self-service BI tools, or a database administrator using BI add-ins of top-tier license versions of enterprise SQL servers (Microsoft BI, Oracle BI, and others).

Now, the BI analyst role is standalone and with affordable BI tools compared to a decade ago. The main distinguishing characteristic of the BI role is that it is highly integrated with technology and often requires the BI analyst to work just as closely with the technology department as much as with the business teams using their final BI reports.

Data engineer

The data engineer role is another new standalone role that didn't exist a decade ago (some will argue to the contrary, so remember it is my perspective that this role was not a standalone role over a decade ago). A data engineer works primarily on pulling data from different sources, transforming that data into a better structured and enriched form, and saving it into an enterprise data warehouse or data lake. A data warehouse is a relational database infrastructure that has been intentionally set up to accommodate business needs and data governance policies, while a data lake is a free-form data storage infrastructure that allows the storage of both relational data and non-relational data. Relational data is data records that conform to traditional database storage rules, while non-relational data has no strict data definition rules. An example of relational data is data stored in traditional accounting software to capture financial transactions. It typically has defined columns and formats. When a data engineer transfers that data into another storage infrastructure – be it in a data warehouse or a data lake – it retains its relational structure. An example of non-relational data is customer support chats and voice calls. They are not expected to have a predetermined structure and are best stored in a non-relational data format.

A data engineer role is a purely technical role with little or no business team interaction. A data engineer must use the best technology tool without bothering about what the business team uses. Currently, data engineers use the Python programming language, SQL, PowerShell, and other scripting languages.

Data scientist

This role was the hype of the early 2010s. It was then classified as the "sexiest" data professional role. Unfortunately, it didn't deliver the promised value to business managers and lost its attractiveness to companies. Data scientists are mostly focused on preparing the business for the future – making automated forecasts, suggesting real-time strategies for operations optimization, or managing risks in a fully automated way.

In an ideal setting, a data scientist would use the output of the data engineer and BI analyst to build machine learning models that will help the company handle the future. So, like the data engineer, the data scientist must focus on using the best technology tool. However, they are judged by how successfully they predict or influence the future for the business team. This makes their value tied to a variable that is never within their control – business users' never changing goals.

Data scientists build machine learning models. I joke that most data scientists try to get a Ph.D. so that they will have some inner inertia to overcome the resistance they eventually face in the corporate world. Their role is one that seems to be valued in some industries – quantitative finance-based companies, AI product companies, precision engineering companies, life sciences companies, and research-heavy companies. However, it is difficult to justify their role in others – retail companies, small-sized companies, and consulting companies. Companies with a lot of human interaction, such as retail companies, deal with a lot of human-influenced parameters that are tricky to mathematically capture. Small-sized companies often lack the internal processes and high-end technology that plugs easily into the output of data scientists' models.

Database administrator

This is a role that has changed immensely over the last 25 years. It used to be a role that worked in core technology alongside network engineers, computer hardware engineers, and cybersecurity engineers. With the large-scale migration to cloud databases and the introduction of data lakes, many database administrators are now database architects or data engineers.

A database administrator role involves designing, maintaining, and securing databases. A database administrator is expected to live and breathe SQL. They may not interact much with the business team except at the start of a database design process.

I think the database administrator role is the most underrated data professional role and that is why many database administrators are becoming data engineers so that they can earn more with less headache. In the days of physical database servers, database administrators didn't go on holidays. Those online memes of database administrators, on New Year's Eve, kneeling in front of servers with raised hands praying nothing goes wrong are not entirely exaggerated.

Now that we have covered all the different data professional roles, it becomes obvious that your role as someone building Excel reports and dashboards is as a data analyst. For your data needs, especially as you trace the best data source to pull data from, you will need to reach out to the data engineer or database administrator. And in situations when the data source is not one you can connect Excel to, you will reach out to the data engineer to create a process for pulling the data into storage you can connect Excel to.

You won't have much to do with the BI analyst and data scientist. For fun, though, you can suggest to a business manager asking for an ad hoc analysis dashboard to reroute their request to the BI analyst. Make sure the BI analyst does not find out what you have done. And if you want to make the data scientist glow red, ask what the business usage is like for their model.

We will now examine the advantages and limitations of Excel dashboards.

Advantages and limitations of Excel dashboards

Now for the moment of brutal truth: Excel is not always going to be the right tool for dashboards even when it is technically capable.

The advantage of Excel is that it is the favorite of non-technical business managers. Most business managers already are comfortable using Excel and often prefer having reports built for them in Excel. This is a boon for a data analyst with excellent Excel skills.

There are, however, some limitations that Excel has that can mean it is not the right tool for some dashboards. One major limitation is that Excel is not mobile device-friendly. If you need dashboards that must be consumed on the fly by users with their mobile devices, then you will find that Excel does not deliver on that. No one enjoys opening Excel on their mobile phone. It is a guaranteed way of frustrating people. For requirements that include mobile device friendliness, you may want to consider using a self-service BI tool such as Power BI.

Another limitation that Excel has is the lack of proper data governance and user auditing. Every dashboard you build with Excel can be seen by anyone who gets their hands on the Excel file without needing any express permission from you. Also, you can't track who has accessed your dashboard or manage access to it.

One more limitation of Excel dashboards is the possibility of fragmentation. Every time you update the dashboard, you have to email it out to users or force the users to access the updated copy via a shared folder. Anyone working off a locally saved copy of the dashboard is not guaranteed to see the most recent copy.

I hope these limitations do not discourage you. The advantages of Excel for dashboards do outweigh the limitations. In fact, with proper education of your users to not bother using their phones to open the reports, to not forward the reports to unauthorized users, and to ensure they access the copy in a shared drive you actively update, these limitations are eliminated.

I have seen companies that have BI tools and other expensive enterprise solutions that are arguably superior to Excel, but the business users actively avoid using those solutions because they already have enough headaches to deal with and are not willing to add more headache-inducing tools to their plate. They would rather pay an Excel consultant (like me) to build them something more familiar and easier to maintain in Excel, which they already use. Also, there are always reports and dashboards that should be built in Excel and not another tool – either because of cost considerations, the technical expertise of the users, or the nature of the source data.

And with that, we have come to the end of this chapter.

Summary

This chapter must feel like ice cream compared to the broccoli you have been having the last couple of chapters. Well, you deserved it! You have earned it and I hope you are motivated to put your dashboard-building skills to use.

Don't forget to properly categorize the dashboard requests you get into one of the three broad categories we covered. You don't want to use the wro ng requirements-gathering approach, and neither do you want to suffer needlessly on throwaway work.

I hope the explanation of the data professional roles has given you clarity on who to reach out to for some help while you carry out your work.

Lastly, don't forget that Excel has some limitations that may need to educate your users about before embarking on dashboard building. All the best in your career. May you Excel!

Index

A

ad hoc analysis dashboards 380
Adventure Works 319
  Enterprise Resource Planning (ERP) 320
  HR schema 321
  human resources (HR) department 320
  person schema 324, 325
  production schema 323, 324
  purchasing schema 322, 323
  sales schema 321, 322
  schemas 320
Adventure Works Cycle Limited (AWCL) 319, 353
AND function 197, 198
Application Programming Interface (API) 39
area chart 262, 263
AVERAGE function 191, 192
Average Revenue Per User (ARPU) 27
Azure Machine Learning 38

B

bar chart 255-260
box and whisker chart 278
bubble chart 270, 271

business data

business data
  connecting, to over 100 different data sources 81-83
business-relevant dashboards
  building 325
BYCOL 238
BYROW 239

C

calculated columns 177
CHOOSE function 215, 216
Close & Load To, Power Query 119-121
cloud platforms 60
  data, importing from 60-65
coauthoring 12, 13
column chart 248, 249
  clustered column chart 249, 250
  example 248
  stacked column chart 251-254
combo chart 283, 284
Component Object Model (COM) 72
conditional formatting 286, 287
  border settings pane 289
  color scales 297-299
  custom formula conditional formatting 302-306

data bars 295-297
fill settings pane 290
font settings pane 288
Highlight Cells Rules preset 291-293
icon sets 299-301
presets 291
Top/Bottom Rules preset 293, 294
COUNT function 188
COUNTIFS function 188, 189
current channel 12
Customer Relationship Management (CRM) 30

D

dashboard requirements
ad hoc analysis dashboards 380
existing established analysis dashboards 378, 379
gathering 377
newly established analysis dashboards 380
dashboards 4
characteristics 7
creating 5
financial analysis dashboard 24, 31
HR dashboard 24, 33
HR dashboard example 6
marketing dashboard 24, 38
sales dashboard 24-31
supply chain and logistics dashboard 24, 35, 36
data
appending, from multiple sources in one data table 85-91
bringing in Excel 47-53
copy and pasting, into Excel 53, 54
importing, from cloud platforms 60-65
importing, from databases 59, 60

importing, from flat files 54-58
merging, from two tables into one table 91-98
transforming, in Power Query 84, 85
Data Analysis Expressions (DAX) 169, 182
databases 59
Data Model 171
connection, closing 172
connection, loading 172
Pivot Table, loading 174, 175
data professionals
business intelligence analyst 382
data analyst 381, 382
database administrator 383, 384
data engineer 382
data scientist 383
overview 381
data transformations, Power Query 326-351
Choose Columns 98, 99
Fill Series and Remove Empty 105-112
Group By 104, 105
Keep Rows options 99
Pivot Columns 102-104
Remove Rows options 99
Replace Values 113, 114
Unpivot Columns 101
DATE function 205
date manipulation functions 204
DATE 205
DAY 207
EDATE 207, 208
EOMONTH 208, 209
MONTH 206
TODAY 204
WEEKNUM 209, 210
YEAR 205, 206

DAX-specific formulas
  ALL 184
  AVERAGEX 183
  CALCULATE 183
  FILTER 184
  RELATED 183
  SUMX 183
DAY function 207
doughnut chart 265-267
dynamic array formulas 217
dynamic array functions 185, 217, 218
  FILTER 221-225
  SEQUENCE 225-229
  SORT 229-232
  SORTBY 233-235
  UNIQUE 218-220
dynamic arrays 16
dynamic reports, with Pivot Table 151-167
  Pizza Inc sales data 152

E

EDATE function 207, 208
Enterprise Resource Planning (ERP) 30
EOMONTH function 208, 209
Excel
  data, bringing in 47-53
Excel 365 10
  reference link, for updates 10
  update history 12
Excel 2007 21
Excel 2010 21
Excel 2013 20
Excel 2016 20
Excel 2019 20
Excel 2021 12
  coauthoring 12, 13
  dynamic arrays 16

  know who's in your workbook 13
  LET function 15
  modern comments 13
  performance improvements 18
  sheet views 17
  unhide many sheets at once 18, 19
  visual refresh 14
  XLOOKUP function 14
  XMATCH function 16
Excel dashboards
  advantages 384
  limitations 385
**existing established analysis
    dashboards** 378, 379
Extract, Transform, and Load (ETL) tool 72

F

filled map chart 282, 283
filter context 183
FILTER function 221-225
financial analysis dashboard 24, 31
  account receivables aging 32
  assets trend 32
  capital structure 33
  cashflow trend 33
  debt service 33
  gross profit margin 31
  net profit margin 32
  operating profit margin 32
  Opex by cost center 32
  sales trend 31
  sample 33
  working capital lines 33
flat files 54
  Comma-Separated Values (CSV) files 54
  data, importing from 54-58

Extensible Markup Language (XML) files 54
JavaScript Object Notation (JSON) files 54
OpenDocument Spreadsheet (ODS) files 54
Portable Document Format (PDF) files 54
XML Paper Specification (XPS) files 54
functional organogram 25, 26
funnel chart 281, 282

G

**General Data Protection
        Regulation (GDPR) 39**
Google Analytics dashboard 40

H

Health Safety and Environment (HSE) 34
histogram chart 277, 278
HLOOKUP function 212
HR dashboard 24, 33
    employee attrition 34
    headcount spread 34
    leave 35
    personnel costs 34
    recruitment 35
    retention and productivity 35
    training 34
HR manpower dashboard
    building 353-355
    icons, inserting 360, 361
    picture, inserting 360, 361
    PivotCharts, inserting 358, 359
    PivotTables, inserting 355-358
    shapes, inserting 360, 361
HR schema, Adventure Works 321

I

IFERROR function 194, 195
IF function 193, 194
IFS function 194
implicit filters 183
INDEX function 212
INDIRECT function 215

J

joins
    full outer join 93
    inner join 93
    left anti join 93
    left outer join 93
    right anti join 93
    right outer join 93

K

Key Performance Indicators (KPIs) 23

L

Lambda functions 235-238
    BYCOL 238
    BYROW 239
    MAKEARRAY 239-241
    MAP 241
    REDUCE 242, 243
    SCAN 243
LEFT function 199
Legacy Excel 185
LEN function 203
LET function 15

line chart 260, 261
LinkedIn analytics 42
logical functions 192
    AND 197, 198
    IF 193, 194
    IFERROR 194, 195
    IFS 194
    OR 197
    SWITCH 195, 196
lookup and reference functions 210
    CHOOSE 215, 216
    HLOOKUP 212
    INDEX 212
    INDIRECT 215
    MATCH 213, 214
    OFFSET 214, 215
    VLOOKUP 211, 212

M

MAKEARRAY 239-241
Manage Relationships tool 342
MAP 241
marketing dashboard 24, 38
    audience reach 42
    cost per lead 41
    customer acquisition cost 41
    customer engagement 41
    customer lifetime value 41
    customer retention 41
    Google Analytics dashboard 40
    LinkedIn analytics 42
    sample 42
    website and app usage 42
MATCH function 213
math and statistical functions 186
    AVERAGE 191, 192
    COUNT 188

COUNTIFS 188, 189
MAX 190, 191
MIN 189, 190
SUM 186, 187
SUMIFS 187, 188
MAX function 190
Microsoft Excel
    Excel 365 10
    Excel 2007 21
    Excel 2010 21
    Excel 2013 20
    Excel 2016 20
    Excel 2019 20
    Excel 2021 12
    versions 7-9
MID function 199
modern business needs
    meeting 6
Modern Excel 185
MONTH function 206
monthly enterprise channel 12

N

newly established analysis dashboards 380

O

OFFSET function 214, 215
Open Database Connectivity
    (ODBC) connector 68
Open Data Protocol (OData) 69
OR function 197

P

person schema, Adventure Works 324, 325
pie chart 263-265

Pivot Chart 151-158

  Field Buttons, disabling 161

  improvement formats 161

  inserting 159

Pivot Table 125

  calculated field 144

  columns 131

  Design menu 144

  dynamic reports 151-167

  Field Settings feature 141

  filters 130

  group and ungroup options 140

  inserting 128, 129

  mastering 126

  PivotTable Analyze menu 140-143

  PivotTable Fields 140

  Report Layout setting 145

  sales report, creating 126, 127

  sample sales report 137-139

  Value Field Settings pane 133-136

  Values quadrant 132

Power Pivot 167

  calculated column 178

  dashboard 170, 182

  enabling 169

  features 169

  KPI, setting up 180, 181

  Pivot Table 181

  profit measure, creating 179, 180

  relationships, creating 177

  sort by column 179

  window launching 175-177

Power Query 171

  Close & Load To 119-121

  data transformation 326-351

  data, transforming 84, 85

  formula bar, enabling 114

  in Excel 2013 72-80

  list 79

  M code, demystifying 121-124

  record 79, 80

  single-entry value 78

  table 79

  tables, importing 173

  tips 114-119

  value types 121

primary data source 65

  connecting directly 65-67

  issues, handling 68, 69

  warnings 65

production schema, Adventure Works 323, 324

purchasing schema, Adventure Works 322, 323

R

radar chart 273-275

Recency, Frequency, and Monetary (RFM) value score 41

REDUCE 242, 243

Remove Duplicates tool 218

reports 4

RIGHT function 200

S

sales dashboard 24-26

  active customers, versus total customers 28

  average order value 27

  average sales per customer 27

  market share 28

  Net Promoter Score (NPS) 29

  productive calls ratio 28

  sales channels performance 27

  sales conversion rate 29

sales cycle length 29

sales growth 26

sales per headcount 28

sales performance dashboard

building 362

measures, creating 363-365

picture, inserting 369, 370

PivotChart, inserting 367, 368

PivotTable, inserting 367

shapes, inserting 369, 370

slicers, connecting to PivotTables
    and PivotCharts 370, 371

slicers, inserting 365-367

timelines, inserting 365-367

sales schema, Adventure Works 321, 322

SCAN 243

SEARCH function 200, 201

semi-annual enterprise channel 12

SEQUENCE function 225-229

shapes 306

categories 306-308

images 312, 313

linking to cell 308

SmartArt 309-311

sparkline 311, 312

symbols 313-316

Slicers 145

additional settings 148-150

customization menu 148

inserting 146

OrderDate field timeline, adding 150

removing 146, 147

Timeline customization menu 150

Software-as-a-Service (SaaS) 25

SORTBY function 233-235

SORT function 229-232

stock chart 271, 272

SUBSTITUTE function 201

SUM function 186, 187

SUMIFS function 187, 188

sunburst chart 276, 277

**supply chain and logistics
    dashboard 24, 35, 36**

capacity utilization 36

days inventory outstanding 37

distribution cost per sales 37

example 38

order cycle time 37

perfect order rate 37

throughput 37

vendor performance 37

supply chain inventory dashboard

building 371-373

company logo, inserting 375

PivotChart, inserting 375

PivotTable, inserting 373, 374

surface chart 272

SWITCH function 195, 196

T

TEXT function 202, 203

text manipulation functions 198

LEFT 199

LEN 203

MID 199

RIGHT 200

SEARCH 200, 201

SUBSTITUTE 201

TEXT 202, 203

TODAY function 204

treemap chart 275

U

UNIQUE function 218-220

V

value types, Power Query
  function values 122
  list values 121
  primitive values 121
  record values 122
  table values 122
Visual Basic for Applications (VBA) 10, 235
VLOOKUP function 211

W

waterfall chart 279-281
Web connector 81
WEEKNUM function 209, 210
Weighted Average Cost of
      Capital (WACC) 33

X

XLOOKUP function 14
XMATCH function 16
XY (scatter) chart 267-270

Y

YEAR function 205, 206

packtpub.com

Subscribe to our online digital library for full access to over 7,000 books and videos, as well as industry leading tools to help you plan your personal development and advance your career. For more information, please visit our website.

Why subscribe?

- Spend less time learning and more time coding with practical eBooks and Videos from over 4,000 industry professionals

- Improve your learning with Skill Plans built especially for you

- Get a free eBook or video every month

- Fully searchable for easy access to vital information

- Copy and paste, print, and bookmark content

Did you know that Packt offers eBook versions of every book published, with PDF and ePub files available? You can upgrade to the eBook version at packtpub.com and as a print book customer, you are entitled to a discount on the eBook copy. Get in touch with us at customercare@packtpub.com for more details.

At www.packtpub.com, you can also read a collection of free technical articles, sign up for a range of free newsletters, and receive exclusive discounts and offers on Packt books and eBooks.

Other Books You May Enjoy

If you enjoyed this book, you may be interested in these other books by Packt:

Data Modeling with Microsoft Excel

Bernard Obeng Boateng

ISBN: 978-1-80324-028-2

- Implement the concept of data modeling within and beyond Excel
- Get, transform, model, aggregate, and visualize data with Power Query
- Understand best practices for data structuring in MS Excel
- Build powerful measures using DAX from the Data Model
- Generate flexible calculations using Cube functions
- Design engaging dashboards for your users

Alteryx Designer Cookbook

Alberto Guisande

ISBN: 978-1-80461-508-9

- Speed up the cleansing, data preparing, and shaping process
- Perform operations and transformations on the data to suit your needs
- Blend different types of data sources for analysis
- Pivot and un-pivot the data for easy manipulation
- Perform aggregations and calculations on the data
- Encapsulate reusable logic into macros
- Develop high-quality, data-driven reports to improve consistency

Packt is searching for authors like you

If you're interested in becoming an author for Packt, please visit `authors.packtpub.com` and apply today. We have worked with thousands of developers and tech professionals, just like you, to help them share their insight with the global tech community. You can make a general application, apply for a specific hot topic that we are recruiting an author for, or submit your own idea.

Share Your Thoughts

Now you've finished *Building Interactive Dashboards in Microsoft 365 Excel*, we'd love to hear your thoughts! Scan the QR code below to go straight to the Amazon review page for this book and share your feedback or leave a review on the site that you purchased it from.

`https://packt.link/r/1-803-23729-5`

Your review is important to us and the tech community and will help us make sure we're delivering excellent quality content.

Download a free PDF copy of this book

Thanks for purchasing this book!

Do you like to read on the go but are unable to carry your print books everywhere?

Is your eBook purchase not compatible with the device of your choice?

Don't worry, now with every Packt book you get a DRM-free PDF version of that book at no cost.

Read anywhere, any place, on any device. Search, copy, and paste code from your favorite technical books directly into your application.

The perks don't stop there, you can get exclusive access to discounts, newsletters, and great free content in your inbox daily

Follow these simple steps to get the benefits:

1. Scan the QR code or visit the link below

https://packt.link/free-ebook/9781803237299

2. Submit your proof of purchase
3. That's it! We'll send your free PDF and other benefits to your email directly

www.ingramcontent.com/pod-product-compliance
Lightning Source LLC
Chambersburg PA
CBHW060649060326
40690CB00020B/4574